# DELICIOSO

FOODS AND NATIONS is a new series from Reaktion that explores the history – and geography – of food. Books in the series reveal the hidden history behind the food eaten today in different countries and regions of the world, telling the story of how food production and consumption developed, and how they were influenced by the culinary practices of other places and peoples. Each book in the Foods and Nations series offers fascinating insights into the distinct flavours of a country and its culture.

Already published

*Al Dente: A History of Food in Italy*
Fabio Parasecoli

*Beyond Bratwurst: A History of Food in Germany*
Ursula Heinzelmann

*Delicioso: A History of Food in Spain*
María José Sevilla

*Feasts and Fasts: A History of Food in India*
Colleen Taylor Sen

*Gifts of the Gods: A History of Food in Greece*
Andrew and Rachel Dalby

*Rice and Baguette: A History of Food in Vietnam*
Vu Hong Lien

*A Rich and Fertile Land: A History of Food in America*
Bruce Kraig

# Delicioso

## A History of Food
## in Spain

María José Sevilla

REAKTION BOOKS

*To my granddaughter Sofía Maria*

Published by Reaktion Books Ltd
Unit 32, Waterside
44–48 Wharf Road
London N1 7UX, UK
www.reaktionbooks.co.uk

First published 2019
Copyright © Maria José Sevilla 2019

Printed and bound China by 1010 Printing International Ltd

A catalogue record for this book is available from the British Library

ISBN 978 1 78914 137 5

# CONTENTS

# INTRODUCTION

The history of Spanish food is a subject that has been neglected in the past by scholars. In Spain, history can be found in every corner of this diverse country. A diversity which is difficult to match in the rest of Europe opens up a world of all things Spanish: land and people, music, tradition, language and, of course, food. From early times, Spanish food has been enriched by the different cultures that arrived in the area where the Basques and Iberians, believed by some historians to have been the original inhabitants of the peninsula, were already living. Cereals and peas moving westwards across the Mediterranean began feeding Iberians along the Mediterranean and southern Atlantic coast and Celts in the north and northwest of the peninsula, where they would settle to raise animals and cultivate the land. From the other side of the Mediterranean came the Phoenicians. They were looking for trade, valuable minerals and, in particular, sea salt to cure fish. The Greeks brought wine to Catalonia, while the Romans looked to 'Hispania' for olive oil, garum, grain and gold. Before the arrival of the Romans, the Jews had already taken refuge in Sepharad, the name they gave to the Iberian Peninsula.

Then, in the fifth century, Germanic tribes crossed the Pyrenees to occupy the remains of what had been the Roman province. Later, Berbers and Arabs would make their home here for almost eight centuries, converting most of the peninsula into a fertile garden of beauty they called Al-Andalus. During the thirteenth and fourteenth centuries, before the Christian *Reconquista* of the land had ended in Castile, expansion of the powerful federation of Aragon, Catalonia and Valencia in the Mediterranean added another layer of flavour and tradition to the food of Iberia – one which was greatly influenced by Italy. From the sixteenth century onwards, exchanges of food with America expanded Spain's larder of ingredients and improved the interest and variety of its food. The arrival of the Bourbons in the early eighteenth century, and the resulting French influence on Spanish life and food, provoked a strong negative reaction in the population.

By the nineteenth century, Spanish authors and restaurant critics had become defenders of the authentic food of Spain. Threatened by the loss of identity, they strongly guarded the concept of a 'national cuisine' which in reality had never existed before. However, it might have been better if they had just championed the 'regional' *cocinas*, or cuisines, of Spain, which had been under threat for quite some time: *Las Cocinas de las Autonomías de España* (The Cuisines of the Autonomous Communities of Spain), as they should correctly be called today. The loss of Cuba and the Philippines in 1898 was a major blow to the pride of Spaniards and the economy of the country, but the years of hunger and deprivation and the terrible experiences of civil war in the 1930s seriously affected agriculture and the *cocinas*.

Writing a comprehensive book about the history of Spanish food has been a challenge. I am a Spanish food writer who lives abroad, fascinated by my own country and my culture, and who has found in social history an answer to the way I cook and like to eat. For the last thirty years, this fascination has created in me an attachment to the subject of Spanish food and wine that, in the way of those in exile (voluntary in my case), has grown stronger through living outside the land of my birth. Sharing Spanish food and wine with others, travelling, cooking and writing books on the subject have helped me along the way and allowed me to keep in touch with my origins at a time when food has been changing dramatically in Spain.

When I left Spain in 1971, Franco's dictatorship was ending, and the road to democracy and favourable economic prospects was already under construction. Only a few years before, J. H. Elliott, the prestigious British historian, had written the following words in an early edition of his book *Imperial Spain*:

A dry, barren, impoverished land: 10 per cent of its soil bare rock; 35 per cent poor and unproductive; 45 per cent moderately fertile, 10 per cent rich. A peninsula separated from the continent of Europe by the mountain barrier of the Pyrenees – isolated and remote. A country divided within itself, broken by a high central tableland that stretches from the Pyrenees to the southern coast. No natural centre, no easy routes. Fragmented, disparate, a complex of different races, languages, and civilizations – this was, and is Spain.[1]

Although things have improved dramatically since the 1970s, some of Elliott's remarks may perhaps remain relevant forever. His words not only describe the fabric of the country but its uniqueness and strong, complex personality. Now more than ever, the necessary acceptance of the plurality of Spain, trying at the same time to effect syncretism, convergence and divergence in society, will also contribute to an understanding of the individual personality of the country's food.

Today's Spain is largely a modern country where motorways and fast trains cross the dramatic landscape much admired by poets and painters. Left behind, hopefully for good, is the chronic backwardness of the rural areas that affected the country badly, a malady which for centuries rendered the life of the Spanish farmer, and a large part of society, impossible.

In 1978, after the death of Franco and the restoration of democracy, the country was divided administratively into seventeen autonomous regions mainly derived from medieval kingdoms: a complex patchwork of different geographical, climatic, agricultural, and food and cookery worlds. The Spanish *cocinas* have their origins in the food of the feudal peasantry of those earlier times. However, what we understand these days as Spanish *cocinas* are not necessarily based on the simple and repetitive daily diet of the poor. Many dishes of that large part of the population were prepared with great economic sacrifice and with quality ingredients, especially for saints' days, festivals and weddings – as recorded by Miguel de Cervantes. Over the centuries, these dishes have been adapted to incorporate changes in local agriculture, new products from the Americas and some influences from the food of the nobility.

Spain no longer needs to prove the existence of a 'National Cuisine' as nineteenth-century critics thought when searching for a national identity. The existence and individuality of the *Cocinas de España* has now been fully accepted. As for the 'international food' of the nineteenth and early twentieth centuries, much dreaded by Spanish food critics of the time, this has been replaced by a rightly admired creative and innovative Spanish *alta cocina* (Spain's version of haute cuisine), prepared in many restaurants which are in a state of constant evolution and now serve outstanding and original food.

Spain is the fourth largest economy in the eurozone with a Gross Domestic Product of U.S.$ 1.1 trillion and a population of 46.4 million people. It is a fully industrialized country and a major exporter of fruit and vegetables, olive oil, cheeses, rice, hams, wines, recipes and even chefs. Coinciding with the industrial and economic advances made by Spain, in the last forty years, creativity and innovation in the professional kitchen – starting in the Basque

Country and followed by Catalonia and the rest of the country – has placed Spanish food among the best in the international arena. As a consequence, many young chefs born in Seville, Madrid, Barcelona or Bilbao, having achieved recognition by following initially in the footsteps of avant-garde Spanish masters of recent decades, have now returned to traditional food, improving and strengthening its character. Those chefs are adopting modernity and adapting it when needed, but now they are also making sure they are keeping those principles and ingredients that maintain the local character intact. What has also happened is that chefs working individually but also in collaboration have established links between the different food traditions that, based on quality, guarantee good food all over the country. These links are so strong that not even politically independent souls would be able to deny their existence.

As for the isolation and remoteness that existed in the past, today millions of visitors, the new temporary invaders, choose to travel every year to that mostly dry but definitely not so barren land where they demand Rioja wines, Manchego cheese, Ibérico ham and Calasparra rice. Unfortunately, they also demand the fast food, industrially made pastries and sugary sweet drinks that young Spaniards enjoy, too.

Long gone are the times when Spain only attracted foreign travellers and writers searching for dramatic and colourful stories to relate when back in their home countries, not always fair or generous but always engaging. As for authentic Spanish food, not so long ago ignored, dismissed or simply compared unfavourably with French or Italian, changes in the opinions of national and international critics have been notable. Admired now all over the world, the food of Spain, traditional or avant-garde, is continuously writing new chapters to add to its long history. The beauty and the diversity of Spain have remained unequalled and a good plate of food is now guaranteed almost everywhere.

ONE

# A Land at the Edge of the Unknown

Food history started early in the Iberian Peninsula. Speaking about Atapuerca, Professor José María Bermúdez de Castro, of the National Museum of Natural Sciences in Madrid, said that this was a good place to live. It was high up so it provided a welcome vantage point for hunters, and there was also a river nearby. Professor Bermúdez was referring to the Atapuerca Mountains situated in the region of Castile-León, a Palaeolithic site where dozens of international archaeologists were undertaking excavation work. They were looking for evidence of ancient Spaniards who lived 800,000 years ago and even earlier. Experts were discovering how people lived and hunted, what they ate, what tools they used, how they died and how they were buried. In one of Atapuerca's caves – known as Gran Dolina – archaeologists have found stone tools which were used to butcher animals and, more importantly, strong evidence suggesting that they cooked their food. They have also discovered here the oldest evidence of human cannibalism. Even more exciting than Gran Dolina, if that is possible, hominid tool-making dating back about 1.5 million years has been recorded at the Orce site in Granada. The Spanish findings are casting reasonable doubt on the dominant view that the earliest stages of human evolution took place exclusively in Africa.[1]

Moving quickly through prehistory, experts are trying to fill the gap between the findings at Orce and Atapuerca and the recent discovery at Capellades in Catalonia dating back to circa 80,000 BC. Capellades is already bringing the food researcher much closer to the diet of the early occupants of the Iberian Peninsula. Here furnaces used for cooking and tool-making have been found, together with a collection of stone and bone tools and wooden utensils.

Archaeologists have established that the diet of the early inhabitants consisted of the meat of animals they could hunt. It appears that they also ate insects and worms, roots, nuts and the wild fruits which they could find on their journeys from site to site, through mountains and valleys covered in thick forests. As they often lived close to the sea, they gathered shellfish and other marine species. Oysters, limpets and sea snails were eaten extensively, both raw and cooked in their shells on stone hearths. Who knows if the traditional fish and shellfish soups that the Basques are so partial to were once a speciality prepared at the local caves? Barandiarán, a Catholic priest and a key figure in Basque archaeology, believed that this was the case.[2] Writing about the excavation of the Santimamiñe cave near Guernica in Bizkaia, he described the discovery of charcoal and ash, a few oyster shells and limpets, and a hearth 115 centimetres (45¼ in.) in diameter made of large stones. Count de la Vega de Sella, another well-known Spanish archaeologist, pointed out to Barandiarán that the shells they had found had not been opened by force, nor had they been placed directly on a fire. He believed they had been boiled in some form of natural utensil.

In 1820, in the magnificent caves of Altamira in Cantabria, northern Spain, artwork was found dating back 14,000–18,500 years. Artists used charcoal and haematite rock to depict bison, horses, deer and wild boar in black as well as intense orange colours. They also depicted men hunting for food and dancing for pleasure, while their other main activity was gathering wild fruits and leaves. Also in Cantabria, the cave of El Juyo (13,350–11,900 BC) is one of the richest Magdalenian sites known in the Iberian Peninsula. El Juyo documents the social organization of activities as well as the economics

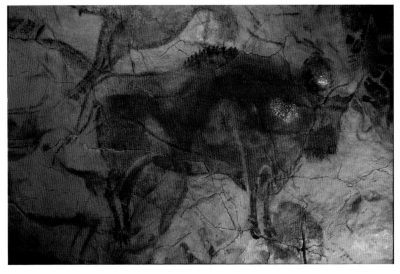

Palaeolithic people hunted bison for food: Altamira cave painting.

*Kaiku*, an ancient Basque cooking utensil (modern reproduction).

of daily life in Magdalenian times. At this cave, more than 22,000 identifiable bones have been found, belonging to deer, goats, lions, horses, wild boar and foxes. Given the number of shells found at the site, it is clear that prehistoric Cantabrians enjoyed the same sea urchins that the people of Asturias in particular still hold in such high regard today.

Archaeologists agree that in the foothills of the Pyrenees wooden utensils called *kaikus* were used for cooking before pottery had been produced in Iberia. The *kaiku*, carved out of a solid log, allowed early inhabitants of the peninsula to boil water using hot embers inside the utensil, a cooking method that tenderized shellfish and roots. Much later, following the same method but using milk instead of water and animal rennet, the same *kaikus* were used to prepare rich junkets called *mamias* or *gaztamberas*.[3]

Agriculture developed in Iberia around two hundred years later than in other parts of the world. The region's geographic and climatic diversity would have determined which crops were grown, particularly in the north of the country where wet Atlantic weather makes growing cereals such as wheat and barley difficult.

In 2015, Mattias Jakobsson of Uppsala University in Sweden and his team analysed genetic material from eight sets of human remains found in Atapuerca dating back to 5500–3500 BC. They came to the conclusion that present-day Basques are the descendants of Iberians living in the peninsula after the transition to farming. Having mixed with local hunter-gatherers further north, they then became isolated for millennia. This group of scientists not only provided information about hunter-gathering and agriculture in early Spain, but contributed to the understanding of the origins of the Basques, one of Europe's most enigmatic people. This is a subject that has puzzled historians for centuries, not only in Spain. 'Our results show that the Basques trace their ancestry to early farming groups from Iberia, which contradicts previous views of them being a remnant population that trace their ancestry to Mesolithic hunter-gathered groups,' affirms Professor Jakobsson. Once they were established in their beloved and difficult to cultivate area and able to conquer further north, they became safe from those who tried to invade their territory and eventually left.[4]

Further east of the Basque country, things were very different. Research carried out in the Pyrenees points to the cultivation of free-threshing wheat, barley and pea crops around 6000–5400 BC. In other parts of the country, especially in Catalonia and Valencia, the early success of Mediterranean agriculture is also well documented.

While the development of agriculture in Iberia came late, it happened quickly and proved to be one of the most varied in Europe. However, the reasons for this are still open to debate. Were different crops grown together in a field to reduce the risk of crop failure? Were early farmers experimenting with different crops? Was the selection of crops determined by their eventual use as food for humans or for animal feed, such as the making of dough or the quality of the straw? Whatever the reason, in the Iberian Neolithic the list of crops available in one region or another was staggering. There was hulled wheat, wheat for making flour and early bread, barley, peas and other pulses such as lentils, as well as flax and poppies. Animal husbandry, another fundamental part of agriculture, also occupied an important part of the lives of the early peoples of Iberia. They reared goats, pigs and bovids according to the climatic and geographic characteristics of the zone and the general lack of fresh grass, except in the very north and northwest.

## EARLY SETTLERS AND NEWCOMERS

The settlers of Spain were made up of different tribes. Early sources described the inhabitants of the far-reaching land at the end of the world as odd. They performed bloody rituals, they fought other tribes, they drank beer, and they danced during the long nights of winter. They also raised cattle, pigs and sheep and cultivated the land. They were the Iberians, probably the oldest known people of a peninsula that would bear their name forever.

The origin of the Iberians is much debated. Some experts believe they could have been North African Berbers, while others are of the opinion that they came from Asia Minor in 6000 BC. Acknowledged by the Greeks and Romans, the Iberians occupied extensive areas in the east and southeast of Spain as well as some parts of Andalusia. They cultivated wheat, barley, rye and oats, and they ate the basic *torta* bread made with ground cereal grains and water then cooked directly over hot embers. They also brought millet and cabbage with them. Meat consumption increased (sheep, goats, oxen and particularly pigs). The Iberians' advances in agriculture and mining in southern Spain attracted powerful traders from the eastern Mediterranean shores. Iberians had discovered the value of salt, minerals and precious metals, and were now interacting with other cultures coming from Europe and Africa.

Celtic tribes of Indo-European provenance had started crossing the Pyrenees as early as 900 BC. This was not a classic invasion – it was a prolonged process of immigration lasting more than six hundred years. That they loved nature as much as war would be proven when the Romans tried to subjugate them centuries later. The Celts were a pastoral people at heart. They loved butter and goat's meat as well as the hams they cured in the high northern hills, where they built their characteristic circular houses with conical thatched roofs. Further east on the coast and in the foothills of the Pyrenees, the Basques

The first-century-BC Celtic settlement of Santa Tecla, Galicia.

cultivated the land and fished close to the coast. The Celtiberians were a group of Celts that, during the centuries before Christ, occupied the central and eastern part of the peninsula. They were the ones who would fight the Romans to the death as their leaders became more determined to stay in the peninsula for good.

## THEY ALL LOVED BREAD

In his *Geography*, the ancient Greek writer Strabo devoted the third book to Iberia, in Book III.1 talking about the simple breads prepared by the Celtic tribes that lived in the northwest of the Iberian Peninsula, today northern Portugal and Spanish Galicia. To make bread from acorn flour was easy. During the winter months, ripe acorns were collected from the trees. If their tannin concentration was high, the acorns were first roasted or boiled. When dried, they were milled to a coarse flour using rudimentary milling stones; then a little water was added, and the dough was ready for cooking.

Spelt, an ancient form of wheat, is used to make *tortas*. These are *Triticum spelta* spikelets containing the wheat grain.

The Celts who had settled in the peninsula were more sophisticated than the Celtic tribes in Gaul; they knew how to make more sophisticated breads by adding ferments to the dough. The result was lighter, more appetizing bread which they often used to mop up the juices from roasted kid and other meats. Known also as *torta*, this type of bread was made further south and east of the peninsula with millet or with other grains of a higher value such as wheat and barley. As they did not have ovens, they placed portions of dough directly on top of the coals, sometimes protected by large maple leaves as the people of Galicia and Asturias still do today when baking cornbread. Sometimes they would bake their breads using ceramic pots, which they placed at the centre of the fire covered with an inverted lid onto which hot coals were placed.

## THEY CAME FROM THE EAST

The arrival of newcomers from far eastern Mediterranean shores brought the Near East closer to the West. By then vines had already been cultivated in some areas of the peninsula for hundreds of years. It is a matter of argument as to whether the vine was a native of the western Mediterranean area or was brought there from the East when man learned about fermentation.[5] The city of Gadir (Cádiz) was founded in 1100 BC by a confederation of maritime traders from Tyre, Byblos and Tripoli – the Phoenicians. Originally they belonged to a civilization centred in the north of ancient Canaan, the area known today as Lebanon. They were great sailors and traders, specializing in textiles, glass and pottery. They also dealt in cedar, olive oil and wine. Their ships were built to sail the Mediterranean and further, around West Africa, always in search of business and profit. They founded colonies wherever they went, in Cyprus, Rhodes, Crete, Malta, Sicily, Sardinia, Marseilles, Carthage and Cádiz. As the oracle of their god Melqart explained, they believed that at the edge of the known world they could find minerals and precious metals which were the most valuable cargo of all, together with sea salt to preserve fish. Southern Spain was rich in silver, gold and copper, and tuna fish was as plentiful as salt. During the Phoenician period, Cádiz also gained control of the commerce in tin from the rest of the peninsula and from the Cassiterides, or the 'islands of tin', a mysterious place further north in the Atlantic Ocean. Ships would sail north along the Portuguese and Galician coast to certain points where they traded with merchants from those mysterious islands, which might have been located opposite the coast of Galicia, Brittany or even further north in the British Isles.

Initially the Phoenicians established a number of colonies to the east and west of Gibraltar. These were small settlements located all along the coast at short intervals which could serve as ports. From the eighth century BC to the middle of the sixth, Phoenician immigrants settled in this region in large numbers. Evidence from tombs excavated by archaeologists indicates that the remains belonged to wealthy families who had lived in the area for successive generations. This was more likely to be a permanent immigration rather than temporary commercial visits. In the settlements situated at the mouths of rivers they could cultivate the land and raise cattle, goats and sheep. They could also easily reach the interior of the country and therefore search for minerals and other valuable commodities. The mild weather and the richness of the seas were other determining factors. Places such as Abdera (ancient Adra), Almuñécar (Sexi), Chorreras, Morro de Mezquitilla, Toscanos and Málaga (Malaka) were all Phoenician settlements.

From the start, the colonists also engaged in intense commercial activity with the indigenous people of the hinterland, although on a much smaller scale than around Cádiz and the other coastal areas. They brought with them textiles, fine jewellery and ceramics. They also brought wine safely transported in the classic earthenware amphorae they had been using for centuries. In southern Spain this idea has been supported by the presence of countless shards from broken amphorae of the period. The amphora was the perfect container, used not just to transport olive oil and wine but also grain and many other products. Later, during Roman times, the classic amphora would be copied by dozens of local artisans with slight variations on the original design. Recent archaeological findings indicate that during the Phoenician period, wine had become the number one export to Iberia. Obviously the native population was developing a taste for the fermented juice of the Middle Eastern grape. Until then beer brewed both by men and women had been enjoyed by the indigenous people. The Phoenicians also developed factories for the preservation of tuna fish and for the production of their purple-dyed textiles. In the town of Cádiz, coins have been found bearing the image of a tuna fish, indicating how important tuna fishing and fish preservation were for the local economy of the time. During these early centuries, exchanges between the indigenous and imported cultures impacted favourably on the development of mining, farming, fishing and trade, and logically on the food prepared in local kitchens. The Greeks, who were great cultural benefactors, were also travelling in the western Mediterranean and establishing trading colonies in Catalonia.

## TARTESSOS

The southwest coast of the peninsula intrigued geographers in antiquity and continues to attract archaeologists today. Some are looking for amphorae, cooking utensils and ancient seeds, while others are looking for treasures such as the El Carambolo, which was found in 1958. Exhibited at the Archaeological Museum in Seville, this is a magnificent collection of the finest jewellery treasures, which confirm the sophistication of the culture they belonged to. Regardless of whether it was the hands of Iberian or Phoenician jewellers that made these unique treasures in the sixth century BC, their discovery on a site located some kilometres west of Seville has been associated with Tartessos.

Until the second half of the twentieth century Tartessos, surrounded by tales of treasure and adventurous voyages, was considered to be a mythical place. It appears that it actually had existed in the southwesternmost part of Spain from the ninth to the sixth centuries BC. Today, archaeologists believe that Tartessos once occupied the same place as the National Park of Doñana in the province of Huelva, in western Andalusia. Doñana is a sanctuary of great beauty and wildlife where birds rest and feed before crossing the Strait of Gibraltar on their yearly journey to Africa. It appears that their territory reached modern Extremadura.

Tartessos is a name given by the Greeks to the capital and harbour of a wealthy state which, having developed both politically and culturally, would become the first known organized far-western civilization. It was also the earliest to trade with eastern Mediterranean cultures, travelling across the sea.

At that time, before reaching the Atlantic Ocean, the Guadalquivir River split into two mouths to form a lagoon surrounding an island where some experts believe the capital city of the kingdom of Tartessos was located, even if recently academics have doubted the existence of a capital as such.[6]

In Book Three, Chapter Two of his *Geography*, Strabo mentioned the austerity of the people living in the centre and north of the peninsula, although he was more interested in the people of the south, especially the people from the Guadalquivir valley known in ancient times as Turdetania, believed by Strabo to be the land of Tartessos. For him, these people had been more sophisticated and wealthier. Their land was more fertile and rich in minerals, metals and sea salt. They mined silver and gold, tin and copper, all much valued throughout the Mediterranean. Strabo's depiction of life as well as the richness and the colour of the land came alive in his writing together with his accounts of the development, all along the Mediterranean coast, of agriculture, fishing and mining. His admiration for Andalusia was obvious, and in particular Turdetania, the land of Tartessos:

Turdetania is marvellously fertile, and abounds in every species
of product. The value of its productions is double by means of
exportation, the surplus products finding a ready sale amongst the
numerous ship-owners.

Further on in the same chapter he continues to describe the same area:
'Large quantities of corn and wine are exported from Turdetania, besides much
oil, which is of the first quality, also wax, honey, pitch, large quantities of the
kermes-berry and vermilion.' Strabo's description of the riches of the Atlantic
Ocean, which he calls 'the exterior sea', is impressive:

Oysters and every variety of shell-fish, remarkable both for their
number and size, are found along the whole of the exterior sea . . .
The same is the case with regard to all kinds of cetaceans, narwhals,
whales.

He speaks of the size of the congers – 'quite monstrous' – and of the lampreys,
and many other fish of the same kind. Nothing is missing from his never-
ending list. Then he touches on the subject of tuna fish, the most appreciated
of all: 'The rich tuna fish that crosses the Straits, fattened with the fruit of
stunted oak which grows at the bottom of the sea'. He also believed that the
beautiful lands of Tartessos must be where the Hesperides had kept their
orchards of golden apples. For Strabo, the connection between Spain and
food had reached the realms of mythology. While he does not shine light on
the food of the Tartessians, he describes with great detail the food prepared
by the Lusitanians in the Duoro valley further north, their diet consisting
of roasted goat and very sustaining *torta* bread.[7]

Eventually the lagoon dried up, and the second mouth of the river
disappeared completely. By the fifth century BC, the title 'most dynamic culture
in the peninsula' switched from the west to the eastern coast, where Iberians
had ongoing access to Greek and Carthaginian trade and were making their
mark. In 1897, the intriguing *Dama de Elche* (Lady of Elche) was found in
an archaeological site in L'Alcúdia, near Valencia. Believed to be a piece of
funerary Iberian sculpture dating back to the fifth century BC, it represents a
woman – probably a goddess of incredible beauty – wearing the most intricate
ceremonial headdress and necklaces. The *Dama de Elche* is the peninsula's most
ancient Iberian icon.

With the demise of Tartessos, possibly due to political divisions and the
attacks from powerful Carthage on the original Phoenician trading posts and

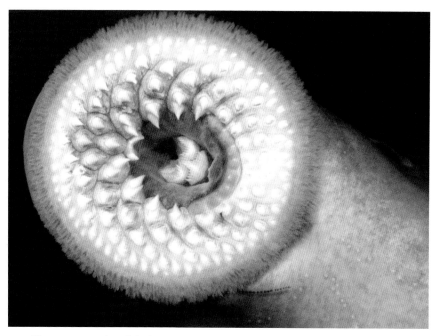

'Quite monstrous', said the first-century Greek geographer Strabo of tasty lampreys; this is the sucker-like mouth of a lamprey.

settlements, the peninsula entered a new chapter. For the first time, foreign domination would impose a pattern of life on the population. From the moment Carthage, itself a Phoenician city-state located on the Gulf of Tunis, gained independence from Tyre, the western shores of the Mediterranean became a theatre of war where Greeks and Carthaginians first, and later Romans and Carthaginians, would fight to the death for power and possessions. Sicily, Corsica, Sardinia and the Balearic Islands as well as the whole of Iberia would be the ultimate reward.

## They Called It Hispania

In the end, Rome was declared the winner. It was almost by default and through sheer determination to end the presence of Carthage in the Mediterranean once and for all that the Romans had decided not to invade Iberia. They finally came in 218 BC. The Romans saw much more than a space to be taken from their enemies and they conquered it. The job was costly. It would take Rome almost two hundred years to subdue the warrior spirit of the Celtiberians. As for the Cantabrians and the Basques, they would remain independent, their spirit never to be subdued.

At Numancia, the last Celtiberian name associated with resistance and valour during Roman times, archaeologists have uncovered undisputed evidence of the diet eaten by the indigenous population of that tragic city. Here it has been possible to establish that two-thirds of the diet was based on grains, nuts such as acorns, and green vegetables and roots. The rest was made up of meat and fish.

In 143 BC, the Roman Senate sent Scipio Aemilianus, grandson of Scipio Africanus, to defeat Numancia. The Romans blockaded the city. Without food, some of the inhabitants succumbed to cannibalism before starvation and sickness. In the end they decided to commit mass suicide.

As recorded by the Greek historian Appian in his *Roman History*, Scipio ordered the reaping of large fields of green wheat to use as animal feed as his army marched towards Numancia, leaving the River Ebro behind. Apart from precious wheat (durum and spelt), other cereals such as barley and millet were also planted by local Celtiberian tribes. Acorns discovered by archaeologists in the flourmills at Numancia had been equally important to the ancient inhabitants while they had been under siege. They could make bread and polenta in their traditional *ollas* (ceramic pots used for cooking and storing food), and perhaps some vegetable dishes prepared with wild herbs and cardoon at the beginning of the siege.

Not until the reign of Caesar Augustus was Rome able to claim the peninsula. Hispania, the name Rome gave to the ancient land of the Iberians, would become not just a provider of gold, silver, olive oil, grain and slaves to Rome but one of the most valuable acquisitions of both the Republic and, later, the Empire, a basic pillar that sustained their growth.

Not only did the indigenous population pay the taxes demanded by Rome, Hispania would become Rome's granary, a province of the Empire where wheat – the most precious of all grains – was produced in abundance. Using wheat, yeast, water and the Roman oven, white bread would become for Spain a symbol of Christian purity and an object of desire and wealth. Hispania grew into into a well-stocked larder that fed the rich Roman aristocracy as well as the soldiers of the legions fighting in Germania. Within a few decades, economic development and consolidation of a successful exchange of goods between Rome and certain parts of Hispania allowed the new province to become an affluent recipient of Roman luxury goods, including fine black glazed and thin-walled pottery worthy of any distinguished household.

There is little evidence of the food prepared in the Iberian Peninsula during the Roman occupation, but this is compensated for by the multitude of agricultural studies and insights from the field of medicine and archaeology. Evidence found in the artistic mosaics that decorate the houses and villas of

Roman Spain, and in numerous eating and cooking utensils and containers, also allows scholars to learn about the culinary traditions in the peninsula between the first and the fifth centuries AD.[8]

At museums in Tarragona, Valencia, Zaragoza, Cuenca or Cádiz are well-preserved amphorae and bottles, pestles and mortars, *patellas* (small dishes or plates), *patinas* (broad shallow dishes), *caccabuses* (wide-mouthed terracotta cooking pots) and other *ollas* (generic terracotta cooking pots). These have been kept for everyone to remember one of the most fascinating periods of Spanish history.

From an early stage, Rome had identified the areas where agriculture could be perfected in the Meseta (Spain's central *altiplano*) and in Valencia, Andalusia and the rich lands of the Ebro Valley, among others. The Ebro, one of the most important rivers of Spain, runs between Cantabria in the north and Catalonia, where it reaches the Mediterranean Sea. It crosses part of today's Rioja, Navarra, Aragon and Catalonia regions, areas well known by the Roman generals and their armies at the beginning of their campaign in the peninsula. Soon they would invest in sophisticated irrigation that would improve Iberian agriculture and also in silos where grain could be protected and kept dry. The word 'cereal' derives from Ceres, the Roman goddess of harvest and agriculture.

*Panis militaris* was a good example of the Roman partiality to grains and especially to warm baked bread. In Roman times soldiers would carry a supply of grain, some salt, a little oil, *posca* (a type of vinegar used to disinfect water and small wounds) and dried sausages to chew during the long marches. Every group of soldiers living in the same tent would also carry a small milling stone to grind flour. This allowed each soldier to prepare porridge, small *tortas* or *galletas* (biscuits) and of course bread, generally a coarse, indigestible brown bread. White bread was baked for the officers, just as it was for the upper classes back in Rome; brown bread was synonymous with the peasantry. It is interesting that until very recently brown bread has never been appreciated in Spain. Originally it was made with a combination of inferior grains, almost black in colour, that even today old people associate with the Spanish Civil War and the 'years of hunger' – a type of bread never to be eaten again, they would say.

Cato the Elder, a Roman writer, politician and soldier renowned for his austere writing and his successful campaigns against the Carthaginians, loved bread. His agricultural handbook includes a recipe for bread baked in a *clibanus*. 'Wash both your hands thoroughly as well as the mixing bowl,' he said. 'Add flour to the bowl, add water gradually, and knead well. When the dough is ready, roll it out and bake it in a pot with an earthenware lid.' The

## The Olive Tree

As children we learned it was an olive branch that the dove brought back to the Ark, proving to Noah that the Flood was subsiding. The olive tree, the 'King of Trees' named in the biblical Book of Judges, would eventually cover large expanses of Spain, which to this day remains the main producer of olives and olive oil in the world.

Olive oil has been an indigenous product of Spain for thousands of years. Ships transported olive oil to Rome in amphorae stamped with the seals of the exporters, a good practice that in the case of Italy today and with the help of EU regulations has, perhaps sadly, been largely forgotten. Even if today millions of bottles of Spanish olive oil produced and bottled in Andalusia, Castile, Extremadura, Catalonia, Valencia or the Balearics are sold all over the world, every season thousands of litres of Spanish olive oil are transported to Italy in bulk by modern tankers, which is not necessarily the best commercial practice. It is then sold on in cans and Italian designer bottles not stamped to show the actual origin of the oil. Even so, business is business, and we have to remember that for centuries Italy has remained a good customer for Spain as well as an excellent marketer and producer of olive oil in its own right.

The olive oil of today has little to do with the oil sold in antiquity and even several decades ago, especially the extra

Latin word *clibanus* has many meanings: oven, furnace and even a tray with a conical lid similar to the North African tagine which was used to bake bread.[9]

In the first century Caesar Augustus increased the original division of Hispania from two to three provinces: Baetica (Andalusia and southern Extremadura), Lusitania (today's Portugal) and Hispania Citerior, as the rest of the peninsula was known. Roman values consolidated in Hispania as towns and cities flourished and moved fully into the orbit of Roman life. Augustus, who understood the power of food distribution among all sections of the population and, most importantly, for the armed forces, remained in charge of the production and transportation of food coming from the provinces

virgin olive oil in which the character of the individual olive variety shines through. There are hundreds of olive varieties in the Iberian Peninsula. Some olive varieties are still milled with conical granite stones turning on a base millstone, as they were 2,500 years ago. Others use more modern methods, but the main difference is in the care given to the tree and the olive as it is gathered in the winter months. Olive varieties include Picual, Hojiblanca, Cornicabra, Manzanilla, Picudo, Carrasqueña, Morisca, Empeltre and Arbequina, among many others. Modern trees, which tend to be smaller, are irrigated at the beginning of their lives. Their fruit is picked by hand. This avoids bruising the fruit and a decrease in quality, which affects the aroma and increases the acidity. This should be avoided at all costs. Good practices are also applied to old trees today but large trees force the gatherer to use more traditional methods such as hitting the branches with large wooden sticks. Bruising is avoided by placing large nets underneath to collect the falling fruit. After carefully transporting the olives to the mill or *almazara* – another Arabic word – best olive oil, *aceite de oliva extra virgin*, is extracted at the beginning of the process, practically without pressure, drop by drop. Other oils sold simply as 'olive oil' have been refined and tend to be used more for stewing and frying.

during his tenure. It was clearly dangerous to leave such a matter in the hands of men with ambition in places as valuable as Hispania or the African colonies. Under his rule, agriculture and trade thrived even further. Apart from wheat from the Meseta, often transported by road to supply the army along the northern borders of the Empire, olive oil and wine were exported in earthenware amphorae to Rome from Baetica via the Guadalquivir and then by sea. Even if the means of production and transportation of goods was limited, it is clear that long-distance commerce was established by the Romans as an economic policy, and even as a means of political control to be exercised in the whole of the Empire. In this respect olive oil was a good example.[10] Baetica produced olive oil in great quantities, practically all of it exported to Rome in an exchange that benefited the elite descendants of Romans living in Spain.

Many of the Roman residents were retired soldiers with an agricultural background, as was the case for the father of the emperor Trajan (AD 53–117). Trajan, born in an enclave just outside the city of Seville not far from the Guadalquivir River, is considered by history as one of the 'Five Good Emperors'. He made certain that the transportation of goods between the provinces and Rome was facilitated by building important *vías de comunicación* – many of these roads are still in use today. Wine, which in those days was consumed hot and blended with pine resin, aromatic herbs, honey and spices, proved to be another profitable business and a fundamental part of this exchange. Initially, Roman merchants in Hispania imported wine from Italy, but as the quality of the wine produced in the province improved, exportation of the local production became the focus of their business. Rome alone consumed more than 25 million litres of oil and 1 million litres of wine per year, of which a very large proportion came from Hispania, often forcing prices in Rome to be reduced considerably. In those cases, and to avoid conflict between markets, production had to be held back from time to time. As already mentioned, goods were transported by sea, which merchants preferred, or by river or land if war or other adverse circumstances dictated. For this purpose and in memory of Caesar they built the Vía Augusta road some 1,500 kilometres (930 mi.) long, linking Cádiz in the Baetica with the Pyrenean border and beyond to join the Via Domitia in Languedoc.

Another important source of wealth shipped from the new province was high-quality garum, a strong condiment made from rotten fish that could be blended with oil, vinegar or water, all well suited to the Roman palate. Garum produced in Cartago Nova (Cartagena) was considered to be the finest and commanded higher prices in the market. Salted tuna and sturgeon, known as *salazones de pescado* and produced using techniques brought to the Iberian Peninsula by the Phoenicians, also made many merchants rich. Sea salt, a precious commodity, was available from the island of Ibiza and from the coast of Cartagena as well as in Cádiz. This was the same salt that was used to cure the hams and shoulders of the Iberian breed of pigs, so often mentioned by Roman food specialists. Although Italy was a major market for these products, they were also sold to other parts of the Empire, such as Britain. It is interesting that, independently of their staggering success as traders, the Romans valued agriculture rather than trade and manufacturing as a source of status and wealth.

Transport of people and goods including foodstuffs: Roman bridge, Cordoba.

With the introduction of the Roman oven, bread, a staple food in Spain since the moment man first blended water and flour, was improved beyond recognition. The art of roasting kid, lamb and suckling pig was perfected. Romans preferred the meat of young animals – well cooked, very tender and sweet – as Spaniards still do. An entire small animal cooked on the spit often featured as an impressive centrepiece at dinner parties. It is known that the art of carving meat was highly developed during the early part of the Empire. Carving was a job always undertaken by slaves, perhaps the same slaves who cleaned floors and furniture as the Roman elite vomited in order to be able to eat even more of the exotic food prepared continually in the kitchen.

Strabo, Pliny the Elder, Plato and Martial all provided an extensive record of life in Hispania, while Varro and Columella, who was born in Spain, wrote wide-ranging texts on agricultural development in the province. Columella's *De re rustica* influenced Spanish agriculture well into the Enlightenment. As if this was not enough, he also wrote widely about Roman villas, the original country houses built for the upper classes in Italy and, later on, in the rest of the Empire, of which thirteen fine examples can be found in Spain. Agriculture was managed from these villas on a large scale. Here professional cooks were employed to prepare recipes recorded in books such as *Apicius* (*De re coquinaria*). The fine mosaics that decorated the main rooms of the villas often depicted food from the larder: ducks, rabbits and cardoons, fresh pork ribs and even the hunting of wild boar for a succulent roast dinner. The

A Roman fish-salting factory near Cádiz.

*haciendas* and *cortijos* (landed estates) of Andalusia, where life tends to move at a slower pace than in the rest of Spain, are in essence the Spanish versions of the Roman *latifundia* (large landed estates) and the agrarian villa. Over centuries they have remained synonymous with the extensive number of contracted workers who still maintain the large estates seldom used by their owners. Even though specific information about the food cooked in Spain in Roman times, especially during the last two centuries of their occupation, is practically non-existent, we can assume that the food eaten in Hispania was fairly similar to that of Rome. Some historians believe that in Spain feasting never reached the extremes that became the norm in Rome. Rome's culinary traditions had evolved and were enriched as the Romans conquered other lands and cultures and brought back products from all over the world, in an early process of globalization that improved the diet of the privileged and eventually the poor.

At the beginning of their success and expansion, things had been very different for most of the Roman population, both urban and agrarian. Their diet was based on *puls* or *pulmentum*. Not unlike porridge, *puls* was prepared by toasting grains of cereal, usually barley or wheat, which were pounded and then boiled in water or milk. In Spain today the dish is called *gachas* and also *poleadas*. Back in Rome, bread eventually became available not only to the well-off but to the wider population as well. Following a Roman custom, it was often distributed free to those who could not afford it, their diet complemented with fresh and dried beans and vegetables such as chard, onions and asparagus, which in those days were associated with the diet of the lower classes. The consumption of meat, which was considered to be a luxury by most people, was rare. The Romans enjoyed cheese as well as salted fatty fish when possible. Mushroom hunting was another custom introduced into Spain by the Romans.

Scholars differ in their understanding of which foreign culture has contributed most to the true personality of the food culture of the Iberian Peninsula. Many point to Islamic influences, yet there is a school of thought based on strong evidence suggesting that the greatest influence came from Rome, especially during the last period of domination.[11] By then Latin had become the official language, and sophisticated irrigation systems allowed the cultivation of crops, vegetables and fruits in places where it would have been impossible to do so without water. The same irrigation systems were perfected by the Arabs centuries later. The deforestation of the land, a controversial issue seldom included in academic texts, is a stain on the unbelievable progress made in agriculture during the Roman domination of Spain. Deforestation, already started by the Phoenicians, had become an imperial Roman policy. This was enforced to such an extent that the scarcity of quality timber needed to shore up local silver mines seriously affected the output of this valuable metal.

A *cortijo* among the olive groves near Periana in Málaga; this could be a modern version of a Roman villa.

Hunting, a favoured Roman sport; mosaic at the Roman villa La Olmeda in Palencia.

## A BARBARIAN WORLD

With Rome's demise in the early fifth century AD, caused by its decadence and by the relentless attacks of barbarian tribes on the northern frontiers, the rich Mediterranean table of Hispania became as impoverished as the land that was once again facing destruction and destitution.

At the beginning of the fifth century AD, a number of barbarian tribes crossed the Pyrenees. Throughout their history they had been permanently on the move, with their ancient nomadic custom of always taking from their surroundings but never contributing anything to them. First the Suebi and Vandals were forced to move south by other barbarian tribes, replacing the Romans in Spain. Not only were towns and villages destroyed, the entire country became a desolate battlefield. The newcomers, for whom the refinement and excesses of the Roman table were completely alien, followed their own customs and food preferences, while the indigenous people, their lives shattered and their crops destroyed, struggled to survive.[12]

On the arrival of the Suebi and Vandals, pork fat was substituted for olive oil and beer substituted for the thousands of litres of wine which had been produced every year in Spain. All we know about food during the early years of the barbarian invasion is that, irrespective of the tribe, pork was preferred to mutton and it was roasted over hot coals. As the Visigoth kingdom extended across Spain in AD 573, agriculture and food improved for Christians and Jews alike, even though the variety of crops cultivated had been considerably diminished by that point.

The Visigoths had evolved from earlier Gothic groups originating beyond the eastern provinces of the Empire, and they had been in contact with and influenced by Roman custom and law. With Visigoth King Reccared's conversion from Arianism to Catholicism and the unification of the peninsula under one church, further progress was made. Unfortunately, with it came new outbreaks of religious intolerance. Once again the Jewish population would suffer as King Sisebut (r. AD 612–21) ascended the throne. He was an educated man capable of fine writing, and a religious man determined to convert or eradicate other faiths from the face of the peninsula. The laws passed by another Visigoth king, Recceswinth, were stricter still, prohibiting the celebration of Passover as well as other ancient Jewish festivals and rituals. It was also during the reign of Recceswinth that a great compilation of Visigoth law, the *Lex Visigothorum* or *Liber ludiciorum*, based more on Roman than Germanic law, was completed.

Nothing can be ascertained about food during the period from reading the *Lex Ludiciorum*, but it provides an insight into the composition of society. The Christian Church, in particular the writings of Isidoro de Sevilla, provides a fascinating account of all aspects of life and food over those centuries. St Isidore of Seville was a prince of the Catholic Church and a prestigious scholar whose work in many different fields is often quoted by academics. Born circa AD 560, he was an instrumental figure in the conversion of Visigoth royalty to Catholicism, and in the work done by the Councils of Toledo and Seville towards the concept of a regional representative government. St Isidore's acclaimed *Etymologiae* is an encyclopedic compilation of all human knowledge, divided into twenty books of which two relate to food matters and even housewares. Specifically, Book 17 deals with the rural world: agriculture, crops of every kind, vines and trees, herbs and vegetables. Entry 68 of Book 17 is particularly revealing: 'Olive oil (*oleum*) is made from the olive tree (*olea*), for as I have already said, *olea* is the tree, from which is derived the word oleum.' Isidore even specified which kind of oil in accordance with the maturity of the fruit was best for human consumption. Book 20, entitled 'Provisions and Various Implements', is a detailed study of meal tables, foodstuffs, drinks and their vessels, vessels for wine, water and oil, vessels for cooks and bakers, lamps, beds, chairs, vehicles, rural and garden implements, and equestrian equipment.[13] Isidore's *Etymologiae* is so comprehensive that it is sometimes heard today that the Pope wishes to make him the patron saint of the Internet!

Starting with King Reccared, and until the Moorish invasion of AD 711, the list of Gothic and Visigoth kings reigning in Spain over a period of two

The Gothic kings loved eating pork and drinking beer: statues at the
Plaza de Oriente in Madrid.

hundred years is extensive. In Madrid, at the Plaza de Oriente opposite the
Royal Palace, the statues of those kings and their names stand as powerful
links between the past and present monarchies.

# TWO

# Moors, Jews and Christians

In the *Amadís de Gaula*, a popular early fourteenth-century tale of a knight errant, Spain is described by the protagonist Amadís as

> a land fertile and beautiful as Syria, warm and sweet as Yemen, abundant in aromas and flowers as is India, similar to the Huyaz in its fruits, to Cathay in its rich metals, and to Aden in the fertility of its coastal regions.[1]

Centuries before the *Amadís* was written, these must have been the thoughts of the immigrant prince as he landed at Almuñécar in Granada. By this time Islam dominated almost the entire Iberian Peninsula.

## THIRTY CHRISTIANS PERCHED ON A ROCK

In the early summer of AD 711, a powerful force of 7,000 Berbers led by a Muslim warrior, Tariq ibn Ziyad, landed in the Iberian Peninsula. They had been summoned by the family of the Visigoth king Witiza, who had died in 710. The family was claiming a right that did not exist in eighth-century Spain: the right to inherit the kingdom of their father. In accordance with the Twelfth Council of Toledo in AD 681, Visigoth kings were elected by a number of bishops and aristocrats, and it was Roderic (Rodrigo), a duke or military commander who would become the last king of the Visigoths, not the son of Witiza, who would be wearing the crown on the Visigoth throne of Toledo.[2] This call for help presented a perfect excuse to further the expansionist policy of Islam as it waited in North Africa. The Visigoths called the invaders Moors, and the Moors called the land they were invading Al-Andalus, a name derived from 'land of the Vandals' or from the Germanic *landahlauts* (allotted territory). Within four years the administratively ineffective last kingdom of the Visigoths would be history. By the time the Moors left almost eight centuries later, they had enriched the land beyond belief with literature and fashion, mathematics, medicine and, most importantly, agriculture and food.

Without doubt the cruelty of war and the extreme violence displayed at times by the invaders, as well as the initial enforcement of a new order and a new religion, brought upon a large percentage of the population of Iberia, especially the Christians, a sorrow and destitution never to be forgotten. The reality and myths of the *Reconquista*, as the reclaiming of the peninsula by the Christians is known, together with the intolerance of the Catholic and Apostolic Roman Church, has never allowed many Spaniards to feel comfortable with such an important part of their history. However, the rich heritage they received in medieval times under the crescent moon of Islam would remain a strong feature of the country's complex personality, including the food that would be cooked for centuries to come. The fact is that for several centuries, the magical world they brought from Africa and from the Middle East, as well as their capacity to develop and even improve what they found, has never left Iberia. Among the gifts left behind are many food traditions, still visible today as part of a rich Moorish heritage in Spain.

By the time of the Islamic invasion of the Iberian Peninsula, matters were at a low ebb in the Spain of the Visigoths. King Roderic was under pressure in the northern territories, where the people of Navarre were once more seeking independence. He was also fighting for survival on many other fronts at a time when treason and division were everyday occurrences. Disaster struck at the Battle of Guadalete, not far from Medina-Sidonia. Here an unstoppable and determined Islamic force defeated Roderic's army. By AD 713, the 7,000-strong original invading forces of mostly Berbers had been reinforced with elite forces from Arabia and Syria. As with the Roman legions centuries before, they decided to stay. They even burned the boats in which their forces had arrived. From AD 711 to 929, the peninsula became a province of the Umayyad Caliphate of Damascus, an empire extending from the borders of India to the Strait of Gibraltar, governed by an emir designated by the Governor of North Africa. Within a few years the Moors had occupied practically the whole of Iberia, with the exception of a few small enclaves in the mountains of Asturias, and in the land of the Basques, where some locals as well as certain Visigoth aristocrats had managed to resist.

The advance of the Islamic forces in the eighth century had forced the Visigoth elite to take refuge in a corner of Asturias. Here the inhospitable

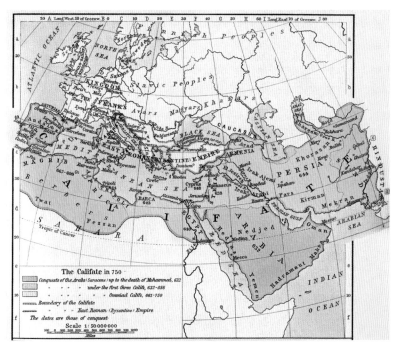

The Iberian Peninsula in AD 750, showing territories occupied by the Umayyad Caliphate and by the Christians.

weather battered a succession of mountains and valleys, and guerrilla warfare had thrived during Roman times. Together with the territories of the Basques and the Cantabrians, this was the only part of the Iberian Peninsula that was never conquered by Rome. Not only was this a dangerous place to settle, the land was mountainous and difficult to cultivate, making it a less attractive proposition to any invader. It was in Asturias where the *Reconquista* of the Iberian Peninsula would start, as recounted in the Ajban Machmuâ, an eleventh-century collected account on the early Al Andalus.[3]

> The same mountain in which the king called Belay (*Pelayo*) had taken refuge with 300 men; the Muslims continued to attack, so that many of Belay's men died of hunger. Others in the end yielded until they were reduced to 30 men and no more than ten women, according to the account. There they remained entrenched, eating honey as they found hives of bees crowded together in the crevices of the rock. It was difficult for the Muslims to reach them so they left them saying: thirty men, what can it matter.[4]

Even if the Christian resistance began almost immediately, the *Reconquista* from the Moors would take many Christian kings and their armies seven long centuries to accomplish. Because of the great speed with which the invasion took place, life under Islam normalized rather rapidly, starting with redistribution of the land. The Moors seized the properties that had belonged to the Church and the Visigoth state, allowing some landlords who had capitulated to retain their properties on condition of paying tributes. A part of the conquered land remaining in the hands of the newly created states would be cultivated by tenants. The rest, the largest section, would be divided among the soldiers who were to be discharged. Many Berbers, considered to be an underclass by the Arabs, were forced to settle on small parcels of land in the mountainous and less fertile lands, where they could resume the pastoral activities they had followed in North Africa before their conversion to Islam. In the cities and the fertile districts of what is today known as Valencia, and in Aragon and Catalonia as well as the lands crossed by the southern rivers of Andalusia, Arabs would be granted Roman *latifundia*. Not only would they enjoy an easier and more prosperous life, they would establish the sophisticated culinary traditions and food that they had brought with them.

During the period of their expansion, Arabs came into contact with Mesopotamian, especially sophisticated Persian, culinary traditions. Until then a simple diet of meat and bread had been at the centre of their nomadic diet. 'Meat to eat, meat to ride and meat to enter meat,' they said. As they encountered other cultures, the original Arab diet changed as new products from different parts of the Middle East and as far away as India and China were adopted. The same products and culinary traditions came with them, already transformed into a sophisticated cuisine, as they invaded Sicily and the Iberian Peninsula. Flat or slightly raised, easily digestible breads made with wheat flour were baked everywhere, and there were many flavoursome pastries and cakes made with eggs or fritters dipped in honey and sprinkled with cinnamon. The original tasteless Arab meat dishes of lamb, kid and game were converted into the distinctively flavoursome, aromatic and cleverly spiced meat offerings that have remained at the centre of the meal. Most importantly, even if the meat melted in the mouth, eating meat was considered to be manly both for warriors and men of peace. To end on a sweet note, they also established a tradition of sweet confections that had never been seen before in Spain. These were made with the thinnest pastry, dried fruits, nuts and the honey of a thousand flowers found locally. As the years passed, the work of farmers, professional cooks and traders resulted in a unique Islamic-Andalusian cuisine that would be enjoyed in a never-ending collection of dishes and cooking techniques with distinct personality. The arrival of sugar cane was going to transform and improve the preparation of sweet and savoury dishes, not only in the Iberian Peninsula but later in the Americas.

Trade between the Middle East and Africa had been flourishing before the arrival of Islam in the Iberian Peninsula. Land as well as sea routes used by Muslims benefited trade significantly. Using the compass and the lateen sail, they navigated the waters of the Persian Gulf, the Red and the Arabian Seas, and the Indian Ocean. They even opened new trade routes between Scandinavia and Russia. Then they sailed to East and West Africa, where gold, salt and slaves would further enrich their coffers. All kinds of exotic merchandise and spices were also transported by land, using caravans across the north and south of the Sahara Desert and heading for the gold-rich kingdoms of West Africa. Rock salt, extracted in large blocks by slaves, became another source of wealth. In southern and eastern Spain, saltpans, a much easier option than salt mining, had attracted trade since the Phoenician period and even before. Eventually the south and east of the Iberian Peninsula would become manufacturing and trading centres featuring crystal, silk, ceramics and gold jewellery – all objects of desire highly valued by merchants on both sides of the Mediterranean Sea. In Al-Andalus, they went beyond trading by creating gardens of vegetables, fruits and flowers to enrich their lives and their tables. For them this was easy. They found in Spain a Mediterranean climate similar to the coastal areas of Morocco, Lebanon and the irrigated lands of Mesopotamia. Furthermore, Greeks and Romans had already advanced agriculture. Arab and Syrian agricultural engineers soon started work on their new lands: Al-Andalus was to share in the agricultural revolution taking place in the Middle East. They analysed different types of soils to suit the crops they wanted to introduce, such as durum wheat, rice, citrus and sugar cane.

Most importantly, they knew how to irrigate their crops efficiently and economically, and in Spain half of the job had already been done by the Romans. Once wells, ditches and water pumps were in place, they transformed large areas of the country into fertile gardens – areas that during the latter part of the Visigoth period had returned to the wild or had never been cultivated in the first place. Wheat and other new and traditional crops were planted, orchards decorated the countryside, and vegetables were sold in abundance everywhere. All the vegetables, herbs and spices we know today were present in the Moors' everyday food, with the exception of course of the products which would begin to arrive from the Americas in the late fifteenth century. They also reintroduced varieties almost lost by then, such as the beloved aubergine of the Jews, believed to have first been planted in Spain in the first century AD, as well as vegetable varieties known since early antiquity, as in the case of lettuce. They loved, as Spaniards do today, chard and cardoons as well as artichokes and spinach, which were also appreciated by the Romans and the Jews.

The Moors planted lemon and lime trees in order to use the juice as a condiment, and bitter oranges for the smell of their blossom, for cooking and to embellish the streets in winter. They also started to cultivate sweet varieties of orange, although they would have to wait a few more centuries for a return on their investment. There were melons and bananas as well as figs, dates and pomegranates – a fruit which Isabella, the Catholic queen, adopted in the fifteenth century as a symbol of her power. They brought a colourful display to greengrocers, market stalls and the palaces of the aristocracy, all to be served in hand-engraved precious metal and crystal bowls, embellished in the autumn with green and black grapes. Wine was not allowed by their religion, but grape vines were tended with renewed enthusiasm. At the end of the summer they were sold fresh or were dried in the hot sun to be enjoyed as raisins and sultanas. *Verjus* or *agraz*, produced with the juice of early unripe green grapes, was equally popular with cooks, as its high acidity meant it was favoured in traditional sweet and sour dishes. Grapes were also the basis for a number of non-alcoholic drinks, mostly sweet, made as *hidromieles* and *vinos melados*, but they also made fermented wine, known as 'illicit wine'. In reality the prohibition of alcohol was never totally enforced in Islamic Spain, as can be seen in the rich poetry Arab writers left behind, particularly during the period of the *taifas* (independent Muslim-ruled kingdoms in Al-Andalus) later on.

Bitter oranges.

The composition of society in Islamic Spain, especially in larger cities, was complex. The Arabs represented the military and landed aristocracy. Lower strata made up of Berbers and *Muwalladun* (Muslims of local descent or of mixed Berber, Arab and Iberian origin, who lived in Al-Andalus during the Middle Ages) worked as merchants and artisans, and in the countryside as farmers and shepherds, especially in the case of the Berbers. Even though they had to pay taxes, both the *Mozárabes* (the name given to Christians who had remained in Al-Andalus) and the Jews were reasonably well treated, especially in the first centuries of Islamic domination. The profitable slave trade and in particular their success in the field of medicine, philosophy and finance would elevate the position of a number of Jewish families, not only in areas dominated by Islam. Further down the scale, slaves worked as servants and cooks in the houses of the ruling classes. This soon brought a regime of tolerance and shared cultural goals to a society that established a unique pattern of civic and intellectual sophistication, and which was envied in the rest of Europe. It was broadly accepted that without some form of tolerance and compromise among all parties, their precious world would end. On the whole, socioeconomic conditions improved considerably, and for the first time individual ownership was encouraged. Agriculture was improved as much as architecture, the arts and the sciences becoming the backbone of the economy. Even if war was to remain a constant feature, during the Emirate and later during the Caliphate of Cordoba, a new-found sense of beauty and internal calm, and above all pleasure, came to be a part of the lives of a large section of the population. In the kitchens of the elite, the food of *One Thousand and One Nights* had reached Al-Andalus.

Although the Moors shared a religion and cultural goals and theoretically were equal before God and the law, in reality they were historically divided into several ethnic groups. Infighting was rife, and the tensions and even war between them would eventually precipitate the end of a Muslim presence in the peninsula. Inequality and internal disputes in the Islamic community would encourage the newly formed Christian kingdoms in the north to venture beyond the borders established by the two forces. Thousands of Berbers who until then had tried to cultivate the land or tend their flocks were forced to flee south or to return to Africa. For the Christians, Toledo, the old capital city of the Visigoths, taken by the Moors at an early stage of the invasion, began to be within reach. This would all happen while a revolt in the Arab world changed the destiny of an Umayyad prince.

## A Prince Reaches Almuñécar

In AD 750, the Abbasids overthrew the Umayyad dynasty, which until then had ruled the Caliphate of Damascus. This was to change the course of history in Iberia. A young Umayyad prince, who had managed to escape the annihilation of most of his family, reached the shores of the peninsula. He was a good speaker, soft and cultivated, and enjoyed poetry as much as war. He was determined and ambitious and never left his business in other people's hands.

News of the prince, whom the Abbasids thought was dead, spread like wildfire throughout the entire Muslim world. He landed at Almuñécar in Granada, having crossed from Africa where he had taken refuge with his mother's Berber clan. Six years later, this prince, the future Abd al-Raḥmān I, *El Inmigrado* (The Immigrant) as he became known in Spain, fought his way to Cordoba, where he installed himself as Emir of Al-Andalus, an emirate of the Caliphate of Baghdad. From that moment in time, most of the Iberian Peninsula, populated by Arabs and Berbers, Visigoth-Christians, Hispano-Romans and Jews, became a haven not only for the few surviving Umayyads looking for a new land but even for many dissident Abbasids. What it was not was a place for rebels and enemies of the young emir, for he was implacable. Having moved the capital of the Islamic world from Damascus to Baghdad, the new Abbasid ruler of the Islamic world had good reason to be concerned. The Umayyad enemy which he thought had been eradicated was rising from

Almuñécar Beach showing the latest incomers, twelve centuries after the arrival in Spain of Abd al-Raḥmān I.

Around the 'Mezquita de Córdoba' were markets selling food and other goods.

the ashes. Some 171 years later, one of the descendants of *El Inmigrado*, Abd al-Raḥmān III, completely severed links with the east when he founded the independent Caliphate of Cordoba in Spain. By then, the daily call to prayers could be heard from the magnificent *Mezquita*, the main mosque at the centre of the capital city.

They say that the most beautiful women in Spain come from Cordoba, a city that became as great as Baghdad during the Caliphate of the same name. Cordoba was equally prosperous and well organized, a city capable of captivating traders, investors, intellectuals and artists from faraway lands. Founded by the Carthaginians, the Romans built one of the most impressive bridges of the time here. This was an inspirational city that in AD 756 pleased young Prince Abd al-Raḥmān, *El Inmigrado*, as he reached the medina of Cordoba, the capital of the emirate he would lead to greatness.

41

## Bitter Oranges from the Past

All through the year, bitter orange trees adorned the streets and the courtyards of important Islamic buildings in Andalusia. They can be found in the Mosque of Cordoba, the Cathedral of Seville and the beautiful streets of Jerez de la Frontera in the province of Cádiz. Planted by the Arabs in Al-Andalus, bitter oranges, also known as Canton oranges, belong to the large group of *Citrus aurantium*. It is believed that *Citrus aurantium*, originating in western India, China and Burma, reached Mesopotamia and came into contact with Rome and later the Arab expansion in the Mediterranean. Bitter oranges from Persia and Mesopotamia reached Syria and, later on, Spain during the Islamic period. Not only were they used to embellish streets and courtyards, they were planted for the fragrance of their flowers and the vibrant colour of their fruit. The juice and even the peel were used in the Andalusi kitchens to produce sweets made with cane sugar. It has been said that, today, bitter oranges signify the purest record alive of the historical presence of Islam in Europe. Contrary to the fate of buildings not so graciously altered by the Christians, or indeed destroyed altogether in the Middle Ages, these decorative trees were never uprooted as Al-Andalus changed hands.

In reality there are two different strains of bitter oranges. The Seville orange strain reached Spain via North Africa. These are the oranges that can be seen on Spanish patios and streets. Bittersweet oranges brought by Crusaders returning from the Holy Land two centuries later belong to the second strain and can be found today in countries in South America.

The use of bitter oranges in the Spanish regional kitchen has been limited to a number of Andalusi recipes. The best-known are a fish soup with a strange name — *caldillo de perro* (dog's broth) — and a rich fish stew, *raya a la naranja amarga* (ray with bitter oranges). Both recipes are associated with the *cocina* of Cádiz and especially with the small historic ports of Sanlúcar de Barrameda and Puerto de Santa María. It is believed that

Aerial view of the orange trees of the Cathedral of Saint Mary of the See (Seville Cathedral) in Seville, Andalusia.

*caldillo de perro*, *perro* being also a derogatory name given to the Moors by the *Mozárabes*, was a well-known recipe of Al-Andalus. Having survived for centuries, these recipes are now in danger of extinction as some of the ingredients, including the juice of the bitter orange, are falling out of favour. The dish is easy to prepare. Chopped onions and garlic are gently softened in olive oil in a deep pan. This *sofrito* is covered with plenty of water, seasoned with a little salt and brought to the boil. Then pieces of white fish, normally cut from a medium-sized hake known in Andalusia as *pescada*, are added and then cooked until tender. Before serving, juice from a bitter orange is poured in. This gives the broth and the pieces of fish a very distinctive flavour. The dish is served accompanied by a fried *mollete*, a small artisan soft bread with an oval shape that is only half baked. Some historians believe this bread was introduced into Spain by the Arabs; others defend the opinion that the origins of the *mollete* are to be found in the unleavened breads of the Jews. The great Scottish invention Dundee marmalade is made with bitter oranges grown in Spain.

## LIFE IN THE CITY

Orange trees bear fruit every year in the courtyard of the Mosque of Cordoba, a colourful bittersweet reminder of its Islamic past. Today *La Mezquita* stands guarding the memory of the Syrian dynasty that ruled Al-Andalus successfully, in times of peace and in times of war, for almost two hundred years. One of the oldest structures still standing from Al-Andalus, the grand mosque sits tall on the grounds once occupied by a Roman temple, later converted into a Visigoth church. With the arrival of Islam this church was transformed into a humble mosque which would be chosen by the Umayyad emirs to be converted into one of the wonders of the world. Part of an elaborate building programme, the project was started in AD 786 by Abd al-Raḥmān I. It was to be expanded by successive generations of Umayyad rulers over the two hundred years that saw them govern Islamic Spain.

In the heart of the main cities of Al-Andalus, the medinas, city life was protected by a high stone wall and by several strong iron gates that were closed at night. This was a world of narrow and winding streets, squares and gardens, mosques and commercial markets that occupied the same spaces as in the former Roman and Visigoth cities. To accommodate population growth, suburbs known as *arrabales* expanded outside the city walls. Here, a certain section of the population, mostly artisans, shopkeepers and farmers, lived, their goods and fresh produce entering the medina's gates daily on their way to the market, the *suq* which they called *zoco*. Everything imaginable could be bought, sold or altered here, including all kinds of foods and services. Hair could be cut, dresses and suits tailored, builders contracted, money-changers found, marriages arranged, gold and silver bought and sold, and land purchased, always supervised by the avid eye of the *Muḥtasib*, the market inspector. The *zoco* was also the place where labourers milling around the busy streets could buy tasty food from street vendors and small restaurants: aromatic lamb and kidney kebabs, fried fish, spicy sausages, roasted lamb heads as well as the traditional coriander *albóndigas* served with egg. The *zoco* was also a kingdom of sweet things. There were puffed fritters and tasty *almojábanas* (*Al-Muyabbana*) made with flour, water, milk, yeast, cheese, olive oil, honey, cinnamon and pepper. The dough of the *almojábanas* would have had the same consistency as *buñuelo* dough (a type of choux pastry).

Even if the *zoco* has long gone, Cordoba, referred to by the poet Razi as the mother of all cities, is still as beautiful as its women, an intriguing city and the guardian of a complex Iberian, Roman and above all Islamic past that refuses to disappear in the modern world.

Apart from Al-Hakam I, a grandson of *El Inmigrado* who had an extraordinary taste for violence, other rulers of the Umayyad Spanish dynasty, such as Abd al-Raḥmān II and Al-Hakam II, were moved by harmony and beauty. For them, music, poetry, good food and even the forbidden fruit of wine were the way to live. Walking today in the old quarters of Cordoba it is easy to imagine life in the city in the ninth and tenth centuries. The high solid walls that protected domestic life around the mosque may have gone, as indeed has the *anafe* stove on which women cooked, but so many things have survived: the taste for flowers, the cool patios bursting with colour, the soothing sound of fountains, and even the passion for the Arab horse are all still imprinted on the fabric of the people of Andalusia.

In Spanish there are 8,000 words and some 2,300 place names of Arabic origin, and many are related to agriculture and cookery. Spanish is more influenced by Arabic than any other language apart from Latin. In Cordoba, an outstanding collection of Arabic books and ancient Greek texts that were translated into Arabic, Hebrew and Latin occupied the shelves of hundreds of libraries located all over the city. Al-Hakam II, the son of Abd al-Raḥmān III, housed in his library more than 400,000 volumes that unfortunately were burned as the Caliphate reached its end. As the Caliphate collapsed, thousands of manuscripts were destroyed in Cordoba and in the Madinat al-Zahra palace at the hands of Berber rebels. In addition to this calamity, numerous volumes were also burned later by the Christians as they took cities and towns, this time in the name of the cross. If some of the works had not been copied and translated into Latin, evidence of the intellectual brilliance that had enlightened early medieval Spanish culture would have simply been swept away in a pile of ashes. Cookbooks were not generally translated, as cookery was considered to be less important than agriculture and above all medicine and dietetics. It is very likely that a number of cookery manuscripts could also have been destroyed forever. Who knows if one day a few more original Arabic cookbooks will be found in the obscure library of a convent or monastery where monks and nuns have kept them in secret.

Ziryab, one of the greatest cultural icons of the Middle Ages, had been invited to join Al-Hakam I at his court in Cordoba. Of Persian or Kurdish origin, the jealousy Ziryab provoked in his music teacher caused him to flee from Al-Ma'mum, the Abbasid Caliph of Baghdad, where he was living. For Ziryab, Al-Andalus may have seemed the perfect place to hide. By the time he arrived in Cordoba, Al-Hakam had died. Panic struck him, but he quickly realized that Abd ar-Raḥmān II would become his greatest protector. Ziryab, a talented musician and singer, would not only enchant Cordoba with his sublime voice, but he brought to the capital city a kind of refinement until then only to be found in the East. Single-handedly he managed to influence the way people looked: how they should cut their hair and even how men should wear make-up, something that until then had been unheard of. However, his greatest contribution has to be his association with food and with the improvement of table manners. Not happy with creating new recipes, he altered the style and content of well-established dishes, reorganizing the order in which they should be served.[5] Until that time dishes, savoury or sweet, hot or cold, would be served at the table haphazardly, a custom that would remain in the kitchens of the Christians in the northern part of the peninsula until the end of the Middle Ages. The new order established by Ziryab controlled the service by grouping dishes with common characteristics: cold starters (appetisers) should be followed by couscous, soups and pies. Lighter preparations with fish should be presented before complex ones made with red meat or poultry, which were often flavoured with garum or vinaigrette. Rich sweets made with almonds and rose water were to be placed on small side tables covered with fine tablecloths made of silk or the finest cotton.

New seeds, plants and spices were brought to Iberia by traders from Africa, the Middle East and even East Asia. These ingredients were in high demand, with cooks aiming to reproduce dishes that belonged to the original Middle Eastern and North African cultures of their ancestors. There were spiced chicken tajines with prunes, partridges with quince and apples, small aubergine omelettes, dishes with asparagus and spinach, fresh cheese and mincemeat sausages known as *mirkas*, and *barmakiya* pies made with chicken and onions and seasoned with black pepper and coriander seeds, ginger and saffron. Saffron imparted to rice dishes a unique colour and flavour. Since the tenth century, rice paddies have painted an almost Oriental picture over large expanses of the Spanish countryside. The Byzantines may have introduced rice in the Iberian Peninsula as early as the sixth century but it is thanks to the Arabs that rice became an important ingredient in the Spanish food tradition.

With the exception of a number of hectares planted in Extremadura in recent times, rice in Spain is still grown in many of the regions selected by Arab agronomists eleven centuries ago: in the deltas of the Guadalquivir and Guadiana rivers in Andalusia, in the delta of the River Ebro in Catalonia, in the Albufera lake in Valencia, and in inland Murcia. These areas attracted specialist Arab farmers who had learned rice cultivation from the Nabateans of southern Palestine and Jordan, as reported by the Al-Andalus agronomist and writer Abu Zacariya writing in the twelfth century. Abu Zacariya had taken reference from earlier Arab agronomists working in Spain and from old Middle Eastern texts.

The Arab farmers found a perfect environment for intensive rice cultivation both in marshland and in drier lands where the Romans had built irrigation systems, although the Romans never used them to cultivate rice. The Romans imported rice from Syria and Egypt, most of which was made into rice water and used for medicinal purposes. In his book about agriculture, Abu Zacariya provides ample instructions about how rice should be planted, when and where. He also mentions how to make rice bread, rice pudding and even rice vinegar.

## Kitchens, Markets and the Water Court

In a typical home, food prepared for the family had little in common with the specialities enjoyed at the tables created by Ziryab at court even if, in some cases, similar preparations were served by the middle classes only slightly differently. They would be prepared with one or two spices instead of seven or eight, or with a cut of meat from a less expensive part of the animal. In the average family home, the kitchen occupied a small space on the ground floor that was accessed directly from the central patio, the heart of the house. Here a small fountain or well and a classic *emparrado* (pergola) provided a cool space to sit under the stars in the torrid nights of summer. In the kitchen, clay *anafes* burning charcoal shared the cooking space with a brick oven where bread was baked, although more often than not, homemade dough would have been taken by a servant to the local ovens early in the morning. The bread-maker, as payment for the service, would reserve a portion of the dough. The custom of using local bakeries not only to bake bread but to roast meat, fish and even rice dishes in communal ovens was still used in some Spanish villages until the late 1960s.

In the medieval kitchens of Andalusia, lunches and dinners were prepared by women, while men often spent the morning doing business, praying and socializing at the mosque, or strolling at their leisure in the market. Here they would drink sweet mint tea and purchase food. In Islamic Spain, men not only kept the key to the larder, but were also in charge of buying food for their families.

The Mercado Central of Valencia is recognized today as one of the best markets in the whole of the Mediterranean world for a very simple reason: the countryside beyond the city is very fertile. Well irrigated since Roman times, this land has been tended for centuries by farmers whose expertise was inherited from Syrian, Berber and Arab farmers who settled in Spain in the early Middle Ages. These days, by eleven o'clock each morning from Monday to Saturday, the narrow streets of the old city of Valencia are bustling with life.

## *Azafrán*

In June 2002, Carlo Petrini, founder of the Slow Food Movement, described saffron as the only drug he knew that was accepted in food, capable of provoking lust, giving beauty to the body, and combining sedative, hypnotic and stimulant capacities. In Al-Andalus, people thought the same.

Saffron, the most expensive spice in the world, has been cultivated in Spain since the tenth century and probably even before. Some historians believe it originated in Crete and Asia Minor; others are more specific, as they are convinced it was in the Zagros, a mountain range in Iran. Berbers planted saffron in La Mancha, Valencia and further north in Aragon. Its name in Spanish, *azafrán*, derives from the Andalusi Arabic word *al-zafaran*, which itself comes from the Arabic *za'faran*. It was initially monopolized by the Andalusi upper classes and used in their kitchens and in trade as a profitable ingredient. Eventually it was cultivated in all vegetable gardens and was used by every level of society in their cooking.

Almost as old as civilization, saffron was used as medicine, in cooking, to prepare drinks and even in cosmetics. Its presence was recorded in Egyptian medical texts, in Greek poetry and in the the Roman *De re coquinaria*. For this reason it is more than probable that in Hispania cooks prepared many dishes with this rich spice.

Numerous recipes with saffron were included in the thirteenth-century manuscript *Anónimo Andaluz* and in the fourteenth-century *Sent Soví*, as well as in the *Llibre de coch*. In the early seventh century, the author of *Arte de cocina*, Domingo Hernández de Máceras, included saffron in meat stews and also in rice dishes such as *Arroz de azeyte, o manteca para los que no comieren leche* (rice with olive oil or pork lard for those who do not drink milk).

In his *Memorias históricas sobre comercio marítímo, comercio y artes de la antigua ciudad de Barcelona* (Historical Records of Sea Trade, Commerce and Arts in the Old City of Barcelona) the Catalan author Antonio Capmany y de Montpalan cites a cargo of 3,060 kilograms (6,746 lb) of saffron destined for the markets of Germany and Savoy in 1427. This quantity was increased to 3,508 kilograms (7,733 lb) in the following year, a large proportion of which would have come from Aragon.

While the production of saffron in Aragon has now practically disappeared, the importance it gained during the expansion of the Crown of Aragon was well documented by the seventeenth- and eighteenth-century Spanish authors Antonio Cubero and Sebastian de El Frasno. They provided extensive information about the main products exported from Spain in the sixteenth century to other countries in Europe and to Central and Latin America: silk yarn, olive oil, white and red wine, pottery, iron and saffron. In the Spanish-American colonies trade was paid in *reales* and *maravedíes*. The *maravedí* originated from the gold dinar, a coin first struck in Al-Andalus during Abd al-Raḥmān III's caliphate.

It was Aragon rather than La Mancha that was destined to become not only the main saffron production area of Spain but the place where the best saffron in the world was produced. Even now it tends to be associated with words such as Moors, *Mancha* and especially with rice dishes cooked in the Spanish *Levante*, including *paella*. Due to a reduction in the area of cultivation and strong competition from other countries, Spain has lost its dominance in the world market.

Saffron fields, largely unchanged since the tenth century.

*Anafe*, a tenth-century portable stove made of bisque clay; see the painting of an *anafe* in use on page 147.

Arabic is no longer the language spoken by the majority, including Jews, Christians, nobles and academics, as it was in the time of the Moors. In matters relating to agriculture, Arabic would also have been the language spoken by local courts such as the all-important *Tribunal de Aguas*, the Water Court. To ensure their crops and the supply of food, in the medieval city of Valencia, men who owned land defended their rights to irrigation by presenting their cases to this respected tribunal.

The *Tribunal de Aguas* was founded in Valencia during the Islamic period to control the use of water in the fertile soils of the Spanish Levant, and is considered to be the oldest democratic institution in Europe. The court still plays a major role today and functions much as it did a thousand years ago. Every Thursday at noon, the Water Court session is held just outside the Apostles' Gate of Valencia's cathedral. The judges, elected from local farmers, sit protected by an ornate circular iron fence, with the public standing close to them outside the fence. The task of this tribunal, which is recognized by Spanish law, is to regulate irrigation and to resolve irrigation disputes. The cases presented to the court are made orally and in person, and the rulings of the judges are final. This is one of the world's few remaining ancestral arbitration practices regarding public property.

The Water Court (*El Tribunal de las Aguas de Valencia*) in 2006: here matters concerning the water supply for agriculture have been addressed since the tenth century.

## THE MADINAT AL-ZAHRA

Abd al-Rahmān III was the red-haired, blue-eyed son of a Basque servant girl and the Emir of Cordoba. As ambitious as *El Inmigrado*, he had declared himself Caliph in the Grand Mosque of Cordoba in 912. By then, the political map of the peninsula had changed. To the north of Al-Andalus, the small Christian enclave of Asturias that had managed to resist the Moorish invasion had expanded into a number of kingdoms both in the north and the east of the peninsula. Twenty-one-year-old Abd al-Rahmān was very aware that the unification of Al-Andalus had become of paramount importance. In the latter part of the Emirate, internal divisions and unrest between the Islamic factions were threatening the survival of Islam in the peninsula. For him, freedom from the restraints imposed by Baghdad was the only way forward, not only to create unity but to be ready to confront a new danger: the rise in Africa of a rival dynasty. The Fatimids of Afriqiye were waiting in Egypt for any sign of weakness. Abd al-Rahmān needed to be totally in charge and he made certain that he was. A new caliphate, *El Califato de Cordoba*, his own creation, had been born.

Did Abd al-Rahmān III order the construction of the magnificent palace-city of Madinat al-Zahra, not far from Cordoba, as a tribute to his favourite concubine named Zahra? Probably not. Historians believe the young caliph was making a serious political-ideological statement. He needed a new urban palace that would become a symbol of his power and superiority over his great rivals in Africa, the Fatimids. In competition with Cordoba, the gleaming white Madinat al-Zahra became not only a vast fortified palace but the diplomatic, intellectual and culinary centre of Islamic Spain. In such a fortified palace of pleasure, beauty and design, food and wine had to be an important part of public relations and diplomatic activity. Lavish banquets and constant entertainment in the traditional Arab way were expected by foreign visitors as well as the Caliph's own family. It is more than likely that both in the kitchens and in the great halls of the Madinat al-Zahra chefs, butlers and maids would follow the teachings of Ziryab.

Within eighty years, Spanish Islam and its caliphate would tremble for the last time, and the civil war which had been contained by the last of the Abd al-Raḥmāns would destroy forever the beloved palace of the greatest caliph of the West, the Madinat al-Zahra. Yet, despite all the years of unrest and desolation, the nearby Grand Mosque in Cordoba would survive.

Even if art, luxury, good food and wine remained as important as before in Islamic society, political life was to change dramatically in Al-Andalus at the end of the Caliphate. In 1031, Islamic Spain was divided into 24 separate kingdoms known as *taifas*, including Seville, Toledo, Cordoba, Valencia, Zaragoza and Badajoz. The rulers, also known as Taifas, were usually young educated men who instigated another period of tolerance with regard to the extraordinary diversity of the population of Al-Andalus left behind as the Caliphate of Cordoba crumbled.

The Madinat al-Zahra, the dream palace of Abd al-Raḥmān III near Cordoba.

Abd al-Raḥmān III receiving ambassadors and drinking with them. Painting by Dionisio Baixeras Verdaguer (1876–1943).

Arab oven in the Madinat al-Zahra.

Most importantly, the Taifas brought with them a renewed fascination for the arts and the sciences, even if rivalry and confrontation between the different Islamic factions would eventually bring them down, with tragic consequences. In Spain, the expression *un reino de Taifas* (a kingdom of Taifas) is still used to define division and by association a loss of power. Politically things would get even worse when military help from North Africa joined the Taifa kings attempting to resist a strong Christian offensive from Castile and León, its army now decisively advancing south of the Douro River.

In 1085, the intention of King Alfonso VI of Castile was clear. It was to take Toledo, the old capital of Visigoth Spain, a city with a strong past and an Islamic stronghold of culture and culinary expertise, especially regarding confectionary. The Castilian king was far too dangerous and had to be stopped. With this call for help from Africa by the Taifas, the end of another fascinating chapter of the history of Spain was fast approaching as horsemen, their bodies and heads covered in black and driven by fanatic fundamentalism, landed again on the white sands close to the Pillars of Hercules. With the arrival of the Almoravids, and later, the Almohads, the dark and fundamentalist face of Islam reached a peninsula in turmoil as thousands of Jews and Christians refusing to abandon their religions would perish or flee north.

## MEANWHILE, IN THE KITCHEN . . .

Throughout Mediterranean Spain, the rhythmic sound of pestles and mortars made of ceramic, wood or metal has been heard in kitchens since antiquity and even before. Different sizes of brass mortars, known as *almirez*, yet another Arabic-sounding word, are still used to pound saffron and cumin, pepper and aniseed, dried fruits, bread or garlic. Apart from its place in the kitchen, there is another function they have always been associated with. Metal pestles and mortars, together with spoons, decorated glass bottles and wooden and metal washing boards, are used as improvised musical instruments played by Spanish communities on festive days. Glazed ceramic green and yellow mortars for pounding ingredients were less expensive than pestles made of wood, and they are still sold in the small shops found outside popular markets. In Andalusia, refreshing soups, made with almonds, garlic, bread, olive oil and water flavoured with wine vinegar, sustained grape and olive pickers as well as labourers who tended the crops and harvested in the summer months. Harissa, the spicy hot paste made with red peppers in North Africa today, must not be confused with the recipe for *harîsa* included in the

*Anónimo Andaluz*, an anonymous thirteenth-century Maghrebi and Andalusi cookery compilation, favoured during Ramadan. This preparation, known in Spain under the name *harisa a las migas de pan blanco*, was made following a simple recipe: in a mortar, pound white or semolina breadcrumbs, soften with water, and then allow this to dry and ferment in the sun. Place in a pan. As *harisa* can only be cooked with lamb and lamb fat, add mince or pieces from the leg or the shoulder. Cover with water and cook until the meat is very tender and has blended with the breadcrumbs. Add bone marrow and some extra crumbs. Pound again to form a dough. Drizzle with hot lamb fat and sprinkle cinnamon on the top.

Apart from mortars, the old-style earthenware cooking pots and *cazuelas* so commonly seen in Spanish kitchens were used in Islamic Spain to prepare rice dishes in the oven and *fideo* pasta with fish on the top of the stove. Couscous, a grain and also a dish prepared with durum wheat in the Maghreb and cooked in the earthenware Moroccan and Tunisian *tajin*, was well known as *alcuzcuz* in Al-Andalus. From Al-Andalus pots and pans, dishes and even stoves would travel all the way to the Americas.

> The phenomenon of emigration of the words *anafe* and *albóndiga* is curious. They started their journey from the Mediterranean coast of Africa towards the West. They settled in Spain. They were incorporated in the Castilian language and then, Christianized, they set sail for the Americas. They crossed the water and spread out into the valleys of this continent. They climbed the most rugged heights, penetrated the densest forests, and we hear them today in the most humble huts in distant corners, on the lips of Aztec descendants.[6]

The Arabic word *annáfih*, represented in Spain as *anafe* and also as *hornillo*, is used for an early form of movable clay stove used in Al-Andalus until twenty or thirty years ago. *Albóndigas* is a popular dish that has been made with minced meat since Roman times. A number of different versions of similar preparations were included in medieval documents of Arab origin relating to Spanish food.

The denial of foods associated with their Islamic past by some Spaniards has been fairly selective, and not too difficult to understand given the strong association of the country with the Catholic Church. It is interesting to note how certain ingredients used extensively in Al-Andalus retained or even gained status in the development of Spanish food, while others were completely

## *Mazapán de Toledo*

At religious and national festivities such as Christmas, Spaniards follow different regional food traditions in which turkey is seldom included. Plates of shellfish and *Ibérico* ham, substantial broths and roasted fish or lamb will be the protagonists of the family dinner at Christmas. During the festivities, *turrón* (nougat) will be served together with candied fruit, pine nuts and the evocative and beautifully decorated *figuritas de mazapán* (small figurines made of marzipan).

In spite of the many theories, so far historians have been unable to obtain definitive evidence about the origin of marzipan and yet the recipe for marzipan itself has managed to remain virtually unaltered through the centuries. So many claims are suggested by history and legend. *One Thousand and One Nights* takes the history of marzipan to the Middle East and ancient times. A religious order in Toledo and a confectioner in Sicily are still claiming the maternity of such a delicacy. Furthermore, Greece, Cyprus, Baghdad and especially Venice, which was at the centre of trading with the Middle East, are also making claims. Lübeck, an important German medieval city founded in the early twelfth century, would play an essential role in the distribution of marzipan in northern Europe. In Venice, marzipan was known as *marzipane*, which comes from *massapan*. This was itself derived from *mawthaban*, a name given by the Arabs to a Byzantine coin, one-tenth of whose value was represented by another coin that the Venetians named a *massapan*.

In Spain, Toledo has for centuries been associated with *mazapán*, its Spanish name. The history of the marzipan of Toledo, as in Venice and in Lübeck, was originally associated with hunger more than pleasure. In Spain, legend associates *mazapán* with the decisive battle of Las Navas de Tolosa in 1212 against the Moors. In Toledo, bread had become very scarce during the battle but local nuns had a solution. The city's *pan dulce*, which did not contain flour, was made with almonds and honey. As plenty of almonds and sugar had been stored at Toledo's wealthy convent of San Clemente, the nuns started to make *pan dulce* with sugar instead of honey. In the kitchen of the convent they pounded almonds and sugar together with a mallet (*maza*) to make a sort of bread (*pan*). With this *mazapán* the nuns helped many of the inhabitants of the city. In Toledo *mazapán* is still prepared as it was centuries before with almonds from Valencia, white sugar, egg yolks, egg whites, a little water, and cinnamon and lemon peel, which are both optional.

Marzipan was made in different shapes.

forgotten. Why has couscous disappeared while rice and pasta forms such as *fideos* (noodles) and *aletrias* (angel-hair *fideos*), both introduced in the peninsula almost at the same time, remained? Why is coriander only used in a limited number of dishes in Andalusia, but not in any other region's traditional cuisine? Why are spices – with the exception of saffron, cinnamon, cumin and aniseed – so seldom used in the regional food of Spain? Why is lamb, the most popular meat in Castile and Aragon, so difficult to find in places like Aracena at the heart of the magnificent Sierra Morena, not far from Seville? In some cases there are perfectly valid reasons; in other cases it is much more difficult to find convincing explanations not associated with old prejudices encouraged by religious impositions. Prejudice, or a lack of understanding of Moorish and Jewish food cooked in Spain during the Islamic period and until the last *Morisco* (converted Muslims living in Christian territories) left, is an essential factor in the regional culinary traditions of Spain, as well as the influence of the period on modern Spanish cooking.

One thing Spaniards would never deny is their passion for sweet things, very sweet things. Sugar, the magic ingredient that would change the face of savoury and sweet food in medieval Spain, had been refined by the Arabs since the tenth century. It was needed for many of their culinary traditions, so once they had settled in the peninsula they started to cultivate sugar cane in the kingdom of Granada and in Valencia. Soon, mills known as *trapiches* were in full production. First the canes were cut down and their roots treated with manure. In November the canes were covered with water, remaining like this until January. Then they were crushed, their precious juice extracted and then boiled in large cauldrons until it was fairly clear. Boiling and reducing the juice for a second time and then letting it solidify yielded a rather rough product which could be used immediately or refined to the desired quality. From that moment sugar became available not only in the kitchens, bakeries and sweet shops of the cities and towns occupied by Muslims but in those taken by the Christians as they pushed further south. Initially and for some time to come, sugar, a very expensive delicacy, could only be afforded by the rich.[7]

## FOOD AT THE *JUDERÍA*

If he keeps the Sabbath out of respect for the law of Moses; which
is proved by wearing a clean shirt and better garments than on
other days, and placing clean tablecloths on his table, and abstains
from lighting a fire in his house and working from the evening of
the Friday before.

If he removes the suet and fat from the meat he intended for his food, and to purify the meat he washes away the blood with water or removes the *landre* or *landredilla* [gland] from the ram's leg or any other dead animal.

If he slits the throat of a ram or birds which were for eating, examining the knife blade beforehand for any damage before he kills the animals, and covers the blood with earth while saying certain words spoken by the Jews.

If he eats meat during the days of Lent and others prohibited by the *Santa Madre Iglesia* [the Saint Mother Church] without needing to do so and believing that it can be done without sin. If he fasts the major fasting day of all, known with the different names *ayuno del perdón, de las expiaciones y del chphurin ó del quipur* (Yom Kippur) . . .

If he blesses the table after the manner of the Jews; if he has drunk of the wine named *caser* [a word derived from *caxer*, which means lawful], and which is prepared by Jews; if he pronounces the bahara or benediction when he takes the vessel of wine into his hands, and pronounces certain words before he gives it to another person; if he eats of an animal killed by Jews; if he has recited the Psalms of David without repeating the Gloria Patri at the end; if he gives his son a Hebrew name chosen among those use by the Jews; if he plunges him seven days after his birth into a basin containing water, gold, silver, seed-pearls, wheat, barley, and other substances . . .[8]

These words, written by historian Juan Antonio Llorente (1756–1823), referred to signs of identity and ritual followed in secret by Spanish *conversos* that the Inquisition had been looking out for since 1492. They were very similar to the rituals that would have been performed by the Jewish population that lived alongside Christians and Moors in Al-Andalus for almost eight centuries.

Tourists visiting the Great Mosque in Cordoba or the Royal Alcázar in Seville tend to wander through the secret winding streets of *las juderías*, the name given in medieval Spain to the quarters where Jewish people lived. Other important *juderías* were to be found not only in towns in Andalusia but in Toledo, Granada, Valencia, Zaragoza and Barcelona, and in the hundreds of villages where Jewish kitchens had shared the aromas of herbs and spices with the rest of the population, as they had been doing since their arrival in the Iberian Peninsula.

If Tarshish, the place where Jonah sought to flee from the Lord, was indeed Spain, one could speculate that the relationship between Spain and the Jewish people could date back to the time of Solomon. Whether this can be endorsed by a reliable source or not, there is strong evidence of the presence of large communities of Jewish people in Spain during the Roman era, especially from the second century. As Roman citizens, Jews living in Hispania engaged initially in a variety of occupations. In the countryside they worked the land, and in towns and cities they worked as traders in goods and slaves, as craftsmen and in finance, their professional lives integrated into the rest of the society. With the arrival of Christianity, things changed. Eventually the Catholic Church began to be concerned about their practices, including the peculiarities of their dietary laws. As a consequence the Church started to show early signs of anti-Semitism. Finally orders came from the Council of Elvira in the fourth century. From that moment Jews could not work the land just as they could not keep slaves, marry Christians (adultery with a Jew would result in ostracism), bless Christian crops or share their meals with the owners of the crops. By the end of the fifth century, Hispania had come under Visigoth rule. As the Visigoths converted to Christianity, things deteriorated even further, and the first edicts for the expulsion of Jews from Spain were published. They had no choice but to convert to Catholicism or to leave. Some converted, others crossed the Pyrenees or left for Africa. As the pressure eased during the reign of Visigoth King Sintila, in the first part of the seventh century, Jewish *conversos* reverted to their religion. The relief was short-lived. By AD 633, yet another Council of Toledo addressed the matter once more. If the *conversos* were found to be practising Jews, their children would be raised in Christian monasteries.

Things improved with the invasion of the Moors in AD 711, and for the next three centuries Jews would frequently be serving the rulers in official capacities, playing a role in political and financial affairs. Medicine was a profession they practised successfully, as were banking and tax collection. During those first centuries of Islamic rule, a regime of tolerance would allow the three Religions of the Book to flourish in an atmosphere of conviviality most of the time. However, Jewish society lived its own life, controlled by its own people, and therefore never became fully integrated, even if along with the Moors they spoke Arabic. Relative calm and tolerance would last for the majority in Al-Andalus, until the demise of the Caliphate of Cordoba in the eleventh century. As the Taifa kingdoms in which the Caliphate had disintegrated became seriously threatened by the Christians, they decided to seek help from fundamentalist Islamic forces waiting across the Strait of

Gibraltar. Life would once again be altered for the worse as the Almoravids and then the sanguinary Almohads would take full control of Al-Andalus. Under threat, Jewish communities decided to venture north, beyond the borders that separated Christian and Islamic Spain, where they could start again, especially in towns such as the old imperial city of Toledo, taking with them their culinary traditions. They could again pray in the synagogue on Saturdays, returning home safely to a warm plate of *adafina*. They could cut cloth to make fine garments, write books and practise medicine. Sadly, their success as traders and especially tax collectors became a reason or an excuse for them to be targeted by detractors and by the Church. As the years passed, further territories were taken by Christian forces moving relentlessly towards the Moorish kingdom of Granada. By the end of the fourteenth century, joyful moments would become just sweet memories for the Spanish Jews.

It all started in Seville, a city already controlled by the Christians. On 6 June 1391 mobs encouraged by Ferrand Martínez, Archdeacon of Ecija, attacked the Jewish quarter located close to the river, lighting a torch of hate. At the same time the 400-year-old *judería* in Barcelona was totally destroyed. Here more than 10,000 people died, and many were converted by force. Within days the same fate was faced by other Jews in Valencia, Majorca and even Toledo. Historians have estimated that before the first expulsion in 1492 there were 250,000 Jews living in Spain and 80,000 in Portugal.

The Synagogue of Santa Maria La Blanca in Toledo (1180), one of the few remaining synagogues in Spain.

Serving from a large cauldron (Hispano-Moresque Haggadah, Castile, 1320).

Since the beginning of their long history and for centuries to come, Jewish people had followed a restricted dietary regime that they took wherever they went for a very simple reason: the Torah said they should. When they left Spain in the fifteenth century they took with them an essentially local cuisine based on products available in the markets, adopted and adapted to their taste, their traditions and their dietary laws. Today many books about Sephardic cuisine have been published in countries where Sephardi Jews settled after their departure from Spain. Specialist food historians maintain that very limited written evidence has been found so far regarding the food Spanish Jews cooked before they left the Iberian Peninsula.

Apart from this, there are valid sources of information that can help to create a picture of the life and food of the Spanish Sephardi Jews before and after their expulsion from Spain in 1492. It comes from the thousands of people who fled to Italy, Greece, Turkey and North Africa, all of them Mediterranean countries that have at one point or another in their history been dominated by Islam. Helped by the memories of their past, Turkish Sephardic dishes are still very close to those that were cooked in the Middle Ages in Sepharad, the name that the Jews gave to Spain.

Just as the Spanish Sephardim would have done before they left the peninsula, women in the Andalusian countryside still dry apricots, peaches and plums in the sun and preserve fruits in *almíbar* (sugar syrup). With the arrival of winter, they cure olives and also make *dulce* or *carne de membrillo* (quince cheese) to be stored in a dry place for the rest of the year. Between November and February quince paste is still prepared in many parts of the country. This is another simple preparation that needs time. Wash four or five quinces. Cook until tender in a large pan covered with water. Remove from the water and let them cool down. Peel, remove the cores and cut into small pieces. Weigh and return the fruit to the pan, adding 80 per cent of its weight in sugar. Cook gently for about one hour until the sugar has been completely blended with the fruit, stirring constantly with a wooden spoon.

In modern-day Majorca, where Sephardic traditions have never died, shops sell colourful *tomates de ramillete*, strings of fresh tomatoes that will keep until Christmas. Before the expulsion, melons and grapes would have been hanging in cool pantries throughout the year. Even today Sephardic communities in Turkey and Greece speak a Romance language derived from Old Spanish, or Ladino. In Spain, vegetarian recipes with aubergines and pumpkin, chard, lentils or chickpeas tend to be associated with the food cooked by the Spanish Jews. Under the influence of Christian culture these recipes may now include small pieces of ham for flavour. It is highly likely that pork, part of Christian cuisine, was used by *conversos* to avoid any dealings with the Inquisition.

The word *almodrote* has always been associated with the Sephardic tradition and with cheese. The word derives from the Arabic *matrup* (pounded). It can be a sauce or a more substantial dish prepared to celebrate the Sabbath. In medieval Catalonia it was a strong sauce made with garlic, eggs and cheese known as *almodroc*, which was often served to accompany game dishes. *Almodrote de Berenjenas* belongs to a group of recipes known by the Sephardim as *kosas d'omo* (gently oven-cooked specialities) in Ladino, a type of gratin made with aubergine puree, cheese and eggs. Another recipe for *Almodrote* can be found in the *Cantiga de las Merenjenas*.

> The third way is that prepared by Ms Joya de Aksote: she boiled them and cooked them after removing the stems, liberally mixing cheese and oil, and she called them by the name *almodrote*, as it can be found in the *Cantiga de las Marenjenas*.[9]

In the region of Aragon, where large Jewish communities were found in medieval times, the Sephardim loved *ternasco en cazuela*, which is slow-cooked lamb with garlic, olive oil and thyme. Here the daily diet of the Jews was based on bread, lettuce, celery, cabbage and olive oil for fried foods, flavoured with vinegar, lemon juice, bitter orange and green apples, and served with wine. They used aubergines in vegetarian stews or stuffed with meat and spices.

Pumpkin, spinach or leek *fritadas* were also favoured at the tables of the Sephardim during the twelfth century. Chickens were roasted or prepared in rich stews, their eggs boiled or served as omelettes. In Aragon, far from the sea, the preference was for mutton, lamb and veal rather than fish, always prepared according to Jewish dietary restrictions and laws. *Cazuelo chico* (small pot) was made with beef, cabbage and one egg. During the Pesah, as an allegory of the building mortar used during the time of their slavery, Jews ate bitter herbs and unleavened bread, served with radishes in memory of the sadness of their exodus, with chopped walnuts, apples and wine. They also ate olives, cured in water and crushed by children using small hammers to shorten the curing process. Rice with lentils and other dishes prepared with their beloved artichokes were also a part of the daily diet. In Mediterranean Spain, Jews ate fish more often than meat as well as bread, eggs and soup, to which they add a little saffron.

Also belonging to the category of *kosas d'omo* were mouthwatering *borrecas o empanadilla* pies filled with cheese, which can also be fried. Tasty pancakes known as *bulemas* in Spain and *premesas* in Turkey could be related to Galician and Asturian *filloas* (laced pancakes).

The complex and strict dietary laws of Islam and Judaism share certain similarities, but both differ greatly from the almost non-existent dietary laws of the Roman Catholic Church. The only dietary restriction of the Church has always been the prohibition of eating meat during Lent, on Fridays and on a few specific dates related to religious festivals. Apart from pork – prohibited for Jews and Arabs – Arabs, Christians and Jews shared a taste for lamb, fish, fresh bread, vegetables, fruit and honey, and even if Jewish and Arabic dietary laws were to a certain extent closer, a clear distinction came with the rigorously controlled laws that ruled the lives of the Jewish population. So many foods were allowed or not allowed and had to be prepared in a specific way; and there were countless ancient precepts and rituals to be followed at certain times of the year. Food was connected permanently with the ancient past, with days of happiness, sadness and exile, with the rituals of Passover, Tabernacles, Purim and Yom Kippur. Orthodox Jews could only eat meat slaughtered according to their custom and with the blessing of a rabbi; the meat of some animals was allowed, and others as established in the Torah were forbidden, especially pork and pork fat, rabbits and hares, as well as shellfish and fish without scales and fins. They could not mix milk with meat or make cheese with animal rennet – possibly one of the reasons why the tradition of making cheeses with the filaments of the wild artichoke continues to live on in Spain. With regard to fruit, it is interesting that grape products such as wine could not be consumed by Jews if they were produced by Gentiles. Today kosher wine is still made in Spain, the fermentation tanks covered and sealed by a winemaker of Jewish origin working under the close supervision of a visiting or local *rabino*. As for the utensils they used in their kitchens, they also had to be kosher or pure, and therefore could only be used for certain groups of food. In the kitchen of a Jewish family the specific use of many utensils was as fundamental then as it is today: some for meat, others for milk. For all Jews since the beginning of their history and irrespective of the country where they were born, the seventh day of the week, known as the Sabbath or *Shabat*, was a day of rest dedicated to God, for no manual work should be undertaken, not even cooking. *Adafina*, a substantial dish that was traditionally eaten at lunchtime on the Sabbath, had to be prepared on the Friday before sunset. Recipes vary for *adafina*, also known as *hamin*, from the Hebrew for hot. Its most simple version contained olive oil, water, vegetables, grain and pulses, especially chickpeas, as well as eggs known by the Sephardim as *haminados*; in the richer version pieces of mutton or kid were added. The earthenware pot in which this dish was cooked was kept warm during Friday night on top of the *enafe* stove, covered with a lid on which hot coals were placed. Some historians believe the *adafina* is a preparation that could easily have been the origin of the ubiquitous Spanish *cocido*, though with a significant difference.

*Cocido* as it is known all over Spain has always been made with pork products. Arguably in the Middle Ages this addition could, as already mentioned, have been a statement that separated Christians from Jews. Hundreds of *cocidos* are prepared all over Spain every day. However, the tradition of the eggs, the *haminados* favoured by the Sephardim on the Sabbath as an important component of their *adafinas*, was one of the secrets they took with them to exile.

The word *haminado* refers to the eggs cooked in their shells inside the *hamin* or *adafina* in Sephardic Spain. During the long cooking process, the egg albumen turned white and the yolk turned a light brown colour, with a delicious creamy texture. Food and cookery scientist Harold McGee has written extensively about the cooking process that turns eggs into *haminados*, also known as 'Brown Eggs':

> During prolonged heating in alkaline conditions, the quarter
> gram of glucose sugar in the white reacts with albumen protein to
> generate flavours and pigment typical of browned food. The white

will be very tender and the yolk creamy as long as the cooking temperature is kept in a very narrow range, between 160 and 165°F.[10]

The Christian custom of having fish on Friday appears to be of Jewish origin. In medieval Spain, Sephardi merchants provided the market with all sorts of fish, especially on Fridays when Christian and Jewish customers would fight for the catch of the day, even if most of the fish was salted. Fresh fish was only available close to the coast. Here the Sephardi cook could fry it from fresh or prepare it in *escabeche* (cooked in olive oil and vinegar), smoke it or preserve it in *salmuera* (salt and water). Fish pies were also considered a delicacy as part of the menu served on the eve of the Sabbath.

The preparation of sweet dishes and cakes marked a time of celebrations and religious festivals in the colourful calendar of the Spanish Sephardi community. Recipes were made with flour or matzo bread or meal, honey, sugar, and orange or lemon peel. Some of them were baked, while others were fried in olive oil, such as the *torrijas* now associated with Lent in Spain. *Torrijas*, also known as *rebanadas* or *fritas de parida*, were prepared by the Sephardim to celebrate the birth of a child, especially if it was a boy (*rebanadas* are slices of bread, and *parida* is a woman who has just given birth). *Torrijas* are still made today with slices of stale bread soaked in milk, coated with beaten egg, fried in olive oil, dipped in sugar syrup or honey, and sprinkled with cinnamon. The light *buñuelos*, made with flour and water and served with honey or sugar syrup, are still fried every day in the city of Valencia and enjoyed with a cup of hot chocolate. They are *bunyols* in Catalan and *buñuelos de viento* in Castilian.

The beloved bread of the Sephardim, leavened or unleavened, played an important role in some of the sweet preparations. Gil Marks in his *Encyclopedia of Jewish Food* includes a recipe known as *pan de España, pan esponjado* or sweet bread, baked by Sephardi Jews.[11] This is the same recipe that Spaniards now prepare in every region under the generic name of *bizcocho*, and a very similar treat is still offered by food sellers in Smyrna, Turkey. Some culinary experts believe that the Galician *tarta de Santiago*, made with almonds, and the Valencian *tarta de naranja y almendra*, a traditional cake made with almonds and egg whites instead of flour, is associated with the original food left behind by the Jews. To celebrate they would prepare almond *arrucaques* and tantalizing *travados* (fried pastries associated with the Jewish community in Rhodes). They also prepared sweet soups known as *hormigos and mustachudos*, both sweetmeats made originally for the festival of Purim with hazelnuts, eggs, lemon peel, cinnamon, cloves, honey and sugar. More and more research into Galician and particularly Majorcan food is shedding new light on the subject of Spanish Sephardic sweet specialities. Jews from Aragon also had a sweet tooth, becoming expert confectioners of nougat, candied fruits and *tortas de pan cenceno* (unleavened bread), prepared during Passover in memory of those flat cakes that the children of Israel carried on their shoulders when they crossed the Red Sea. It is believed that a list of Spanish pastries was associated with Sephardic festive days: Rosh Hashanah was associated with *mogados de almendra*, and Yom Kippur with *hojuela* pastries first fried in olive oil and then soaked in sugar syrup or honey. *Roscas* and *antchusas de leche* were prepared to celebrate Sukkot, while *buñuelos* and *bizcochos de pasas* (sponge cakes with raisins) were associated with the feast of Hanukkah. A rich paste made with walnuts (*pasta de nuez*) was enjoyed at Passover.[12]

An emotive source of information about Jewish Spain can be found in the material obtained by force or fear of the Inquisition (1478–1834) during the trials of the Crypto-Jews or *conversos*. By the time the Catholic kings came to power, tolerance and the modern term *convivencia* had become part of the past. After all, it had always been an unequal relationship. The winners were the Christians, the losers the rest of the population, including those who had converted but decided to carry on practising their religions.

One thing is certain: like the Muslim population, Portuguese and Spanish Sephardi Jews loved sweet things, fruits and nuts as much as they loved the smell and taste of rose water. After Yom Kippur, a day of strict fasting and penitence, the Spanish Jewish population celebrated with a feast which included figs, dates, nuts, sweet pomegranate seeds and other fruits dipped in honey. In 1581, almost a century after the initial expulsion, King Philip II enjoyed a banquet in the town of Valencia that started with prunes, sultanas, sweet candied oranges and dried peaches.

Having become very popular all over Spain, pastries and other sweet specialities from Arab and Jewish traditions are still sold today by Catholic nuns, especially from enclosed orders. While some of their recipes have now been published, the most distinguished have remained secret. More often than not, exact measures and methods are known only by the cook in charge and passed on by word of mouth.

## In Castile

At the end of the eleventh century, King Alfonso VI of Castile faced a serious dilemma: carry on fattening the coffers of his kingdom with the benefits received from his vassal the Taifa of Toledo, or simply force the city to surrender. It was not only that Castile would lose the *parias* (tribute money);

*Vizcocho:* cake made following a Jewish recipe.

he was aware that Toledo, one of the great cities of the Western world, still surrounded by enemy land, would have to be protected at all times at a high cost. Hungry for recognition, he could not resist the temptation of the latter option. Some of the most determined Christian forces would depart from Castile and march all the way to Toledo, the former capital city of the Visigoths and now one of the jewels of Islamic Spain.

As the *Reconquista* gained momentum and the strength of the Christian forces grew, Taifa rulers became threatened not only by Christian warriors but by their own people as internal divisions grew and Al-Andalus spun out of control. As a result they started to seek help, turning to different camps. A costly protection racket was on offer, from Christian mercenaries such as Rodrigo Díaz de Vivar, the famous *El Cid*, and even from King Alfonso VI, whose father Fernando I had originally introduced the practice. King Fernando had advanced the frontier to south of the Douro, often raided by both Moors and Christians. Both he and other Christian kings started to force the Taifas of Badajoz, Seville, Toledo, Granada, Málaga, Denia, Zaragoza, Valencia and the Balearic Islands to pay *parias*. The alternative was to lose their cities and land. The *parias* were high and had to be paid in silver or gold. The historic city of Toledo would remain in Christian hands until the end of the Islamic presence in Spain. As a result the balance of power in the peninsula appeared to be changing in favour of the Christian world, but this was just an illusion.

Under Islam, Toledo had become an intellectual centre, a place of tolerance where three religions co-existed in peace and prosperity most of the time, as they had done before in Cordoba or Seville. Toledo was a city where classical and Arabic manuscripts were translated, where synagogues, mosques and churches flourished, and the best marzipan was made in local artisan shops similar to the ones that today sell small half-moon *figuritas* and large *anguila* or eel-shaped ones now associated with Christmas.

After King Alfonso took Toledo, the Taifas realized that the advance of the Christian enemy was unstoppable. They needed help from Africa, even though they knew this was potentially dangerous.

For fifty years, Berbers in the Sahara had been following a powerful fundamentalist sect permanently ready for war, the Almoravids. Their laws forbade any relaxed customs which were not in agreement with the Koran, customs that were by then accepted in multifaceted and culturally sophisticated Al-Andalus. As the Almoravid armies, their faces covered by black veils, landed in the peninsula in June 1086, the drums of fear sounded again across the sand, the mountains and the valleys cultivated by the *mozárabes* (Iberian Christians who lived under Moorish rule), *moriscos* (former Muslims who had converted to Christianity), Jews and *moros* (Muslim inhabitants of the Magreb, Iberia, Sicily and Malta). The death sentence of the Taifa world had been signed. Leaving devastation behind, Almoravid forces moved fast across the Guadalquivir and Guadiana rivers. Before winter came, King Alfonso would be defeated north of Badajoz, at the Battle of Sagrajas. The ultimate Taifa sacrifice had been made, but the Christian advance had been stopped just as they were regaining control. Accused of moral corruption and subservience to the Christians, one by one the princes of Islamic Spain, the Taifas, would be deposed as the Almoravids took control of Seville, Cordoba, Granada, Málaga and Murcia. Soon the independent Zaragoza as well as Valencia would also succumb. The Christian forces realized that they had to start all over again.

During the eleventh century, new links were established with medieval Europe and the papacy by Christian Spain. The *Camino de Santiago* attracted pilgrims, monks and even passing Crusaders, some looking for salvation, others a place to start a new life. Via the peninsula, Arabic Hispanic culinary traditions were spreading beyond the Pyrenees, while other culinary influences were also contributing to the creation of the regional food of Spain.

In the twelfth century, the Almohads, having taken control from the Almoravids, had become a serious menace to Toledo, to the whole of the Tagus Valley and to Alfonso VIII. By the time Alfonso VIII, one of the great kings of medieval Spain, met his death on 6 October 1214, the border between

Christian and Islamic Spain had moved further south to the River Guadiana. A controversial, powerful and ambitious figure, Alfonso would be instrumental in the final outcome of the *Reconquista*. Having been defeated at the Battle of Alarcos, he made certain this would be the last time that a Christian force was defeated by the Islamic enemy. Helped by the Pope, who believed passionately in the *Reconquista*, and with a strong force of French Crusaders and armies from other Christian Spanish kingdoms, Alfonso stopped the advance of the Almohads at Las Navas de Tolosa. As Seville and Cordoba fell to the Cross, the final chapter of Islamic Spain was beginning to be written.

## THE WRITTEN WORD

The two surviving culinary manuscripts of the time of the Almohads, depicting dishes prepared in the kitchens of the urban elite in Al-Andalus, have been at the centre of academic attention since the 1960s. They have contributed significantly to Spanish culinary history and the development of Spanish *cocinas*.

Born in Murcia in the early part of the thirteenth century, Ibn Razin al-Tuyibi was a learned jurist and poet with a passion for food and cookery. Food was associated with distinction in the Islamic world, as were drink, sex, clothing, scent and the gentle sound of water. The earliest manuscript of the period, the *Fuḍālat al-hiwan fi tayibat al-taʿām wa-i-awan* (Delicacies of the Table and the Finest of Foods and Dishes), has been attributed to Ibn Razin. It is a compilation of early texts, probably dating back to the late ninth or tenth centuries, and produced by Ibn Razin between 1243 and 1328. Little is known about the life of the author, although it appears that he had left Murcia when the Christians annexed the city in 1243, travelling first to Ceuta, where he lived for a number of years, and then to Algeria, where he settled and brought up his family, living among the intellectual elite of the day. In the tradition of the other Arab medieval texts that had become so fashionable in Baghdad, the *Fuḍālat* is a well-organized manual containing more than four hundred recipes divided into eleven different sections for food, plus one for soap and perfumes. The food content includes bread and other recipes made with grains, meat, poultry, fish and eggs, dairy products, vegetables, pulses, sweets, pickles, preserved foods, oils, locusts, prawns and snails. The section for bread and other recipes made with grains contains the highest number of entries, followed by the recipes with meat and vegetables, in which aubergines are notoriously present. The section dedicated to pastries is the closest to the pure Andalusi tradition, a fact mentioned by the author, who at times appears to discriminate between the food of North Africa and that of southern Spain, in favour of the latter. Some of the recipes are simple and others require professional skills. The manuscript also includes recipes presented in two different versions, one more expensive than the other using, for example, better cuts of meat and a greater variety of spices. This manuscript is much more than a cookbook, as Ibn Razin included extensive information about the order in which food should be served, as well as ample advice on the importance of cleanliness in the kitchen.

The second of the surviving Arabic manuscripts has attracted the attention of a number of historians specializing in Arabic texts. The *Kitāb al tabikh fi-l-Maghrib wa-l-Andalus fi ʿasr al-muwabhuadin Ai-muʿallif maybul*, better known as the *Anonymous Andalusian Cookbook* or *Anónimo Andaluz*, is a rather disorganized collection of five hundred recipes that sheds light on the food served in Al-Andalus as the sun set on the Islamic period.

The *Kitāb* is a valuable and unique source of customs and culinary tradition in Islamic Spain, in which regional aspects, utensils used and recommended dishes, even for the sick, are as important or even more important than the recipes. Apart from the recipes cooked by the majority of the population, this manuscript also includes a number of Jewish recipes of enormous value, as we have little valid information about the eating habits of the Jewish community in Spain. This was a community of great historical value, despite representing just a small percentage of society. The Jewish recipes included in the *Kitāb* confirm the culinary adaptation of the Jews to the food consumed by the majority, in terms of the ingredients and style of the dishes, even if dietary restrictions would have always applied as they had done before and have done ever since. The Jews had a passion for pomegranates and aubergines, artichokes and quinces.[13]

These manuscripts appear to be the only sources where a number of recipes belonging to the Spanish *dulcería islámica* are to be found. The word *dulcería* is used here as a generic name encapsulating all sorts of preparations in which sugar played an important role, including pastries and cakes, confectionary, sweets and even savoury dishes. As sugar became available in Spain, professional cooks began to use it in recipes that until then would have been made with honey. There were recipes made with an array of ingredients such as butter, rose water, yeast, milk, cheese, almonds, hazelnuts, walnuts and honey of course. Sometimes, whole eggs or just the whites were used, their flavours enriched with an equal array of spices. Cooks could select from lavender, cloves, cinnamon, saffron or pepper, among others. Sugar would normally be sprinkled on top of the particular dish they had prepared. Often items made with dough were first fried in olive oil and then dipped in honey;

others were baked. Many of these recipes have sadly been lost forever while others have continued with their original names or have, in true Christian fashion, been baptized with the name of a saint, town or village.

The tragic expulsion of Jewish people who decided not to convert came in March 1492. They were farmers, tailors and traders, doctors and scholars, administrators and bankers who took their memories and their recipes with them as they left, leaving behind some strong physical and cultural characteristics that can still be found everywhere in Spain. They also left their own style of cooking, reflected in the recipes that would still be defiantly prepared by the thousands of Iberian Jews, Crypto-Jews who had converted to Catholicism under duress and therefore been allowed to stay. Kashrut (Kosher), the Jewish dietary law which dictates the nature of foods eaten by Jews on their long migrations, would threaten the security of the Crypto-Jews as Christians took over the entire country.

Although they ate pork in public, they never stopped eating Jewish traditional food such as the *adafina* of the Sabbath. Their homes smelled of fish and meat cooked in olive oil instead of pork fat, and of garlic and onions, all of which Christians were averse to. Andres Bernáldez (*c.* 1450–1513), a chaplain to one of the Spanish inquisitors who wrote in his memoirs about the food habits of the converted Jews in the Kingdom of Castile, complained bitterly about the Jewish style of cooking:

> They never stopped eating *adafina* and fried garlic and onion
> dishes in the Jewish way. They cook meat with olive oil and avoid
> pork fat or fatty pork meat. The smell of meat cooked with olives
> and other dishes they cook give the Jews bad breath, and make
> their houses and doors smell bad . . . They only ate pork meat when
> forced to do so. They ate meat in secret during Lent and during the
> days of abstinence and fast. During the time of the Jews they ate
> unleavened bread and kosher meat.[14]

Orthodox Jews believe that food is not just meant to satisfy hunger; the act of eating is a ritual that follows tradition and benefits spiritual and physical equilibrium. They follow a strict and unique culinary model, and a religious calendar that dictates their lives. This was clearly understood by the medieval Jews who lived in certain areas of Spain, such as the island of Majorca in the Balearics and in Valencia after their expulsion in 1492. Sources related to the food prepared by the Spanish Jewish population shed light on the impossible life and times of the Crypto-Jews, and the role played by the food they were not supposed to eat if they wanted to remain safe. *Spill* (Mirror) or *Llibre de les dones* (Book of Women), written in the early fifteenth century by a doctor and influential writer, Jaume Roig, specifically talks about recipes prepared in the commercial district of the city of Valencia by Jewish women using tender beans, onions, garlic and *carn a tassals* from the Castilian *tasajo*, a cut of smoked beef.[15]

Dishes which actually have a Jewish past, cooked with broad beans, aubergines and artichokes, lentils or chickpeas, are still associated by young Spaniards with the best their mothers cook for them. They contain onions and garlic and probably a piece of tasty chorizo, now added without any religious significance just to enhance the flavour. The Jews also left behind poetry and music preserved in an extensive collection of poetical texts and gentle ballads.

### Tears for the Alhambra

During the last two centuries of Islamic presence in the Iberian Peninsula, the Kingdom of Granada became one of Europe's centres of culture, fashion, trade and food excellence. This was a fertile land between the high mountains inland and subtropical beaches kissed by the Mediterranean Sea, a place where sugar cane thrived and advanced irrigation systems performed miracles. In the thirteenth century, Christian advances in Andalusia had forced the Sultan of Granada and founder of the Nasrid dynasty, Muhammad Ibn Yusuf Ibn Nasr al-Ahmar, and his forces to establish a stronghold high above the rich valley of the River Genil, a safe refuge in a magnificent enclave protected by one of the main sierras of the peninsula, the Sierra Nevada. Here they built the fortress of the Alhambra.

In the latter part of the fourteenth century, the Kingdom of Granada, extending originally to Gibraltar and the important trading ports of Málaga and Almería, had become the last bastion of Moorish Spain. Until then Castile, already in control of the north and parts of the south, was not in a hurry to complete the *Reconquista*. The high tributes being paid monthly by Granada were helping to finance an ambitious Crown. The Catholic monarchs were also aware that, by taking control of Granada, they would have to face another problem they had been trying to resolve with limited success as the *Reconquista* was drawing to a close: the depopulation of extensive areas of the peninsula as the Moors and Jews started to leave for good. In the Spain of Isabella and Ferdinand, especially in Aragon, there were not enough people to settle and, most importantly, to take over the array of administrative and intellectual jobs until then dealt with efficiently by Jews. The tending and cultivation of large stretches of land was also under threat. As in Seville and Cordoba, as well as in Zaragoza and Valencia, a large percentage of the Moorish and Jewish population was not prepared to abandon their religion even if they were aware of the consequences. In Christian Spain, tolerance had become a thing of the past, and the inhabitants of Granada knew the *Santa Inquisición* would be hot on their heels even if they decided to convert. The survival of Islamic Spain faced serious danger for the last time as the circumstances which until then had prevented Castile from taking Granada changed. Ridden with dynastic troubles at the heart of the Alhambra, and with growing popular discontent in the whole of the kingdom, Boabdil, the last king of magnificent Al-Andalus, signed the terms of the capitulation of Granada on 25 November 1492. According to legend he left the city in tears when his mother said to him, 'Cry like a woman as you could not defend your kingdom like a man.' Soon Boabdil's bitter tears would be shared by the thousands of *Morisco* farmers forced to depart to unknown Christian territories. They knew they were leaving behind the fertile valleys in some of the richest land of the entire Iberian Peninsula, made prosperous by their work.

# THREE

# Life in the Castle

The number of castles that have been keeping a silent vigil over the Iberian Peninsula for the last six or seven centuries is staggering. Centuries earlier, the same castles built as a defence against the Moors would give their name to one of the most powerful kingdoms of medieval Europe, Castile. For some of these silent witnesses, all that remains is weathered stones, decaying walls and perhaps memories of a succulent roast turning on a spit. Others, still intact, stand tall on hilltops like sentinels watching over fields of wheat and barley, yellow in the summer, green in the spring. They are all reminders of a time when fighting to the death, hunting and banqueting were the only ways those who ruled passed their time and reinforced their power and authority, a time when food was all about meat, bread and wine for the few who could eat well.

All over Spain, hunting, considered by physicians as a desirable exercise and one of the most enjoyable medieval pastimes, was an easy way to provide meat for the noble kitchen although it was forbidden for the rest of the population. Poaching activities were heavily penalized and even subject to the death penalty. Apart from the benefit and pleasure this sport could provide, game was also served by kings and noblemen to impress friends and even enemies. Lavish banquets were held with the main aim of breaking the monotony of daily life. These followed the canonical hours, a series of prayers established by the Church in medieval Europe which grew out of the Jewish practice of reciting prayers at set times of the day. The first meal was taken after mass between the third and the sixth hour, and the second after sunset, at vespers, when the men of the family, their male guests and even some male servants ate together. Noblewomen ate in a separate room, apart from occasional banquets when they were invited to court but had to eat from their husbands' plates. In those days forks and spoons did not exist, only knives

Almodóvar Castle in Cordoba.

were used, and even these were often brought by the guests. Also, the popular shallow bowls, or *escudillas*, were used at the table, as both plates and cups. From the word *escudilla* comes the name *escudella*, the ubiquitous Catalan stew prepared with pasta and small meatball *pillotes* and cooked in a substantial meat and vegetable stock.

During court banquets in the Kingdoms of Navarre and Aragon, women and men sat at tables on alternate chairs, following a French custom associated with class and good taste. In these matters of etiquette France was already setting the trend. On the tables, lace tablecloths were as fashionable as showy decorative ceramics, including the very ornate *Mudéjar* from potteries in Manises and Paterna, both places close to Valencia and at the time belonging to the extensive Crown of Aragon. In Paterna, excavations have revealed two main production sites, where evidence including kiln sites, wheel pits and tools suggests that pottery was made from the early twelfth to the late fifteenth centuries. Here an array of blue-and-white glazed pottery, lustreware and, above all, tin-glazed tableware decorated with copper green and manganese brown was found; this was crafted by *Mudéjar* potters who stayed behind after the Christian conquest of Valencia in 1238.

In the medieval Christian kingdoms of Spain, the diet centred on large quantities of meat, quality white bread and wine – at least, that is, on the tables of the king, the nobles and the upper clergy. Meat represented more than 50 per cent of the cost of food in any privileged household, even during Lent when fasting and abstinence were imposed by religion. During Lent it

Hunting hare at the Hermitage of San Baudelio, Casillas de Berlanga (Soria), *c.* 1125.

*Escudilla de orejetas*, a traditional fifteenth-century Aragonese dish.

was always possible to purchase a few birds with the excuse that the elderly and the sick needed to be fed, especially out of sight of the family's confessor. The local lord would also dine on a few forbidden roasted legs and breasts of a succulent capon or two.

In the lands belonging to the Crown of Castile, as well as in Navarre and Aragon, some animals from itinerant flocks were bred to address the demand for meat required by the kitchens of the nobility. Lamb and mutton were preferred for roasting while pork, mostly salted pork, was used to enrich *ollas* and stews. A rich variety of sausages were prepared with pork meat and fat seasoned with the same spices which were abundant in all the recipes of the time, especially cinnamon and pepper. Easily digestible meat from chickens, capons and ducks was recommended by doctors and dieticians for poorly members of the family, as was fish. Live poultry, bought several times a year at the local markets, was kept near the kitchens in pens. As the Christian kings and their royal courts, itinerant for most of the year, moved around their own kingdoms, either meat or live animals were purchased en route. More often than not this produce was received as obligatory gifts from local farmers. Fish was eaten salted or freshly caught in local waters. Apart from rather boring vegetable and pulse stews, fish remained the only choice that complied with the strict dietary regulations imposed by the Catholic Church, not only during Lent but on the many days when meat was forbidden. If meat was the sole prerogative of the rich, bread and wine remained the salvation of the poor, even if there were great differences in the quality and quantity eaten and drunk at the tables of the various classes: white *candeal* loaves made with the best wheat produced in Castile were baked for the enjoyment of the rich; grey bread made with cereals of dubious quality was baked for the rest. In the Kingdom of Aragon, bread was often supplied as dues to the Crown or the local lords by the *Mudéjar* vassals working the land or building incredibly ornate churches.

Castles and the many medieval monasteries still standing – occupied or unoccupied by their original congregations or converted into modern hotels – have remained keepers of history and custodians of records about everyday life, including cooking traditions. Monasteries have always been associated with culture, food and wine production. They have also been associated with the political and military past of a country riddled with conflict, both internal and with the rest of Europe, since the Visigoth period and well beyond.

Monastic life in the peninsula goes back to the early centuries of Christianity, although its expansion and development coincided with the arrival of the Order of the Dominicans of Cluny from France in the eleventh century during the *Reconquista*. Subsequently, further religious orders such as the Cistercians, Carthusians, Augustinians and Camaldoleses, including a number of military orders, founded their monasteries north of the boundary that separated the Christian kingdoms from Al-Andalus, north of the River Douro and all along the *Camino de Santiago*. Eventually the expansion of monasteries moved south and east as the *Reconquista*, viewed as a Crusade by the Church and the Pope, gained pace. The monasteries were in charge of the best libraries in the country and the most beautifully illustrated sacred texts that have ever existed. Monks divided their time between prayer, study and tending their animals or cultivating gardens. In these gardens a great variety of fruits and vegetables, not only local but brought by monks moving from other areas or even countries, allowed the kitchens to feed their congregations and the poor. Monasteries were also the recipients of large areas of land, buildings and other valuables offered by benefactors seeking a free pass to salvation. In a country that would become seriously devoted to Catholicism and the most powerful in the world, monastic power and authority would become accepted by all, both in Spain and, later, across the Spanish Empire. Catholic nuns associated with many of the male orders, having opened numerous convents, would become instrumental in the production and transmission of Spanish culinary heritage. Monasteries would also become synonymous with the cultivation of the grape, and the production of wine and a number of liqueurs.

## Venturing into the Mediterranean: The Crown of Aragon and the Italian Connection

While Castile remained deeply involved in the slow process of the *Reconquista* and the social and political framework would remain almost unchanged for decades to come, things were very different to the east of the country. Freed from the invaders by the thirteenth century, cultural and culinary changes had taken root in Mediterranean Spain, where the feudal world was beginning to be questioned. Here an incipient bourgeoisie had started to grow while agricultural production expanded across the land, bringing an improvement in the diet and general standard of living. Finally the population was growing. Old towns, new settlements and universities sprang to life, while trade became a fast track to richness.

The powerful Crown of Aragon, a confederation formed by the union of the Kingdom of Aragon and the County of Barcelona which also ruled parts of southwest France, was to become a Mediterranean sea empire extending as far east as Greece between the twelfth and fifteenth centuries. Trade had become a solution and a source of wealth that justified the investment in naval power for the Crown. First, Valencia and the Balearic Islands became part of the Empire, then Sardinia, Sicily, Naples and, briefly, Athens. With the expansion came an exchange of products and culinary expertise that would add another layer to the original Roman-Moorish foundation of Spanish food. Apart from physicians and dieticians, cooks also travelled with kings and nobles, adding new ideas and recipes to their repertoires.

In the Mediterranean, the Muslim monopoly had been broken by Pisa, Genoa and especially Venice, allowing new routes to connect ports between Italy, Spain and Africa. Barcelona, Tortosa, Sicily, Corsica, Tunis, Tripoli and the Balearic Islands (where Islamic piracy had been stopped by Jaime I, *El Conquistador*), all became major ports. Investment from the northern Italian ports had been instrumental in furthering the development of a flourishing local shipbuilding industry in Spain. Some ships were built for battle and others for cargo, transporting grain, olive oil and figs, rich silks and fine pottery exported from Tortosa, Valencia, Denia and Cartagena all along the Mediterranean. The same ships would return to the Spanish ports carrying spices, slaves and advanced medicines. Practising medicine and dietetics had become a respected way to climb the social ladder.

## To Eat or Not to Eat

Having become fascinated by food-related matters, Catalonia's intellectual and professional elite was approaching the subject from many different angles. Some were based on morality, others on medicine and notably tailor-made dietetics, a discipline that had become fashionable among people who could engage the services of renowned physicians, many of them Jews.

For most people living in medieval Spain, constant war and the obligation to supply animals or meat, cereals and fruits to local lords resulted in hunger for the peasantry. For them health was not important, hunger was. The lack of food also affected the diet of the growing urban population: as this grew, people become more concerned about health. Health and its relationship with food became a public issue shared by a growing number of physicians working for the upper classes as well as those in academia.

Those in positions of influence and the nobility were affected by food in a very different way. It was not the lack of cheese and wine, meat, fruit, spicy or sweet things but their over-abundance that brought constant misery to the rich, who became more and more dependent on the advice of their physicians. Doctors were paid to prepare strict healthy diets based on the group that their patients belonged to: sanguineous, phlegmatic, choleric or melancholic. Influenced by Hippocrates, Galen and Avicenna, as well as by further Arab and Jewish teachings, dietetics enjoyed a high status that attracted many to the medical profession. Doctor Arnau de Vilanova, a Valencian or Aragonese doctor-professor at the University of Montpellier, was engaged to prepare a *regimen sanitatis* for the sanguineous King James II of Aragon at the beginning of the fourteenth century, a dietary regime and a guide to correct his way of living. His contribution to the world of medicine and dietetics would influence the medical profession until well into the seventeenth century in Spain and beyond. Following the path established by Greek and Arab authors, as well as others belonging to the Salermo School, which was the most advanced teaching institution of the time, Vilanova's comprehensive work was followed not just by the noble classes and princes of the Church but also by the newly created bourgeoisie. From the quality of the air a man needed to breathe, to the physical exercise a man should do, as well as the way he should eat and drink, nothing was left to the imagination by Dr Vilanova. In his regime he also covered other aspects equally important to a man's wellbeing, such as the need to rest and the manner and frequency of taking baths, including treatment for changes of mood or even for piles, a discomfort suffered by the king of Aragon. The sections dealing with the effect of different foods on the human body – as ingredients or as dishes following ancient groupings of cold, hot, dry or humid – were equally impressive: cereals, pulses, fruits, vegetables and roots, meat and fish, stews and, most important of all, spices and marinades were covered.

Vilanova also looked at drinking in detail. He believed that man feels two different types of thirst. The first one he called 'natural' thirst, resulting from the heat brought about during digestion. This was simply calmed by drinking water. The second, or 'unnatural', was a consequence of doing exercise, eating spicy food or breathing dust. For Vilanova this thirst could only be quenched by clearing the throat with *vino aguado*, wine blended with water. Since antiquity and even during the Arab occupation of the peninsula, wine mostly blended with water was drunk in significant quantities not only by the upper classes but by most people, including men of the cloth.[1]

## CATALAN AND CASTILIAN COOKBOOKS

Early Catalan food manuscripts are fundamental to the understanding of the Spanish medieval kitchen, and to a certain extent the food eaten during the fourteenth and fifteenth centuries in other parts of Europe. Some reflect the food cooked for the clergy, while others are the work of professional cooks working for the nobility.

Two different versions of what is known as the *Llibre de Sent Soví* (*c*. 1324), written in Catalan by an unknown author under the original title *Llibre de totes maneres de potages de menjar*, set the food scene not only in Spain but elsewhere in Europe, especially in France and Italy. In 1979 the American academic Rudolf Grewe edited a complete version, adapting the texts to the old Catalan language.[2] In *Sent Soví*, Roman and Islamic influences are clearly present, both in the list of ingredients and in the method of preparation of many dishes – two hundred recipes in total. Reading the book, it is easy to understand life, food and above all the economic prosperity attained by the Crown of Aragon during its expansion in the Mediterranean world. It was thanks to extensive Mediterranean trade that spices easily reached eastern Spain where there was already a plentiful supply of local fruit, vegetables and meat as well as fish. It is interesting that a comprehensive although rather capricious selection of fresh and salted fish was included in the local diet, with the exception of species found in deeper waters that required the use of bigger fishing boats. Perhaps the author was aware that the Mediterranean, a seemingly gentle sea, often becomes a treacherous world, its powerful short waves capable of damaging the fragile boats used at that time. Equally capricious was the list of shellfish, from which both Dublin Bay prawns and lobster, highly regarded all along the Mediterranean coast and in particular on the island of Menorca, were excluded.

Live eels have always been available in the markets of Valencia and from time to time in Barcelona or Tarragona, their acquired taste seldom being appreciated in other parts of the country. In *Sent Soví*, a simple and yet sophisticated recipe is cooked with eels and with a number of ingredients which were very popular in the area at the time, such as saffron, garlic, toasted breadcrumbs, almonds, sea salt and a rich fish broth. For this broth, grilled or roasted pieces of conger eel were gently simmered in an earthenware *cazuela* covered with a rich almond sauce, which was prepared in a pestle and mortar with the rest of the ingredients. Other festive medieval Catalan dishes included much more sophisticated combinations of spices or dried sauces with fanciful names such as *salsa fina* (ginger, cinnamon, black pepper, cloves, macis, nutmeg and saffron). A simple formula for *polvora duque* was made with cinnamon, ginger, cloves and sugar; another more complex one was prepared with galangal, cinnamon, cardamom, ginger, nutmeg, black pepper and sugar. The *broete de madama* is a classic medieval Catalan dish made with almond milk, chicken broth, pine nuts, eggs, vinegar, ginger, pepper, galangal and saffron, as well as parsley, mint and oregano. *Sent Soví* also included several recipes for *morterol*, a type of thick creamy soup (velouté in French) from the Castilian word *mortero* (*morterol* in Catalan). They all included different types of meat boiled in water with the addition of pork fat and almond milk pounded to a paste in a pestle and mortar, together with an onion *sofrito*, garlic, cloves and saffron. The mixture was then blended with beaten eggs just before serving.

Francesc Eiximenis, a late fourteenth-century Franciscan writer of Aragonese or Valencian origin, opens further doors on the subject of food and Christianity in his *Lo Crestià* (The Christian), a thirteen-volume morality study he wrote in 1384, of which only the first, third and twelfth volumes saw the light of day. As a member of the powerful Franciscan Order, the largest in the world, he had been encouraged to undertake studies at the universities of Oxford, Paris and Cologne in order to obtain a degree in theology at the University of Tolosa. In Europe he acquired extensive knowledge that would make him one of the most respected writers of the Middle Ages. He returned to Spain with new concepts of sophistication and decorum that influenced the way rich and poor behaved in fulfilment of their destiny and in accordance with their class. In the medieval mind, including the mind of the Catholic Church, equality among men did not exist. By birth the members of the aristocracy were simply superior. In *Com usar be de beer i manjar 4,* a section of the third volume of *Lo Crestià* known as the *Terc del Crestià*,[3] Eiximenis stated that people should behave in a Christian manner at all times, even when sitting at table. In the same section,[4] this author reaffirmed the importance of bread and wine in the Mediterranean diet, defending moderation where there was excess and instructing in the art of good manners and in the fight against greed, a capital sin to be avoided at all cost. Apart from providing an extensive general guide, the author entered into detail about food, asking, why is roast meat better than boiled? Why is it a sign of bad taste to pile the plate high with common bread *sopas*, eaten day in and day out in convents and monasteries?

Bread remained an essential part of the diet for the lower classes. Usually milled by hand, flour for the Spanish medieval loaf was made with different blends of wholegrain wheat, rye, millet or barley. Once the dough was ready it was taken to the local bakery, a tradition that would last in many areas of the country until well into the twentieth century. Simple dishes belonging to the group of *papillas* (porridge) were prepared with grains that had been boiled until tender, or made with flour of lower quality. Included in this group were the inferior *gachas* and *poleadas* that kept the body warm during the long winter months, made with water, cereal and little else. On festive days the same dishes, made with the addition of milk, almonds and if possible a little sugar and a dash of ground cinnamon, were enjoyed by the few who had managed to improve their standards of living by trading or by having found work in the cities.

It was not until the early fifteenth century that the culinary traditions of Castile, an extensive part of the peninsula, were recorded. Requested by Sancho de Jarava, official carver-at-table to King Juan II of Castile, Enrique de Aragon (better known as Enrique de Villena) wrote a manuscript entitled *Arte cisoria* in 1423; this was mainly a celebration of meat and also included some fish recipes.[5] Don Enrique dedicated the entire book to the art of cutting, carving and serving food at the table of noblemen, reflecting the taste and customs of a kitchen characterized by quantity, spices and sugar. It does not include recipes for pulses or for rich meat stews where meat had been cut into smaller pieces before cooking. We also know that, although all the dishes were intended for the tables of the aristocracy, some of the dishes were, in a simplified form, adapted for the food of the peasantry as well as for the food that was typically starting to be seen in the cities.

In Villena's recipes, large pieces of meat and game were roasted or served in rich pies, or braised in large earthenware *cazuelas* with elaborate sauces. The wide range of ingredients available to the author at the time is remarkable. Some of the well-seasoned dishes were artistically decorated using birds' feathers, as was the case with the strangely insipid peacock dish prepared as a feast for a medieval and mostly carnivorous society. The dishes that were sliced or filleted and presented on the plate also included vegetables, fruits and fish: trout, grouper, bream, lobster, oysters and even whale meat. More often than not, in fifteenth-century Castile, apart from river fish caught locally, when seafood reached the interior of the country it was already salted. It was served boiled, baked or fried. Even though Villena didn't include them, snails from the fields and freshwater crayfish were also popular. In *Arte cisoria* nothing is left to the imagination. The author instructed servants working in the dining halls in the art of peeling and cutting fruit in a very sophisticated way, helped by an implement he called the *perero* which appears to derive from the word *pera*, pear in English. The *perero* supported the piece of fruit securely while the servant peeled it with a small knife.

## THE TRASTÁMARAS AND A HEAVENLY BANQUET

By the time the *Arte cisoria* was written, Castile was ruled by the House of Trastámara, a dynasty that having started in a controversial way would be instrumental in the development of the Spanish Empire, the discovery of America and, most importantly to this book, the American and European food exchange. The House of Trastámara was to unite the crowns of Castile and Aragon.

It all started with an extramarital love affair between a Castilian king, Alfonso XI, and a woman of noble descent called Leonor de Guzmán, who bore him ten children. His legitimate heir, Pedro el Cruel, the son of a Portuguese princess, had died violently at the hands of Enrique de Trastámara, one of Alfonso's illegitimate sons with Leonor. In 1369, Enrique would be crowned Enrique II of Castile, to be followed by Juan I, Enrique III, Juan I, Enrique IV and Isabel I of Castile, the Catholic queen who would become betrothed to the future king of Aragon, Ferdinand II.

The accession to the Crowns of Castile and Aragon by the Catholic monarchs Ferdinand II and Isabella I in 1469 was the result of a convoluted and unlikely succession of events, in true medieval style. Both Isabella and Ferdinand, who were first cousins, were direct descendants of two different branches of the House of Trastámara.

Earlier, at the beginning of the fifteenth century, Castile and Aragon had faced dynastic troubles. In Castile, Henry III had died, leaving behind a minor as his heir; both his wife and his brother Prince Ferdinand, known as Ferdinand de Antequera, were left in charge of the kingdom. In Aragon, King Martin I had died childless, and there were several conflicting claims to

Queen Isabella of
Castile and León.

the succession including one by Prince de Antequera, whose mother was an
Aragonese princess.

Was devotion or sheer opportunism the reason behind Prince de
Antequera becoming a particularly strong defender of the Virgin Mary? Why
have historians drawn attention to a chivalric order founded by this prince
and a spectacular coronation banquet? One way or the other, the Virgin Mary
would play a decisive role in the life of the Castilian prince who was destined
to reign over the Crown of Aragon as Ferdinand I.

The founding of chivalric orders had become a tradition in Prince
Ferdinand of Antequera's family, at least for any man who sat on the throne.
His grandfather Alfonso XI of Castile had been the first European monarch
ever to create one, establishing a new fashion to be followed by European
kings. His father, John I of Castile, had founded several orders, and even if
young Ferdinand was only a prince he was determined to have his very own.
He hoped to be king one day, when he might need it. His victory over the
Moors at Antequera (Granada) was not enough to ensure this. The Order of
the Jar and the Griffin was founded by him on 15 August 1403 at the Church
of Santa María de la Antigua in the historic city of Medina del Campo; this

was not only a symbol of status and chivalric virtue, it was also associated with the Virgin Mary, a powerful ally in medieval times. As Martin I, the king of Aragon, had died without an heir, Prince Ferdinand of Antequera – who was, after all, the son of a princess of Aragon and a Castilian king – made a claim that was also made by others; these other claimants were equally entitled to a powerful crown which at the time dominated half the western Mediterranean world. The issue was resolved by a special group of electors, who chose Ferdinand as their king at the city of Caspe. Was Ferdinand de Antequera's accession to the crown of Aragon the result of political manipulation, as some thought, or was his destiny influenced by the intervention of the Virgin Mary, as he was sure had been the case? At his coronation and at the banquet that followed, he made certain his authority would never be doubted.

Put the word *entremés* into a search engine and a number of definitions are given, starting with the most common one: 'light dishes served just before lunch or dinner'. The same name is also given in Spain to a burlesque theatrical piece, played out between the different acts of a comedy, which became an integral part of any banquet worthy of the name. At the coronation banquet of Ferdinand de Antequera, now Ferdinand I, which took place in the city of Zaragoza in 1416, a number of these theatrical pieces, all related to subjects relevant to the new king, were performed, to the astonishment of all present: the Moors he had fought, the castles where he had lived, the chivalric order he had founded and of course his devotion to the Virgin Mary. Fine food featured throughout the entire proceedings along with the best wine that could be found. Elaborate stages were created at a grand banqueting hall, together with spectacular floats where musicians and actors performed together, some dressed as angels, others as apostles. A fabulous dragon with fiery breath in the shape of a gold griffin took centre stage, opening the way for servants to present the different courses. The king would have demanded a similar degree of imagination and creativity from the kitchen, many centuries before Heston Blumenthal would try to recreate similar medieval celebratory dishes for a television series. There were peacocks and capons covered in gold, pies stuffed with various living birds that would fly around the griffin, roasts, boiled spicy meats, exotic fruits and sugary treats, all served with the best wines produced in the land.[6]

## La Mesta

The shepherds are going to the Extremadura
The Sierra is now left sad and in darkness
The shepherds are going away towards the sheepfold
The Sierra is now left sad and silent
– Traditional Spanish children's folk song

It is highly probable that the meat served at Ferdinand's banquet would have come from lambs raised in the valleys of the Pyrenees, from the wind-battered plains south of Zaragoza or even from Castile, for lamb, not beef, has always been at the centre of Spanish cuisine. It was not a question dictated by taste or even economics – the reason can be found in the geographic and climatic conditions across most of Spain and by other determining factors such as war, traditional animal farming, and above all wool production. The life of the shepherd today has changed beyond recognition, but the spectacle of large transhumant flocks moving along well-established routes, the *Cañadas Reales*, in search of fresh pastures has remained as evocative as it was in the twelfth, thirteenth and fourteenth centuries, and even much earlier. Evidence of extensive sheep raising and of the production of quality wool has been a Spanish feature since early times. Breeds included the Basco-Béarnaise, Churra, Manchega, Alcarreña and the gentle, long-haired Latxa. From Africa came the most successful breed of all, the Merino.

The determination of the Castilian monarchy to control the tax-profitable production of raw materials, and the role played by an association of the wool industry known as La Mesta, ensured a high demand for wool. Wool, a very profitable international business, would be supplied from Castile-León and eventually from other Iberian kingdoms including Navarre and Aragon.

Since Roman times, Spain had been renowned for the quality of the wool produced from indigenous breeds of sheep. During the Visigoth period in Spain, the production of and trade in quality wool gained strength. Later, with Islam and the expertise of Berber tribes who were forced to settle close to the dangerous frontier areas around the River Douro, the wool industry grew even further. The introduction of the Merino in Castile, a breed of sheep capable of producing high-quality wool, would be responsible for major changes to traditional agricultural patterns and even the economic outlook of medieval Spain. It is believed the Merino was introduced into southern Spain and Extremadura by the Beni-Merines, a Berber tribe that reached the peninsula when it was ruled by the Almohads in the twelfth century. They brought with them advanced pastoral practices that would improve the local stock.[7]

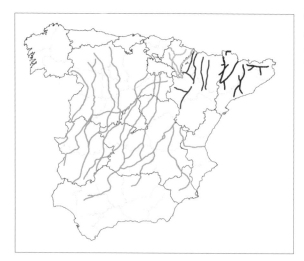

The *cañadas reales*, showing transhumance routes for the movement of sheep.

The Festival of the Trashumancia in Madrid: there is a traditional right of way for sheep to pass through the middle of Madrid.

In 1273 it was King Alfonso X the Wise who, partly as a result of unification of the different local associations of shepherds (*mestas*), approved the foundation of the *Honrado Concejo de la Mesta*, a sectorial institution that would become the catalyst for the development of *ganadería lanar trashumante* (transhumant sheep rearing) in large areas of Spain. The original *mestas* had been trying to resolve the issue that ownership of a large number of animals was lost sight of during the long summer and winter migrations. By the thirteenth century, as the *Reconquista* gained momentum as it moved south, migratory flocks began to cross the borders between the land of the Christians and Al-Andalus: thousands of animals moving almost at the same pace at which Christian forces were taking over lands that until then had been efficiently cultivated by the Moors. These were extensive areas to be placed in the hands of the monasteries, the powerful military orders and the local oligarchies. They were granted land in return for services rendered to an impoverished Crown trying to regain control of the peninsula. This was the same Crown that had become aware of the economic power and fiscal advantages of transhumance, as the wool industry grew and gained importance in the export markets which Castile would control during the sixteenth and early seventeenth centuries. Spain maintained the exclusive right to breed Merino sheep until well into the seventeenth century.

On 19 October 1469 another Ferdinand, the king of Sicily and heir to the throne of Aragon, married Isabella, the sister of the king of Castile. With their marriage the supremacy of the Crown of Castile became a potential threat to its traditional enemies, France and the Castilian feudal lords. The power of the latter had been growing even more as a result of endemic wars between the peninsula's medieval kingdoms: Castile, Aragon, Portugal, the small kingdom of Navarre, the Basque provinces and the last enclave of Moorish survival, Granada. The destiny of the peninsula would change dramatically when in 1474 Princess Isabella became Queen Isabella I of Castile, and her husband Ferdinand inherited the Crown of Aragon in 1479. For them, the unification of the entire peninsula would become a priority. Only Portugal would remain outside the dominion of the Catholic kings. The union of the crowns of Castile and Aragon started the chain of hereditary links that brought Spain's Empire into being. Even if the history and legend created by Franco's regime tried to depict the Spain of the Catholic kings as a unified country, the reality was different. Aragon and Castile were markedly different in size and strength, and in cultural and historical development as well as in food and agriculture. In size

Vines at the former Carthusian monastery of Scala Dei in Tarragona.

and strength Castile was undoubtedly the dominant side of the partnership, but the very sophisticated Mediterranean Crown of Aragon would prove superior in other spheres. During the thirteenth and fourteenth centuries, Castile had remained a pastoral and nomadic society while the Aragonese and Catalans had been deeply involved in their commercial interests in the Mediterranean. By the fifteenth century things were changing in Castile. Trade had become the name of the game as the economy had been substantially developed by the growth of the wool trade.

The expulsion of a large proportion of the Moorish and Jewish population from 1492 onwards resulted in one of the most tragic periods in the history of the country in terms of human suffering, the economy and losses to academia and medicine. Agriculture, at the hands of the aristocracy and other landowners, was also severely affected. In barren Castile, wool instead of grain would become the all-important commodity that sustained the needs of the Crown. For the majority of the population the demise of agriculture would prove to be a serious threat, but La Mesta was to be protected at all costs.

As a consequence of the Crown's erroneous policies, and of giving precedence to wool-producing stock rather than the cultivation of the land, the supply of wheat became chaotic in Castile. Wheat could always be imported from the Spanish territories in Italy, especially from Sicily, thought the over-optimistic Catholic monarch. The picture was completely different for wine production; this flourished in the peninsula during the period much as in the rest of the Mediterranean world, where consumption reached all levels of society. Inferior-quality wine for the peasant in the countryside and the lower classes in towns and cities was purchased at local tavernas. The 'best' wines were produced for the upper clergy, the aristocracy and wealthy citizens, although it was usually served blended with water and in some cases flavoured with expensive spices and aromatic herbs in the traditional Roman way. Wine was basic food with a difference. It provided pleasure at a reasonable price. In Castile grain was in short supply from the twelfth century; however, economic policies were put in place that encouraged the cultivation of the vine, with a legal framework supporting the processes of production and even its distribution throughout the peninsula. Furthermore the vine could be planted in areas where little else would grow. When drunk in moderation, wine was a joy not only for the body but for the soul, a reference to the alliance between God and men and therefore a Christian practice to be encouraged.

On the subject of wine, Francesc Eiximenis thought that drinking wine was a response to the human need for enjoyment and happiness. It could be produced by the peasants in limited quantities for their own supply or could, with minimum effort, be produced on the large estates controlled by the nobility to supply old as well as new cities emerging from the *Reconquista*. It is worth remembering that vines can adapt to extreme climates and poor soils as well as drought. Issues relating to the nature of wine and its effect on men were looked at from different angles: from dietetics to fashion, from morality to order. Most importantly, in Christian Spain wine as much as wheat was associated with the body and blood of Christ. At a time when water was frequently unsafe to drink, its association with the upper clergy, the powerful military orders and the monasteries encouraged its consumption. Dangers associated with excessive drinking were fully understood and criticized, not only by doctors and dieticians but by the same thinkers who praised moderate drinking in the first place, such as Eiximenis or Arnau de Vilanova. Images of grapes and the cycle of grape cultivation and wine production carved into the walls of magnificent Romanesque and Gothic buildings bring a medieval past to life that can still be found by modern pilgrims and tourists throughout Spain.

## Looking for Pepper

Since ancient times, Europeans had become accustomed to the taste of valuable Oriental spices well known to Greeks, Romans and Moors. In the Middle Ages spices had already become a sign of abundance and status: nutmeg and cinnamon, ginger, mustard, cloves and peppercorns grown primarily in a number of islands in the western Pacific, the Spice Islands. Traditionally, spices had reached western Europe with the caravan trade via Arabia and North Africa, or via the Mediterranean Sea. By the thirteenth century traders dealing with Venice had found an easier route across Asia and Mesopotamia. The shortening of the journey and the elimination of the middleman brought prices down and consequently increased consumption. Venice would become the centre of the world for the spice and silk trade. A revolution in China and the Turkish expansion in the Mediterranean resulted in a return to the original journey across Arabia and to the ports of Alexandria and Cairo, where distribution became centred. Prices increased substantially again, and the need to find alternative routes became a priority. The Portuguese ventured south down the African coast while the Spanish set sail across the Atlantic Ocean. Both were looking for lands where spices flourished, for white and black pepper and more besides.

Following in the footsteps of the Crown of Aragon, Castile had started to acquire maritime experience that would allow its expansion across the seas but with a difference. Castile's navigators would not sail in the already congested

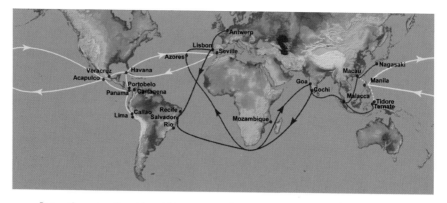

Sixteenth-century Spanish and Portuguese trade routes across the world (white represents Spanish routes).

Mediterranean, nor would they follow the African route already opened up by intrepid Portuguese navigators down the African coast, all the way round the Cape of Good Hope and to the rich spice lands of Asia. Castile would set a course across the Atlantic Ocean, heading into waters of potential danger but with potentially rich rewards. The contribution and expertise of Catalan and especially Basque mariners would also guarantee a succession of great adventures. The navigators were to discover silver, gold and an array of new foods that was to change the diet of the entire Old World within decades. With the discovery of America in October 1492, the dream of a Genoese mariner, Columbus, and a Castilian queen, Isabella, became a reality.

This discovery of America in 1492, followed by the succession of the Habsburgs to the throne of Spain in 1516, were two major events that catapulted Spain into the forefront of international affairs.[8] A steady flow of new products came from the Americas from 1493 and until the nineteenth century. Apart from precious metals, the Spanish galleons returned to Europe with potatoes, tomatoes, maize, peppers and beans among many other goods, including the intriguing and valuable seeds from which an unpalatable drink would be made into the world's most desired treat – chocolate. In fact it was the search for black pepper, not gold and silver, which was the main reason why the Spanish crossed the Atlantic in the first place. In an unequal process of exchange, Spaniards introduced a 'language' to the New World which was not limited to vocabulary and grammar but also involved culture and religion. This incorporated plants, animals, methods of cooking, and above all the capacity to transform raw materials into highly valuable foods.[9]

Christopher Columbus was convinced that, if his calculations were correct, Asia could be reached by sailing west from the Canary Islands. All he needed was financial backing, and Portugal had already refused his project. Now the success of the expedition lay in the hands of the Spanish monarchs. Isabella and Ferdinand were preoccupied with the last stages of the *Reconquista* in the peninsula, and delayed their decision while a commission investigated the mariner's claims. Eventually, during the siege of Granada at the beginning of 1492, an initial agreement between Columbus and the Catholic kings was reached. Castile would help to finance the project that already had the backing of a number of Genoese bankers.

On Friday, 12 October 1492 a Spanish caravel reached the islet of Guanahani, which is part of today's San Salvador. It lay due north of the Windward Passage between what we now call Cuba and Haiti. Then in 1519 Cortés arrived in the Gulf of Mexico, and two years later Pizarro arrived in Peru. In the end the conquistadors did not find pepper, or '*pimienta*', in the newly discovered land; instead they discovered an amazing array of unknown plants and foods whose benefit they could never have imagined. It is important to remember that these products arrived from the Americas at a time when the majority of people living in Spain ate a perpetually frugal and uninspiring diet. It consisted largely of *gachas* (porridge) and *tortas* (savoury biscuits), created not with wheat but with coarsely milled, low-quality flour made from barley, rye or millet and water. Vegetables and pulses, which were less attractive to the lord of the land they belonged to, were a welcome addition as were small pieces of dried salted pork fat which they could store all year around if they were able to keep a pig. To raise money to pay the high taxes imposed by the king, the Church and the nobility, they had to sell their pigs' hams and shoulders as well as other quality cuts. Practically all the food they produced went elsewhere including wheat, milk, cheese and above all meat. By and large they hardly ever ate meat. It can be argued that the major benefit brought by the discovery of the Americas was not the gold or silver that arrived with the galleons, but the improved diet of impoverished rural societies, at first all over Europe, and then gradually eastwards across Europe and Asia: peppers, maize, beans, vanilla and chocolate found early appreciation back in Spain, but other products such as tomatoes and potatoes were only accepted over time. Botanists and doctors believed that potatoes and tomatoes were poisonous, and that tomatoes were even an aphrodisiac. As a result, for decades and even centuries to come, they would face refusal and prejudice among the upper classes. However in Andalusia, where they arrived soon after their discovery, tomatoes were accepted much earlier by the lower classes, and this can be seen in sixteenth-century Spanish literature and painting. In Galicia and in Asturias, potatoes saved the poor from famine, as was the case in Ireland (though in Ireland overdependence led to famine).

At different rates the American plants started their unstoppable global journey, each one with a very different history to tell.

Was it out of ignorance or was it a deliberate mistake on the part of the Spaniards that they gave names they already knew to some of the plants they found in the land they would called 'the Indies', especially if they were associated with the names of valuable spices? Whatever the reason, by doing so they caused confusion in the world of food that would take botanists centuries to correct. The word for pepper, the vegetable, is *pimiento* in Spanish, a word very close to *pimienta* (peppercorn) – one of the best examples to illustrate this confusion.

## A MATTER OF TASTE

Having survived the crossing of the Atlantic on rotten biscuits and several casks of dubious wine, it is curious that, even though they were starving, the newcomers initially contemplated New World foods with such disdain. In their defence, large fat spiders and white worms may not have looked too appetising either.

But the Spaniards quickly developed a liking for sweet potatoes, among other things. They had a very pleasant taste reminiscent of the nutty flavour and texture of the traditional European chestnut. However, maize (corn) would never take the place of wheat. For the Spaniards, wheat meant bread, leavened bread, but corn did become widely accepted, especially when made into tasty hot flat *tortillas* and *tamales* (dumplings). American products arrived in the peninsula with interesting notes written by chroniclers who carefully described the plants and fruits they were finding, comparing them with those they grew back home. Some of the best-known chroniclers were the Franciscan ethnographer Bernardino de Sahagún; the historians Fernández de Oviedo and Francisco López de Gómaral; the missionary and naturalist José de Acosta and the narrator Bernal Díaz del Castillo. The colonist and historian-turned-friar Bartolomé de las Casas, Bishop of Chiapas, should also be included in the list. Unfortunately the local recipes and the people who followed them were left behind.

By 1500 both sweet potatoes and maize had been successfully planted in the Canary Islands, Andalusia, Castile and León. However, in the case of maize, a failure to understand how crucial it was to apply the method of preparation followed by the Native Americans would bring misery to the poor of Europe. In the mountains of Asturias, and later in Italy, in areas where the American crop thrived while other cereals failed due to climatic conditions, pellagra would strike with a vengeance. Pellagra, a nutrient-deficiency disease, would become unfathomable for scientists. Although Gaspar Casals, a Spanish scientist working at the University of Oviedo, was the first to link corn with pellagra in 1735, the mystery wasn't solved for nearly two more centuries. Casals had observed that all patients suffering from this unknown illness were found in parts of Asturias where the diet of the poor was based almost entirely on maize. The symptom of the disease was a reddish rash on the hands and feet – Casals called it *el mal de la rosa* (the rose illness). Pellagra was fatal. Not only did it affect the skin and the digestive system but it also provoked dementia. A few years later an Italian, Francesco Frapolli, called it by the name we know today, pellagra, meaning 'rough skin'. It was in America in the first part of the twentieth century that scientists finally demonstrated that a vitamin deficiency was the cause of the epidemic both in Europe and in North America. Its tragic consequences could easily have been prevented by an improved diet and notably nicotinic acid (vitamin B3). Corn was considered to be a fabulous crop, but it had been travelling the world without a safe recipe since the fifteenth century. Both the Aztecs and the Mayans treated maize before preparing the recipes which were at the base of their diets. They softened the maize to make it edible with an alkaline solution, limewater, which released the missing nutrient niacin and an all-important amino acid, tryptophan, from which niacin is made. Even if Europeans eventually enjoyed some corn dishes while staying and living among the indigenous people, they never paid attention to or recorded the way that corn had to be treated before it was cooked.

In Spain maize was mostly used to feed animals. However, in areas where other cereals such as wheat or rye produced only very small crops or simply failed, local people started to prepare traditional recipes with the new crop. Maize was cheap and abundant. These days, in Galicia and Asturias, many small growers still protect their crops from damp and rodents by storing their corn in magnificent stone *hórreos* that decorate the countryside. At local fairs and artisan markets, large round loaves of *pan de maíz* wrapped in maple leaves and baked in wood fires are sold to the delight of visitors, as are the maize *empanada* pies filled with cockles and even sardines. Unfortunately delicious and esteemed Indian *tamales* stuffed with delicate bean paste, and hot tortillas cooked over the fire in a *comal*, never reached Europe. Capsicum peppers, *pimientos*, followed another interesting path. 'In those islands there are also bushes like rose bushes, which give fruit as long as cinnamon, full of small seeds; those Caribs and Indians eat that fruit like we eat apples', wrote one of Columbus' crew as he sailed back to Europe. It was Diego Álvarez Chanca, a physician on Columbus' second voyage to the West Indies in 1493, who brought

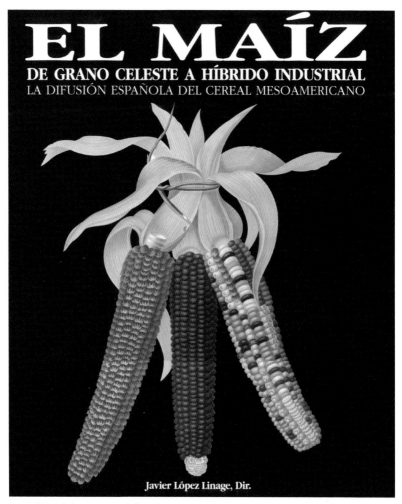

# EL MAÍZ
## DE GRANO CELESTE A HÍBRIDO INDUSTRIAL
### LA DIFUSIÓN ESPAÑOLA DEL CEREAL MESOAMERICANO

**Javier López Linage, Dir.**

'*El maíz*': front cover of *El maíz de grano celeste a hibrido industrial, la difusión española del cereal mesoamericano*: so many more varieties of maize were available than in Spain.

back chilli peppers for the first time.[10] Even though Diego Álvarez wrote about their medical virtues, he did not know that wild chilli peppers had been part of the diet of the Americans of the Andes since at least 7500 BC, and had later been cultivated by the Mexicans more than 6,000 years before his writings. A self-pollinating crop, chilli peppers were being grown in Mexico and other parts of Central and South America when the Spaniards reached the new continent.

Even if many species of chilli peppers are grown in the Americas, only the Mexican species, *Capsicum annuum*, belonging to the large Solanaceae family, were initially introduced into Spain. In Spain and Portugal monks grew chilli peppers in the vegetable gardens of their monasteries to enhance their food, while in municipal botanical gardens they were planted as curiosities. The Monastery of Guadalupe in Extremadura (Hieronymites), to which Columbus brought some seeds as presents after his return to the peninsula, would become instrumental in the expansion of the American pepper. In Spain it was treated as a vegetable, a spice and a medicinal wonder that travelled from monastery to monastery throughout the land. From Spain peppers travelled to the Middle East including via the routes established in the Mediterranean through Aragonese and Ottoman expansion. Within two decades of their arrival in Spain, farmers were growing more than twenty different varieties of

Fresh chillies known as *guindillas*.

peppers. The hot varieties were usually used as a spice, a new spice that could be used instead of the more expensive black and white Asian pepper enjoyed by the upper classes and the aristocracy.[11] As they did not arrive with recipes from their countries of origin, they were used to add flavour and colour to the brownish appearance that onion gave to the base of many Spanish preparations, including the *sofrito* sauce so admired by Rupert de Nola among other medieval food writers and cooks. Soon *pimientos*, and chilli peppers (*guindillas*), were incorporated into many recipes prepared by Spanish cooks. They used them raw, fried, stewed or pickled for the winter months. They could also be dried and kept all year round. Once dried in the sun, peppers and chillies could easily be pounded into a thin powder which would become the magical – sweet or hot, smoked or unsmoked – spice of intense red colour that Spaniards named *pimentón*. Without *pimentón* many regional dishes, from Valencian *paella* to Asturian *fabada*, from the *pulpo à feira* of the Galicians to the *sopas de ajo* of the Castilians, would never have been the same, nor indeed would chorizo. Would it be possible today to imagine any tapas bar without *pimientos del piquillo* stuffed with cod, or a piping hot plate of sautéed *pimientos del padrón*, brought to Galicia by monks five centuries ago?

Compared with the easy ride that peppers enjoyed on their way to European aristocratic and popular tables, tomatoes faced a journey guided all the way by ignorance and prejudice. This was only to be compared with the equal suffering potatoes would have to endure later on along their journey, this time from the Andes.

Tomatoes, cultivated by the Aztecs, were discovered by the Spaniards at the time when Cortés was enjoying Montezuma's hospitality, around the 1520s. Tomatoes were used by the Aztecs in their cooking according to two distinguished chroniclers, Bernardino de Sahagún and Bernal Díaz del Castillo. More than a century later, Father Bernabé Cobo in his *Historia del Nuevo Mundo* (History of the New World) provided further information:

> The tomato plant is small and grows as a calabash, but it does not
> spread out much; its stem is more slender than a finger, but from
> its branch shoots out many others which are yet thinner. The leaves
> are similar in shape and size to those of the mulberry bush. The
> fruit known as the *tomate* is round and brightly coloured, and the
> small ones are the size of cherries. There are also green and yellow
> ones the size of plums and even lemons. Inside them is a reddish,
> watery substance and seeds somewhat smaller than sesame. The
> skin is as thin as that of a grape.[12]

Father Cobo reported that tomatoes were never eaten raw due to their sharp taste. 'They are mostly used in soups and stews,' he said. One thing none of chroniclers knew was that the tomato's origin lay not in Mexico but further south at the heart of the Andes in Peru, Ecuador and Chile. These were places where wild tomatoes thrived, although it is thought that they were not cultivated or used in indigenous kitchens. From there turtles had carried their seeds to the Galapagos Islands, and from this point they started their long journey to Mesoamerica and to the rest of the world. On the other hand, the Aztecs cultivated tomatoes and cooked with them in rich sauces which the Spaniards would have certainly eaten as they proceeded to annex the land.

It is important to note that there was a period of significant scientific progress in the field of botany in Europe in the fifteenth and sixteenth centuries. New plants were arriving, not only from the New World but from Asia and Africa. Many botanists and members of the medical profession were once again adopting the classical thinking of Dioscorides or Galen. Religious beliefs, old and new prejudices, and Greek and Roman myths were also part of the mix. They even revived the names of plants and fruits that had no relation either to each other or to those coming from across the Atlantic. In the specific Spanish case it should be remembered that in the sixteenth century, Spain was marked by the exodus of Moors and Jews, and by the scourge of the Inquisition. There was a fear of all that was new and untried, especially among the upper classes, and this delayed the use of American plants in their kitchens in spite of, for example, tomatoes' versatility and the ease with which they could be grown in subtropical regions, both of which should have encouraged their development as an ingredient in country cooking.

Why do Spaniards call tomatoes *tomates* and not golden apples or love apples, the names given to the new arrival by Italian and Swiss botanists such as Mattioli? Surprisingly, this time Spaniards used a name quite close to the one they would have heard from indigenous people, though yet again they caused confusion by giving two different fruits the same name. The Aztecs called the tomato we know *xitomalt* and they often blended these with chillies and ground pumpkin seeds to prepare a tasty sauce, or salsa, that they served with fish and even turkey. This sauce could easily have resembled the fresh and cooked sauces so fashionable today in fusion food. At the same time Spaniards found another very different but equally attractive fruit which the native population used to make sauces: the *tomalt*. Despite the similarity of the name, this fruit was botanically totally unrelated to the *xitomalt*, the tomato as we know it. In reality the *tomalt*, also known as the tomatillo, green tomato or husk tomato, is a *Physalis* (*Physalis ixocarpa*), while the *xitomalt* belongs to the group of the *Lycopersicon esculentum*. The acknowledgement of the use of tomatoes (tomatillos would never cross the Atlantic) in the Spanish kitchen would have to wait for the Spanish Golden Age and the poetry of eminent late sixteenth- and seventeenth-century writers including the playwright Tirso de Molina:

> Oh salad,
> of rosy-cheeked tomatoes
> so sweet, and yet so piquant.

Lope de Vega's daughter, Sor Marcela de San Félix Carpio, wrote in her colloquy 'The Death of the Appetite': 'Some cold meat I fancy / and a salad of tomatoes and green peppers.'[13]

With the discovery of the New World, the river port of Seville became the point of entry of all goods coming from the Americas, including foodstuffs which had never been seen before. They were brought by sailors and traders and, most importantly for their connection with botanical gardens and monasteries, by many members of the Catholic Church. Seville, on the River Guadalquivir, was 50 kilometres (31 mi.) away from the Atlantic Ocean, and had been a historical city and an important trading centre for Christians, Moors and Jews as well as for foreign bankers and entrepreneurs in general on the look-out for a good return. La Casa de Contratación (The House of Trade) was set up in Seville in 1503 by the Crown of Castile, and the Crown also granted the city the exclusive right to trade with the New World. The decision to move the focal point of trade with the Americas from Cádiz to Seville, only a limited river port, and the fact that the Crown of Castile treated the Americas as their own personal property, would prove to be a serious mistake. Ultimately the move denied the entire Spanish economy the giant boost that it desperately needed. And there was more. Defending the huge empire that the Habsburg dynasty had inherited had already become Castile's number one priority, instead of protecting the human and economic interests of the peninsula. Within two centuries the vast quantities of gold and silver mined in the Caribbean and Central and South America were invested mostly in armaments, soldiers and national debt payments. Spain did not realize that new seeds, vegetables, cereals and fruits, including chocolate and tobacco, transported to Europe would eventually yield as many tangible and intangible benefits as could be obtained by growing and transforming Old World goods such as sugar and coffee into rich commodities. Eventually other countries did. Spain realized too late that the exchange of foods taking place across the Atlantic was to be the most successful outcome of the entire discovery.

Seville in the second half of the sixteenth century: a great trading port. Oil painting
attributed to Alonso Sánchez Coello (1531–1588).

## THE ANDEAN CROP

It is highly likely that Seville was the first place where potatoes were planted,
not just to combat the endemic hunger suffered by the poor in the south
of the country but for their lovely flowers, which were widely appreciated
in local gardens. The people who brought them across the Atlantic in one
of the small caravels could never have imagined the place the beloved food
of the Incas would occupy in the lives of people all over the world one day.
Nor could they have imagined the travails the poor potato would endure
before reaching the table of the aristocracy.

*Patatas fritas* (fried potatoes), *papas arrugadas* (wrinkled potatoes),
*patatas a lo pobre* (poor man's potatoes), *patatas a la importancia* (very
important potatoes), *asadas* (roasted), with *al-i-olí* (garlic and olive oil
sauce), *tortilla de patatas* (Spanish omelette) or even *panadera* (breadmaker's
potatoes): these are all names of dishes prepared with the *papa* the Spaniards
first encountered not in Peru but in Colombia, around 1530. A staple part
of the indigenous diet, potatoes were rejected at first by the conquistadors.
However, hunger and malnutrition soon forced them to change their minds
as they moved south through Ecuador, Peru, Bolivia and the north of Chile.
In Peru the Incas prepared *chuños* to be used in stews and other recipes.
The *chuño*, very much still in use today, is a freeze-dried potato that can be
stored in good condition for months. The Incas ate them like bread and as an
accompaniment to other foods. They also ate quinoa, sweet potatoes, yucca
and especially the *papa*. Inca Garcilaso de la Vega, a descendent of the royal

Inca rulers, gave the most riveting first-hand account of Inca traditions and customs. In his *Comentarios reales de los Incas*, Garcilaso speaks passionately about the *chuño*:

> Throughout the province named Colla, over a distance of more than one hundred and fifty leagues, maize does not grow because the earth is very cold: much quinoa is harvested, which is like rice, along with other grains and pulses that thrive below the ground and amongst these, there is one they call *papa*, which is round and, because it is very moist is prone to going bad quickly. To stop it going bad they lay it on the ground, on a kind of very fine straw that grows there; it is left out for many nights in the frost, for there is heavy frost all year round in that province, then once the frost has done with it, as if it had been boiled, they cover it with straw and tread on it carefully and softly to dispatch the water the *papa* naturally contains and that which the frost has created. Then after having pressed it well they put it out in the sun and leave it to rest until it is shrivelled up. Prepared in this manner it keeps for a long time and changes its name and is called *chuño*, and this is what they did to all crops that were harvested in the Lands of the Sun and the Inca, and they kept them in the *positos* [stores] with the rest of the pulses and seeds.[14]

Although the taste and texture of the *chuño* has never been appreciated outside its original area of production, Spanish women who had emigrated to the Americas used the flour obtained from the *chuño blanco*, also known as *Moray* or *Tunta*, to prepare cakes and other recipes. By the time the Spaniards arrived in Peru, more than 150 varieties of potatoes of all colours and amazing shapes were being cultivated in the Andes.

The arrival of the potato in Europe has been the subject of much research and debate. It is unknown who brought it, when and from where exactly. Redcliffe Salaman in his *History and Social Influence of the Potato* assumes that potatoes arrived firstly in Spain, the only country that had a connection with the area of production in the second part of the sixteenth century. This was around the critical years of 1573–5 when it is believed the potato reached Seville.[15] Earlier records can be found in the Canary Islands where 'patatas' were exported from Gran Canaria to Antwerp in 1567. From Spain, the potato started its journey to the rest of the world. Today potatoes rank fourth among the world's foodstuffs behind wheat, rice and maize.

Other edible roots and nuts were also being consumed by the indigenous population of the New World upon the arrival of the Europeans. Known as *camotli* by the Aztecs and *apichu* by the Incas, sweet potatoes were rapidly and eagerly incorporated into the Spanish diet, unlike potatoes. *Batatas*, as the Spaniards have called them ever since, have an attractive colour – salmon, ivory, purple and yellow – as well as a sweet taste and a soft nutty texture similar to the chestnut, especially when roasted in their skins.

## CHOCOLATE AND THE EMPEROR

'A crazy thing similar to the coca of Peru', cried Father José de Acosta in 1590 in his *Historia natural y moral de las Indias*. He was talking about chocolate. Regardless of whether Father de Acosta could have known that the far-from-sweet bean would end up as one of the most desired treats a man can wish for, the cacao bean would become one of the most successful products in the economic history of the whole food exchange with the Americas.[16]

According to many books and articles, Hernán Cortés offered chocolate to Charles I, his king, but no one knows for sure exactly when cacao first reached Spain, and there is no historical basis to validate this account. The first documented support of the arrival of cacao and chocolate in Spain is linked with Prince Philip the future Philip II, the Dominican Order and the Maya, not the Aztecs.[17] Arranged by the Dominicans in 1544, a delegation of Maya nobles in their native costumes visited the young prince, bringing with them their most valuable presents: quetzal feathers, copal incense, chillies, maize, sarsaparilla and beans. They also brought decorative clay pots, including some containing beaten chocolate which Prince Philip may have politely tasted. Perhaps it could be agreed that away from tangible documentation and historical facts, chocolate is a subject in itself that allows the imagination to fly free.

Following ancient belief, Quetzalcóatl, the creator of light, had decided to offer a gift to the noblemen of Tula, a Toltec city he loved. The gift was a precious and sacred plant – *Cacau-quauiti* – which he had stolen from another god. The Toltecs made a divine drink from the seeds of this plant which they called cocoa. It was the Toltecs who introduced the cacao plant into Mayan culture. They would use the seeds to prepare a ceremonial drink, and for them it was also a currency that would support trade in Mesoamerica.[18]

*Theobroma cacao* is the Latin name given to the cacao tree by Linnaeus in the eighteenth century. It is a plant native to Mesoamerica, the area occupied by Mexico, Belize, Honduras, Guatemala and El Salvador. With the seeds of this plant, a dark drink had been made for centuries by different civilizations before the Spaniards first arrived. Cacao refers to the tree, its fruits and the seeds before processing. The Aztecs called a drink made with cacao beans *xocoalt*; and taking the sound of the word, the Spanish called it *chocolate*, a name which until the eighteenth century in Europe referred to the drink made with water and cocoa powder with the addition of flavourings. These flavourings would change with the passing of the time.

The Maya, who managed to control the production of cacao beans until the arrival of the Spaniards in the sixteenth century, also used cacao in many culinary preparations made with maize, the principal staple of their diet. A number of recipes with cocoa (the powder) were reported by Fray Diego de Landa, a Franciscan who became Bishop of Yucatán. Deep down, Landa was a man full of contradictions, an Inquisitor guilty of the destruction of invaluable Maya books, and yet he became responsible for saving much of the pre-Columbian Maya culture by recording the daily life of the ancient people. He wrote, among many other things, about a refreshing drink which the locals drank warm in the morning, made from roasted maize, cocoa and chilli, which he called *pimienta de las Indias*:

> Men return from the fields at dusk and then the family eat the
> main meal of the day. Men separate from the women and children
> in different rooms: fresh tortillas and frijole beans, a little meat if
> they have it, perhaps some other pulses and chocolate.[19]

Other Maya recipes of the time used *aguacate*, papaya, *anana*, *siricot* (*Cordia dodecandra*), *chayote* (*Sechium edule,* a type of squash), *ají* peppers and *xitomate* (tomato in the Nahuatl language). They also ate fish and shellfish, which they brought from the coast, and meat seasoned with salt, chillies, herbs and *azapote* (*Pouteria viridis*, a fruit) as well as *achiote* (*Bixia orellana*), which they used as a condiment and colorant.

Columbus was the first European to come across cacao beans in a Maya trading canoe in Guanaja, an island in the Caribbean, during his fourth and last trip to the Indies. He was surprised to see the high value that the natives attached to such a humble, dark bean. Cacao beans where not only important in the kitchen but valuable as currency. Spaniards were very partial to the sweet flavour of cocoa butter. The fat extracted from the cacao bean was, in fact, very similar to the delicious lard Columbus had left behind in Spain. Ground and blended with a little water, this fat was used locally to cook many different dishes. This was the same cocoa butter that the Europeans would become so addicted to at a much later time.

Once the nutritious value of cocoa both as a drink or mixed with other ingredients became well-known, this new food soon came to the attention of the Catholic Church, which was by now well established in the New World. Fasting was considered at the time to be an important matter, and the question of whether chocolate could be allowed or not during the fast became a serious debate for men of the cloth.

Eventually the case was referred to Rome. In the late sixteenth century, Pope Gregory XIII declared that chocolate, as long as it was just a drink, did not break the fast. The news was welcomed by the convents, where Spanish nuns were praying as well as working on new recipes that would change the bitter character of the original Mayan and Aztec drink. They would add vanilla, sugar and cinnamon and remove the spicy chilli. Today in the Mexican city of Oaxaca specialist shops roast and grind the beans selected by their clients before their preferred flavourings are added. But the time when women used to spend their lives on their knees in Puebla, Jalapa or Oaxaca grinding cacao beans or corn kernels on the traditional *matates* or grounding stones has practically gone.

The discovery of chocolate proved to be a wonder for the Spaniards, even if it has rarely been used as an ingredient in Spanish traditional food, with the exception of cakes and confectionary. In contrast, Mexican cooks still commonly use it in all sorts of recipes, including the rich sauces or *moles* so reminiscent of those prepared by the ancient Aztecs before the arrival of Cortés. This is the case with the succulent *mole poblano de guajalote*, one of the best-known recipes associated with the city of Puebla. *Guajalote*, also known as *pavo* in Spain and as turkey by English-speakers, is a descendant of the wild *Meleagris gallopavo*, of the family Phasianidae. Apart from cooking the bird, the old Aztecs used its feathers in their headdresses and for making arrows. Turkeys became so important in their society that they were included in the festivals in which they worshipped their gods. They called the bird *huexolotli* – the modern Mexican name *guajalote* derives from this word.

Hernán Cortés saw these exotic birds for the first time at the court of Montezuma. They were large animals, being tastier and much meatier than the *pavo real*, as the Spanish called the peacock, which had been known in Europe since antiquity.

## Cisneros's Dream

Based on his positive and negative contribution to the history of Spain, the figure of Cardinal Cisneros, Gonzalo Ximénez de Cisneros (1436–1517), still moves between the realms of reality and legend. As Queen Isabella I of

Castile's confessor and as a man of political influence and clear vision, he would be instrumental in the decision process that ended successfully in the discovery and the evangelization of the Americas. Unfortunately he was also associated with the introduction of the Inquisition in Spain.

Having become aware of the negative effect the *Reconquista* had on agriculture, especially in Castile, Ximénez de Cisneros decided to commission a specialist treatise that could be followed by farmers and men of letters for centuries to come. It was fundamentally a book written in correct and yet simple language which was easily understood by the men and women who tended the land and by those who could make a difference in matters related to the same subject. The author was Gabriel Alonso de Herrera and his work would help to advance Spanish agriculture at a desperate time for farmers. While following a life in religious studies in Granada, Alonso de Herrera, a Castilian, had become fascinated by the advanced agricultural practices introduced by the Moors in the fertile valleys of the kingdom of Granada, the last bastion of Islamic Spain. Muslim agriculturalists had flocked to this area, bringing with them know-how inherited long before in the fertile valleys of the Middle East. Furthermore, Alonso's progress in the Church and his interest in agriculture would lead him on an extensive journey, not only through the rest of Spain but to Germany, France and Italy, where he would also become acquainted with classical teachings. *El libro de agricultura* by Herrera was printed in Alcalá de Henares (Madrid) around 1512. It comprises six books. The first one is a general view of agriculture and soil variation, although the main subject is the cultivation of cereals without irrigation. The second book deals with vines and the third one with trees. In the fourth book, his focus turns to vegetables and in the fifth, livestock. The final book is a farming calendar based on Palladius' work. For Alonso, classic knowledge was as relevant as Arabic teaching and the modern approach brought about by the Renaissance.[20]

By the time the Catholic king Ferdinand II died in 1516, the road to the Spanish Empire had been built. His great capacity as a warrior and his belief in the benefit of European marital alliances would prove to be a successful strategy as both the Tudor and the Habsburg dynasties became the centre of his attention. His daughter, the Infanta Catherine of Aragon, married Prince Arthur, the elder son of King Henry VII of England. It was a great political move but destined to end in disaster. Most importantly, over in the Netherlands, the Infanta Joanna married the handsome Archduke Philip of Burgundy, son of Maximilian I, Holy Roman Emperor. Death and tragedy would initially affect King Ferdinand's plans, but the birth of Charles, the son of Joanna and Philip, would guarantee a successful outcome. Charles became the heir of three of Europe's leading dynasties: the House of Habsburg, the House of Valois-Burgundy of the Burgundian Netherlands, and the House of Trastámara of the Crowns of Castile and Aragon. Destined to be an emperor, Prince Charles could not have imagined that he would be instrumental in the publication in Castilian of a very important Catalan cookery book.

## DE NOLA'S ART

In Catalonia, the sixteenth century started with the publication of a Catalan cookbook which would become a great success and a benchmark for other publications in Europe. It appears to have been written around 1490 by Mestre Rupert de Nola under the title *Llibre de Coch*. It was published in numerous editions starting around 1520 first in Catalan and later in Castilian. This book is considered to be a fundamental text in the history of Mediterranean cooking. De Nola presents himself to the reader as a true Renaissance man who writes about Catalan food and its introduction to the refined Court of Naples. It is clear that he was also interested in other food traditions. While it is obvious that De Nola's book followed in the footsteps of Martino, a fifteenth-century Italian cook, *Llibre de Coch* is a song dedicated to Mediterranean food. It is full of Catalan, Aragonese, Valencian, Provençal and Italian recipes in particular, going back to Roman times, inherited from Moorish, Christian and Jewish traditions, and adapted to a renaissance in the Mediterranean world. Prominence is given to fish, meat and spices, but the work also includes an array of vegetables, fruits and nuts grown in the Mediterranean in general and in Catalonia in particular – almonds and hazelnuts, rice, aubergines and lemons, figs and lettuces – at a time when Castile was still looking for black pepper across the Atlantic. The fact that De Nola had not selected any recipes from Castile could be interpreted as a sign of the antagonism and rivalry that had always existed between the most powerful areas in Spain. As his success was unstoppable, he soon attracted the attention of professionals and kitchen novices serving the nobility not only in the lands of the Crown of Aragon but in Castile, in both Toledo and in Logroño, where it was published under the title *Libro de los guisados, manjares y potajes* (Meat Stews, Delicacies and Lesser One-pot Meals Based on Vegetables). It has been said that the publication of the book in Catalan and in Castilian was made possible by the patronage of both the king of Naples and Emperor Charles V, who might have tried De Nola's food during a visit to Barcelona.

Who was Rupert de Nola exactly? Who was Ferrante, the king of Naples whom he served as mentioned in the 1520 edition? Here the matter gets

*El Llibre de Coch*, a sixteenth-century cookery book.

complicated. Some historians believe he was a professional Catalan cook who could have been born in Italy, in the locality of De Nola. His parents could have been Catalan, or perhaps he had simply learned Catalan during his service to the Crown of Naples. As the king did not include a number after the name Ferrante, which king was De Nola serving? Ferrante I, a natural son of Alphonse I of Naples, or Ferrante II, grandson of the same king? Although it has not been proved, it appears that it could only have been the first, as he was the only king who stayed in Italy long enough for De Nola to be able to write such an accomplished record of the world of food.

Above all, *El Llibre de Coch* is a cookbook designed as a guide for young apprentices, both inside and outside the walls of the kitchen. Apart from an extensive recipe list it includes ample information on what is expected from butlers, chefs, carvers, sommeliers and waiters. Even the duties of those in charge of the king's horses were recorded by De Nola. Another important aspect of this book is the light it sheds on the precepts of the Christian *Cuaresma* (Lent) as they were before 1491. This was the year the Church made radical changes to the number of foods that could be eaten during the main period of fasting in the Catholic calendar. These included milk, cheese, eggs and fish as well as olive oil, which was to replace the popular pork fat (a true giveaway of one's religious beliefs) at a time when religious tolerance had become a thing of the past.

A recipe from the book that would have been served during Lent is the *manjar blanco de pescado*, a variation on a popular recipe cooked with chicken in many other countries in medieval times and known in English as blancmange. First recorded in Spain in the Catalan *Sent Soví* in 1324, the dish could have been based on a similar preparation of Arabic origin known as *tafaya* and also cooked in Al-Andalus. *Tafaya* was a meat stew cooked very slowly with flour and almonds and flavoured with rose water and spices. It was also recorded as *mangier blanc* in *Le Viandier,* a recipe collection credited to Taillevent (thirteenth to fourteenth century), and *blancmangieri* in the Italian *Anonimo Toscano.*

In the section related to food in Lent, De Nola wrote:

> We have spoken, and in the briefest way that we could have
> done, on the art of cooking in regard to the foods and dishes for
> meat days. Although the foods that you can make for meat days
> are infinite, many of them can be made in Lent, because in the
> chapters on those foods where I say to blend them with meat
> broth, those sauces or pottages can be thinned with salt, oil, and
> water, but first you have to boil it; and in this manner, it is as good
> as meat broth if it is well-tempered with salt, and if the oil is very
> fine. And in this manner, many foods which are served for meat
> days can be made in Lent, and this is nothing but the custom of
> men to alter foods from one thing to another. And because of this,
> it seems to me that I have spoken enough on this topic of dishes
> for meat days.[21]

Although De Nola's book includes a comprehensive list of recipes cooked with fish, he considered that the three best preparations in the world were *salsa de pavo*, *mirrauste* and *manjar blanco*, which are all cooked with poultry. *Salsa de pavo* is not quite a sauce – it is a type of thick soup made with almonds, chicken or turkey liver, bread soaked in orange juice or white vinegar, ginger, cinnamon, cloves and saffron, all sprinkled with sugar. *Mirrauste* is a dish made with roasted pigeon and chicken cooked in a sauce made with toasted almonds and bread, soaked in a substantial broth and all pounded in a pestle and mortar, flavoured with plenty of cinnamon. To

## *Manjar Blanco de Pescado*

To prepare a good *manjar blanco de pescado*, De Nola in *Llibre de Coch* recommends the following:

You must take lobster and snapper, and although they are by necessity of different qualities, they are required; but the lobster is much better than the snapper; and from these two take what seems to you to be best, and cook it in a separate pot; and when it is almost half-cooked, remove it from the pot and set it to soak in cold water; and then take the best of the white meat of the lobster, and you must cook it more vigorously. And put it on a plate and shred it thus like threads of saffron. And cast rose water over this shredded white fish. And then for eight servings take four pounds of almonds, and a pound of flour, and a pound of rose water. And then take two pounds of fine sugar, and take the blanched almonds, and pound them in a mortar in such a manner that they do not make oil; and to avoid this, moisten the pestle of the mortar frequently with rose water. And when they are pounded, blend them with lukewarm water, which should be clean. And when they are strained, take a very clean pot which has not been recently tinned, nor which is made of copper, and take the shreds of the lobster, and let them go into the pot with the rose water. And then cast in the milk you have obtained. And not all of it, but that which you know will suffice for the beginning; and afterwards add the milk in two turns rather than in one; but if you add in everything together you cannot well know if the *manjar* will thicken. In the same manner you put in the flour little by little so that it doesn't clump; and beat it or stir it constantly with a stick until it is cooked; and then prepare dishes. And upon them cast fine sugar; and in this manner the *manjar blanco de pescado* is perfectly made.[22]

prepare the classic medieval *manjar blanco*, a recipe already included in the *Sent Soví*, De Nola selected a good-sized hen, rice flour, rose water, sugar, goat's milk and eggs.[23]

# FOUR

# A Golden Age

This describes the food eaten habitually by Emperor Charles v before his death at the Monastery of Yuste in Extremadura:

> At dawn he took breakfast: capon or chicken broth with milk and sugar. He took twenty dishes at noon for lunch. At mid-afternoon he ate *merienda*: fresh or preserved fish and salted shellfish to awaken the appetite. Already into the night he ate dinner: sweet pastries, preserves, fruit and *empanada* pies. He was partial to beer and wine from the Rhine.[1]

## SPICES, ETIQUETTE, BEER AND WHEAT

Charles I (1500–1558) was king of Spain from 1516 when his father died, and from 1519 he was also Charles v of Germany, Holy Roman Emperor. Not much is known about what the future emperor thought about the culinary traditions of the country he inherited from his father. His mother, Queen Joanna, with whom he shared the Crown, was still the queen of Castile but had become unwell. Charles was a Habsburg. What is known is that Charles's life would become ruled by politics, religion, war, debt and a massive appetite for good food, wine and beer that would cause him to suffer for the rest of his life. He struggled to chew his food properly and consequently suffered from indigestion, which was aggravated by his passion for meat – whether game, pork, veal, mutton or black pudding – which he would demand constantly during the never-ending journeys to defend his Empire and his faith. Incidentally, Charles's problem with chewing was caused by the Habsburg jaw. Too much inbreeding meant that the lower jaw stuck out way beyond the upper jaw, a family trait which afflicted various Habsburg monarchs.

Apart from bringing a large number of advisers from Ghent, where he was born, who provoked serious grievances with his Castilian subjects,

*The Inn's Menu*: painting of 16th- or 17th-century food preparation by
Juan Manuel Pérez, 1995.

the young king also brought cooks, butlers and even brewers to Spain, who
equally offended those responsible for the palace kitchens and drinks cellars.
Furthermore, as he found Castilian court etiquette to be lacking and rather
vulgar, he introduced a stricter, rather sophisticated etiquette that he had been
accustomed to since he was a child: Burgundian etiquette.[2]

Charles had been raised in Mechelen, a town in Flanders associated with
excellent beer. As he preferred beer to wine, he imported beer from this city
during the short periods he lived in Spain and even when abroad fighting his
enemies. In the land of his father, beer made with hops had been perfected
since the thirteenth century to allow transportation and a longer life in the
barrel. To ensure a steady supply, he brought a number of prestigious Flemish
brewers to his court in Spain, which is the reason why his subjects started to
hate the foreign dark brew. After his abdication and final retirement to the
monastery of Yuste in Extremadura decades later, Charles would still enjoy a
jug or two from one of his barrels. Even though more than five centuries have
passed since he ruled, one of the most popular beers produced in Belgium
today is sold under the name Charles Quint Blonde or Keizer Karel Blond.
During his reign, Santander, Castile's main seaport on the Bay of Biscay and

The 'Habsburg jaw' caused difficulty in chewing (portrait of Charles V, c. 1491–1542).

the most direct line of communication by sea with the Low Countries, became not only an important trading port for wool but for wine and beer.

A major problem King Charles inherited in Spain, at a time when the population was growing, was the high price of wheat and other cereals due to poor harvests. His subjects needed bread and feed for their animals. Cereals were the main agricultural product in large areas of Castile, once considered the granary of Europe. Although population and economic growth had been evident in all areas of cereal production, Castile had been losing its capacity as a major agricultural area since the reign of the Catholic kings. To make matters worse, La Mesta, a prolific source of tax revenue, was in control of half of the land. Wool had become more important than food and sheep more important than farmers. To aggravate the situation even further, with the gold and silver coming from the Americas, the rich and powerful acquired large swathes of land for animal rearing as opposed to planting cereals and other crops. This was the same land where not only had depopulation occurred after the expulsion of Arabs and Jews but much of the male population had been sent away to fight for the Empire. Olives planted in Andalusia, on the other hand, and vines in Castile and Galicia, had proved to be good businesses to invest in. Sugar cane produced in Granada and silk in Murcia and Valencia were equally in demand.

Hunger forced the peasantry to move to the cities, increasing not only the demand for cereals but the price. Speculation and food shortages became a fast track to riches for a few but hunger for the rest. Attracted by the situation, English and Dutch merchants moved down to the Mediterranean, causing prices to rise even further.

For hungry Spaniards the rich soils of the Americas could have been their salvation. However, for the early Habsburgs, defending the faith and the borders of their Empire, along with the gold and silver needed to do so, had taken priority. Apart from these precious commodities, only wool and spices were considered to be of any importance.

The need to find an alternative route to the riches of the Spice Islands (now Indonesia) dominated by the Portuguese forced Spaniards to venture further west across the seas, beyond the newly discovered world. In September 1519 five Spanish ships left Sánlucar de Barrameda, a small fishing village to the west of Cádiz. As Columbus had done before, they sailed towards the Canary Islands and the favourable trade winds needed to push them across the Atlantic. They were sailing under the command of Ferdinand Magellan, a prestigious Portuguese explorer contracted by Charles I. Magellan knew that the land Columbus had discovered was not in Asia. Bound by the Treaty of Tordesillas signed in 1494, in which newly discovered lands outside Europe were divided between Portugal and the Crown of Castile, the Spaniards had agreed not to follow the route to Asia via Africa and the Cape of Good Hope. They needed to find an alternative commercial route as soon as possible, and the most famous European naval exploration of all time had begun. Within a year four of the five ships had found a way through the windy straits that separated the southernmost tip of South America from the rest of the continent. They had reached a new ocean they called *El Pacífico* (the tranquil

Looking for pepper: a replica of the *Nao Victoria*, the only one of Magellan's five ships to return to Spain in 1522 after circumnavigating the globe.

one) as it appeared to be calmer than the Atlantic Ocean they had just crossed, having encountered serious difficulties and even tragedy.

After weeks at sea with food and water running low and no further sight of land, they became aware of the enormity of their enterprise. In March 1521 Magellan was killed by a poison arrow on the island of Mactan in the archipelago that would later become known as *Las Islas Filipinas* in honour of Philip II. Having lost a further two vessels, the two remaining ones, named *Trinidad* and *Victoria* and now under the second-in-command, Juan Sebastián Elkano, sailed south towards the island of Maluku in Indonesia. At Tidore they managed to load up with spices from Portuguese traders. From here they set out again, continuing their long circumnavigation westwards across the Indian Ocean towards the Cape of Good Hope and finally back into the South Atlantic. In the end, Castile had made its dream a reality. Now the Spaniards could sail in the waters of the desired Spice Islands without contravening the Treaty of Tordesillas because Tordesillas did not include the Pacific. Their joy did not last. Gaining a handsome prize, Charles I signed a new agreement with Portugal to be known as the Treaty of Zaragoza that would not favour Spain. A new line of longitude was drawn in the Pacific, 2,975 leagues to the east of Maluku. From that moment Spanish vessels would not be able to operate to the west of the line. Spain had relinquished any claims to the riches of the Spice Islands, even if the Philippines and New Guinea would later on be incorporated into the Spanish Empire. Spaniards had proved to be excellent navigators and truly adventurous souls, but traders and visionary businessmen they were not.

Years later, riddled with gout, the emperor sat alone at Yuste close to the chapel where he attended daily mass. He was 58 when he died. Even though bullion was still coming from the Americas, he was handing on a Spain in debt to his son Philip. All his life he had too many frontiers to defend and too many armies to feed and pay for. He was now leaving the defence of the faith he had fought to protect with such ardour to others. He was no longer the enemy of Francis I, king of France, nor of the papacy. He had fought Algerian pirates in the Mediterranean, the Turks in the East, rebellious nobles in Spain, the French in northern Italy and Protestant insurgents in Germany. At Yuste he was just waiting for his next meal and for God.

## THE DARK SIDE OF SUGAR

By the time the Moors introduced sugar to Andalusia, around the tenth century, sugar cane was already a well-travelled plant. It is believed that it had first been domesticated in New Guinea, although it was in India that the process of refining cane juice into granulated crystals was developed. From the subcontinent of India it travelled to Persia and with the Arab expansion in the Mediterranean to Spain, where only the rich could afford it. The climatic conditions they found in the coastal area of the old kingdom of Granada were perfect for the cultivation of such a valuable crop, and sugar cane was later introduced into the Canary Islands. Strategically located, the Canaries became a new destination for European goods and also played a crucial role in the American-European exchange. Cargo ships leaving the Canaries, helped by the favourable northeast trade winds, faced a shorter and safer crossing of the Atlantic Ocean than from other ports on mainland Europe. Within a few decades the Canaries would become a substantial production centre for sugar.

As the production of sugar gained momentum in the Caribbean it became available to a much larger section of the population including many convents in Central America and in Spain. Here nuns, following the traditions inherited from the Middle East, specialized in making sweets and pastries and adapted local preparations to new ones suited to the Spanish palate such as drinking chocolate. With the addition of sugar, the drinking chocolate of the Aztecs became in Spain the thick *chocolate a la taza*, at first appreciated by the rich and by the *madrileños* at large a few centuries later.

Sugar cane.

Apart from the fundamental role sugar would play in making food palatable, the development and success of the sugar industry would bring tragedy to Africa. As the indigenous population in the New World perished, the local work force which was so vital to the development of new industries started to be substituted by African slaves.

Trade in humans, a practice known since the beginning of time, together with the Inquisition, become one of the darker aspects of European trade. By the end of the sixteenth century, 250,000 Spaniards had emigrated to the Indies. In addition, 100,000 Africans were transported in appalling conditions to work on the newly established sugar plantations, ranches and other economic enterprises.

As a result of the Spanish Crown taking the view that slavery was unjust, Spain became the first European country to legally abolish it in the New World in 1542. Sadly in many cases the abolition was too late or ineffectual. Furthermore it only addressed the abuse that the native population of the New World had suffered since the arrival of the Europeans.

Slavery had been endemic in the Iberian Peninsula since Phoenician times. The peninsula as a centre of operations for invaders and businessmen alike became a perfect platform to deal with a silent work force that could make no demands. The Romans encouraged it and Moorish and Jewish merchants enjoyed a healthy trade in European Christians. Helped by Portugal, the country in control of the eastern sea routes to the Spice Islands, Spain would join the African slave trade later destined for the West Indies. Portuguese traders would bring slaves to Seville from West Africa, where they would be auctioned outside the cathedral. From there Spanish merchants would transport them all over their new territories across the Atlantic – after all, the Pope had given them permission to do so. In 1452, with parts of the peninsula still under Moorish occupation, Pope Nicholas V issued the *Dum Diversas*, a papal bull that granted Portugal the right to enslave enemies of the faith. The bull, later extended also to Spain, read:

> We grant to you [kings of Spain and Portugal] for these present
> documents, with our Apostolic Authority, full and free permission
> to invade, search out, capture and subjugate Saracens and pagans
> and any other unbelievers and enemies of Christ wherever they
> may be, as well as their kingdoms, duchies, countries, principalities,
> and other property . . . and to reduce their persons into perpetual
> slavery.

Even if the Pope at the time could have acted to protect the Catholic faith, the result of *Dum Diversas* in the Americas amounted to a catastrophe for thousands and thousands of human beings transported from Africa.[3]

While the conduct of the Catholic Church was often questioned where morality, greediness and even cruelty were concerned, the work done by some of the religious orders in the Americas should not be underestimated. Although the foundation of Catholic missions did not become a priority for the Crown until 1609 when Mexico was designated a royal colony, members of the main religious orders had reached the New World before that time. The Franciscans had arrived first in 1524 followed by the powerful Dominicans in 1526 and seven years later by the Augustinians.

They all came with a single purpose: to save the souls of the indigenous people. But they also started to record life and events as they happened. For them this was as important as ensuring that native peoples could produce food to feed themselves and therefore survive while also having to work for the newcomers. Missionaries would take seeds and plants to other missions in the Americas and monasteries in Europe as gifts for monks in charge of kitchen gardens. This is how *pimiento del padrón* arrived in Galicia. Five hundred years later this small green pepper – which can be sweet but also at times truly hot – has become a permanent feature on the menus of tapas bars and restaurants across Spain and beyond. The religious orders would also play a very active role in the planting of grapes destined for wine making in South America and in California.

For Spaniards already living or travelling in the Americas, wine would become almost as important as wheat or meat. It was also a profitable business. Because wine transported across the Atlantic became sour and the *flota* (fleet) system would prove inadequate to provide suppliers to the colonies, vines were planted wherever possible. This was a job well suited to the religious orders traditionally associated with the production of wine and liqueurs in their own monasteries. Most importantly, wine was needed to celebrate mass. Certain parts of Mexico and Peru would prove to be perfect for vine cultivation.[4]

## WARRIORS, DREAMERS AND TRADERS

Back in sixteenth-century Europe, thanks to the production of high-quality wool as well as olive oil, economic and trade relations between the Crown of Castile and other European countries had intensified during the reigns of Charles I and Philip II. Indeed Spain became the number one exporter to northern Europe and Italy. This was helped by a diminished English wool industry and by the growing demand for Spanish merino wool. In this case, Flanders and not Spain gained the most from highly prized Spanish wool. Shipped from the Spanish port of Laredo on the Cantabrian coast to the ports of the most efficient and industrial part of the Empire (the Low Countries), wool became a success story from which Spain should have learned a lesson. Even if trading proved to be profitable for exporters and importers, once in the hands of the most efficient and evolved textile industry in the world, the value of the finished goods tripled overnight, giving northern European bankers and lenders another reason to celebrate. They knew their profits would triple once more when used to rescue the Spanish economy again. High-value raw materials would leave the peninsula to be transformed into warm blankets and robes in Flanders, and into valuable fine tapestries to be hung on the walls of its bankers and aristocrats. Lacking mercantile vision, Spain was again far too preoccupied with holding onto the Empire and defending Catholicism. Manufacturing was a matter for others. Apart from wool, further profits would also be secured by Spanish and northern European merchants as new business opportunities presented themselves in Atlantic trade: tobacco, sugar, wine and salt cod could also be transported in wooden barrels and ceramic containers.

Pottery played a decisive role in the trade between Europe and the New World, particularly in the transport of goods and notably olive oil, wine and vinegar, as is stated in the third section of the Archivo General de

Indias housed in the ancient Merchant's Exchange of Seville. Pottery shipped to the Americas, made mostly in Andalusia, was divided into three large groups: building materials, domestic pottery and decorative objects as well as containers for agricultural and artisan products such as the *botija perulera*, a type of ceramic container used to transport all sorts of goods across the seas. The distinctive word *perurela* clearly refers to Peru, one of the most important centres of colonial Spain.[5]

## A Taste for Cod

For centuries, the love Spaniards have for fish and shellfish has remained a strong element of their food culture. Being a peninsula surrounded by the Mediterranean Sea and the Atlantic Ocean, in Spain fishing would become a profession shared by an important part of the population from early times, their expertise as sailors and fish hunters acknowledged across the seas. In the early North Atlantic race, Basques in particular would prove to have the strength of character and fishing techniques to make them deeply respected by their competitors, especially by British, Dutch and French fisherman and merchants. As their whaling activities, which had started in the eleventh century, were under threat due to over-hunting in the Bay of Biscay, Basques were forced to travel further and further, first towards Scandinavian waters and then across the Atlantic Ocean.

By the middle of the sixteenth century the Basques had ventured into the rich fishing banks off North America where cod swam in abundance. A sea adventure and a passion for fish without equal had started. In the rich cold waters of the North Atlantic, cod salted at sea and dried back in Europe proved to be a successful business and a welcome addition to the restricted diet of Catholic Iberia during the long periods when the Church imposed constraints. The saltpans around Cádiz and other areas of Mediterranean Spain were instrumental in the success of this venture while it lasted. Cod fished on the rich Grand Banks of Newfoundland would become a complicated issue for Spain and Portugal, as France and England decided to enter an enduring race.

The Norwegians also had renowned fishing expertise; they had arrived first to the rich banks of the northern Atlantic, and most importantly they had abundant stocks of sea salt in their countries – in the final race for cod the Spanish and the Portuguese would never have the upper hand. In the case of the Spaniards, not only was trading not their forte, they did not feel the need to claim the land on behalf of their king. The short fishing season (limited to the months of summer), the limitations of the Spanish fishing vessels against the versatile 'sack ships' of the English, and above all the claim by the English and French to the better natural harbours close to the rich Newfoundland banks were also against them. A constant need for salt was an expensive drawback. However, for those who claimed the land, fish could be dried ashore in the fresh air, a technique that had been used by the Vikings for centuries. The larger and stronger sack ships were used by the English to carry all kinds of spare parts and other goods from Europe to the New World. Fish and, later, cotton and tobacco were some of the commodities they could bring back to Europe. With a greater economy of scale, they could guarantee the profitability of both journeys.

It would take another century for Spain to ensure a constant supply of the fish that had caught the imagination of Spanish sailors and cooks. The solution was to establish a triangular trade of wool, wine and cod between England, North America and Spain. The Basques in particular had developed a strong taste for cod and they knew how to cook it in many different ways; they were prepared to travel across the Atlantic to catch it in substantial numbers.

It is rather difficult to establish with authority why the Basques have such a strong affinity and culinary expertise with salt cod, *bacalao*, only equalled or even surpassed by the Portuguese. The simple explanation that the dietary rules of the Catholic Church were largely responsible for salt cod's popularity has been challenged by a number of historians. For them the story of cod and its relationship not only with Spaniards but with many other countries appears to be much more complex. It has been argued that the introduction of salt cod made a limited but nonetheless significant contribution to altering the southern European diet.[6] In the Iberian Peninsula *bacalao* became a solution for the poor and a way to improve the diet, especially during periods when the Church dictated what could or could not be eaten. In a mountainous country with extensive areas located far away from the sea and with no decent roads, the inclusion of salt cod to the rather unattractive list of fish available inland was more than welcomed by many, excluding the upper classes who took the view that salt cod was a vulgar addition to the same list. Castile's main exits to the sea were to be found in Andalusia as well as the ports of Santander, Laredo and Bilbao on the northern Cantabrian coast. Fish was transported inland by muleteers who risked their lives and their fish cargo on the tortuous roads, each journey taking between seven and ten days. Unlike fresh fish, salt cod could be carried long distances with a minimum loss of quality; it was inexpensive and a long-lasting source of nutrition. As a result consumption increased steadily over a period of two hundred years, culminating in the improvement of the roads in the eighteenth century and the opening of the railway in the nineteenth. By then the supply of lesser-quality salt cod by the English, caught off Virginia, had become another success story. Still having the advantages of superior ships and cheap supplies, the English would take control of the cod-fishing trade to the detriment of the Spanish, Portuguese and even the French. The northern town of Bilbao, a place where trade links with the English had always been strong, became the permanent residence of English merchants and suppliers, contributing even further to the attachment the Basques had for salt cod. Also in Castile and in the Catalan lands, not only urban communities, the main consumers of *bacalao*, but also the majority of the population had learned how to desalt, hydrate and cook each part of the *bacalada*, the name given in Spain to the whole fish once salted and dried. Different parts of the *bacalada* commanded higher or lower prices, allowing the cheaper cuts to be purchased by the poor. Properly treated it could be fried in olive oil, made into omelettes, and, most importantly, improve the traditional vegetable and chickpea stews, the staple diet of the poor. During Lent and other fasts pork fat, sausages and meat were simply substituted by a nutritious piece of *bacalao* that added flavour to any popular dish. In Spain cod that is unsalted has never been called just cod, unlike in England; instead it is known as *bacalao fresco*, a fish rarely seen in the markets.

In 1977, after five hundred years of fishing in the rich waters of the North Atlantic Grand Banks, the 322-kilometre (200-mi.) fishing limit established by the Canadians would end a fascinating history of Spaniards catching fish there in which the Basques had played a leading role.[7] Today the Basques are no longer searching the seas for the best cod, but they are still demanding the quality of *bacalao* that Basque fishermen used to catch and cure. They still buy *bacalao* in huge quantities at prohibitive prices as long as it is salted with sea salt and dried in the sun to their taste. Chefs and amateur cooks, men and women, still cook salt cod in Spain following distinguished traditional or modern recipes. Those recipes are not only of Basque origin, for the Catalans and the people of Andalusia have also remained faithful to salt cod.

## FASTING, ABSTINENCE AND CARNIVAL

'La Cocina Española está llena de ajo y de preocupaciones religiosas' (Spanish food is full of garlic and religious concerns), wrote the unique Julio Camba while talking, not always with generosity, about Spanish food.[8] Even if parts of modern Spain are now in denial, most Spaniards have always been Catholic by choice or fear and, by passion and tradition, devotees of the Virgin Mary. As Catholics, the Church imposed upon them centuries of abstinence and fasting. On the other hand, Mary, Mother of God, is still a perfect excuse for a calendar full of *romerías* and local festivals where food, wine and beer are consumed in abundance. Meanwhile *Carnaval* has returned to modern Spain despite the efforts of the Church.

Although half of Europe was ruled by the Habsburgs, a dynasty of healthy appetites to say the least, the acceptance of the Counter-Reformation in Spain had a lot to do with the strict implementation by the Catholic Church of ancient practices intended to curb human desires and excesses. It is important to remember that Luther and Calvin rejected fasting as a means of salvation, while in the Catholic faith, the individual path to salvation depended heavily on ascetic practices that could control lust, anger, pride – and gluttony of course. Fasting and abstinence from eating meat had been followed by early ascetics and by members of religious orders in recognition of the forty days Christ spent in the desert in preparation for his last days on Earth. We now know this period as Lent, *Cuaresma* in Spanish. It is fair to say that when it comes to obligatory religious dietary restrictions, Spaniards had an advantage over other Catholic countries for many centuries, thanks to the *Bula de la Santa Cruzada* or Bull of the Crusade. Dating back to the reign of the Catholic Monarchs, this Bull was originally granted by the Pope to Spain in recognition of the country's achievement in the fight against Islam.

The Bull, which had to be purchased from the Church by the faithful of Spanish origin in accordance with their means, allowed them to eat meat throughout Lent and other days of fasting and abstinence, except Ash Wednesday, the Fridays of Lent, the last four days of Holy Week, the vigils of the feasts of the Nativity, Pentecost, the Assumption and the Festival of Saints Peter and Paul. Abstinence in Catholic countries was finally regulated in a less severe way by canon law, during Benedict XV's papacy in 1918. It prohibited the consumption of meat and meat broth for 21 per cent of the year, an improvement on the third part of the calendar to which it applied in the sixteenth century.

Before Lent came *Carnaval*, the ancient celebration of life, excess, political criticism and satire dating back to Roman Hispania and the days of the popular *Baccanals*. In Spain, from time to time and for several centuries these festivities met with resistance and prohibition from the Church, kings and dictators. In 1523 Charles I forbad the use of masks. The Carnival encouraged subversion, he was told by his courtiers. It was also prohibited several times during the eighteenth century, in the belief that it could unsettle the population at a time too close to the days of prayer and abstinence. From 1937 to 1947, under Franco's rule, the celebrations simply had to be stopped and not only in

*The Fight between Carnival and Lent* by Pieter Bruegel the Elder, 1559.

Cádiz where the most colourful festival of all was held. In reality this never happened completely. Carnival continued to take place in Spain in secrecy and in defiance of the Church. For the men and women of the cloth it simply could not be tolerated. For the people, it wasn't just about masks, sweets, confetti and satire; they wanted meat, wine and sex.

The dichotomy between Carnival and Lent as a battle of opposites (carnality versus purity and abstinence) has been treated by European painters and writers throughout history. In Spain the theme first appeared in a book by a fourteenth-century Spanish poet, Juan Ruiz El Arcipreste de Hita, a collection of poems under the title *El libro del buen amor* (The Book of Good Love).[9] The same theme was to be depicted in a splendid oil on canvas by the Flemish artist Pieter Bruegel the Elder in 1559. Bruegel's painting represented a transition between two different seasonal cuisines: one meatless, austere and rather unappetizing, the other prepared for those who could afford it: rich, full of hope and with plenty of meat.

## A Golden Age: *Pícaros*, Painters and Writers

Spain enjoyed a magnificent and lengthy literary and cultural period known as *El Siglo de Oro*, the Spanish Golden Age, which coincided with the rise and fall of the Spanish Habsburg dynasty or, to be more precise, from the beginning of the sixteenth century to the middle of the seventeenth century. As to who first coined this phrase, the answer remains in the hands of academics. They still need to work on the country's literary historiography including the concept and origin of *El Siglo de Oro*.[10]

In the sixteenth century, literature was moving away from the romantic approach that had diverted attention from the serious difficulties experienced by a large section of society. Themes that were previously considered unattractive started to be used by artists and writers as powerful statements: illness, abuse, injustice, survival and, above all, hunger. The ideal of a fantastic and plentiful world offered by courtly literature became a thing of the past. Work such as *La Lozana andaluza* (The Lusty Andalusian Woman) and, notably, *El Lazarillo de Tormes* (The Life of Lazarillo) were published with great success. An era of intense literary innovation had started, and even woman were involved!

In the fifteenth and sixteenth centuries Spanish women featured a great deal in literature, and the power they could exercise over men by cooking became another subject of interest, even if it only reflected a man's point of view. In Venice, Francisco Delgado, better known as Francisco Delicado, a Spanish *converso* destined to become a Catholic priest, was working on a manuscript under the title *La Lozana andaluza*, to be published in 1528. *Lozana* is one of the earliest manifestations of the *picaresca* (picaresque) novel, a new literary genre that became dangerously popular in the opinion of the Church and the Inquisition. After their expulsion from Spain in 1492, many thousands of Jews, later followed by *conversos*, took refuge in Portugal, the Low Countries and in a number of Mediterranean cities – among them Rome, Venice and especially Naples, an important enclave belonging to the Spanish Empire. Delgado decided to follow his friends to Italy, settling in Rome where he started a career in writing for economic reasons. In *Lozana*, the amoral and the erotic are as essential to the story as is the sense of being in exile and the memories left behind, including memories of food. Lozana, an ambitious Andalusian woman born in Cordoba, a *converso* of devious virtue and limited physical attraction, uses her ability as a cook in Italy to satisfy the needs of her clients. In one of the early chapters, during a conversation with her aunt that took place while still in Cordoba, she reveals not only how she became a cook but which dishes her grandmother taught her to prepare before she decided to embark on a life of adventure abroad. Lozana says:

You see my lady I am more like my grandmother than I am to my mother, and for the love of my grandmother they named me Aldonza. If she would have been alive I would have learned more of the things I do not know. She showed me how to cook; under her guidance I learned how to make *fideo pasta*, small pies, couscous with chickpeas, rice – whole grain, dry, oily, small meat balls round and firm with coriander. Everybody admired the ones I made. Look, my dear aunt, this is what my father's father, who is your father, used to say, 'These are from the hand of my daughter, Aldonza. And you think she didn't make *adobado* [marinade].' You know how many rag-and-bone men in the men's quarter of Heria want to try it particularly with a tender piece of mutton. And what honey! Just imagine Señora, that we had it from Adamuz, and saffron from Peñafiel, and the best of Andalusia came though my grandmother's house. She knew how to make *hojuelas* [thin fried pastries], honey-sprinkled fried dough, almond biscuits, sesame meringues, hemp seed, fried flour and honey *nuegados*...[11]

In *Lozana*, the extensive list she recites provides the reader with a clear picture of Andalusian food, still fully influenced by Jewish and Arabic traditions. Lozana's larder is rich in cheeses, semolina and *fideo* pasta, capers from Alexandria, almonds from the Mediterranean and raisins from Granada.

A harsh life leads Lozana into a world of corruption, violence and prostitution in Rome. Eventually she becomes the madam of her own brothel thanks to her ability in the kitchen. This was a skill Lozana used to control men in order to exercise power over them. Lozana's sexuality invades the entire novel in a complex relationship with food and cookery, ending surprisingly on a happy note as she finds some form of respect. She is an expert in rich traditional Judeo-Arabic-Andalusian cooking prepared with the best ingredients money can buy, including pepper, garlic, cumin and caraway, spices that reveal her Sephardic lineage – men cannot resist.[12]

Lozana's tale would have scandalized the humanist Juan Luis Vives, who wrote extensively in defence of woman seeking perfection and respect. He wrote: 'When pondering upon the diet of an honest, virtuous woman, spices, along with wine and sweetmeats, are recognized as being undesirable elements that dull the consciousness.' In 'The Education of a Christian Woman', a manual he wrote for the education of Henry VIII's eldest daughter, the future Mary I of England, Vives continued along the same lines as he emphasized the importance of humility and sobriety in the fairer sex:

## *Frutas de Sartén*

*Frutas de sartén* is the name of a group of traditional Spanish recipes made with a dough of flour and water and deep fried in olive oil or lard. Sometimes the dough is enriched with eggs and milk. They are often served coated in honey, dipped in syrup or sprinkled with sugar. Many of the recipes are associated with religious celebrations such as Christmas, Lent and the never-ending list of saints' days.

The origins of the *frutas de sartén* are uncertain. Small portions of dough made from flour and water have always been fried by Spanish shepherds to treat themselves during the winter months. Some of the recipes were already eaten in Imperial Rome while others have a clear Andalusi or Jewish connection. A number of *frutas de sartén* recipes appeared in early Spanish cookbooks and in novels written in Castile during the Spanish Golden Age. The Portuguese claimed that they were responsible for bringing some of these preparations from remote places in China.

In Spain the list of the *frutas de sartén* is extensive: *almojábanas, enmelados, melindres, cohombros, angoejos, rosquillas de anís, hojuelas, buñuelos, pestiños, torrijas, churros, porras* and *flores de sartén* are some of them. Angel Muro, the nineteenth-century author of *El practicón*, includes in his book a recipe for *flores de sartén* which he calls *Rosas*. He complicates things by comparing the Spanish recipe for *Rosas* with the French *gauffre*. In Spain *flores de sartén* are made using an iron mould with a long handle forged in the shape of an open flower. The mould is heated first in hot oil, then dipped in a light batter made with flour, eggs and milk and then dipped again in the very hot oil. As the *flores de sartén* cooks, it frees itself from the mould. Once prepared by home cooks for days of feasting and celebration all over the country, the tradition is maintained today by a generation that is fast disappearing. Thankfully these delicacies are still made in local patisseries.

Rather unhealthy but totally 'Moorish' *churros*, having survived changes in the Spanish way of life, have been able to

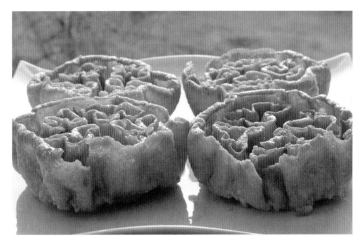

*Frutas de sartén*, sweet fried pastries still cooked during Lent.

retain their popularity. They are made with a fairly consistent dough of wheat flour, water and salt which is piped into deep pans of hot olive oil using a *churrera* fitted with a star-shaped nozzle that gives *churros* their thin corrugated shape. *Churros* and *porras* (a variation on the theme) are two of the very few Spanish specialities that belong to what is known in English as 'street food'. In the streets they are both eaten very hot sprinkled with sugar and served in a paper cone, rather like British fish and chips. More often than not they are prepared in permanent or mobile *churrería* shops that sell directly to the public and also in numerous *cafeterías* and *chocolaterías* where they are eaten for breakfast and for the *merienda*, in the late afternoon. They must be crunchy and never doughy. A range of *frutas de sartén*, including *churros*, are very popular in many countries in South America.

Losing ground are the *torrijas*, which are square or oval pieces of bread dipped in egg and milk or even wine, fried and then dipped in syrup or just sprinkled with sugar and cinnamon. They cannot deny their medieval past. They are still prepared by home cooks as well as in pastry shops and in local cafeterias, especially during Lent.

Along with this the young damsel will learn how to cook to eat, not in the manner in which chefs cook, and neither sweetmeats nor frivolities but how to cook simply, modestly and cleanly and this so that she might as a girl make content her parents, brothers and sisters and once married her husband and children. In this way she will win the praise of them all.

The Humanist Vives was obviously defending a position only a woman of the cloth or the privileged could follow to the letter. This was a world that was no longer prepared to be silenced and would use the best that Spanish literature could offer to voice anger, hunger, injustice and even comedy.[13]

For the next century, the *picaresca* would draw attention to the reality of a country without a bourgeoisie, polarized from an economic point of view: aristocracy and *pueblo* (the rest), richness and misery. In the *picaresca*, to talk about hunger became as fashionable as to criticize the excesses of the Church. Characterized by being strongly realistic and with a critical view of society, the new genre introduced hunger for the first time as a common denominator used by different authors to depict life. *La picaresca*, from the Castilian world *pícaro* (rogue, rascal), was an early form of novel, usually a first-person narrative that in time became a progressive ironic or satirical survey of the corruption in society which lasted until practically the end of the seventeenth century. The reader finds a world of observations concerning people in more humble walks of life, as well as a unique and faithful picture of Spain during the reigns of Charles I, Philip II, Philip III and Philip IV. For most experts in the field, the new genre dates back to the publication in 1554 of *El Lazarillo de Tormes* and ends with the publication of Quevedo's *Buscón*, another masterpiece of the Golden Age.

Written by an unknown author, *El Lazarillo* relates the life and times of a young rascal who had suffered from hunger and misfortune since childhood. He tries to overcome this by working as a companion and servant to a variety of mean characters whom he constantly tries to trick by way of retaliation. A literary jewel, *Lazarillo* is a lesson in resilience, and a story of hope and disenchantment which ends in high moral cost. What it achieved was to shame those in powerful positions, society and the Church. Soon it would become clear that both the Church and the Inquisition disapproved. The author had gone too far, and the popularity of such a critical work had to be stopped. As a consequence, soon after the publication, *Lazarillo* was banned but not silenced. Following in the footsteps of the *novella picaresca*, Miguel de Cervantes (1547–1616) in his acclaimed novel *Don Quixote* confirmed the significance achieved by food or the lack of it in sixteenth- and seventeenth-century Spain. From the first page the reader becomes submerged in the world of food surrounding the two main characters. Don Quixote is a dreamer and a gentleman who has lost contact with reality by reading chivalry novels. He does not even need to eat to fulfil his dreams. He is tall, lean and marvellously eccentric. The other character, Sancho Panza, is a down-to-earth suffering servant who is short, fat and never dreams, for he is forever hungry. Considered to be the first modern European novel and one of the best works of fiction ever written, *Quixote* begins with a well-known sentence that offers a clear idea of the social position occupied by an ageing Castilian *hidalgo* of lesser means. At this early stage, the fragile gentleman who would become, as the story progresses, the perfect anti-hero has already decided to solve the injustices of the world as an errant knight, giving up a peaceful life and even the pleasures of the rather frugal and earthy local table with forced moderation. At the beginning of the book Cervantes mentions a number of dishes served at his table. An occasional stew (*olla podrida*) of beef more often than lamb *salpicón* (made with meat leftovers from the *olla* cooked with onions and dressed with olive oil and vinegar) most nights, on Saturdays *duelos* and *quebrantos* (eggs and abstinence), lentils on Fridays, sometimes squab as a treat on Sundays. While *Don Quixote* is far from being a book about food, it gives the reader a detailed and fascinating insight into the larder and popular culinary traditions of La Mancha, the large Castilian expanse of the southern Meseta. More often than not, food in this part of the country was not only scarce but rather unappealing. It was normally prepared by women at home or in the infamous inns scattered along the dangerous roads or in local villages. On some occasions the same dishes became rich and flavoursome, especially when converted into the kind of meals dreamt of by muleteers, farmers, shepherds, *pícaros* and even bandits. It was the food eaten by lesser noblemen and by merchants returning from abroad. There were, however, recipes prepared at festivals and celebrations, historical recipes which are still used nowadays by prestigious chefs: *gazpachos galianos* made with small game and unleavened bread; *duelos y quebrantos* prepared with eggs and bacon and even lamb's brains, seasoned with salt and a little black pepper. Some recipes were often given ingenious and descriptive names such as the potato and salt-cod preparation known as *atascaburras* from the words *atascar* (to get stuck) and *burras* (donkeys). The *tiznao*, which refers to the dark colour given to the dish by dried red peppers and *pimentón*, was made with salt cod and potatoes as well as onions, garlic and olive oil.

Throughout his famous work Cervantes insisted on keeping his heroes in a perpetual state of hunger and deprivation, but for a few generous

Young beggar living on whatever scraps of food he could find; painting by Bartolomé Esteban Murillo, *c.* 1645–50.

moments, he allowed excess to be portrayed even if frustrated by ongoing circumstances most of the time. This is the case in Part II of the novel on the occasion of Camacho's wedding, when the heroes arrive invited by two students they have met on their travels. 'Your Grace should come with us,' they say, 'and you will see one of the finest and richest weddings ever celebrated in La Mancha, and for many leagues around.' Here, for the first time, Sancho, tempted by the superb display of food served by the caterers of the rich Camacho at his wedding, takes sides publicly against his master. He defends the right of a rich man such as Camacho to wed a young local girl,

Quitea, who has always been in love with Basilio, a handsome, well-built lad of even more limited means than Sancho, if that were possible. As it happens, by staging an astute plot of deceit, Basilio finally manages to wed the heroine while pretending to be dying. The ingenious plot, fully justifiable in the eyes of the *hidalgo*, ended the dreams of his squire. Just that morning, Sancho had been awakened by the heavenly smell of a roasting joint of bacon. This was only the beginning of the amazing display of food waiting to be served by more than fifty chefs to hundreds of guests invited to the promising feast. As they arrived at the site of the celebrations Sancho could not believe his eyes. There it was,

> an entire steer on a roasting spit made of an entire elm; and in the fire where it was to roast, a fair-sized mountain of wood was burning, and the six pots placed around the fire which were not made in the common shape of other pots, because these were six cauldrons, each one large enough to hold the contents of an entire slaughterhouse: they contained and enclosed entire sheep, which sank out of view as if they were doves; hares without their skins and chickens without feathers without number were hanging from the trees, waiting to be buried in the cauldrons; the various kinds of fowl and game hanging from the trees to cool in the breeze were infinite.

The *frutas de sartén* made of dough to be fried at the end of the banquet were already another cause for celebration, as were the hundreds of litres of wine waiting in wineskins; there were piles of rich Manchego cheeses as well as hundreds of loaves of white bread that poor Lazarillo could not even have imagined. At the end, with desperation, poor Sancho had to leave the place with his stomach as empty as it was when he arrived, for his master, in true *quijotesco* style, had decided once again to follow the wrong party.[14]

## All the Way to El Escorial

The empire Philip II inherited, apart from Germany which was inherited by his uncle, was still one of the most extensive that would ever be seen in history. This was an empire that would demand a lifetime of commitment from the new king just as it had from his father, in order to defend the

Catholic faith, to ensure Castile's hegemony, and to desperately avoid becoming the vassal of an economy frequently in disarray and in the hands of foreign bankers most of the time.

As in his father's time, the tons of gold and silver coming from Mexico and from Peru were not enough to finance the huge expenses the sovereign had to face. As soon as the fleet bringing the precious cargo arrived in Seville, the same cargo would leave the country to pay for the endemic, heavy foreign debt that would eventually bring the Spanish Empire to its knees. During Philip's reign Spain defaulted on the payment of its foreign debt several times over. The economic consequences of this default would be felt by Spain's most needy, especially in Castile.

The new king did not share his father's taste for travel and desire to be seen as events unfolded in the international corridors of power or on the battlefield, nor did he inherit his father's notorious appetite. Even if he had tried hard to become a Spaniard, Charles I, a Francophile from birth and a polyglot by destiny, had remained a foreigner. On the other hand Philip II was a Spaniard or, better said, a Castilian through and through even if, like his father, he was blond and blue-eyed. He had also inherited the unattractive Habsburg shape of the head from his father, as well as a healthy appetite for perfectly cooked game, but the similarities ended there. He was not a glutton. He wore black, which did not help his image, enjoyed a life of austerity and was associated with the Inquisition. All of these aspects would be used effectively by his enemies to the detriment of his image. Justly or unjustly, the *Leyenda Negra* (Black Legend) reputation would follow him until his death and forever after. Obviously for many of the right reasons, not often mentioned, he remains the best-known Spanish royal that has ever existed, admired by his own people and detested by the rest of the world. The loss of the *Armada Invencible* or, better said, *vencible*, caused by the British weather and the Spanish commander's lack of maritime experience and indecision, did not help either. Philip's enemies were numerous: England, France, the Reformation and even his own son – another Charles. Charles, a sickly and devious character, would be remembered for treason and for his association with the uprising in the land that his grandfather loved most of all, the Low Countries. Philip loved Madrid better than any other place.

It was not the first time that the king and the entire court had arrived at La Villa de Madrid, a relatively small Castilian town of Moorish origin, perfectly located at the centre of the peninsula. For inconclusive reasons often discussed by historians, Philip had decided he would stay here for the rest of his life. It is well known that the queen hated Toledo, and Seville was too far to be contemplated. From the Alcazar in Madrid, a nineteenth-century Moorish fortress where the royal palace, El Palacio de Oriente, now sits, he would govern not only Spain but the entire Spanish Empire. Later he would build El Escorial in the foothills of the Guadarrama mountains: his own palace, monastery and royal mausoleum where he would live, die and be buried close to his father. The king's decision to move to Madrid permanently would improve both his family life and the state of the country's coffers, for a court constantly on the move was a costly affair, not only for the Crown but for the locals, as they were obliged to provide most of the food consumed by such a large entourage as it passed through villages and towns.

Later, at El Escorial, the king would become isolated and out of touch with his people. The oak table at the centre of his spartan office became the centre of operations where he would plan expeditions to the New and to the Old World; he would deal with mundane issues as well as with matters of the soul, and constantly try to assess where he could win and lose distant wars and battles. Meanwhile Madrid was growing out of all recognition as outsiders started to occupy the space where artisans and farmers, as well as the very limited number of civil servants and provincial nobility, had lived until then. The grandees still lived on their estates in the countryside, but now courtesans and lesser aristocrats, ambassadors and bankers, bookkeepers and shopkeepers, barbers, professional cooks and even beer-makers had found a new place to prosper. As a consequence demands on the supply of food and wine became a serious matter for the local authorities.

The social and economic transformation of Madrid in the sixteenth and seventeenth centuries would result in changes in the production and distribution of food. It would also alter the culinary traditions of the town as a new order influenced by the cooking of other regions of Spain, and even other countries, was established. The importation of food became a necessity that converted the new capital into the most important food market of Spain. One thing was clear: *madrileños* could live without fruit and vegetables, fish and meat, that is if they could afford it, but they could not live their daily life without the two main components of the traditional diet of the majority – bread and pulses. Even wheat, a crop that had until then been cultivated locally in sufficient quantities to supply the requirements of the town and even to export for a handsome profit, had to be imported. Not for the first or last time during the Habsburg period, crop failure and the government's inability to control the supply of grain would provoke social unrest. The imbalance between food supply and demand pushed prices out of control while encouraging speculation and greed among producers and traders, a practice that soon became endemic.

King Philip of Spain banqueting with his family and courtiers
(Alonso Sánchez Coello, *The Royal Feast*), 1579.

As the population grew in size and diversity, the demands for different foods, in addition to grain for flour, necessitated further imports. Muleteers brought an extensive range of foods to the markets each day, but more often than not the produce was in less than acceptable condition, especially in the case of fish but also meat. Located at the heart of the peninsula, Madrid, surrounded by high mountains and difficult terrain, was a long way from the coast. River fish caught locally was generally preferred by the *madrileños*. However, other species such as conger eel, sardines, octopus, tuna and even bream – mostly salted and dried or smoked – reached the kitchens of the well-off. Bream, *besugo* in Spanish, simply baked in the oven with a slice of lemon on top, would become, for good reason, a dish traditionally served in Madrid on Christmas Eve. Every year large schools of bream reached the northern Spanish coast during the winter months. In early seventeenth-century Spain this was the only time of the year when a limited number of fresh fish with a good firm texture could reach their final destinations in a more or less acceptable condition. For the rest of the year fresh fish, without exception, would have reached Madrid in a condition practically unfit for human consumption, especially in summer. In winter, snow from the mountains gathered by muleteers and mixed with straw to make it last longer helped to protect, at least for a time, their fragile cargo during a journey lasting over a week. Five centuries have passed since then, but today *madrileños* are still prepared to pay for the freshest and largest bream at Christmas time, whatever the price.

Goya's *Still-life with Golden Bream*, 1808–12.

Fish shop in the
Central Market of
Bilbao.

In the Madrid of the Habsburgs, ice-cold drinks and cold dishes became very popular as *madrileños* developed a passion for them. Snow from the Sierra de Guadarrama was stored underground outside the city mixed with straw and with blocks of ice made in large, shallow metal containers during the Meseta's freezing winter nights. The result was an unpalatable, unsafe ice that could not possibly be used in a drink if one valued one's life! It was bought from ice stalls located in the main streets of the city that were supplied by a local *obligado*, the name given to a trader who was in charge of a particular business. This form of monopoly maintained the whole chain of supply: from collection in the Sierras to storage and then distribution to the public. Chefs to the royal palace and to the wealthy frequently used ice to cool large serving plates for elaborate dishes. Ice was also used by palace servants and sommeliers to bring down the temperature of water, beer and jugs of wine to be enjoyed by royals and courtesans. It was towards the end of the seventeenth century when an entrepreneur, Pedro Xarquies, decided to open a number of ice wells in Madrid to provide ice for making fashionable cold drinks as local doctors debated their benefit.

Although Philip II preferred the austere and silent setting of El Escorial, the pomp, ceremony and etiquette of his Burgundian background could be seen in Madrid at the Alcazar, the place that would become the permanent residence of the Spanish royal family for centuries to come. This contrasted noticeably with the provincial populist Spanish lifestyle of his vassals, even if the king often enjoyed simple fare such as a substantial *olla* for lunch. He also relished several helpings of dishes such as *manjar blanco*, as described by Mestre Rupert de Nola a century before. One thing was clear: Philip II did not need the capon boiled in milk which his father had demanded from the royal kitchen every day to get him through the night.

## At the Royal Kitchens

Apart from a general attachment to a plentiful table, detailed information about the food served at the table of Charles I or at the table of his slightly frugal son Philip II is limited. At this time, the Inquisition and the Index of Forbidden Books were the only two initiatives affecting the history of food; obviously they did not encourage any form of writing, not even books about food. We know that Philip II hated fish as much as fruit and that he enjoyed Rupert de Nola's old recipes. As no other cookbooks were to be published after the death of the king in 1598, De Nola's book was used as the court chef's bible. As with his father, Philip suffered from gout, an affliction common to those who ate rich food in excess, which in the case of Philip II appears to be a contradiction due to his apparent frugality. During the period of the Habsburgs, more can be ascertained by looking at other aspects related to food and food service such as financial, everyday family peculiarities or the organization of the complex royal household caring for two houses: one of the king, the other of the queen.

The *oficio de boca* was the name given in the Alcázar to all sections, buildings and people involved in the provision, content, preparation and service at the king's table every day of the year, including banqueting. Apart from the *guardamanxier*, the area where all foods were delivered and controlled, there were the kitchens and pantries, the bread bakery, the *cava* (where drinks were stored) and the *sausería*. The last was where certain valuable ingredients and spices were kept and distributed, together with the limited cutlery used at the time, but other specialist tasks were also included in the *oficio*. There were makers and repairers of furniture, carpets and tapestries in charge of both the decoration and preparation of the rooms, while the candlemakers provided lighting. Breakfasts, lunches, dinners and the capricious demands of the royals in between times occupied the lives of hundreds of servants. This obviously included festive food and the food to be served at official banquets and celebrations at which the whole court would be present. In the kitchens, where large fires and enormous ovens never went out, a wide selection of earthenware, copper and iron utensils were ready for use. Cooks, kitchen hands and pot washers worked under the eagle eye of the *cocinero mayor*, today's executive chef. He was in charge of all matters related to the kitchen as well as receiving all ingredients arriving from the store and, most importantly, making sure that the dishes were properly prepared and seasoned before they were dispatched to the royal table. The *cocinero de servilleta*, who perpetually carried a large napkin over his shoulder, was a senior sous-chef with extra duties such as carrying the dishes to the refectory and serving the royals himself several times a day.[15]

Diego Granado's *Libro de arte de cocina* also coincided with the death of Philip II at El Escorial. It was an extensive collection of recipes, more than seven hundred, many of them influenced by De Nola's work, for which he was strongly criticized by other writers and chefs and especially by the master of all masters, Francisco Martínez Montiño, a distinguished royal chef. Bartolomeo Scappi's *Opera dell'arte del cucinare* was another source from which Granado lifted ideas and recipes.[16]

In less affluent kitchens things were changing as the country moved through the seventeenth century, particularly for those who were looking to move to a city having lost their jobs in the countryside. The extreme polarization between the noble table and the 'less well-off table' that had existed for centuries was changing slightly, as long as less well-off people including some poorer nobles had a secure job or were studying in well-known institutions. To illustrate this point, a tasty recipe for spinach recorded at that time shows how some cooks and authors started to provide 'recipes in between'. This refers to preparations originally created for the royal kitchens that could easily be prepared by other classes in cities and towns which were sprouting up all over the country. It is worth remembering that in the sixteenth and seventeenth centuries, industry scarcely existed in Spain, and that the concentration of arable land in the hands of a few had altered the fabric of life in the countryside. Here the nobility, exempt from taxes, lived for war, privilege and ownership while the others – the destitute, tax-bearing and hungry – started moving to the towns in search of work, venturing to sea or joining the army. The progress made in cities and towns was reflected in the improved way that people lived, the food they could buy and the recipes they were able to follow.

Make the spinach dish mentioned above as follows. Wash the spinach. Boil in some water with salt and spices. Drain and chop the leaves on a board. Fry chopped garlic in a *cuartillo* of oil before the spinach is added. Sauté together with raisins and honey, a very sweet mixture. To flavour the dish more, crush some spices and extra garlic, and dilute with a little water before pouring this preparation onto the spinach. Serve it dry. During Lent you can serve it in place of soup or with a splash of vinegar. A modern translation of this recipe, excluding the honey and possibly the spices, is still prepared by chefs. The original comes from a book published in 1607 and written by Domingo Hernández de Maceras, a cook working for San Salvador de Oviedo College at the University of Salamanca. Clearly of Jewish or Arabic origin and therefore using olive oil, this recipe could also have been served at the table of Philip II or even Philip III by the very renowned Francisco Martínez Montiño, *cocinero mayor* of these two monarchs.[17] In the hands of both Maceras and Montiño, the recipe would have been very similar, although it would have differed in the variety and quantity of spices used as well as the frequency with which the dish would have been served. Hernández de Maceras was cooking on a restricted budget for the sons of the educated as well as the offspring of magistrates and bankers. Martínez Montiño was cooking for the king in a kitchen with the most plentiful larder, and where meat was far more in tune with the taste of the monarch, especially Philip II, who detested vegetables all his life.

Domingo Hernández de Maceras's *Art of Cooking* is a revealing book dedicated to Don Pedro González de Arzuelo, the Bishop of Plasencia. He described the way to prepare food during the whole year, meat as well as fish, pies, flans and sauces, different courses and desserts in the Spanish tradition of the time. The book is divided into four chapters. The first chapter includes winter and summer appetizers made with fresh and dried fruits, as well as with vegetables such as frisée lettuce leaves or carrots cooked with oil and vinegar and lots of sugar and pepper, following a very distinctive method of cooking. Henández de Maceras cooked the recipe as a hot salad in an earthenware pot covered with a plate. Then the pot and the plate were inverted, placed in the centre of the hearth surrounded with hot coals and cooked for two hours. In the second chapter he includes a fresh salad made with a combination of ingredients that only a talented fusion-food chef could match: different vegetables (it does not give the names) are flavoured with desalted capers and then dressed with olive oil and vinegar. He plated the salad before serving, enriching it with slices of fatty ham and cured tongue and with trout and salmon (we assume also previously cured), egg yolks, *diacitrón* (candied citron peel), manna, sugar and pomegranate seeds as well as borage flowers which he uses to adorn the dish. By contrast, the salad included in Chapter Three is just made with cooked desalted capers dressed with olive oil, vinegar and sugar. He dedicated Chapter Four to desserts served in winter, summer and during Lent: fragrant apples, known as *camuesas* in Spanish, cherries and peaches, apricots and wild pears, each preparation providing evidence of the taste of a growing section of the population who enjoyed a certain standard of living in the world of Imperial Spain.

Hernández de Maceras proceeded with the all-important and disproportionately large section on meat, starting with carving and followed by an extensive collection of meat and game recipes. Classic recipes were featured such as the medieval *manjar blanco* prepared with chicken and rice, and the *manjar real* traditionally served at royal tables with mutton. The popular *empanadas inglesas* were also included, as well as game *pastelones* made with puff pastry in different sizes and shapes (pies and flans), and sweet and savoury marzipan *tortas*. The *olla podrida*, one of Sancho Panza's favourites, was another 'must have' as were the *guigotes* and stuffed capons and partridges prepared in a tasty *escabeche*. There were also recipes for meat and game: roasted, stewed, marinated or made into small balls known as *albondiguillas*.[17] Another section was dedicated to Lent and featured recipes prepared with eggs or the vegetable stews still known today as *potages*. There were also dishes made with fresh or salted seafood and river fish. Eels, conger eels and the odd-looking lamprey – still so popular in Galicia – shared the pages with tuna, bream, sardines and even lobster, first boiled in water and then served with pepper, salt and orange.

Some of the fish dishes were grilled while others were roasted or made into pies. The list of desserts was notable, particularly the *tortada* pies made with dried or fresh fruit, honey and spice compotes.

If Charles v was impressed by the banquet prepared in Bologna by Bartolomeo Scappi, the well-known chef of Cardinal Campeggio, to celebrate his coronation as Holy Roman Emperor, he would have been equally impressed by Francisco Martínez Montiño, a young man who had entered the service of his son Philip II at a tender age. Montiño would not only become the chef de cuisine, or *cocinero mayor*, at the kitchen of another king, Philip III (1578–1621) but also one of the most influential Spanish chefs of all time thanks to his *Art of Cooking and Making Pastries, Biscuits and Conserves*, a book published in 1611. Written for people cooking for the king, Montiño's *Arte de cocina* is a clear example of the court cookbooks published during the Spanish Baroque period. It was destined to become the reference for Spanish cooking well into the nineteenth century.

Little is known about the life of this royal chef and author par excellence. It is known that he trained in Portugal, where he had been working in the kitchen of Joanna, a sister of Philip II. Joanna had become wife to the heir of the Portuguese throne, and she needed a talented chef at her service. It is important to remember that Portugal had always been associated with the best patisseries of the time. A perfectionist with a clear vision, Montiño believed the kitchen of a *gran señor* should be run following three principles: cleanliness, taste and ability. He was adamant that only staff who could be trusted should be hired, avoiding at all cost dreaded rascals or *pícaros* in the kitchen. Montiño, following the party line of his employer, appears to have been politically and religiously correct. He cooked with 'Catholic lard' instead of olive oil, which was traditionally associated with Arabs and Jews. He made puff pastry with lard, one of his highly acclaimed dishes. Philip III was particularly partial to his chef's very tasty *empanadillas*, made with a very light pastry, a type of brioche or fermented dough he called *ojaldre*. Montiño's pastry, wonderful as it may have been, was not the superior puff pastry we know today, which is wrongly assigned to him by some enthusiastic authors and known in Spanish as *mil hojas* or *hojaldre* (thousand leaves) and to the French as the very Gallic *millefeuille*. Other court chefs attempted to reproduce Montiño's recipe without success, and even Montiño, as was common practice among chefs, would have omitted an ingredient or even part of the method in his book, whereas in the case of such a complex pastry precise instructions must always be followed to the letter.

Here is an adaptation from his famous *empanadillas*: Take a pound of the finest flour, place it on a board and make a hole in the middle. Add half a pound of ground and sifted sugar, a quarter pound of lard, eight eggs (two whole and six yolks only) and a little salt. Knead your dough until it becomes smooth. Make a filling with rashers of bacon. First grill the bacon, ensuring it does not dry out, and sprinkle with a little wine while still hot. Leave to rest for half an hour. With the dough rested, make four circular patties and from these make four *empanadillas* (half-moon-shaped small pies stuffed with a rasher of bacon cut in half). *Empanadillas* should be equal in size so that they don't need to be trimmed, nor should you need to dampen them with anything to crimp them. Montiño also gave recipes for pies stuffed with pigs' trotters and sardines, as well as the local *criadillas de tierra* (*Terfezia arenaria*) he used instead of truffles. Given the number of sweet recipes included in his *Art of Cooking*, particularly those cooked for religious festivities such as Christmas, it can be assumed that Philip III and his family had a very sweet tooth.

Montiño's Christmas feast served at the king's table included ham as an entrée, followed by a first course comprising the following: both *olla podrida* and roast turkey with its gravy, veal pies, roast pigeons and bacon, small game *tartaletas* over a whipped creamy soup, roast partridges with lemon sauce, *capirotada* (a topping) of herbs and eggs with pork loin, sausages and partridges, roast suckling pig with cheese, sugar and cinnamon soup, leavened puff pastry made with pork lard and roast chickens. The second course was equally substantial: roast capons, cake with quince sauce, chicken with stuffed endive, English *empanada* pies, roast veal with sauce, seed cake of veal sweetbread and liver, roast thrush over *sopa-dorada* (golden soup), quince pastries, eggs beaten with sugar, hare *empanada* pies, German-style birds, fried trout with bacon fat and puff-pastry tart.

The third course followed the same lines as the two before: chicken stuffed with bacon, fried bread, roast veal's udder, minced bird meat with lard, 'drowned' pigeons, roasted stuffed goat, green citron tarts, turkey *empanada* pies, ring-necked dove with black sauce, the famous *manjar blanco* made with chicken, milk, rice and sugar, and different fritters. In his book Montiño also provided a recipe for nougat.

At the height of his career, the royal chef's food was reigning supreme at court. His influence and writing were being followed by professionals all over Spain, the rest of Europe and the Americas. Unlike Diego Granado, thought to be an opportunist, Montiño was an original chef who was copied even when preparing very traditional and simple food. He was a humble man capable of combining simplicity and sophistication who included in his repertoire recipes favoured by the whole of society and not just by the elite. In the seventeenth and eighteenth centuries this might have been considered an oddity by

European society and by those who travelled in Spain and wrote about food. Helped by the most influential chefs in Spain, the food of the people was filtering up to the food of the rich and powerful.

## CARROTS AND PINK CARDOON

If the Spanish heart beats to the rhythm of art, it must have been beating out of control from the late sixteenth to the early eighteenth centuries, especially during the Spanish Golden Age. It was not only the sheer number of talented artists who were trying to be recognized and earn a decent living. It was the originality and personality of their work that separated them from other talented artists who had been appearing in different countries since the Renaissance. For some the representation of live or dead objects including flowers and food, especially in paintings commissioned by the ruling classes and the rich, had become a very decent way of earning their living. In a sphere of extremes represented by religion, gluttony and hunger, food came alive in art in the shape of a new genre. This form of art, known as still-life, had appeared independently in Spain, northern Italy and the Netherlands at almost the same time, and was displayed by collectors in all three areas, all of them rich in artistic talent and all of them under the domination of the Spanish Empire. At the beginning of the sixteenth century, Spanish artists started to follow in the footsteps of the Italian masters, but as the century progressed the originality of Spanish art became apparent, especially with Juan Sánchez Cotán (1560–1627), considered by many as the most original still-life painter of all. He was a Castilian, born in Orgaz, Toledo. Although Philip II liked illustrations, especially those of American birds and fruit trees, natural history in art was not as highly developed in sixteenth-century Spain as it was in northern Europe and in Italy. Soon things would change. Cotán's artistic virtuosity, as well as his remarkable capacity for observation and attention to detail in common foodstuffs, would alter the status quo in the early seventeenth century. From 1606 a number of Cotán's most acclaimed canvases appeared, arousing controversy and admiration among critics. He depicted fruits, vegetables and fowl – quinces, apples, melons, carrots, cabbages, cardoons, cucumbers, pigeons and ducks – simply and almost geometrically arranged. Painted on dark canvases and displayed in virtual well-lit window frames, Cotán's irresistible, ingenious compositions marked a complete departure from the flamboyance of Flemish still-life paintings. Philip III, among others, took a liking to them; they were simply unique. A painting described as 'a small fruit still-life with a black and gold frame and an open melon in the centre' by Cotán, believed to be part of a group of five, was bought by the Spanish king from a collection belonging to the estate of Cardinal Bernardo de Sandoval y Rojas, the powerful Archbishop of Toledo. Other Spanish painters, also fascinated by the natural world, would contribute to the genre too.

## A Very Spanish Still-life, the *Bodegón*

Thirty-nine years younger than Cotán, Diego Velázquez, a name that attracts a spectacular number of art followers to the Prado Museum every year, is admired for his figurative work, especially the magical *Las Meninas*. Yet his *bodegones* (the generic name given in Spain to food-related still-life works) have gained wide acclaim over the last fifty years. In reality *bodegones* differ greatly from the *lienzos de frutas* (fruit canvases) of Cotán and others. Velázquez started life as a painter under the close supervision of Francisco Pacheco, a renowned painter and author belonging to the school of Seville whose daughter he would later marry. It was Pacheco who would give Velázquez's genre paintings the name of *bodegones*. They were so different from any others that they deserved a specific name, Pacheco thought. In his early career as an artist Velázquez produced a stunning collection of *bodegones*, 'the best of which have never been surpassed' to quote William B. Jordan and Peter Cherry, two great specialists on the subject.[18] As part of Pacheco's circle, the young painter would be influenced by Italian artists such as Benadino Campi and especially by Flemish still-life painters of the calibre of Pieter Aertsen and Frans Snyders, whose influence is easily detected in Velázquez's work.

Velázquez's three early still-life paintings depict themes he saw at local *bodegas*, taverns where food and drink was served. While Cotán's still-lifes usually depicted ingredients, in his *bodegones* Velázquez included people, artefacts, ingredients and even dishes set in kitchen scenes typical of daily life. A technique of dramatic lighting known as *tenebrismo* or tenebrism, also used by Caravaggio, would bring him fame and grant him entrance to the Court of Philip III in Madrid. Velázquez's talent was unquestionable: *Las Meninas*, *The Crucified Christ*, the portraits of the king and the *Infante Don Carlos*, among many others. Two impressive *bodegones* are today acknowledged as masterpieces: *The Waterseller of Seville* and *An Old Woman Frying Eggs*. In the long and brutal summers of Seville, the waterseller, usually represented in imagery as a marginalized figure, often a beggar or, even worse, a cheat, was a

*Still-life with Game Fowl, Vegetables and Fruits* by Juan Sánchez Cotán, 1602.

welcome figure that Velázquez depicted with dignity. Even more impressive, if this is possible, is an oil on canvas that brings art lovers to the Scottish National Gallery in Edinburgh. *An Old Woman Frying Eggs* is also known as 'An Old Woman Frying a Couple of Eggs, and a Boy with a Melon in His Hand', which is a better description of the real scene Velázquez was seeing. Here art critics differ in their understanding of the painting. Were the eggs fried in olive oil or poached in water? Was the young boy who was holding a melon, which was to be kept for Christmas, a *pícaro* or her grandson? Another *bodegón* oil on canvas, known as *Christ in the House of Martha and Mary*, introduces a further element of vital importance in the Spain of the Habsburgs: religion. Velázquez depicts two maids in the foreground of this painting. The older is giving advice; the younger is pounding garlic and chilli pepper in a heavy metal mortar, or *almirez*, to marinate some bream. The brightness of the eyes of the fish is a sign of freshness that the painter catches instantly. At first glance the painting appears to be a contemporary genre work – it has all the simplicity that characterizes Spanish still-life – but through a serving window, Mary is listening to Christ. Leaving the religious content to one side and coming back to the subject of food, the Velázquez painting reflects scarcity and simplicity and the use of ingredients such as garlic and a New World chilli pepper that Mary is pounding in the *almirez*, as Spaniards still do today in order to cook bream.

It is fascinating how the scarcity and simplicity referenced in Velázquez's *Christ in the House of Martha and Mary* can be contrasted with the abundance and opulence present in another masterpiece painted in the Low Countries, the fabulous *Cook with Food* by Snyders. Here a young woman is also pounding food in a metal pestle and mortar very similar to Mary's, but she is surrounded by the most expensive food money can buy: rib of veal, a duck, fresh asparagus and a hare, large Dublin Bay prawns, grapes and chestnuts or even hazelnuts, which are probably what she is pounding as she prepares a dish for a rich family in Flanders.

*An Old Woman Frying Eggs* by Diego Velázquez, 1618; the woman is using an *anafe* similar to the one on p. 50; these remained in use in some parts of Andalusia until the 1940s.

Velázquez, *The Kitchen Maid*, 1618, oil on canvas.

## OLD AND NEW CHRISTIAN FOOD

One of Philip III's first domestic changes was the issuing of a decree in 1609 for the expulsion of the *Moriscos* from Spain. In Aragon the significant presence of *Moriscos*, the original Moorish population that had converted and therefore been allowed to stay, also known as 'New Christians', precipitated a revolt with serious social consequences for the former followers of Islam. There was tension and prejudice between the *Moriscos*, a competent force behind efficient agriculture, working on the rich banks of the River Ebro, and the so-called 'Old Christians', who were mostly shepherds coming down yearly from the Pyrenees looking for fresh pastures for their sheep, and this tension was about to reach boiling point. As the population at large became freed from the Black Plague and started to grow, trouble broke out between the lords and their old Christian vassals, who sought work on seigneurial lands traditionally tended by *Moriscos*, who enjoyed the protection of the nobles. It was not the first or the last time this question would bring social unrest to different parts of the country. It had happened in Granada and Valencia sometime before and also with tragic consequences.

Initially, in the final capitulations signed in 1492 by Boabdil, the last Moorish king of the Nasrid dynasty, and the Catholic monarchs, the Moorish population were allowed to retain their houses, to practise their religion and to be governed by their own magistrates. Queen Isabella's confessor, Cardinal Cisneros, and the Inquisition would make certain that the terms of the capitulations would be violated by the triumphant Christian forces. On 11 February 1502 a royal edict gave all followers of Islam two choices: to accept the Christian religion or to leave the country, dispossessed of their houses and of the land they themselves and their ancestors had been cultivating for several centuries. The implacable response to the strong negative reaction of the Moorish population to the violation of the terms forced more than 50,000 Muslims to accept baptism under duress. Some left, but the majority were forced to move away from their beloved Al-Andalus, to other areas of the peninsula, searching for fertile lands, watered with traditional *acéquias*, to convert into vegetable gardens and fruit orchards, and to prepare the rich dishes that constituted their cultural heritage. Dishes such as *tafalla* had two rich variations, the 'green' with kid and fresh coriander, and the 'white' made with dried coriander seeds. Another popular preparation, known as *mayabanat*, was a type of hot bun stuffed with cheese, sprinkled with cinnamon and coated with honey. They also enjoyed sausages they called *mirkas* which they bought from the local markets, as well as *buñuelo* fritters and a dozen different types of pies made with rose water and almond or date paste.

In 1612 the Duke of Lerma, one of the king's ministers, ordered the final expulsion of all descendants of Hispanic Islam. By 1614 some 250,000 *Moriscos* had left Spain, mostly from the areas of Aragon and Valencia. Even the extensive rice paddies which had been cultivated by them for over six centuries stopped production. From that moment food in Spain had to become Christian and cooked with lard, butter and olive oil. As much as the *frutas de sartén*, the rich and delicious *morteruelo* is a good example of an 'Old and New Christian dish' from La Mancha in central Spain. To make it, take pig's liver, loin of pork and a whole bird. Sauté in olive oil and garlic. Add some stock and cook together until the meat of the bird falls off the bones and the other meat becomes as tender as butter. Pound all the meat in a pestle and mortar, and pass the mixture through a sieve to form a creamy texture, helped with stock from the pot. Add some breadcrumbs and season with a number of preferred spices, the rest of the stock and the creamy meat. Using a wooden spoon, blend the mixture together as for a classic pâté that can be kept fresh until needed.

In 1609, Spanish agriculture, which for over two centuries had been in the hands of the *Moriscos*, faced its darkest moments as Philip III signed their final expulsion order. Partly as a result and until well into the twentieth century, Spanish agriculture – including the production of rice – would remain almost locked in a feudal system that would severely affect its development. Some progress would be made at the end of the seventeenth and especially during the eighteenth century, but it was not enough. In the case of rice, a renewed interest in the crop brought it back to life in newly established and forgotten paddies. It was not always planted in areas that could be considered safe. Malaria and other illnesses would affect not only farmers but some of the population living nearby.

# FIVE

# Madrid, Versailles, Naples and, Best of All, Chocolate

Described by historians as a great century with a disastrous end, the eighteenth century, *el siglo ilustrado*, started in a complicated fashion for Spain. In November 1700 Charles II, the son of King Philip IV, died in Madrid without a direct heir. He was the last king of the Spanish Habsburg dynasty. Philip of Anjou, a French prince born in Versailles, was destined to inherit the crown south of the Pyrenees. He was a grandson of Louis XIV. As a result, years of bloody dynastic turmoil would taint the soil of Europe as Charles, Archduke of Austria, challenged the final will of Charles II. The archduke's claim to the Spanish throne was backed by the powerful Spanish Church and the Grand Alliance of England, Holland, Prussia and Austria, against a possible alliance between France and Spain. Fourteen years later, at Utrecht, an agreement was reached in favour of Philip of Anjou that would bring peace to Spain at a very high cost. On 1 November 1700 he was crowned Philip V of Spain. As a consequence Spain lost most of its European territories and even Gibraltar. Life for the new king should have been more focussed at home in Spain and in the Americas, and yet he felt driven to maintain Spanish involvement in the European arena, especially in Italy – a serious error of judgement that would accelerate the end of the Spanish Empire. Inevitably French political and social innovation became a model to be followed although it would never fully replace Spanish law or most of the local traditions enjoyed by the *pueblo*.

### Out with the Old and In with the New

Defined by the Spanish food historian María de los Angeles Pérez Samper as 'opulent, refined and cosmopolitan',[1] having become fashionable all over Europe, French food would also reign supreme in the kitchens of the Spanish

Bourbons. It would soon feature in the kitchens of the top end of society as well as those of the growing bourgeoisie. To the dismay of the Spanish kitchen brigades, the arrival of the Bourbon dynasty at the Royal Palace, El Palacio de Oriente in Madrid, brought inevitable changes as French chefs started to dictate the style of food to be served at the palace. Not only were there new recipes, methods of cooking and favourite ingredients '*a la francesa*', the dress code had to follow fashion too. Chefs' heads had to be covered with napkins used normally at the table – a custom that would later evolve into the traditional hats used by chefs all over the world.

During the eighteenth and nineteenth centuries, abundance and refinement at the table were manifestations of power that would be maintained at court. As before, the Spanish royal table had to fulfil a double function. First it had to feed the royals in accordance with their tastes, which at the beginning of the century were mostly French and later also Italian, at least in public. A number of traditional Spanish dishes were also included on the menu. Secondly, it had to respond to the institutional demands of the Bourbon dynasty. Interestingly enough, pomp and ceremony would remain attached to the rituals of the old Court of Burgundy. Eva Celada's *La cocina de la Casa Real*,[2] based on the extensive documentation found in the royal archives, provides unedited information on informal and formal dining.

Philip V, an unusual French prince with little appetite for food unless it was part of the pleasures *dans la chambre à coucher*, suffered from melancholy all his life. The king and his second wife, the Italian Elisabetta Farnese di Parma, did not share the same passion for a good table, with the exception of poultry dishes and especially eggs, which they both enjoyed. Early Spanish Bourbons would frequently eat whole raw eggs, including the shells if the eggs had been laid the same day, in the belief that it was good for their health. Queen Elisabeth, a powerful woman with a healthy appetite, was the only one making constant and capricious demands on the royal kitchen. Rich broths and tasty consommés were also highly appreciated by the royals. At the time, food preferences were changing drastically, starting with meat – red meat to be precise. Poultry and small game shot locally or raised at the palace would take centre stage, particularly pigeon and partridge. Veal, beef, lamb and kid would be demoted to second place, while the selection of rich and very Spanish cured pork products, including the highly prized Ibérico hams and rich chorizo sausages, would remain very much in tune with the royal palate. Also considered as delicacies, *menudos* or *menudillos*, a generic name given to what can be thought of as light offal, were equally appreciated. There were sweetmeats, brains, trotters and *mollejas*. The *mollejas*, a small gland obtained from young calves, was the most expensive delicacy of all.

The kitchens in the Royal Palace in Madrid.

Independent of the taste of a particular royal and the preference of those who never work for exotic and exquisite food, bread, meat and wine remained at the centre of Spanish cuisine during the eighteenth century. Looking at the diets of different classes, the largest proportion of bread was associated with the lower ones. Wine was enjoyed by all. Pulses and pork belly, mostly salted, has to be added to the list as well as confectionary and chocolate for those with more money. Food was cooked in all types of fat although butter, produced in the peninsula in very limited quantities, had become increasingly popular at court and among the upper classes. Dishes prepared by the *pueblo* were typically cooked with olive oil in the south and in coastal areas of Mediterranean Spain, while lard was favoured in areas in the very north of the country where the olive cannot be cultivated, including inland northern Catalonia. In Andalusia, a region that has always produced large quantities of olive oil, this was used particularly for frying, while lard was preferred for making pastries and baking in general.

Recognized in history as the 'true saviours of hunger', a malady never associated with the nobles, pulses in Spain did not have the same stigma attached to them as in other countries, and had always been eaten by rich and poor. It would be fair to say that, in general, dishes based on pulses were associated with the peasantry and urban common food and were used to feed the kitchen brigades of the well-off. Until the arrival of American beans (*Phaseolus vulgaris*), chickpeas and lentils were mostly used, but at La Granja

## Forgotten Cuts of Meat: Offal

Offal is found in many recipes of the *Cocinas de España*. There are liver, kidneys, trotters, black pudding, tripe, brains, oxtail, fresh and salted bones, and sweetbreads, among others. Offal has always been available from specialized local shops known as *casquerías*, located normally in covered markets. They still attract a segment of the ageing population who grew up eating and cooking offal with regularity.

As the country progressed and the diet of Spaniards improved in the early 1960s, offal started to lose popularity in large towns and cities, especially with the middle classes and the young: *manitas de cerdo o de cordero* (lamb or pig trotters) are delicately prepared in La Rioja; marrow bones and other bones, fresh or salted, are favoured by those who enjoy marrow and gelatinous textures. Lamb brains, *sesada*, are sold nowadays individually packed in small purpose-made containers that protect the delicate skin. Long gone are the days when fried brains, coated with flour and beaten egg, were given to children and the infirm. They are now only demanded by those with a discerning palate. Tongue is normally stewed with carrots, onions and white wine. Veal liver still commands a fair price in the markets, while pig's liver is fast losing ground as are lamb kidneys, even if they are prepared *a la Jerezana*, cooked with a generous glass of sherry.

Many recipes calling for offal can be found in books dedicated to the food of Spain. In Andalusia salted bones and pigs' trotters enrich soups and *pucheros*. *Chicharrones* (fried pork belly or pork rind) are still used in the preparation of a sweet *torta o pastel*, sold in bread shops on saints' days. *Carrilleras de cerdo o ternera*, pork or veal cheeks cooked for hours at a low temperature with a glass of Amontillado or Oloroso sherry, and *rabo de toro* (bull's tail), have now been included in the menus of influential chefs, not only in Andalusia where they have remained very popular but in the rest of the country. The authentic recipe for *rabo de toro* is made when bull fighting takes place in towns where the meat is sold in specialist butchers. (It can also be made with oxtail.) Strictly speaking *botillo*, a speciality of the Comarca of El Bierzo in Léon, does not belong to the family of offal. It is a large sausage made with the caecum of a pig, stuffed with pork meat, ribs, tail and spices. This is also the name of a flavoursome dish of intense red colour prepared with *botillo*, and with local chorizos, potatoes and cabbage. In Navarre, *txangur* belongs to the *cocina de aprovechamiento* (leftovers). This is a dish cooked once or twice a year in farmhouses and villages after most of the meat of a ham has been eaten. It is made with the little meat still attached to the bone of a cured ham or shoulder, once it becomes dry and difficult to carve any further. The bone is soaked first in water to allow the detachment of any remaining pieces of ham. These are then cooked in a rich *sofrito* made with onions, red peppers and tomatoes.

For how long will many of the recipes cooked with these products survive? The answer must rest with the modern professional chef, who is capable of using these products and making local recipes lighter and easier to digest, or by creating new ones which look much more appetizing than before. Home cooks are now saying, 'Children don't need liver. Iron is contained in many other foods,' while grandmothers may add, 'They are brainy without eating brains. It is much better for them to eat fish.'

La Granja beans in the market of Oviedo in Asturias.

de San Ildefonso, not far from Madrid, buttery and utterly delicious American white beans had been added to that list since the sixteenth century. During the hot summers of the Meseta regions, Elisabetta Farnese, mother of the future Charles III, enjoyed living at the palace in La Granja de San Ildefonso. This was on the way to the city of Segovia where the king enjoyed hunting. It was a very charming and very French palace where pheasants were fed with tender American beans. At La Granja the same beans have been growing successfully by the banks of the River Eresma since the sixteenth century.[3]

As with all dried beans, La Granja beans, or *judiones de la Granja*, would have been soaked overnight and then simmered very gently for at least two hours, together with some beef shank, chorizo sausage and bay leaf. Once tender but still holding their shape, they would have been flavoured the same way as is done today with a *sofrito* of onions and a little flour as well as some garlic, parsley, sea salt and pepper pounded in a pestle and mortar. Did Elisabeth Farnese's kitchen, the queen's kitchen, headed by two well-known French chefs, Pedro Benoist and Pedro Chatelain, ever serve beans? The French detested beans but the Italians and Spaniards did not. Spanish chefs would have retained some influence even if they were working under the French. Small game and tender beans are a heavenly combination, and the Queen was very partial to pigeon, quail and partridge. After all, La Granja were extremely good beans, and they had come from the Americas.

French taste and food traditions were by no means enjoyed by all in eighteenth-century Spain. Most of the population remained fairly sceptical about the arrival of a glamorous French take on life and on food. Ordinary Spanish food, already coloured and flavoured with red peppers, tomatoes, *pimentón* and a strong taste of garlic, had almost become a political statement.

Recognized today as the greatest Spanish still-life painter of the eighteenth century, Luis Egidio Meléndez was no longer interested in becoming a court painter. Due to his father's and his own vanity, his promising career as a figure painter and portraitist had vanished before it had even started. Having been excluded from the Real Academia de Bellas Artes de San Fernando and a possible endorsement by the king, he was forced to look into a genre easier to sell among less privileged classes. Following in the footsteps of Cotán and Velázquez but with a unique style, Meléndez became a master whose artistic ability allowed him to transform the most mundane of kitchen ingredients and foods into powerful still-lifes: fruit, bread, meat, vegetables, quince paste

Luis Eligio Meléndez, *Still-life with Box of Gelatine, Bread, Salver with Glass and Cooler*, 1770.

and other preserves and confectionary boxes, as well as copper pots and glass and ceramic ware, especially jars. The body of work he left, which comprises well over one hundred still-lifes, constitutes one of the greatest achievements of eighteenth-century Spain and places him alongside the finest still-life painters of Europe. These were all pieces of skilled art in which light magnifies the different elements of the composition in a bold but never vulgar fashion: *Still-life with Quince, Cabbage, Melons and Cauliflower; Still-life with Game, Vegetables and Fruit; Still-life with Cardoon, Francolin, Grapes and Irises.*

## Power and Struggle

With the exception of the Basque Country and Navarre, which had retained their *fueros* or medieval rights in exchange for supporting Philip v during the War of Succession, the rest of the country fell under the government of Castile in the eighteenth century; this was a government in flux, strongly influenced by France. The Age of Enlightenment, *El Siglo de las Luces*, would influence the governments of the three Bourbon kings who were to reign in Spain during that period.

Until then Castile had been ruled by a powerful 'conciliar' form of government inherited from the Habsburgs: the Council of State was in charge of diplomacy and war, the Council of Castile acted as a high court and consultative body, and the Council of the Indies dealt with matters related to the Inquisition, the military orders and the finances of the realm. Now political and economic responsibility would be shared mostly by the Council of Castile and a body of secretaries or ministers (French style) that would transform the administration with some success, establishing a contemporary style of government which lasted for centuries. The reformers faced an arduous job as they had to confront a fragile economy almost entirely dependent on a deficient agrarian output. The aristocracy, the Church and even the municipalities stood in the way. They were the owners of the land and the recipients of most of the taxes, from which they themselves were exempt. The economy was affected by the appallingly low standard of living of the majority, by delayed economic and technological development, and also by the contrasting rates of these developments in different parts of the country. Trade with the American colonies was another cause for concern. The Castilian trade monopoly across the Atlantic was under increasing threat. The Spanish Crown's determination to maintain a policy based on restriction and monopoly did not work. It affected more than mercantile activity across the Atlantic Ocean for products of European origin. The trade in American goods, including foodstuffs such as cacao and maize, between Nueva España and the South American Pacific coast, would result in a network of efficient contraband practices almost impossible to restrain. The fast-growing interest of the Dutch and English in the New World was in evidence, as much as their mercantile expertise and less desirable maritime practices. Futhermore, business in the major Mediterranean Spanish ports, Barcelona and Valencia, was in the hands of foreign merchants and intermediaries. The insistence in the corridors of power on pinning all hopes on the improvement of medieval agriculture, instead of on trade and manufacturing, would delay the modernization and industrialization of the country for decades. Luxurious merino wool, the economic engine of Castile, had started to be substituted by cheap imports from the Netherlands and England.

On a positive note, between 1712 and 1798 the population of Spain increased in certain areas by as much as 40 per cent, growing from 7.5 million people at the end of the War of Succession to 10.5 million in 1797. Unfortunately this population increase was not enough to resolve the situation in large parts of the country where hunger was ever-present.

With the war in Europe over and decades of plague and desolation now thought to have been left behind, the health of the nation gradually began to improve. An advance in agricultural techniques and the introduction of new crops may have helped, but epidemics – this time typhus, cholera and smallpox – broke out again in 1769 with serious consequences. By then the Spanish peasantry, particularly in the Meseta and Andalusia, was as desperate as it had been in the sixteenth century or even very early medieval times. Here the peasants rented the land they cultivated for the sole benefit of the local lord or the Church. Even the meagre benefit they could obtain, usually by selling the limited food they produced for their own consumption, was taxed. Little was left to improve their standard of living and to secure the future of their families. They could improve neither the condition of the land they tended nor the quality of the crops they planted, and yet the general policy of the country would remain the same: to treat agriculture as the route to prosperity even if this was extremely challenging. Again the interests of the aristocracy, the Church and La Mesta were under threat. To complicate things even further, due to adverse weather conditions consecutive crop failures provoked further unrest among the poor, especially in the cities. Even if their intentions were honourable, and improvements had been achieved, king and government faced a difficult task.

A large percentage of the fertile land was still in the hands of absentee landlords who, favouring life at court, were incapable of managing their properties efficiently. The percentage of the land in the hands of the Church was equally high. In Castile, apart from titles, stipends and rural and urban properties, the Spanish Catholic Church and the religious orders held one-seventh of the region's agricultural and pastoral lands. Even though they produced one-quarter of the area's income from agrarian resources, critics felt the return on the investment was too modest compared with the income the same lands could obtain if they were privately owned rather than Church-owned. Perhaps the same critics of properties being in the hands of the *manos muertas* (lands held in mortmain) were forgetting how serious the agricultural situation inherited from the old regime, the Habsburgs, was. Furthermore they also overlooked the fact that the Church, growing in strength in eighteenth-century Spain, was the only organized body which, as part of an international institution, was still capable of being a serious threat to royal absolutism and government plans.[4]

Believing in the positive effect of the growth of the population on the economy, the government introduced a number of measures aiming to improve the birth rate and the production of food. Privileges would be granted to *familias numerosas*, families with large numbers of children. (Franco introduced a similar policy after the Civil War.) Much later a further measure was introduced. Depopulated land which had never been cultivated or had been neglected would be colonized by foreign workers from other parts of Europe. Some of the measures worked; others, such as the decision to substitute wheat for higher-yielding lower-quality cereals, proved to be yet another error that delayed economic growth.

Spain, a superpower in the sixteenth and seventeenth centuries, would only have second-rate status by the end of the eighteenth century. The main reason would become clear: the government's endemic and incompetent fiscal management. Gold and silver were still coming from the New World, but the political class was simply incapable of planning for the future. They never thought of investing in the economic development of the colonies. Silver and gold were plentiful. In the unpublished text *Considérations sur les richesses de l'Espagne*,[5] and later on in *De l'esprit des lois* (The Spirit of the Laws),[6] Montesquieu asked himself if gold and silver were a fiction or a sign of wealth. He concluded that as signs were very durable but represented fewer things, they became less and less valuable as they multiplied. Spain should have listened to one of the true luminaries of the time, even if he was a Frenchman. With a faulty fiscal system largely propped up by the less able, borrowing from foreign banks and investors was the only solution that Spain had to finance the high cost of wars in Europe. The national debt started growing out of control just as it had done during the reigns of Charles I and Philip II. In some parts of

Europe things were different. A financial revolution based on a combination of direct and indirect taxation had taken place first in the Low Countries in the sixteenth century and in England in the seventeenth century. This had allowed both countries to deal efficiently with the cost of war. But Spain, having failed to introduce a single tax that would simplify her complex system of revenues, including all kinds of indirect taxation, had continued to cripple the life of the middle and lower classes. Even olive oil was heavily taxed.

As before, exhausted Castile was the place where the government obtained most of the funds needed to maintain the extensive borders of its decaying empire. The fiscal system affected two areas directly linked to the livelihoods of the peasantry and the small businessman – trade and the production of food. On food, the *millones*, a tax introduced by Philip II in 1590 in order to replace the 10 million *ducados* lost by the Armada disaster, were applied to the sales of wine, vinegar, oil and meat. The sizeable revenue obtained from this 'temporary' tax soon made it a permanent one. Both the *millones* and the *alcabala*, which was an indirect levy on trading, affected the price and availability of food. In the seventeenth and eighteenth centuries taxation became another significant cause of poverty in the Castilian population. Meanwhile in the coastal north and eastern part of the peninsula the future was looking brighter. Having been denied a share in the Empire's profits, these areas had been spared the human and financial costs brought by constant wars that were crippling Castile. At least in the north of Spain, maize, with its constantly improving yields, had saved both poor people and animals. Beans from the New World (*Phaseolus vulgaris*, also known as common beans and green beans), planted among maize fields and dried, had also become a solution in the north of the country. Catalonia had a fairer contractual tradition of land tenure which protected the smaller farmer and was already producing steady growth in agriculture. Watering systems were modernized, and alternative crops were encouraged to grow in appropriate soils. Large areas of vines were planted, and the production of wine and liqueurs increased substantially. Near the delta of the River Ebro, rice paddies followed suit. However, upriver almonds, hazelnuts and orchards could be seen everywhere. Wine, brandy, cotton, linen and silks were now exported to the rest of Europe and the New World from ports such as Barcelona, Valencia and Alicante.

In other parts of the country the production of wheat, barley and rye occupied three-quarters of the total productive land of the country, but was insufficient to feed the rest of the population. Without even mentioning crop failures, the lack of manpower in many areas of the country, added to the limited availability of seeds and limited investment in modern agricultural equipment, rendered Spanish agriculture as a whole inadequate to resolve hunger and poor economic development. In the rest of the country changes were too slow. Eventually, faced with harsh reality, politicians decided that a solution could be found for the difficult task of converting barren land into agricultural land, forgetting that, among others issues, the powerful Mesta would still be a formidable obstacle.

## Food 'in its Own Ink'

This is an intriguing title used by the Spanish National Library for an exhibition dedicated to food. It is of course a play on the name of a classic Basque recipe, *calamares en su tinta* (squid cooked in its own ink). As it is, the title was not related to any given recipe, but to cookery writing during an extraordinary period starting at the end of the seventeenth century and lasting until the nineteenth century. It stretched from the Baroque period up until some time after the Peninsula War, from the influences associated with past cultures and invasions affecting Spain to further influences from France and other countries. These changes affected the food eaten by the aristocracy, the food that shared many characteristics with the aristocratic tables of other European countries. It was not a classic or national cuisine – it was the food prepared by well-known chefs influenced primarily by the traditions of two countries distinguished by the quality of their food – Italy and particularly France. This explains the lack of court cookbooks published in Spain in the eighteenth century of the calibre of the *Llibre de Coch* by Rupert de Nola in the sixteenth century or the *Art of Cooking* by Martínez Montiño a century later. By the eighteenth century Spain had lost the international prestige it had enjoyed in the past. Court food had largely become a synonym of French food and therefore rather ineffectual; it was an imitation and in the main not a very good one. The time had come for local tradition to present itself as an original alternative, but it would take another century for it to do so with gusto.

Independently from the above, some eighteenth-century published writings relating to Spanish food have been studied by modern historians and food writers. Others kept unedited in public and private libraries are now beginning to see the light of day. Some of these writings originated from the kitchens of religious orders working in Spain and in the Americas during the Spanish colonial period. They relate to the work of members and non-members of their orders, both men and women, who lived under the roof of convents and monasteries cooking simple and very tasty food. Published in

1745, *Nuevo arte de cocina sacado de la escuela de la experencia económica* (New Art of Cooking) is an original cookbook written by a humble Franciscan friar, Raimundo Gómez, known as Juan de Altimiras, a cook who managed to achieve a fame which was only enjoyed by court writers until that point.

As a friar cooking at the friary of San Diego in Aragon, Altimiras wrote a comprehensive study not only of the food eaten in the refectories of religious orders but at the tables of ordinary people living in Spain, both in towns and in the countryside. In *New Art of Cooking*, provenance was not given in the recipes, which probably indicates that the recipes were gathered in different parts of the country.

The author's main intention was to instruct newly professed members of the Franciscan Order who, having been assigned to a Franciscan kitchen, had little understanding of food, food preparation or hygiene, while dealing with the arduous task of feeding the congregation and guests on a very limited budget. Addressing his readers Altimiras wrote:

> From the moment that, forced by obedience, I found myself in the kitchen without a teacher from which to learn everything I needed to do, I decided when fully instructed to write a small cookbook. A book to help newly professed monks leaving the noviciate with little experience, and save them the embarrassment of having to ask everything they may need to do their tasks.[7]

This included the preparation of the *sopa boba*, a thin broth of little substance, a duty normally added to the apprentice's daily routine. It was destined to feed thousands of professional beggars knocking at the back doors of monasteries and convents. Every day after the Angelus, at noon, baskets of bread and heavy cauldrons of hot broth were brought from the kitchen to the doors of the monasteries by members of the congregation. Here long queues of men out of work, women and children, disabled soldiers and half-starved students waited patiently for the only sustenance of the day. In seventeenth- and eighteenth-century Spain, the *sopa boba* prevented a section of the population from dying of hunger in the streets.

All the recipes included in Altimiras's book were prepared by him with fresh ingredients grown in the vegetable gardens of the conventual kitchens in which he worked, including products from the New World, ingredients gaining popularity but still scorned by the nobility. The eggs he used were from the convent's chickens, and the red and white meats were also from animals cared for by the friars. Altimiras made certain that the recipes he included in his book were both simpler and more economical, even if still heavily influenced by the very Baroque and regal Martínez Montiño. Altimiras, for instance, still used sugar, cloves and cinnamon indiscriminately in both sweet and savoury preparations, but his recipes prioritized local seasonal ingredients of good quality to please the palate more than the eye. They were also very much in tune with the many days of silence and fasting and the days of silence and moderate feast in a Franciscan convent where the preparation of festive food required imagination. To perform miracles with a moderate budget was never easy, even for a man of the cloth. Altimiras prepared tasty fish *en adobo*. He fried the fish without flour before he started preparing the *adobo* sauce or marinade. He brought to the boil a mixture of bay leaves, crushed cloves of garlic, thyme, fennel, oregano and small pieces of orange in vinegar. He then placed the fish into the sauce and advised adjusting the salt if needed. Altimiras also included in his book flavoursome *potages de vigilia* for Lent with salt cod, spinach and chickpeas, flavoured with garlic and sweet *pimentón*. In his kitchen modest stews such as *pepitorias* and rabbit and chicken *cazuelas* were as tasty as the humble *potage de judías* prepared with beans, garlic, saffron, pepper, grated cheese, bread and mint. Many vegetable dishes were as welcoming as the lamb *calderetas* that he created to feed pilgrims from time to time. It is also obvious that he was more partial to sausages, lard and crackling than to the hams poor Sancho Panza dreamed of as he arrived at Camacho's wedding in Cervantes's *Don Quixote*.

The manuscripts written at the time by monastic or lay brothers contained popular recipes that had usually been transmitted by word of mouth, as well as more elaborate ones copied from the more prestigious writings of the time. *El cocinero religioso* (The Religious Cook), containing 318 recipes, was written in Pamplona around the beginning of the eighteenth century by an unknown lay monk writing under the pseudonym of Antonio Salsete.[8] Salsete's manuscript, while still in tune with some early medieval, Renaissance and Baroque traditions, is also an indication of how the Spanish popular kitchen was modernizing. Some of Salsete's recipes are original; others clearly belong to writers such as Altimiras. This manuscript and other religious cookbooks not only illustrate local food traditions of the region where they were written but include recipes from many other regions of Spain. Members of different religious orders moved around the country, bringing with them their own traditions as well as new recipes. Eventually a writer among the cooks would take time to update a manuscript with new recipes which were still influenced by Christian and Arabic traditions but also included new ingredients from the New World. As a clear indication of how the products from the New

World had already been integrated into common and monastic food, Salsete's manuscript included several recipes with peppers and *pimentón*, chocolate and of course the novelty – tomatoes. He used tomatoes in salads and in meat and fish stews, and in the belief that tomatoes delayed the cooking process he made certain they were added after the dish had been cooking for a while. To prepare a *cazuela*, the Spanish name for an earthenware pot and a stew, Salsete first sautéed the tomatoes before adding onions, garlic, some breadcrumbs, salt and a dash of *agrio* (vinegar, lemon juice or verjuice, which is also known in Spain as *agraz* or *verjus*). He prepared his *salsa de tomate* with roasted peeled tomatoes, flavoured with ground cumin and coriander seeds, and blended with a little vinegar and salt. Salsete recommended the reader to serve the sauce with a little oregano on top.

The breakdown of ingredients in *El cocinero religioso* is as follows: meat dishes 30 per cent, fish dishes 17 per cent, soups and other dishes made with bread, dough and/or flour 9 per cent, eggs and *lacticinium* 9 per cent, seeds and dried fruits 7 per cent, sauces 6 per cent, conserves and preserves 5 per cent, *arrope* (boiled must), sugar and honey 1 per cent, pickles, olives and marinades 1 per cent and others 15 per cent.[9] It is interesting that in the meat section, lamb and mutton were the most valued, followed by beef and veal, kid and poultry. Pork, associated with the food of the poor, occupied a secondary place in the number of recipes but the last in the mind of the cook. Other cuts were minced to prepare meatballs and *gigotes*, or they were chopped for *pepitorias* (with egg and almonds) or *salpicón* (with onions). There were also recipes cooked with offal – brains and tongue, feet and trotters – which were very popular. Sometimes the names of the recipes derived from the method of preparation: *mechado* (with lardons), *estofado* (stewed), *con masa* (in a pie), *asado* (roasted) or *cochifrito* (pieces of beef, lamb or kid first boiled and then fried with olive oil, garlic, vinegar, spices, parsley, rosemary, bay and mint).

## FUSION FOOD IN NUEVA ESPAÑA

Still under the influence of Martínez Montiño, the food eaten in eighteenth-century Nueva España was recorded for posterity in a number of cookbooks known as *recetarios*, written by both male and female Spanish and *criollo* authors. (The name *criollo* was given to those born in the New World of pure Spanish descent.) Although the original intention had been to preserve the traditions of both Spanish regal and common food, it became clear that what was being recorded was the result of an evolving process which had started in the sixteenth century, a process of juxtaposition using a larger of American and European food products. Furthermore the *recetarios* reflected the extent to which indigenous cultural traditions had influenced the kitchens of Spanish origin in the Americas.

## A VALLEY OF RICH FOOD

Between 1535 and 1821, all Spanish territories in North and Central America as well as in the Philippines and in Oceania were under the control of the powerful Viceroyalty of New Spain with Mexico City, the old Aztec Tenochtitlán, as the capital. Mexico City, built in a magnificent valley known as the Valley of Mexico, was largely a lake until the thirteenth century when the Aztec leaders ordered the centre of the lake to be filled in and the capital to be constructed on the site.

In the sixteenth century the supply and distribution of food was well organized in the Valley of Mexico. Food was brought to the capital across the lagoon from other parts of the extensive Aztec territory as well as from the *chinampas*, floating parcels of land efficiently cultivated by the Aztecs.

Sixteenth-century Aztec agriculture as reported by Spanish clerics was efficient, advanced and sophisticated. In their lands climatic conditions were very diverse; the soils were mostly rich, and, contrary to what was happening in Spain at that time, its development was in the hands of highly qualified horticulturalists. They knew where, how and when to plant an array of crops that could be harvested several times a year. As in Europe, famine would strike from time to time with devastating consequences in the Valley of Mexico, but here the reasons were always related to crop failure and never to the wrongdoings of those in power, as was often the case in Castile. Aztec rulers, undoubtedly expansionist and also empire builders, understood the importance of feeding the whole of the population effectively and at a minimum cost.

In the Valley of Mexico, the land could be owned by communities and then parcelled out to individual families, or by large privately owned estates where resident tenants worked the land. Furthermore, individuals could also work on small plots used for their own consumption, their spare produce sold at the local markets.

The colonists may not have been surprised by the extensive use of terracing they found in Mexico. This was, after all, an agricultural system that had been known in Europe since antiquity. Nor would they have been surprised by the extensive knowledge the Aztecs had about irrigation. Spaniards had inherited advanced Roman, Arab and Berber agricultural practices starting before the first century, yet not even the *Moriscos* could have made the fertile lands of

The Aztec canals at the floating gardens of Xochimilco.

Valencia or Aragon produce five or six crops a year. By using the *chinampa* system of cultivation, the Aztecs achieved what could only be considered an agricultural miracle.

At the height of the Aztec Empire, thousands of *chinampas* were constructed on the bed of the shallow freshwater lake situated around the capital city of Tenochtitlán, today's Mexico City, as well as on Lake Texcoco and further south on Lake Xochimilco and Lake Chalco. Separated by canals that provided access and irrigation, these artificial islands were built above water level, supported by a wooden structure fixed to the lake bed by posts and joined together by wattle. They were filled with layers of dried vegetation and rich mud until fairly compact. A willow tree was planted on each *chinampa* to give the construction stability as well as to prevent soil erosion. Then they were planted with different crops, originally maize, beans, peppers and aromatic plants, but later with all sorts of fruits and vegetables growing irrespective of the wet or dry seasons. Experts believe that even today the *chinampa* system could be a way of avoiding hunger in many areas of the world.

The Mexico of Cortés on the mainland was very different from the world Columbus first encountered in the Caribbean a few years before, even if geographically and botanically they were both exotic and magnificent, and so very different from any place either had ever seen before:

> I walked among the trees, which are the most beautiful I have ever seen. I saw as much greenery, in such density, as I would have seen

in Andalusia in May. And all the trees are as different from ours as
day is from night, and so are the fruits, the herbage, the rocks and
everything.

Even though this was written by Columbus in his log while in the Bahamas
on Wednesday, 14 October 1492,[10] it could also have been a description of
the land conquered by Cortés years later. It has to be said that Mexico's
geographic and botanical diversity is far superior, without mentioning
its potential for exploration and exploitation. The Aztec world which the
Spaniards disrupted belonged to a strong, sophisticated and cruel civilization
which had been constantly evolving, taking by force and absorbing other
cultures that had been equally advanced. While growing strong, they created
their own food culture based on maize, beans, chillies and chocolate,
complemented by turkeys, lizards and spiders, grasshoppers and worms,
snakes and wild pigeons, all of which the European invaders did not
necessarily care for.

In 1529, Cortés's ambition became a reality when Charles I granted him El
Marquesado del Valle de Toluca, a rich and beautiful expanse of land located
not far from today's Mexico City. Until then he had been keeping European
livestock in Toluca. For Cortés this was much more than a dream and a Spanish
title; he knew this was a perfect place to become rich and powerful. It was just
the beginning of a successful business career. He invested in the production
of wheat and sugar and the extraction of precious minerals, while also trying
his hand at mercantile activities across the Pacific Ocean.

The change from crop production to livestock in some parts of the valleys
became a serious problem for the indigenous population as they saw their
fields of maize and beans transformed into prairies. As Caesar has done in
old Hispania, Cortés could feed armies and *colonos* on their way to discover
and settle new territories, this time in the name of the Spanish king. Even if
Cortés's enterprises were far from altruistic, he gave Spanish food culture a
chance to take a firm hold in the Americas. Eventually ingredients, methods of
cooking and the regional character of Spanish food would become an integral
part of Mexican cuisine.

With the weakening of the initial resistance to European foodstuffs
now successfully produced in Nueva España, more European products were
adopted by native cooks. Sugar cane, which centuries before had rescued the
rather unsophisticated early medieval diet in Europe, was now growing well
in the Americas – not only in the Caribbean but in Mexico, where sugar
would transform the bitter chocolate drink the Aztecs loved into one of the

most desirable and palatable treats that Europeans could ever have imagined. Eventually honey would be replaced by sugar in the Mesoamerican diet as well.

One particular factor that separated eighteenth-century Spain from Nueva España was the sheer extent of the land and the potential offered by agriculture. In Nueva España, land was at least initially free from the tight man-made restraints that had affected agriculture and the food of the poor since early times in Spain and other European countries. In principle, away from the cities anyone could take fruit from the abundant trees, and sweet-tasting insects made palatable by roasting were free for all. Maize, the basic food of the Mexicans, could be planted in all types of soils and different levels of humidity. The production of wheat, while modest in comparison with the production of maize, was staggering compared with European output. In Nueva España wheat productivity would become six times greater than in France, a major producer of quality cereals. Even so, in 1785 famine struck in Nueva España with devastating effects: crop failure, depopulation of large areas and mining were among the reasons behind the suffering and death caused by the lack of food in a land of plenty.

Mexico City, already a magnificent city before the arrival of the Spaniards, would become under Spanish control one of the largest and most affluent places in the world. It was a trading paradise where jade, cotton and precious metals were traded, as were meat, sugar, maize, wheat and *pulque*, a popular alcoholic drink made from the pulp of the maguey plant. Wine was also now consumed by those of European origin. Here people from different cultures could also buy salt, live animals and slaves. In Mexico City most of the population were native Mexicans, with a minority of powerful colonial Spaniards, members of the Church and *criollos*. Slaves were brought from Africa to strengthen the workforce needed by the colonials to produce European crops, especially sugar, and even cocoa, and these made up another large section of the population. Each group would sit in front of a plate of food in which quantity and quality more than diversity were defined by racial and social status. In sheer contrast to Spain at the time, in Nueva España eating meat was not an indication of social status or race – the type of meat was. All inhabitants had meat in their diet, because meat had become one of the most successful areas of trade. Lamb and chicken were associated with the top end of society, beef with the middle class (comprised mostly of Spaniards and *criollos*), pork for the rest, and goat for those who could not afford pork. By the eighteenth century El Mercado Central de la Ciudad de Mexico had become the largest and most important market in the whole of the American Spanish Empire, 'a market that reflected the richness and diversity of the food consumed by its inhabitants'.[11] The food trade had been very successful in Mexico City. This was reflected in the hectic activity of hundreds of stores trading in the central market. Here the enriched list of foodstuffs produced already in Nueva España was filling the baskets carried by women: live chickens to cook with almonds, turkeys with a rich *mole* made with chocolate, pig's trotters for a substantial stew, a pomegranate to refresh a hot pepper dish, maize flour to make tortillas, wheat flour for white bread or to make light *buñuelos* fried in olive oil. In the following century these were all dishes that would evolve into the elaborate, colourful and unique Mexican national cuisine we know today, neither Spanish nor native, just original and very *mestiza*.

## A Fusion of Culinary Traditions

In Mesoamerica food exchange had existed since the beginning of the discovery of America by Europeans, while the fusion of culinary traditions, or *mestizage*, would take several centuries; the indigenous population remained closer to their own culture. For the Spaniards, accepting new foods and adapting their diet had been a necessity, particularly when they first arrived and were expanding the area of discovery into mainland America. Either they ate as the locals did or they starved. Once settled, they encouraged the indigenous population to grow the list of foodstuffs they were accustomed to, especially wheat to make bread. As meat was another essential part of the European diet, in high demand among the Spanish elite, colonial traders embarked on breeding the animals brought by Columbus on his second voyage. This became a successful and profitable business. In Nueva España the introduction of meat and lard into the diet of the indigenous population would encounter less resistance than other products of European origin. As they started to produce their own animals, they would sell the best cuts to Spaniards and *criollos* in the markets while keeping the lesser cuts for themselves. But wheat or barley could never compete with maize. For the indigenous population, bread baked in an oven, even if it was made with best *candeal* wheat, would never taste as delicious as the hot corn tortillas made for their meals on the *comal*, the traditional flat earthenware griddle where tortillas were cooked on top of the stove.

The fusion of food cultures between the New World and the Old had become a reality in Nueva España and further south including Chile and Peru. By then the population of the *Indias Occidentales* had grown substantially not only in size but in ethnic diversity. They consisted of indigenous people, mestizos, blacks, mixed race people and whites, of which many were *criollos*.

They were living side by side in towns and in the countryside now adorned with olive groves, vineyards and wheat fields. In Nueva España recipes included in manuscripts and cookbooks were already showing a much more prominent element of fusion, as was the food prepared by cooks serving in Spanish or *criollo* households. The recipes prepared with very basic facilities in the houses where indigenous families lived were still following ancient Toltec and Aztec traditions, their mattresses sharing living space with artistic earthenware such as the stone *molcaljete* (mortar) or the clay *comal*. With the passing of time these recipes incorporated many of the ingredients brought by the Spaniards: for example *tamales* (maize-based dough wrapped in leaves and steamed), stuffed with sweet or savoury ingredients, including beef, and tortillas served with refried beans in pork fat. Other recipes of Spanish origin were prepared in the convents and large colonial houses occupied by the white population, mostly of Spanish descent. These houses were built in the image of those of Andalusia or Castile. Here the kitchens, even in the most modest colonial houses, occupied a large space, separated from the rest of the house and with their ovens inside or outside. They were tended by native cooks trained in the culinary traditions of Spain and capable of adopting or adapting recipes from the two worlds. Mexico City had become a centre of integration and adaptation of all aspects of culture.

Apart from making fascinating reading and providing the most extensive record of life and food across the Atlantic, three manuscripts – *El recetario*

*Molcaljete*, the ancient Mexican pestle and mortar: a similar solution was found on both sides of the Atlantic.

*novohispano*, *El recitario de Dominga de Guzmán* and *El libro de cocina de Fray Gerónimo de Pelayo*[12] – put the fusion of two strong culinary cultures into context, revealing at the same time the extent of the influence of Spanish food.

A good example of the above can be found in the recipe for a chicken stew, *guiso de gallina*, included in *El recetario novohispano*: Cut the chickens into quarters and wash them, add lard and salt, and sauté until golden in colour. Add chopped garlic, onion and parsley. Cover with tomatoes (*jiyomate*) and season with *especias finas*. As the author does not give the names of the spices added to the chicken, the composition probably followed the medieval *salsa fina*, which included cinnamon, pepper and saffron, among others. In today's Mexico the parsley would be exchanged for coriander.

Another recipe cooked with chicken comes fom *El recetario de Dominga de Guzmán*. This is a perfect example of a *mestizo* or *criolla* recipe written by a woman. It contains lard, wheat bread, chorizo, fruit, sugar syrup and *acitrón*, all of Spanish origin. Dominga prepared this in a *cazuela*, the traditional earthenware pot used both in Spain and in Mexico, covered with an indigenous *comal*. She toasted some bread spread with lard. She then prepared a watery sugar syrup and dipped the toast in the syrup. She placed a layer of the bread in the *cazuela* and another layer of chorizo with toasted sesame seeds, sultanas, almonds and *acitrón*, then another of bread and another of the chorizo. She worked this way until the *cazuela* was completely full, then she cooked the dish on top of the stove covered with a *comal* on which hot embers had been placed. She would serve this dish with roasted chicken.

## WOMEN'S PAGES

It is undeniable that the strong relationship between women and food has existed since the beginning of time, yet examples of women actually sharing their knowledge about food and culinary traditions in writing have been scarce. In Spain the main reason was simple: a high percentage of women could not read or write properly until well into the twentieth century, particularly if they belonged to the peasantry or the lower urban classes. Since medieval times, the percentage of women who had access to some form of education was to be found only among the aristocracy and the Church.[13] Here, listed together with reading and writing among the subjects any young lady should master before entering married life, were sewing and of course cooking. It is also known that another source of recipes would have been distinguished Spanish *damas* entering convents after becoming widowed, or when seeking protection from the outside world. They brought with them family recipes and more often than not a servant to cook for them. This way, knowledge and new techniques were added to those already well established in the New World. Here novices and experienced religious cooks were working, both of Spanish and indigenous origin.

'A Tablecloth-stainer'

*Manchamanteles* – from *mancha* (stain) and *manteles* (tablecloths) – is the name of a Mexican festive recipe, a sweet and sour stew cooked with chicken, pork or both in a rich sauce or *mole*, which has been recorded by different writers since the seventeenth century. The recipe usually contains meat, tomatoes, plenty of fresh fruit and sugar as well as a number of spices originating in the New and the Old Worlds, the list of ingredients changing from writer to writer and becoming more and more *mestiza*. It is thought to have been recorded first by a nun, Sor Juana Inés de la Cruz, another Mexican food writer working around 1678. Sor Juana prepared *manchamanteles* with chillies, sesame seeds, chicken, plantain, *canote* (sweet potato) and *panochera* apples – a cooking apple which tastes far better than it looks. In the eighteenth-century *El Recetario de Dominga Guzmán*, Dominga kept the chillies and sesame seeds, although she specified that the chillies should be *chilcoscle* (yellow chillies) and added black pepper. Later in the same century, Brother Jerónimo de San Pelayo added bread, lard, tomatoes, the very Spanish cumin seeds and the very Mexican *epazote*. By the twentieth century the recipe had been enriched by the inclusion of pork, pineapple, plantain, cinnamon and even vinegar from Castile, keeping the chicken and chilli of course.

Some modern authors associate *manchamanteles* with one of the seven *moles* claimed by the city of Oaxaca as its own. Zarela Martínez, a great authority on the subject of Oaxacan food, associates this recipe not only with this city but with the city of Chiapas, although for her the Oaxacan version is more fruity and spicy. Zarela's recipe contains two types of chilli – *ancho* and *guajillo* – garlic, onions, tomatoes, *tomatillos* (*Physalis ixocarpa*), oregano, fresh thyme, bay leaves, cinnamon, cumin seeds, black peppercorns, pieces of chicken and pork ribs, pineapple and green apples. It follows a complex method of preparation that requires lots of patience and skill.[14]

## A Matter of Sweet Things

Understandably, pastries, biscuits, sweetmeats and milk puddings were included in the American manuscripts, many of them made with bread, and the majority belonging to the monastic Spanish tradition. Nuns had needed to support themselves and their convents since their orders had been founded. Working by the motto *oro y laboro* (I pray and I work), they soon found an easy way to obtain generous donations and favours from new patrons. They could prepare the most delicate selection of pastries and sweetmeats, inherited from the array of cultures that had passed through the Iberian Peninsula. The nuns had the time, patience and above all the discipline and knowledge that pastry experts needed. And they had the most important quality of all, the soft and feather-like touch so envied by pastry chefs. In Spain, religion was never far away from the kitchen: the Spanish mystic and Roman Catholic Saint Teresa of Jesús wrote in the sixteenth century in *The Book of the Foundations*: 'También entre los pucheros anda El Señor' (The Lord God can also be found among the pots). In Spain, a certain number of prayers have traditionally ensured that a dish is not overcooked or undercooked: ten Credos to stir the quince paste, three to boil an egg, and a Hail Mary for a more simple operation.

To fully understand the relevance of the extensive group of manuscripts and published sources dealing with *dulcería* and *pastelería* (sweets, confectionary and pastries) in colonial Spain in the eighteenth century, it is important to go back to sugar and to a number of early Spanish books and manuscripts associated with cookery not only within the religious orders.

The expansion of sugar plantations and the profitable return on the investment obtained by Spaniards first in the Canary Islands and then in the New World changed the face of Spanish sweet and dessert traditions. With better distribution and consequently lower prices, sugar began to replace honey in recipes prepared by chefs, religious cooks, laywomen and even doctors, and yet there were very few books that acknowledged its importance.

A number of unpublished anonymous manuscripts of the sixteenth and seventeenth centuries are fundamental to understanding the Spanish sweet tradition, its development and its association with refinement and luxury – something delicate and noble. Furthermore there was a close relationship between confectionary, gastronomy, medicine and dietetics.[15]

*El Vergel de señores en el qual se muestra a hacer con mucha excelencia todas las conservas, electuarios, confituras, turrones y otras cosas de asucar y miel.* (The Gentleman's Orchard, in which it is shown how to make with much excellence all the conserves, electuaries, jams, nougat and other things of sugar and honey) is considered the oldest Spanish manuscript on the subject of sweet things and even drinks. It was written in the Castilian language between 1490 and 1520. This is a complete book that, apart from a comprehensive list of ingredients and cooking methods, includes a long section on kitchen utensils and different containers needed to prepare the recipes. The complete list reads: brass pestle and mortar, ceramic mortar with a wooden pestle, a silver spoon to remove hot quince paste from the pot, a number of *almorfías* or large serving dishes, several ovens, a metal or cotton strainer, a number of wide and shallow wooden boxes for jam, *un meneador* or wooden stirring stick, as well as many other utensils commonly used in traditional Spanish kitchens. Following in the medieval tradition, *Gentleman's Orchard* also provides detailed information on the preparation of oils, beauty products and perfumes. The section about aroma, taste and colour is a sophisticated piece of writing not often seen in this type of book.

Little was known about the contribution of another sixteenth-century author, Juan Vallés (1497–1563), who worked on the subject of body care and refinement, sweet things and their benefits to health. Vallés was a diplomat in the service of Charles I. Until fairly recently there was only one copy of Valles's *Regalo de la vida humana* (Gift of Human Life), kept at the Austrian National Library in Vienna, which had been available for research. Recently the academic Fernando Serrano Larráyoz has transcribed the original manuscript, shedding more light on a subject that fascinated sixteenth-century Spain at a time when in Navarre the preparation of sweets and preserves was the responsibility of *boticarios* or pharmacists.[16]

Miguel de Baeza's *Los cuatro libros del arte de la confitería* (Four Books on the Art of Confectionary), published in 1592 in Alcalá de Henares, is thought to be the first book published in Castilian dedicated to confectionary. De Baeza was born in Toledo, a city renowned for quality Arabic and Jewish confections, as clearly reflected in the book. Full of interesting details and facts, it firstly describes how sugar is produced from cane and then the different qualities which could be obtained from it. In the rest of the book the author provides recipes and notes for all kinds of preparations made with sugar as well as honey, including sophisticated jellies, preserves, jams, marzipan and sweetmeats of all shapes as well as *turrón*, a special nougat. De Baeza's book also includes a copy of the official regulations to be followed by professional confectioners, later signed by Philip III in 1615.[17]

Back in the eighteenth century, Spanish books about confectionary came at a slower pace than their French equivalents. Written by professional cooks,

*Turrón*, the Middle Eastern sweet treat adopted by the Spaniards.

these books were less well known in the international arena, with one important exception. Juan de la Mata's *Arte de repostería* or 'The Art of Pastry', published in 1791, became an instant success at home and beyond the Pyrenees. Written in Castilian, this was a book specializing in pastries and desserts, cold and hot drinks, cream, nougat and even fresh fruit, and instantly won the approval of Domingo Fernández, the king's master pastry chef, a difficult thing to do. De la Mata was a qualified pastry chef and confectioner working in a completely different environment and with a different approach from Altimiras, Salsete and the many cooks in religious orders, even if similar recipes were included in texts by all of them. He was a modern chef in the service of the court who had previously been influenced by modern Italian and French chefs, and would influence thousands of professional and non-professional kitchens for over two centuries. Divided into two chapters, his book was presented in a style that was easy to read and accessible to all. The first chapter is an extensive introduction dealing with the organization of the kitchen, table service, and the menus to be served at banquets and large celebrations. The second is a collection of 507 recipes. Some are Spanish recipes while others originated from France, Italy, Portugal, the Netherlands and even Asia. De la Mata used an abundance of fruit to be served fresh or made into jellies, jams and compotes following De Baeza's school of cookery. Some products were European while others came from the Americas, a novelty that distinguishes his book from the unedited manuscripts previously mentioned. He rejoiced in traditional Portuguese and Spanish pastries and cakes, biscuits and sweetmeats: *mazapanes*, *rosquillas*, *mostachones*, *merengues* and delicious *yemas* (a speciality of many prestigious convents made with egg yolk and sugar syrup). He went much further by including all types of drinks such as liqueurs made with alcohol and grape juice known as *mistelas*, cold and frozen fruit juices, chocolate and even coffee. The first mention of coffee in Spain actually appears in this valuable book. On coffee De la Mata believed that it diluted and destroyed the effects of wine, helped digestion, strengthened the spirit and prevented excesive sleep.[18]

## Down-to-Earth Food at the Palace

More culinary influences, this time Italian, came when Charles III ascended the throne in 1759. Charles was the son of Philip V of Spain and Elisabetta Farnese di Parma, an Italian princess. His reign saw complexity and excitement in the kitchens of the Royal Palace in Madrid. As in the rest of Europe, by the middle of the eighteenth century people were developing a taste for new ideas and a desire to break with the old system that would also influence food.

A number of societies, created to encourage agriculture, industry and commerce and above all the arts and sciences, became an inspiration to the population at large. The most famous of them was the Basque society La Real Sociedad Bascongada de Amigos del País (the Royal Society of Friends of the Basque Country), founded in 1764 under the auspices of the illustrious Count of Peñaflorida. This society or academy aimed to encourage the agricultural, scientific, cultural and economic development of the Basques, and would be followed by many others all over the country (not be confused with the popular gastronomic societies that would appear a century later in San Sebastián). The introduction of social reforms became a possibility in this changing climate, which the new king recognized and acted upon. With a momentary peace with Europe and the domestic economy in some form of limited expansion, the time to introduce practical new ideas and social reform had come. Even food improved for a large part of the population as enlightened politicians such as Jovellanos o Cadarso became aware there was a clear relationship between happiness and food.

Unlike his father, Charles III (1716–1788) was a man who favoured a relatively simple life and enjoyed people of all classes, even if he could not avoid the extravagance, pomp and ceremony attached to the Spanish Court inherited from the former Habsburg period. Wealth, excess and even greater

Charles III dining before the court, 1775; painting by Luis Peret y Alcázar (1746–1799).

distance between the court and the people had arrived with the Habsburgs. The food they preferred, influenced by European tradition, would remain isolated – even from the food enjoyed by the Spanish aristocratic class – for centuries to come. This had changed to a certain extent with the arrival of the Bourbons and their populist take on life.

A number of favourable circumstances and his mother's capacity for political intrigue and manipulation had given Charles first the Kingdom of Naples and then the Crown of Spain and its domains in the Americas. As protocol demanded, grand French and Italian food was prepared for lunch at the Royal Palace of Madrid. It was served in the huge *comedor de gala* (formal dining room) with strict ceremony, an obligation Charles III did not enjoy. Here the king sat alone at the table in the presence of his ministers, ambassadors, servants and favourite hunting dogs. In the evenings Charles tried to live a very different life. As a man of simple taste who was rather partial to ordinary Spanish food, his perfect dinner consisted of roast beef, one egg, salad, a glass of wine from the Canary Islands and some biscuits to accompany the wine.

### A Social Reform Doomed to Failure

In the 1760s, three consecutive wheat failures had resulted in a sharp increase in the price of bread. Landlocked and far from seaports bringing in major wheat supplies from Italy, food prices rose out of control. Madrid was in turmoil and this wasn't just due to the lack of bread. Even if the king enjoyed ordinary food, *madrileños* felt that foreign influence at court was threatening the traditional life, values and even the style of clothes worn by people living in the capital city. Claiming the need to ensure civic security in the streets, Minister Esquilache's ban on the traditional cape and hat worn by men in winter ignited the flame of insurrection, and Esquilache had to resign. There were other issues too, including the permanent threat of hunger due to failing crops and the ancient privileges enjoyed by La Mesta and the feudal landlords. These were the same privileges that for the benefit of rearing sheep and producing wool had kept a large percentage of the land unproductive. The unfair distribution of land needed to be resolved once and for all! In response, Charles III ordered the municipalities to divide common land into small farms to be distributed among landless peasants. Persuaded by his ministers, he also ordered the creation of new communities to be built beside the newly opened roads.

Although the first law soon proved to be a failure, as corruption in the municipalities landed the farms in the hands of the already privileged, some newly formed colonies in the area of the Sierra Morena in Andalusia flourished, at least for a time. Minister Olarvide was given the responsibility of carrying out an ambitious project aiming to bring uncultivated or abandoned areas of Andalusia to life. Villages such as La Carolina in Jaén, La Luisiana in Seville and La Carlota in Cordoba were created with more than 6,000 Austrian, German and French workers looking for a new life. To avoid accumulation of land, they were not allowed to purchase further property. They would be exempt from the taxation that for centuries had crippled the advance of the agrarian population in the country. It is important to remember that neither the aristocracy, nor the Church or the municipality, had ever paid these taxes. Today some traditions such as the 'day of the painted eggs' and the Fasnacht (Carnival) have been preserved by locals, many of whom still have blue eyes and blond hair. The Sierra Morena project, the subject of Olarvide's dream, was studied in detail by Joseph Townsend, the author of *A Journey through Spain in the Years 1786 and 1787*, as he travelled between Madrid and Seville in 1787. Having spent a night at lodgings at La Concepción de Almuradiel, a little village within the new settlements of the Sierra Morena, he was supplied with dirty linen that he immediately rejected. He bought his usual wine, bread and mutton because beef, his favourite food, was not available at the local *venta*. The following morning he continued on his journey south in the company of his fellow travellers, going through Santa Elena, where

> the country is highly cultivated yet many trees are left, so that the whole, at a little distance, appears like an extensive forest. In one cottage we saw tame partridges. They are trained, like decoy ducks, to collect others.[19]

On the outskirts of another foreign settlement, La Carolina, Townsend talked to D. Pablo de Olarvide, the man behind the project. Whilst employed by the Governor of the Council of Castile, Count d'Aranda, Minister Olarvide had came up with the idea of introducing agriculture and arts in the deserted mountains of the Sierra, where rape and violence had long been widespread. The difficulty was to produce settlers. One Turigel of Babaria was hired to contract 6,000 men for husbandry. But instead of men trained in agriculture, he brought only vagabonds, who all either died or were dispersed without doing the work for which, at immense expense, they had been brought. Settlers were then invited from all parts of Germany, and, in order to encourage immigration, on application every newcomer received a plot of land, a house, two cows of which one was pregnant, one ass, five sheep, as many goats, six hens with a cock, a plough and a pick-axe. They each began with 50 fanegas of land (929 sq. m/10,000 sq. ft), and when they had cultivated that, they received fifty more, free of all rent for the first ten years, and after that period subject only to royal tithes.

## Fashionable Drinks

As the distribution of cocoa improved, the fashion for drinking chocolate had moved from Madrid to other parts of the country. Soon the new drink became fully integrated and adopted by Spanish culture, becoming a new national symbol, the Spanish drink par excellence! This development had been helped by a multitude of factors. Some were related to economics, trading issues and colonial politics. Others, notably after the 1660s, were influenced by cultural, scientific, medical and of course religious thought. In sixteenth-century Mexico Hernán Cortés had discovered the high value given by the Aztecs to the cocoa bean and to their drink, chocolate. For them, these beans were not only of divine origin, they provided energy and sustenance, another reason why the popularity of cocoa began to spread in Europe with such speed.

By the end of the same century, cocoa consignments had increased progressively between the ports of Veracruz, Cádiz and Seville and become a highly profitable business. As expected, the first chocolate factory soon opened its doors in Seville. By then the unpalatable recipe Cortés had tasted at the court of Moctezuma, a cold and bitter drink made with powdered roasted cocoa beans, chilli pepper, *achiote* and *orejuela* (known in English as ear flower), had drastically changed. The first recipe for a chocolate drink was published in Spain in 1631 by Antonio Colmenero de Ledesma in his book *Curioso Tratado de la Naturaleza y Calidad del Chocolate Dividido en Cuatro Puntos* (Curious Treatise on the Nature and Quality of Chocolate Divided into Four Sections). His recipe, still made with chilli, which he said could be substituted for black pepper, included roasted and ground cocoa beans, aniseed, a vanilla pod, cinnamon, almonds, hazelnuts and sugar, as well as the original *achiote* and *orejuela*. *Orejuela* (the petals of the flower of the *Cymbopetalum penduliflorum* tree) was and is still used in Mesoamerica to flavour chocolate. It was highly appreciated by the Aztec and the Maya for its spicy aromatic fragrance. Both *achiote* and *orejuela* were left behind as chocolate as a drink became fashionable in Spain. In *Food Matters*, Carolyn A. Nadeau makes an interesting comparison between the arrival and acceptance by different social classes of a number of Central and South American products, such as tomatoes and potatoes, as they reached Spain and the rest of Europe. Chocolate, protected by the Church and the aristocracy, crossed the Atlantic as an already sophisticated drink, along with recipes which, having originated in the Americas, would change or increase many of their original ingredients while preserving the original preparation method.[20]

The Spanish created many recipes with chocolate. They were mostly hot and stimulating, invariably ending up as a drink that contained cocoa and a number of spices well adapted to the European palate: aniseed, sesame seeds, vanilla, and usually cinnamon and sugar. Sugar had altered the palate everywhere and was associated with wealth. In *Sweetness and Power: The Place of Sugar in Modern History*, the American anthropologist Sidney Mintz argues that sugar 'embodied the social position of the wealthy and powerful'.[21] Undoubtedly chocolate had followed the same path. Cacao would become for the Spanish Crown the second most important product of the Americas, only surpassed by silver. For economic reasons and to the detriment of the Mexican plantations, by the seventeenth century cacao cultivation had extended successfully to South America, especially to Caracas, Maracaibo and Guayaquil. In Mexico, mines were more important than cacao for businessmen and the Crown.

## *Jícaras* and *Mancerinas*: A Little More about Drinking Chocolate

Chocolate has become a powerful tool in the hands of avant-garde Spanish pastry chefs. Chefs such as Oriol Balaguer, Enric Rovira and Albert Adrià have revolutionized the Spanish world of chocolate by breaking down the frontiers between sweet and savoury and looking back into the past. Even if the chocolate they use in their pastries, cakes and *bombones* is far removed from the chocolate prepared by the Maya and the Aztecs – a drink made with cacao powder and other indigenous ingredients – Spanish chefs have successfully started to use some of the original ingredients in their preparations, especially chilli pepper.

Half a millennium has passed since the first Castilian recipe for making drinking chocolate was written down. The recipe prepared by the Spaniards contained 795 grams (1¾ lb) ground cocoa, 55 grams (2 oz) vanilla, 400 grams (14 oz) chilli pepper, 14 grams (½ oz) cloves, 700 grams (1½ lb) sugar and a dash of *achiote*, which was the seed used by the Aztecs to paint their bodies red. The chronicler Bernal Díaz del Castillo (1490–1584) reported that chocolate was drunk in cups of gold at the palace of Montezuma and that it was a very frothy bitter drink, having been well beaten with a *molinillo* (a wooden whisk) in the traditional Mexican *chocolatera*, a pot that incorporated the whisk. The first version of the recipe written in Castilian was quickly changed to please the less sophisticated taste of the Spaniards. Out with the chillies and the *achiote*, in with the cocoa power, milk, sugar or honey, vanilla pod and sometimes cinnamon. In Spain cocoa seeds were ground by hand using similar grinding stones to the original *matates* of the Aztecs. Eventually industrialization came to the rescue in the eighteenth century but even then local artisans went house to house with a grinding stone while the method of preparation still followed the Aztec way. In Spain and in Nueva España chocolate was served in a ceramic *jícara* cup. The word *jícara* comes from the Nahuatl *xicalli*, a little utensil made from the fruit of the calabash tree. Later on it was served in a clever device called a *mancerina* invented by the Viceroy of Peru, the Marqués de Mancera. It consisted of a combined food plate and cup holder made of ceramic or metal to hold the cup, or *jícara*, of hot chocolate, thereby avoiding accidents.

Even if chocolate was already known in Madrid in the sixteenth century, it was during the seventeenth and especially in the eighteenth that it became part of the life of the capital. Chocolate was introduced to Italy in 1606 and in 1616 to France during the wedding of Louis XIII and the Spanish princess Anna of Austria. At that time chocolate as a drink was enjoyed several times a day. Whether at the palace, in the convents or in middle-class homes or inns, the sweet smell of chocolate, vanilla and cinnamon added an exotic touch to daily life. Until the appearance in the nineteenth century of *cafeterías*, drinking chocolate was served to the public in shops known as *botillerías*.

The Spanish hot chocolate for drinking, *a la taza*, is much thicker than the hot chocolate favoured in France, and the reason is simple. Spaniards like to dip all sorts of pastries, biscuits and *churro* fritters in the thick chocolate.

*Mancerina*, a clever utensil for enjoying hot chocolate and biscuits during animated conversation.

At the beginning, chocolate was only served in noble Spanish households. With time it would also become popular with the aristocrats of Europe, competing all the way with coffee and with tea, drinks that, unlike chocolate, Spaniards could not rightly claim as their own. Today the chocolate that Spaniards enjoy as a breakfast drink or as an afternoon treat, *chocolate a la taza*, follows a much simpler recipe.

Antonio Lavedan, a doctor writing in 1796 about the uses, abuses, properties and virtues of tobacco, tea and chocolate, provided extensive information on how these drinks were prepared and served in Spain. After all, he thought chocolate was a divine, heavenly drink as well as a panacea and universal medicine. He reported that to obtain the cocoa paste or powder needed to prepare the drink, the cocoa seeds had first to be separated from their hard shells by roasting, using a type of iron or copper griddle, or large pan known as a *paila*. To avoid burning the beans, white sand was first heated in the griddle, and then the beans were placed on top. This method enabled the separation of the hard shells from the beans, and also ensured the preservation of the cocoa fat and the fragile aromatic components inside the beans, essential for making high-quality cocoa paste. Once the beans were separated from their shells and the sand, they were crushed between two stones, which were first slightly heated in a brazier. This turned the beans into a thick paste which was then blended with sugar before being crushed for a second time. Still warm, this paste was allowed to harden in metal or wooden tins, or it was shaped individually into chips resembling the original beans. Some doctors believed that chocolate blended with a little vanilla and cinnamon improved digestion. Pepper and ginger were also used by some producers, although their flavour and aroma were not so popular in Spain. Lavedan went even further by including two different methods of making chocolate. In the first, the hard chips or small blocks of chocolate were broken into pieces and put into a *chocolatera* (chocolate pot) with cold water. Then it was gently heated while constantly beating the mixture with a traditional wooden *molinillo* by rolling its handle between the hands, until the paste had dissolved completely. Lavedan insisted that it was essential to maintain a gentle heat during the whole process, so as to prevent the paste from separating into its solid and fatty components and becoming a rather indigestible drink. The Spanish doctor also recommended drinking the chocolate when just made, and never reheating the *chocolatera* for a second time. He believed a second method of preparation was even better. The cocoa beans were first pounded to a fine powder and then added to the water in a *chocolatera*, stirring the mixture constantly while heating with the *molinillo* to create a perfect blend. Made this way, the different components of the chocolate paste did not have enough time to separate.

*Xocolatada*: twentieth-century tiles showing chocolate being served in 1710, in the Museu del Disseny, Barcelona.

### REFRESCOS AND AGASAJOS

Another characteristic of life in Spain in the eighteenth century was the social and cultural change taking place, particularly in larger cities. Any excuse was valid to organize a *tertulia*, as they were known: a literary gathering or political discussion in one of the fashionable cafés that were springing up all over the country. Equally representative of the time were the frequent social gatherings of women or men and women taking place at court, as well as in wealthy private houses, where a selection of sweet pastries and biscuits, ice creams and sorbets, ice cold and hot drinks known as *refresco* or *agasajo* were served. The *refrescos* were similar irrespective of where the gatherings took place, or the financial and social position enjoyed by the host or hostess. Hot or cold chocolate was always the centrepiece, even if during the long, hot summer months all kinds of waters flavoured with fruits and spices were offered first: fresh almond *horchata*, lemonade and orange juice were followed by granitas and sorbets. Fresh milk was also served as were ice creams made with eggs, nougat or even the delicious *leche imperial* made with milk, eggs and almonds to the consistency of De Nola's *manjar blanco*.

Social events were very popular, and not only in Madrid; they were equally popular in Valencia, Seville and particularly among the Catalan elite. Barcelona was a city gathering momentum; its port was gaining importance thanks to the American trade, and was already free from the Castilian monopoly. A city with a unique mercantile spirit, the Catalonian capital was trying to follow in the footsteps of the English and Dutch, while remaining attached to the old aristocratic ways imposed by the Spanish court, as the *El Calaix de Sastre* reveals. This is a well-documented testimony of the life and tastes of the provincial aristocracy in Catalonia. Written by Rafael d'Amat i de Cortada, Barón de Maldà, during the latter part of the eighteenth century, it centres on the best of life and food in quality and quantity.

El Barón spends page after page describing the pleasures to be encountered at breakfasts, lunches, dinners and social events: five-course lunches and dinners, chocolate in the morning and in the afternoon, rice and omelettes for excursions, cod for Lent. The Barón de Maldà also includes ample details about the food element of the *refresc* (*refresco* or *refresc* in the Catalan language means food and drinks offered during a social gathering or party), especially the tantalizing selection of pastries and fairy cakes: *melindros* also known as *bizcochos de soletilla* (ladyfingers), *catanies* (small balls made with almonds, hazelnuts, milk, cocoa powder and sugar), *besquits* from Mallorca, the light *ensaimada* pastry also from the Balearic Islands, as well as the sweet buns known as *brassos* and *pans d'ou* or the *pessic* (made with flour, eggs, sugar, lemon and butter), among many others. Wine, perhaps less popular than soft drinks, was also served as well as coffee during the numerous gatherings taking place in the mansions of Catalan Society, while the diet of a large majority of the population was based on potatoes, onions and also wine.[22]

Coffee, a drink that initially had only been consumed at the royal courts, would garner a strong following among intellectuals and discerning bourgeoisie all over Europe. People could gather at cafés to hold public meetings and to exchange news and thoughts over a cup or two of the most fashionable and rather addictive drink. Having been discovered in Ethiopia in the sixth century, coffee had come to Europe from the Arabian Peninsula via Turkey in the sixteenth century. Chocolate had become popular with every level of society while coffee, the fashionable dark, bitter and invigorating drink, would soon become a way of life in Spain. In the eighteenth century, the fashionable cafés attracted the political class and the intellectuals of the day. They were places of idleness, social and political discussion. Since then coffee has become an after-lunch or -dinner treat, and today millions of cups of *solo, cortado, con leche* or *con hielo* (black, with a drop of milk, with milk or iced) are also enjoyed for breakfast, elevenses and the *merienda*, the snack or afternoon tea that Spaniards enjoy between lunch and dinner. In reality in Spain coffee is enjoyed at any time of the day at home, in bars and especially in the popular cafés that adorn streets and squares all over the country, for this is a drink that does not require a specific time or excuse – it only requires sugar, for some.

In the Americas, Cuba was lost to Britain as a consequence of the Seven Years' War, which ended in 1763. However, on the signing of the Treaty of Paris in 1783, which ended the American War of Independence, the island was returned to Spain with certain conditions. Charles III could sleep again even if Florida was a high price to pay to reclaim the island. Not only was Cuba a major producer of sugar, a commodity increasingly in demand, it was a strategic point for Spain. The island had to be re-armed again. Among different concessions, Cuba was to be freed from the trade monopoly established by Spain in the Caribbean. Spain would be able to buy grain as well as agricultural equipment from the United States in return for sugar. The final chapters of Spain's dominance in the New World were beginning to be written.

Another consequence of the Seven Years' War in Europe would be the introduction of thousands of black slaves to the island by the British, a strong force of cheap labour that would change the face of the sugar plantations. For more than a century Cuba, helped by new refining technology, had been the main sugar producer of the world. Coffee was to become another crop to enrich the coffers of powerful traders who by now also had Spanish names.

## The 'Grand Tour'

The great efforts made by eighteenth-century Spanish intellectuals and politicians to catch up with advances made by other European countries were not enough to convince well-to-do British families to include Spain in the foreign journey their offspring would venture out on after they finished their studies. Such a journey was known as a 'Grand Tour'. For them France and Italy had enough beauty, history, art and good food to last them a lifetime. As far as they were concerned Spain, in the hands of absolutist kings, inadequate governments and a still intolerant Catholic Church, had been left behind by modernity. Spain was a country lost in a glorious past that was never going to return. Eventually travellers started to cross the Pyrenees, not as part of the Grand Tour but as travel writers with a critical eye, looking for an original story to tell, and simple spectators usually in need of recognition or money. The contribution of writers such as Arthur Young, William Beckford, Joseph Marshall and Alexander Jardine was much more positive, as they tried to understand the intriguing side of the Spanish soul and to appreciate its originality and uniqueness. Meanwhile others came, Bible in hand, to save souls from the tyranny of the Catholic Church. Among them were Joseph Townsend and George Borrow. Finally there was another group which included a few adventurous travellers with money to spare and who just wanted to be intoxicated by the exotic and the unknown.

### A Foreign View with an Attitude

Food served at local and country inns – *ventas and posadas* – was still severely criticized by foreign writers who had begun to travel in Spain from the early seventeenth century, and some even earlier. They were all attracted by the exotic land beyond the Pyrenees which they could not resist, even if their adventures may not always have matched their expectations. Eating a decent plate of food on arrival and resting in a comfortable and clean bed and at a local *posada* were, alas, very rare experiences. As it was not enough for a travel writer to record things as they were, they needed to use their imagination to embellish their stories. In Spain they found fertile ground to do so. In the foreword to David Mitchell's *Travellers in Spain* Tom Burns wrote: 'Almost as soon as they reached their first *posada*, they felt compelled to write about their experiences.'[23] He noted the rather sad encounters of these travellers with the food served in *posadas* and other local inns, if food was served at all. They presumed that living standards in Spain had to surpass the standards they had left behind in their own countries. 'You must buy first in one place your fire, your meat from the butcher, your wine from the tavern, your fruits, oyle and herbes from the botega, carrying all to your bed-lodgings,' commented the well-seasoned traveller William Lithgow in the 1620s.[24] While in some cases their strong criticism was unjustified, generally their comments could not have been closer to the truth. Writers from Italy, France, Britain and Germany knew that their stories and articles would bring healthy returns. Discomfort went hand in hand with a large number of exciting adventures. As these writers became better known, once home they would attract people from all spheres of society to their drawing-rooms or to the drawing-rooms of distinguished names, all eager to listen to their experiences.

Spain was a Catholic country with an intriguing and very powerful past and governed by absolute monarchs – from which lessons about despotism and religious intolerance could be drawn. Both these subjects contributed even further to the attraction of a long list of authors specializing in empires,

A travellers' *meson* (inn) in Andalusia.

climate, geography, local customs, politics, passion and even food. A century earlier and from perhaps a lesser intellectual position, two of the most famous accounts of journeys in Spain had come from France. Written by a woman whom modern historians believe had never set foot on the peninsula, Madame d'Aulnoy's *Mémoires de la court d'Espagne* (Memoirs of the Spanish Court), written in 1690, and *Relation du voyage d'Espagne* (Travels in Spain) in 1691 proved to be instant successes in fashionable Paris.[25] The way Spanish men talked to women or related to other people, the way women dressed and decorated their hair with the traditional *mantilla*, or sat on the floor while eating in the Islamic way at a social gathering, were all considered by her followers as the most fascinating stories of the time. She wrote that she was served chocolate and sweetmeats, and enjoyed partridge even if cooked in the Spanish fashion, tasty but slightly dry. Whether Madame d'Aulnoy, considered the most prolific of the fairy-tale writers of late seventeenth-century France, had ever been in Spain or not, she managed to have access to the most detailed information to be found regarding the Spanish lifestyle, included in manuscripts or in articles and essays published by writers with first-hand experience. She even copied, in a clever and rather attractive way and with considerable literary freedom, the personal memoirs of the French ambassador or perhaps, to be more precise, the work of one of the ambassador's assistants at the court of the Spanish king.

Writers from the British Isles looked at Spain in a different way from the French. Half the time they set out on their journeys with extreme caution; after all they were travelling in unknown territory, in terms not only of geography but of cultural variation and behaviour. Religion was a subject never to be touched! Some of them detested everything they saw; others became accustomed to such a different world and developed an attraction that was not difficult to explain. In many cases Andalusia was the region that attracted them most. The call to Spain was so strong from the balmy south that cities and towns such as Seville, Granada and Málaga were often favourite places for their families to stay, and perfect bases from which to move around the country searching for yet more stories to tell.

## PEOPLE'S FOOD

By the end of the eighteenth century, the political scene was far from settled in Spain and the economic situation was still cause for concern for the government, but there was optimism in the streets and in the many cafés and *mesones* where people enjoyed their leisure time. Foreign travellers were acknowledging an improvement in Spanish food and in the advances and individuality of the regional traditions. The bread was good and people already enjoyed the colour and flavour of red peppers and *pimentón*. Tomatoes and even potatoes had already been incorporated into local dishes. Dried beans, lentils and chickpea stews were still flavoured with shin of beef and sausages, made with garlic and spices or without garlic and *pimentón*, as was the case in Catalonia. People knew how to roast lamb to perfection and how to cook small game, which they prepared in rich stews or gently cooked in olive oil and vinegar. The food of the *comarcas* (geographical divisions within regions sharing agriculture, markets and food), where the true regional food of Spain originated, was already showing its diversity and personality in Galicia and the Basque provinces, as well as in Navarre and Valencia. In Catalonia writers talked about the *cocido* known as *escudella de can d'olla*, broth and meat and vegetable stew with beans and *butifarra* sausage, a regional variation on the many Castilian *ollas* and *cocidos* loved by both kings and peasants. Capons were roasted with lard, pine nuts and sultanas, and partridges were stewed with wine and a little chocolate for extra flavour. Chefs and home cooks often prepared *fricassée*, a French method of cooking that had crossed the Pyrenees. Sweet things were in abundance. There was nougat and quince paste; sweet dough fritters called *buñuelos*; sugared almonds; fruit *confituras* and light milk puddings. Across the Pyrenees in fashionable Paris, potatoes, already widely used in ordinary Spanish food, had become the talk of the town.

By the end of the century, as reality dawned, dreams of creating a fairer society soon vanished. Spain was to embark on a rollercoaster ride of social and economic decline, despite the efforts of the enlightened and lovable Charles III. Both the effects of the French Revolution and the inability of the king's successors to adapt to the country's modern needs led to the demise of the Spanish Empire. Between 1731 and 1829 the Crown's expenditure in Spain showed no appreciable movement. With a proportion of the population still hungry, 75 per cent of public expenditure continued to be allocated to the defence of the realm.

# SIX

# Politics at the Table

The Spanish custom of eating twelve grapes as the clock strikes twelve at the start of each New Year is meant to bring good luck. However, the grapes failed to bring luck at the dawn of 1800, at a time when the French and all things French were omnipresent in Europe.

### THE FRENCH ARE HERE, THERE AND EVERYWHERE

After the Spartan approach to food of some leaders of the French Revolution and the resulting disruption of food production and its distribution, the pleasures of the table slowly returned to Paris and across France. It was at that point that the words *gastronomie* and *gourmand* started to be seen in the French capital. Prestigious chefs, no longer working for the aristocracy and seeking employment, had been joining or opening restaurants serving food that, contrary to what had happened before, could now be enjoyed by many and especially by the growing bourgeoisie. Furthermore, new investors looking for profitable business had discovered the potential of *la restauración*, as the restaurant business is called in Spanish. 'Fine cooking had moved from the palace to the street', wrote Néstor Luján in his *Historia de la gastronomía*, adding that the number of restaurants in Paris had already reached the healthy figure of 2,000 in 1810.[1]

This was the time when chefs such as Marie-Antoine Carême (1784–1833) chose to establish the principles of what is known as classic cooking. To this day a good schooling in French classic cuisine remains virtually essential for anyone who wants to master the 'art of food', even if they intend to follow a different style of cuisine afterwards. Carême was much more than a renowned chef working for the top end of a new society. He was a chef in many kitchens not only in Paris but among the aristocracy around Europe. He cooked

Francisco Goya, *Charles IV of Spain and his Family*, 1800–1801.

in London for the future English king George IV, for the court of Vienna and for Alexander I in Russia. The British Embassy in Paris and the Baron de Rothschild were also among his employers. Carême went further in his aspirations by becoming a prolific author whose body of work brought classic French food to many areas of the world, including Spain. Of humble origins, he had started his career as a pastry chef. This was reflected in *Le Pâtissier royal parisien* and *Le Pâtissier pittoresque*, two of his numerous books. He also produced several kitchen compendiums to be studied by professionals across Europe and far beyond. By then French food had become universal. In Spain, thanks to the French and to an ineffective Spanish monarchy, people were still fighting wars instead of cooking.

As he posed with his entire family at Goya's studio in 1800, Charles IV of Spain, another Bourbon, appeared to be a peaceful and contented king who enjoyed the pleasures of a good table. The reaction to the large oil on canvas – which was never to become one of Goya's most popular works – by art critics was as harsh as it was controversial. In an article published in Paris, the Belgian journalist Lucien Solvay wrote: 'The Spanish royal family has numerous points of resemblance with any decent family of grocers who might have had themselves portrayed on a lucky day, still and formal, in their Sunday best.'[2]

Charles IV loved a cup of hot chocolate before breakfast, and tasty partridge and quail dishes for lunch. Surprisingly, he did not enjoy alcohol, not even the rich Canary Island Malvasía wines diluted with a little water that his father, Charles III, had relished. Nor would he share the moderation and restraint his father had shown at the table during his lifetime. He was a glutton who made constant demands on the palace kitchen, where well-known *cocineros de la servilleta*, the only cooks allowed to prepare the food of the royals, would do the honours. Names such as Manuel Rodríguez, Gabriel Alvarez and Francisco Valeta were all, perhaps surprisingly, of Spanish origin. Often, even when the royal household budget could not cope with his extravagant demands, Charles IV would ask for dishes off the menu – extra dishes which had to be paid for by him personally. Even then these were sometimes not enough to satisfy his great appetite and certainly never enough to calm his desire for meat. He was, after all, a keen hunter. While big helpings of meat had become rather unfashionable, the king could not live without them. At his table there was turkey stuffed with chestnuts and sausages, duck with turnips, fillet of pork with toasted croutons, fried black pudding, tripe Spanish-style, turkey with

Red-legged partridge; like his father, Charles IV was a enthusiastic hunter and loved eating partridge.

*macarrones*, pork cutlets with chive sauce, roast goose, marinated pork with fried eggs or veal *fricando*. He was also rather partial to a tasty chorizo sausage.

Charles IV would not be remembered for the numerous paintings he posed for at the studios of the famous artists of the time. Instead he would become known for his ineffectual reign, his early abdication and the tragic consequences of his association with France, which ended with the invasion of his country by Napoleon's troops in 1808. As if this were not enough, during his reign the complicated agrarian situation Spain had been facing would remain almost unchanged. In his magnificent large canvas portraying the execution of Spaniards by French fusiliers on 2 May 1808, Goya displayed his artistic and unique creative ability by painting the horror of the event in the most dramatic way.

The nineteenth century found Spain fighting to defend her remaining possessions in Europe and in the colonies yet again. In the European theatre of war the main players of the day were Britain, France, Portugal and Spain, all of them changing sides and alliances when required. In the colonies the wind of independence was blowing strongly. At sea, Spain had lost supremacy to Britain and trade across the oceans was permanently under threat. The alliance between Britain and Portugal was going to complicate things even further. France was feeling uneasy. Napoleon Bonaparte and Godoy, a highly questionable Spanish First Minister, decided on behalf of the king to frustrate Britain's trade aspirations. Portugal, the historic ally of England, had to be invaded. The French crossed the Pyrenees to join the Spanish army. By the following year they had conquered Portugal. With its army now in place, France conveniently decided that her troops would remain in the peninsula. Forced by the country's unrest, and under duress, the irresolute Charles abdicated in favour of his son, Ferdinand VII, a decision soon to be regretted by all.

Serious political and social disagreement confronted father and son. General Murat, Marshal of France, convinced both to travel to Bayonne to try to resolve their differences. Instead they were forced to renounce their rights to the Spanish throne. Joseph Bonaparte, Napoleon's brother, who would be known in Spain as 'Pepe Botella' for his apparent attachment to the bottle, was proclaimed king. Spain had finally been conquered and it seemed that the hopes of the French had at last become reality. In fact this was far from the case. Napoleon had underestimated not only the people's reaction in Spain but Britain's determination to avoid the consequences of such a dangerous alliance. Even if political and economic failure had bred indifference, Spaniards would strongly react to the threat of yet another invasion. Once more guerrilla warfare, a rather unorthodox but effective way to deal with the enemy, would not only capture the imagination of the country but, at a price, that of the Duke of Wellington.

On 2 May 1808 the people of Madrid rebelled against the French invaders, followed by other people all over the country. They demanded the return of the Spanish royal family. Spain embarked on a five-year war never to be forgotten. By the time Ferdinand VII, *El Deseado* (The Wanted), finally returned to Spain in 1813, the weak infrastructure of the country had been destroyed. With Ferdinand's return came peace with France for a while, but political freedom in Spain and the chance to join the economic advances already achieved by other countries in Europe would suffer a serious setback. Despite the efforts made towards a fairer society by the emergency government running the country while he was held in France, the young king decided to return to a radical form of absolutism. As expected, the Church and the aristocracy, owners of a high percentage of the land, supported him. In 1812 the Spanish parliament, the Cortes, the only existing legitimate authority during the absence of the king, had drawn up a constitution in Cádiz. As far as the king, the Church and many of noble blood were concerned, the Constitution of 1812 went too far towards freedom and liberal thinking. In 1814, Ferdinand VII declared the meeting of the Cortes in Cádiz illegal and abolished the new constitution. Consequently, the enlightened ideal of a more liberal and egalitarian society that would have allowed people to vote ended. Little did Ferdinand know that the same ideals that he had repressed in Spain would pave the way for democracy in many other countries of the Western world later on.

## THE SPANISH RECIPE AND THE GENERAL'S WIFE

During the Peninsular War, also known as the War of Independence, many monasteries and convents were sacked or destroyed by the French army. It was only the beginning of a sorrowful chapter in the history of the Catholic Church that would end in a process of disentitlement once again. In 1807, on their way to Portugal, Napoleon's troops ransacked the monastery of Alcántara in Extremadura. It has often been written that a recipe for partridges, *Perdiz al estilo de alcántara*, from the monastery's cookbook landed in the hands of General Junot's wife, the Marquise of Abrantes. As the Marquise never spoke about this preparation in her memoirs, controversy has surrounded the recipe ever since. Did this recipe, or indeed the monastery's cookbook, ever exist? Apart from partridges, which are abundant in central Spain, the recipe included a large number of highly valued ingredients such as foie gras and truffles. Did the monks use foie gras and truffles or was their dish prepared with local products? Since the region of Extremadura is situated in the path of migrant birds on their way to and from Africa, instead of foie gras monks could have used duck liver, and the local truffle-like *criadillas de tierra* (*Terfezia arenaria*) as a substitute for truffles. Port wine, another crucial ingredient in the recipe, was produced across the border, in Portugal.

It could also be argued that perhaps a visiting French friar brought the recipe to Alcántara, or that this was a French recipe which had been named by a chef following fashion and had nothing to do with Alcántara. Other recipes of unproven origin were also described in France as being prepared 'à la catalana', 'à la valenciana' or even 'à la albufera'. The great Carême created a dish to honour Mariscal Suchet, a hero of the Peninsular War who was made Duke of La Albufera. Much later, Auguste Escoffier's *Guide culinaire* (1903) would also include recipes for pheasant, snipe and partridge 'à la mode d' Alcántara'. To prepare this controversial recipe the partridges – one per person – are stuffed with foie gras and truffles and then marinated in port wine overnight. They are drained and then browned in duck fat at a high heat until golden and then placed in a large oven dish with some stock as well as port wine. The birds are cooked in the oven at a moderate heat until tender and then served with some of the sauce. By 1814 the Peninsular War was over. Wellington's troops and the *guerrilleros* celebrated a great campaign with wine and the little food still available. Even if French troops were known for their skills of extracting provisions locally, the fact that they never brought provisions with them to the peninsula would be another cause contributing to their defeat. The Spaniards made certain that the French soldiers could not find food, and Wellington had efficient ways of ensuring that the allies, especially the British, had their own supply lines permanently guaranteed.

## To Be or Not to Be: A Failed Spanish Bourgeois Revolution

The end of the War of Independence started a new chapter in the history of Spanish food. A new middle class, *la clase media*, was introducing a third way of doing things in the Spanish kitchen for people at neither the top nor the bottom of society. It is important to understand that the Spanish middle class was not strictly speaking what was considered a bourgeoisie in the rest of Europe. Initially Spain's middle class lacked economic independence in the majority of the country. While the food of the upper class was strongly influenced by French cuisine, lacking a political, social or kitchen revolution the food of the incipient Spanish middle class was influenced by tradition, especially at the beginning of the nineteenth century. This was particularly the case in Madrid, Barcelona and also Cádiz, the city that would play such a significant role in Spanish politics, at least for a while.

During the first part of the nineteenth century, modernization and the true establishment of the middle classes followed different paths in France and in Spain, two countries entangled in war and involved in a lively exchange of ideas, most of them coming from France.

Similar to what had happened in France at the end of the eighteenth century as a result of the French Revolution, the War of Independence also brought calamity to the upper end of society. As a consequence of the war, Spanish and many French chefs who had arrived in Spain after the French Revolution had to leave their privileged kitchens and look for new positions. They would eventually find work in the households of some of the landed aristocracy that, protected by the Church and the king, had managed to remain untouched. Some chefs had also opened modern restaurants with French flair, but not even in Madrid or Barcelona could they match the fabulous Parisian food scene. They tried to copy French style, recipes and professional service, but with a few exceptions they failed. The impact of the War of Independence on Spanish food could never be compared with the impact on cuisine in France after the Revolution.

Far from responding to the process of modernization and liberal thought brought about by the 1812 Constitution, the much-heralded return of Ferdinand VII from France proved to be a great disappointment. Once again Spain was beset by division and unrest. The *afrancesados* who followed progress and liberal thinking were on one side while the *tradicionalistas*, along with the king, defended the ways of the past and of absolute power on the other. Contrary to popular belief, many *afrancesados* did not necessarily follow post-Revolutionary French ideas and fashion to the letter. They were more concerned with the positive effect of the Revolution on a modern world, and for that they had to leave the country.

## Larra's Dream

In 1818, after years in exile, the *afrancesado* family of Mariano José de Larra returned to Madrid. Mariano José was to become a brilliant journalist and a political critic and activist. Soon the young Larra would become aware of the lack of freedom and the general backwardness that characterized his country. The romantic Larra would dedicate what turned out to be a short life to a relentless attack on political incompetence and to the defence of social renovation. He would always hold on to his belief in Spain and his patriotic dreams. Satire and irony were powerful tools in the hands of the accomplished liberal essayist, and he wrote extensively for the *Revista española* under the name of 'Fígaro'. In some of Larra's essays food became a powerful instrument used to serve his purpose even it was rather unfair. Sadly he committed suicide at the age of 28.

The way in which the early nineteenth-century Spanish middle class conceived all forms of social activity, including eating, was addressed sharply and critically by Larra in three major essays: 'Correspondencia del duende', 'La fonda nueva' and 'El castellano viejo'. For Larra, food was culture and refinement, and these elements were missing in the Spain he found on his return from France, especially compared with the food scene to which he had become accustomed. In the first two essays his protagonist Fígaro bitterly complains about the poor quality to be found at many inns and restaurants in the capital city. Not only was the food mediocre, he could not stand the unprofessional calibre of the waiters and their customers' low expectations. In 'La fonda nueva' (The New Inn), the protagonist is a French visitor looking for an excellence that he cannot find in Spain. 'In Madrid there are no horse races, no carriage rides, no public dances, no inns serving refined food as it should be served,' Fígaro says. In his brilliant article 'El castellano viejo' (The Old-fashioned Castilian), Larra's critical view of the hobbies of the Spanish middle class could not be harsher. The protagonist of the essay was invited to lunch by a civil servant, Braulio, 'an extremely crude man, ignorant of the most elementary rules of civil behaviour'. It is clear that from the very beginning nothing pleases Fígaro at Braulio's house, including the food served. For him the whole experience is a total disaster. Even if he admits that some of the food is tasty, Fígaro describes the *cocido* as a rather baroque dish impossible to serve with any form of distinction. He dislikes the *carne mechada* as much as he does a tough capon which is impossible to carve, probably cooked days before by a servant with little expertise or, even worse, brought from the local *fonda* for the occasion. His description of the lady of the house is no better, nor any of the wines selected by the host.[3]

In reality Larra's criticism of food eaten by the Spanish middle class was rather unfair. For the first time tasty and nutritious, well-balanced dishes were being prepared by family cooks for this new level of society, even if in the first part of the century Spanish cookery books were still scarce.

## HOME COOKING REVISITED

Perhaps Larra would have changed his critical views if he had been living and writing in late nineteenth-century Andalusia, where tasty recipes written in old and new *recetarios domésticos* (home cooking manuscripts) had become fashionable. These documents were allowing the follow-up of culinary traditions, and were an important source of socioeconomic and cultural information. The fashion had been helped by the inclusion of cooking classes in the curriculum imparted to young women by religious orders and lay educational institutions.

Some of the manuscripts were copied from originals which had been passed down from mothers to daughters for generations, while others were written at that time. Isabel González Turmo, a professor of anthropology at the University of Seville, has been studying a revealing collection of 43 manuscripts covering almost two hundred years of the history of Andalusian food in villages and towns in the provinces of Seville, Cádiz, Huelva and Granada. In González Turmo's opinion, domestic manuscripts provide information about the food that should be eaten, rather than the food eaten in the family in reality. They also provide insights into the food people preferred, the ingredients home cooks could find in the market and those they could not find. New kitchen techniques were also included in the manuscripts. Furthermore they demonstrated how culinary knowledge was transferred down the generations and by whom. While González Turmo's book, *200 años de cocina*, emphasizes the role women have always played in the transmission of culinary knowledge in Spain, it clearly separates this from the art of cooking. In home cooking this has always been considered as a '*don*', a divine talent some people are born with but which is not necessarily inherited or transferable. Independent of the above, *200 años* provides the reader with a faithful account not only of the evolution of life and food in Andalusia over a long period of time but of the travails of a country trying to catch up with the advanced green as well as the industrial revolutions that were taking place in northern Europe. In the words of González Turmo: 'In Spain the nineteenth century was as complicated and irregular as it was reformist and reactionary.'[4]

Contrary to the success cookbooks had in the previous century, the publication of cookbooks in the Castilian language in the first part of the nineteenth century lost momentum, apart from several reprints of two acclaimed seventeenth-century books: Martínez Montiño's *Arte de cocina* and Juan de Altimiras's *Nuevo arte de cocina*. In culinary terms Catalonia would become the centre of attention again.

## LA CUYNERA CATALANA

Since medieval times, cookbooks had been mostly published in Castile and Catalonia. Now the spotlight was moving more towards the latter. While the Castilian economy seemed to be in permanent disarray, development in Catalonia, especially Barcelona, was notable. A successful textile industry and a growing middle class with cash in hand and a taste for the good things in life had resulted in a growing interest in local food and recipes. *La cuynera catalana: o sia, reglas utils, facils segures i economiques per cuinar be, escudillas dels autors qui millor han escrit sobre aquesta materia* (The Catalan Cook: That Is to Say, Useful, Easy, Safe and Economic Rules for Cooking Well Written by the Best Authors on the Subject) is the title of an anonymous cookbook and practical guide written in verse and printed in Barcelona in 1851. This book has to be considered a ground-breaking publication in the field of regional food in general and Catalan food in particular. It purposely targeted Catalan women cooking and entertaining at home, which was rather unusual as the majority of cookbooks written at the time addressed the needs of the professional cook, always a man.

In one of the verses, *La cuynera* recommends the use of plenty of olive oil in the preparation of rich *sofritos*, as well as explaining how to prepare dishes for partridges, lamb, chicken and beef:

> *No mires nostre profit*
> *ni menos nostra ganancia*
> *gestalt oil en abundancia*
> *no t' saps tourer del pregit*
> *aten á lo que t' tinch dit*
> *mira lo que est llibre te diu*
> *sabrás de guisar perdiu*
> *moltó, gallinas y bou*
> *Va, mentressa i tinch prou,*
> *de gustos ningú n' escriu.*

> Don't look for benefit
> Nor for gain
> Using oil in abundance
> The *sofrito* won't die
> Listen to my words
> See what the book says

You will know how to cook a partridge
Lamb, chicken and ox
Yes madam I have enough
Nobody writes about taste.[5]

The 'Catalan Cook' makes it easy to understand the principles on which today's Catalan food is based. It was published in four two-part instalments in pamphlet form: one for guidance and practicalities, the other for recipes. How to become an accomplished home cook and how to clean and maintain order in the kitchen are two themes treated with care and attention in Part I, together with thirty recipes for broths, soups and stews, another twenty for vegetables and greens, and a further fifty for meat and offal dishes. Part II is a guide to etiquette and the best practice to be followed when entertaining guests at home. The section dealing with sweet and savoury pastries and pies made with all kinds of ingredients, as well as sweets and desserts, follows a good old-fashioned medieval method, never to be forgotten in the Catalan world of cooking. One of the recipes included among the desserts is *mató de monja*. This is a rather confusing title as it does not actually include *mató*, a type of ricotta. Originating from the medieval *manjar blanc*, listed in both *Sent Soví* and the *Llibre de Coch*, *mató de monja* does not include chicken breast, which is one of the main components of the medieval recipe. By the nineteenth century the recipe had evolved from being a rather sweet main course to being a proper dessert. *Mató de monja*, also known these days as *Mató de Pedralba*, is made with almond milk, cow's milk, lemon peel, cinnamon, sugar, water and a little corn flour. The almonds are first peeled, ground and covered with water for several hours. When the almonds are tender they are pressed to obtain as much almond milk as possible. When it is ready the cow's milk, together with the sugar, lemon peel and cinnamon, is brought to the boil and then sieved. Then the flavoured milk is blended with the almond milk and the cornflour, which has been dissolved in fresh milk. Stirring constantly, the blend is slowly brought to the boil, sieved again and poured over the dish.

## A HANDBOOK FOR TRAVELLERS IN SPAIN

'The national cooking of Spain is Oriental and the ruling principle of it is stewing,' wrote Richard Ford in his *Handbook for Travellers in Spain and Readers at Home*.[6] Ford (1796–1858), a gentleman of independent means, had returned to England from an extensive journey in Spain carrying a manuscript to be published. He was an Oxford graduate, a lawyer, and above all a travel writer who loved to collect art. He was also stoutly anti-papist and a Francophobe. He had settled in Seville with his family while writing a travellers' guide that would bring him fame.

As mentioned before, from the seventeenth century and especially during the nineteenth century, foreign travellers, with one or two distinguished exceptions, criticized Spain mercilessly. They included Americans, Frenchmen, Britons and even Danes. Despite their critical accounts, many of them became addicted to an original, colourful and unspoilt world which had all but vanished from their industrialized and money-driven societies. Upper-class British travel writers in particular found a rich source of deficiencies to find fault with in Spain. As had been seen two centuries before, critical writing assured the writers' approval from both their publishers and their bank managers. They would mock the powerful Spanish clergy, the inadequate aristocracy, the self-destructive male pride and, above all, the dangerous roads with real *bandoleros*. In most cases they were abusive and eloquent but they were never indifferent. These writers were, among others, Alexandre Dumas, Théophile Gautier, George Borrow, Hans Christian Andersen, Lord Byron, and above all Richard Ford, the author of *A Handbook for Travellers in Spain*. To many followers of the subject, Ford's handbook was and still is one of the most compelling recollections to be found. Well researched over many years of living and travelling throughout Spain, and published in London in 1845, it would become an instant success. His travel book was full of humour and fine detail covering politics, history and art, people's food and the *refranes*

Gustave Doré, *A Scene from El Tío Caniyitas in the Zarzuela de M. Soriano Fuentes*, 1874.

(local sayings) he learned at country inns. There is no doubt that for Ford, a traveller who appreciated the pleasures of life, food mattered as much as the network of hotels and inns to be found scattered around the countryside. Even if Spanish inns never met the expectations of the foreign traveller, they proved to be a valuable source of new and exciting material, just as they were places to meet the most fascinating characters. Ford's perfect use of the extensive *refranero español* in his writing provides a clear picture not only of his deep understanding of the language but of the precise way Spaniards quote from the *refranero*. He had learned to use the *refranes* over a glass of *tinto* with local travellers sitting comfortably in front of a fire.

The collection of recipes Ford included in his book is a comprehensive list of Spanish traditional dishes, written in a precise way. This was the same food that was served at his family home in Seville by one of his servants, the same style of food he probably would have tasted in one of the *ventas* or *posadas* he mentions in his book. As in the past, good food was not necessarily associated with the lodgings which affluent foreigners had to endure when in search of something to eat or some rest, ideally free from fleas. For this reason he recommended hiring a good local servant who could fulfil certain important credentials. Cooking and purchasing food were high on the agenda. The innkeeper usually provided cooking facilities, but the food he supplied, if available, was rarely of good quality.

Ford's recipe list starts, unsurprisingly, with the most traditional preparation of all, the *olla*. For the author this was a synonym for the dinner of the Spaniards although his version was prepared in a rather original way. He recommended that the reader use two pots instead of one. This missed the point of the exercise completely, which was the benefit of cooking all sorts of meat, pulses and vegetables in the same pot. Ford's *olla* was a rich preparation with chickpeas, pumpkin, carrots, chard, *fideo* pasta, beans, celery, garlic, onions and a few leaves of *escarola* or frisée lettuce in the first pot, covered with water. In the second pot, chorizo sausage from the town of Montánchez, Catalan *longanizas* from Vic, black pudding, half a salted head of pork (already desalted), a chicken and a piece of beef were all simmered for hours in plenty of water. As with all *ollas*, this is a dish served in three courses. The first is a substantial soup or broth followed by the pulses and the vegetables as a second course. The tender sausages and meats are served as a third course. Ford also included in his book recipes for onion soup, a vegetable-and-meat omelette, marinated and fried brains, and a salad flavoured with tarragon and onions dressed with a vinaigrette.

Ford also included a partridge or hare stew and added a recipe for *gazpacho*, which, he wrote, in its early form was of Roman and Arabic origin, made with onions, garlic, cucumber and peppers, bread, water, olive oil, vinegar and salt, but without tomatoes. By then tomatoes were being eaten by the locals but not by the upper classes. Ford went even further by adding another preparation of Arabic origin known in Spain as *agraz* or *verjus* (verjuice) that had frequently been used in medieval cooking in Europe as an ingredient in sauces, as a condiment or to deglaze preparations. It was and still is obtained by pressing green grapes. *Agraz* was also prepared in Andalusia as a refreshing drink made with sugar, water, and crushed and filtered grapes; the drink was served with ice and even with a drop or two of Manzanilla sherry.

Ford was also interested in the type of fats used in different parts of the country, including olive oil and lard. Even if the quality of the butter in Spain could not be compared with the butter produced in Ireland or in Flanders, he appeared to be surprised by the widespread use of olive oil instead of butter in the peninsula. Ford asked himself, were the ancient *Iberos* not great users of butter, as Strabo had recorded? Surprisingly he did not include a recipe for the humble *tortilla de patatas*, a dish always cooked in olive oil and included in nineteenth-century Spanish cookbooks. The inclusion of two recipes using olive oil is very revealing: *huevos estrellados*, eggs fried in olive oil, and *pollo con arroz* cooked in the Valencian style confirmed Ford's belief that the regional recipes he selected were the best examples of Spanish food of the time.

Spanish omelette, showing what Richard Ford's omelette would have looked like.

## A Lady with a Good Appetite

Another war, this time a civil war, was brewing as little Isabella, Princess of Asturias and the oldest daughter of Ferdinand VII, played in the royal gardens. The year was 1833. Thinking he was dying, the king abolished the French Salic Law with regard to female succession first introduced by Philip V. This would allow Isabella to ascend the Spanish throne under the regency of her mother. Under no circumstances would Don Carlos, the late king's brother, accept this. As a man he considered himself to be the rightful heir to the crown. As a consequence of Isabella becoming queen, a disastrous period of civil wars followed, as old and new values confronted each other; the absolutism and clericalism of Don Carlos versus the queen and the liberal tendencies of the country. People in the Basque Country, some outposts of Catalonia and Aragon, and especially those in profoundly Catholic Navarre, backed Don Carlos. The strengthening of a depleted royalist army needed to defend Isabella's rights required strong financial support the country could not afford. As a consequence, the fate of a large percentage of ecclesiastical property was sealed, and the principle of liberal thought as established in the 1812 Constitution had finally to be accepted by the Bourbon monarchy. From now on the sovereignty of the nation would reside with the Crown together with a bicameral parliament: El Congreso de los Diputados and El Senado. For all the players, the ending of the First Carlist War (1833–40) became a priority. Minister Mendizábal, in charge of the finances of the country, found a solution. He would implement a liberal programme of agrarian reform starting, once again, with the disentitlement of municipal and Church property, as well as the transfer of tithes and other contributions historically owed to the Church. The state would then redistribute the land at a handsome profit. The war stopped, but the selling of the land would never accomplish the social benefit heralded initially by Mendizábal. A very high proportion of land still ended up in the hands of the less needy. There was to be further deprivation with laws introduced in 1855, which legislated for the sale of common land. The rights of the people to use those lands for hunting food, to make charcoal or for pasture, would be lost forever. However, Navarre was the exception. Thanks to Vergara's peace agreement, signed between General Espartero on behalf of the queen and the government and the Carlist general Maroto, not only did the war end but Navarre managed to retain its ancient *fueros* and communal lands.

Although liberal ministers had again succeeded in the unification of the country and to a certain extent in the redistribution of the land, they did not manage to obtain their goal: the higher agrarian output so badly needed to bring the country more into line with the demands of a free market, even if the country's wheat supplies were guaranteed at least for the time being.

This was good news for bread-loving Spaniards. As a consequence of the enlargement of cultivated land, wheat shared equal status with potatoes in people's diets, and started to replace cereals of lesser quality. In the north of the country, in green Spain, corn destined for animal feed would become a nineteenth-century agrarian success, only to be surpassed thirty years later by a huge increase in vine planting in La Mancha, Rioja, Valencia and Catalonia. The French wine crisis brought about by phylloxera resulted in the destruction of 40 per cent of France's vineyards. As a result, Spanish wine exports enjoyed a highly profitable period between 1877 and 1893. Later the American plague would also reach Spain with equal devastation. After that, and for a long period, Spanish agricultural exports, fighting strong competition from North America, Argentina and the Balkans, would face a very serious setback as the country entered into one of the worst periods of its long history.[7]

Queen Isabella II, a passionate woman with more than a healthy appetite and a sweet tooth, had introduced some changes to the informal kitchen of the palace. These changes were more in tune with the changes taking place in the kitchens of the middle class. All Spaniards loved bread as well as other simple but tasty food, and Queen Isabella was no exception. As a result bread-making benefited hugely during her reign. She also favoured well-known regional dishes prepared by professional chefs. This also brought some changes to the specialities associated with the very French Bourbon table which always featured on formal and state occasions. She loved *albóndigas en salsa* (meatballs in a rich sauce), cod in a rich tomato sauce, and chicken with rice and saffron, often eating several helpings for lunch. She also enjoyed *paella*, *cocido* and above all *callos a la madrileña*, or tripe Madrid-style. Another favourite dish was *croquetas*, a Spanish version of the popular French dish with the lightest and most flavoursome *salsa bechamela*, and fried in olive oil. The queen enjoyed hunting, as did her ancestors, but she did not share their passion for eating game. What she inherited from them was a strong taste for chocolate and above all for rich biscuits made with cream.

Isabella was a frequent visitor to the most fashionable restaurants of the capital, and restaurants were springing up all over Spain. The fashion had developed for them to serve French food as well as a number of Spanish regional recipes that were popular with customers. Lhardy, a restaurant destined to become very popular with the royals as well as with the aristocracy, opened its doors in the Carrera de San Gerónimo in Madrid in 1839. It belonged to Agustín Lhardy, a Swiss entrepreneur who also owned restaurants of the same name in Paris and Bordeaux. In Madrid the fame of its rich consommé, its traditional *cocido*, and the sweet and savoury pastries that are still served today was unsurpassed. Other restaurants such as Fornos, El Hotel Inglés and El Viejo Botín, also in the capital, were attracting an equally healthy clientele. In Barcelona, the Grand Restaurant de France and the 7 Portes had also become very successful. At the same time, thanks to the egalitarian spirit that would characterize nineteenth-century Spain, restaurant food started to influence the traditional fare offered by the *mesones* and *casas de comida* favoured by the lower middle class in a positive way. However, excellence in the kitchens in these establishments still had a long way to go.

The railway, making previously impossible routes viable, had started to transport passengers who, as they arrived in towns and cities, required food and/or refreshments. Coffee shops were rapidly becoming popular. They were a sophisticated alternative to the old *botillerías* and *chocolaterías* that had served chocolate and other refreshments up until then. Reading the words written at the end of the eighteenth century by Jean-Marie-Jérôme Fleuriot de Langle in his acclaimed *Voyage de Figaro* it was not surprising that his own countrymen, normally so critical of all things Spanish, had to agree that the coffee in Spain was truly excellent:

Lhardy in Madrid, Queen Isabella II of Spain's favourite restaurant.

208

I believe Madrid is the place on Earth where you can taste the best coffee. A delicious drink a hundred times more delicious than all the liqueurs in the world . . . Coffee makes you happy, gives you energy, electrifies you. Coffee fills the head with ideas . . .[8]

By the nineteenth century coffee had become associated with the political and intellectual Spanish classes, and especially with the informal political debates known in Spain as *tertulias* that, taking place in famous cafés all over the country, attracted liberal and conservative discussion. Spanish cafés were elegant, well-decorated places where comfortable sofas shared the space with small, feminine tables. Competent waiters served coffee sporting fashionable white shirts and long black aprons *a la francesa*, an outfit that would have met with the approval of the critical Mariano José de Larra a century before. In the streets the atmosphere was tense, and after the short revolution of 1868 Queen Isabella and her family left for Paris, never to return.

Despite its short length, this revolution has been described as the most interesting period of Spanish modern history. It marks the transition from the Spain of Ferdinand VII to that of his daughter Isabella II and his grandson Alfonso XII. Edward Henry Strobel, an American diplomat serving at the time as First Secretary of the American delegation, reported that on 30 September 1868 the royal family, amid the silence of the assembled crowds, left San Sebastián for a life in exile in France. At Biarritz, Eugénie de Montijo, the wife of Napoleon III, was waiting for Isabella II of Spain.[9] Strobel and other historians concur that Isabella had failed to deliver on the expectations she had created in the country. Her indulgence in political and personal excesses, including food, would result in her downfall. The navy rebelled in Cádiz, the city associated with freedom and with the Constitution which she had failed to respect. The army and the rest of the country also rose up in rebellion. Two years later in Paris, on 24 June 1870, Queen Isabella abdicated in favour of her son, Alfonso de Bourbon. Meanwhile, in Spain politicians, permanently in disagreement, were confronted with the difficulty of finding a substitute. Their decision to install as king a prince of the House of Savoy, Amadeo I, would end in a republic which would also fail to stabilize the country politically and economically. Another monarchy seemed to be the way forward.

A well-known politician, Antonio Cánovas del Castillo, who would later become prime minister, played a major role in the restoration of the Spanish Bourbon monarchy. The long period of *La Restauración Borbónica* started with the arrival from exile of King Alfonso XII. Alfonso brought renewed optimism

The sculpture *La Tertulia* in front of the modern Café Moderno, Pontevedra.

to the country even if, during the king's honeymoon, a pastry chef named Otero shot at the king's carriage as it passed through Madrid's El Retiro park.

Minister Cánovas del Castillo was also responsible for drafting legislation which formalized a new constitutional monarchy. Regrettably the well-intentioned but badly designed democratic political system, based on the British system, was flawed. In Spain the two most influential parties would alternate in government, helped when needed by the intervention of military coups – *pronunciamientos* – from that point onwards.

## Sopa o Soupe

Richard Ford had rightly criticized the efforts made in Spain by professional chefs to achieve success by copying and serving French dishes to the upper classes. He believed that the desire to imitate foreigners had ruined Spanish cooks. It can be said that, apart from the honesty and simplicity to be found in local and regional traditions, Spanish food created in the shadow of France was made to impress more than to please the palate. Paris, and not Madrid, was still the main cultural reference for the Spanish urban and fast-growing middle classes.

Badly executed French recipes, often cooked with the wrong ingredients, not only in reputable restaurants but also in the home, would give Spanish food a bad name that would last at least for another century. This was further aggravated by the impact of French cookery books on Spanish food writing. The majority of the books published in the first part of the nineteenth century in Spain were translations or practically copies of original French texts. In response to this, Spanish regional food – the real food of Spain – started to seek its own identity. Could the regional food of Spain ever be considered as the 'national cuisine' of the country? This was a question that started to be strongly debated by food writers and critics. With time, some of these critics become the authors of the most representative cookbooks written during this era. Helped along by the efforts of a number of well-known Spanish novelists who were using food as an intrinsic part of their stories, food writing would enter into the world of political and social discussion. The country had to move forward and try to catch up with modernity and the progress that other European countries had already made.

Towards the end of the nineteenth century and the beginning of the twentieth, Spanish food texts written by experts, critics and publicists reflected the conflict that existed between different philosophies. Some writers were defenders of French and cosmopolitan styles and their influence on popular culture; others saw French food as a serious threat to the tradition they believed represented the culinary heritage of their nation.[10] For the latter group, regional food represented the national cuisine of Spain, full of promise and indigenous character, but suffering from years of neglect. They had convinced themselves that the individuality and diversity found in different parts of the country were not an obstacle to their claim. A further group, perhaps thinking in a more realistic way, was trying to find a place for Spanish regional signature dishes that were slowly positioning themselves among authentically French dishes or those of other countries without substituting for them completely. A long list of names – mostly writers and a limited number of kitchen professionals – defended their position forcefully in newspapers, essays and books. These included D. Mariano Pardo y Figueroa (1828–1918), José de Castro y Serrano (1829–1896), Angel Muro (1839–1897), Emilia Pardo Bazán (1851–1921) and Manuel María Puga y Parga (Picadillo) (1874–1918). Working well into the twentieth century, another equally important group has to be added to the list: Dionisio Pérez, known as Post-Thebussem (1872–1935), María Mestayer de Echagüe, also known as Marquesa de Parabere (1877–1949), and two eloquent chefs and prolific authors, Ignasi Domènech (1874–1957) and Teodoro Bardají (1882–1958).

*La mesa moderna* (The Modern Table), published in 1878 at the heart of the Bourbon Restoration, highlights the strong nationalistic view needed in Spain. The country was in the hands of a failing political class incapable of implementing the right strategies and was in search of an identity. *La mesa moderna* is not a cookbook or a cook's dictionary, nor is it a satire. It is a compilation of letters exchanged between two writers and friends who were well aware, as were others, of the poor state of the food they defended as being the true cuisine of Spain, against the dominance of French food. Mariano Pardo de Figueroa, known as Dr Thebussem, an anagram of the Spanish word *embuste* (lie) to which he had prefixed the letters THE to add an international flair, was a lawyer and a food writer. José de Castro y Serrano was a judge and gastronomic critic who wrote under the unusual pen name Un Cocinero de Su Majestad (His Majesty's Chef). Both admirers of King Alfonso XII, they decided to dedicate their epistolary exchange to him. Both authors were well-known literary figures who in their letters appear to have taken opposite views on the subject of the food eaten in nineteenth-century Spain: traditional fare versus the modern intruder. Dr Thebussem was fanatical in his defence of the glorious regional food of the country; José de Castro y Serrano apparently positioned himself with France and its haute cuisine, while still realistically defending the best dishes of the Spanish regions. Eventually they came together as strong critics of what they considered to be a threat to the real food of Spain and the wellbeing of the nation. After all, didn't French tradition include numerous unhealthy practices undesirable at any cost? The letters were published four times a year between 1869 and 1921 in *La ilustración española y americana*, a Spanish magazine modelled on other prestigious European magazines such as *L'illustratrazione italiana* and the French equivalents *L'Illustration* and *Le Monde illustré*. In their quest, Dr Thebussem and 'His Majesty's Chef' (or 'HM's Chef') had two main objectives: first, to analyse the poor state of Spanish food, and second, to encourage writers and cooks to defend the original and authentic character of the Spanish kitchen, dismissing the influence that the French Revolution and the Belle Époque had on the elitist Spanish table.

'Why does celebratory food served at the palace have to be written in French?' asked Dr Thebussem. 'If Roast Beef is served happily at the English court, *Sauerkraut* by the German and *Polenta* by the Italian, why cannot the *Olla Podrida*, the saviour of the nation, be present as it was once, at the tables of the king of Spain?' he added. The reply came emphatically from HM's Chef:

French is the language of the modern table as much as it is the language of diplomacy . . . France is the only language that speaks the true language of gastronomy; the rest of the nations only cook in dialects.[11]

As the exchange progresses, the position of the authors becomes clearer. While HM's Chef does not object to the original names of dishes from different countries appearing in their respective languages, he does object when practically all the dishes, the table decoration, the way the food is served, the way it is carved and the way it is eaten follow French custom. He considers unnecessary the *plateau* (a large flat tray for decoration which took up the centre of the broad table's surface) and its flowers, the fruits and the lights, as the only thing they do is hinder gentlemen from admiring the beauty of a lady sitting across the table. HM's Chef dislikes the long rectangular tables that so limit the possibilities of conversation with several people during lunch or dinner while defending small round tables where eight or ten diners can easily converse together. He also dislikes the waiters, often dressed better than the guests, serving food from large dishes and exercising portion control. For HM's Chef the same serving dishes should be placed on the table so people can serve themselves as often and as much as they want, while helping others to do the same.

Nothing escapes the attention of HM's Chef, including the order in which the different courses are served. Why should all fish be served after the soup and before the meat? Why should fried food, one of the best examples of culinary chemistry, be avoided? In his opinion French people do not really know how to fry; they are simply worried that fried food, one of the pleasures of life, cannot be covered with yet another rich sauce that hides lack of freshness. He is equally determined to comment on another subject of similar importance at any respectable dinner: the wines to be served. First, he defends the inclusion of wines on menus, where people can read what they will eat and drink; then he once again advocates freedom at the table by adding that each person sat at the table should be allowed to choose the wines they want to drink from those on the menu. He recommends the use of small notebooks, similar to the ones used by ladies at a dance, to request the order in which they wish to receive the wines. In this way the waiter could easily read each person's choice of wine with each dish, avoiding unnecessary exchanges between waiter and guest. For HM's Chef, using notebooks would also allow some form of order that could improve the chaotic way wines were usually served by the country's elite: with oysters, Sauternes; with the soup, sherry; with the fish course, beer; with the entrées, Bordeaux; with poultry, Tokay; with roasted meats, Champagne. He was convinced that in the Spanish world of wine a radical change was needed. Dr Thebussem, who would disagree with HM's Chef about some of his statements while agreeing over many others as they proceeded on their epistolary exchange, was delighted. Despite the efforts of the authors, *La mesa moderna* would not achieve recognition as a ground-breaking work although it would later influence such inspired writers as Dionisio Pérez, who adopted the pseudonym 'Post-Thebussem'.

*El practicón: tratado completo de cocina al alcance de todos y aprovechamiento de sobras* (The Practitioner: A Complete Cookbook for All and Use of Leftovers), written by Angel Muro in 1894, is considered by many scholars to be not only culturally relevant but the 'best-selling' Spanish cookbook of all time. Muro, who was born in Andalusia, was not a chef but a publicist and journalist who wrote for newspapers and magazines such as *Blanco y Negro*, *La Esfera* and *La Monarquía*. In South Africa he became foreign correspondent for the Puerto Rican daily *El imparcial*, but it was in Paris, where he lived and worked for a number of years, that he would finally develop a strong passion for all things food-related. A prolific writer of great intellect, he left an extensive collection of essays and recipes, as well as practical recommendations that shed light on the food eaten by the Spanish establishment and the upper middle class during *La Restauración* (1874–1931). In accordance with the tastes of the times, *El practicón* defends both

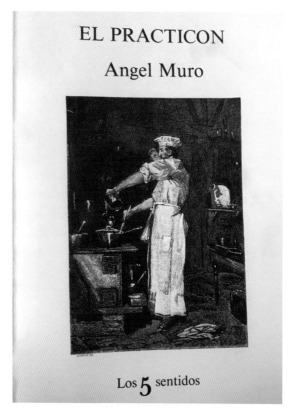

*El practicón* by Angel Muro, 1982 edition.

the virtues of Spanish traditional food and those of the cosmopolitan kitchen, which were not only French in influence but Italian and even German. Nothing escaped the attention of the author. Together with hundreds of recipes, Muro included a dictionary of culinary terms, a guide to wines and hygiene, and a compendium about manners.[12]

Countess Emilia Pardo Bazán (1851–1921) was a well-known novelist and an admirer of the French philosopher Émile Zola. Among many other books dealing with all sorts of topics not necessarily associated with women, she had been working on a series of books published under the generic name *Biblioteca de la mujer* (Women's Library). Here her intention was clear. She would provide Spanish women with up-to-date information on the progress of feminism in Europe. In an unusual move by a successful novelist, she decided to write two cookbooks, or *libros de fogón*, as she called them: *La cocina española antigua* (1913), and *La cocina española moderna* (1917).[13] By mentioning the slightly derogative word *fogón* (stove), it appears that she was purposely detaching herself from the serious matters her readers had been accustomed to, entering into an indisputably female world. In reality she was joining the national intellectual debate about food. Following Muro's way of thinking in a realistic manner, Pardo Bazán covered the food eaten in Spain from all possible angles: from the regional and the traditional to the modern approach to food and cookery represented by France.

Rebecca Ingram of the University of San Diego defines Pardo Bazán's culinary project as 'coherent with wider nation-building discourses, reviling

Emilia Pardo Bazán, an exceptional writer. Her statue is in Galicia.

the class divisions at the heart of Spanish liberal nationalism'.[14] Her *La cocina española antigua* is an extensive compilation of recipes representing an idealized *pueblo*. Some of the recipes are from Galicia, the birthplace of the author, and others are taken from different parts of the country. A third group are borrowed from prestigious writers and chefs working and writing in Spain at the time such as Domènech, Muro or Puga y Parga (Picadillo). Again in the words of Ingram:

> The modern cuisine Bazan presents in *La Cocina Española Moderna* becomes a practice of anxious middle classes, in which she substitutes tradition for elegance as the defining characteristic of Spain's national prominence.

Is Pardo Bazán pro-French or decidedly pro-Spanish? Some experts have been asking this question, with most taking the view that she leaned more towards Spain. Lara Anderson, an expert on Spanish and South American studies at the University of Melbourne, disagrees. She believes that Pardo Bazán contradicts herself as a serious writer and thinker. She has a clear desire to proclaim the virtues of Spanish regional food, but to respond to her literary needs she also needs to borrow from modern French culture.[15]

## A YEAR TO FORGET: 1898

It had become clear that the Empire was crumbling. By the 1820s, with Ferdinand VII still on the throne, Argentina and Chile had gained independence and Simón Bolívar was gaining ground in the northern territories of South America. All that was left were the Philippines, Puerto Rico, Cuba and the sugar-rich plantations of the Caribbean Islands, with their own interests at heart. Things would change dramatically during the period 1895–8, three years that the Spanish political and intellectual classes probably wished had never happened. The loss of Central and South American colonies had serious commercial consequences for Spain, particularly for the wheat and textile traders in Castile and in Catalonia, yet Spain reacted in a positive way by increasing its trade interests with Europe as well as in Cuba, its most important trading base. However, sugar had become a very important commodity, not only for Britain but for the United States. *La suerte estaba echada!* (Luck was running out). In 1898, Spain lost the war with the United States. Her forces, *los últimos de Cuba, Filipinas y Puerto Rico*, 'the last ones', had to return to their garrisons in a defeated and humiliated Spain. What is interesting is that the economic implications of the loss of the islands were less severe than the loss of the mainland American colonies. With regard to Cuba, as most of the merchant firms and properties owned by Spaniards on the island were unaffected by independence, most Spanish shipping companies managed to remain in business.

The Spaniards had lost face and they could not cope with being defeated. For Spain, America had been an exciting and costly adventure that had lasted over four hundred years. In the end, the drama and serious consequences of the events of 1898 should not be entirely and exclusively associated with the loss of the war with the U.S. nor with the loss of the last colonies. Some modern historians are of the opinion that the excessively negative reaction of Spain, and the decision to close Spain's borders to international markets, delayed the industrialization and progress of the country even further. As economic history teaches, protectionist measures do not guarantee success – the contrary is often true. Incapable of maintaining the speed at which other countries in Europe were moving towards prosperity and the modern world, Spain was left behind yet again. This was almost a repeat of what had happened two centuries before. Now the Spanish nation was in tatters and needed to be rebuilt. To an interesting degree, help was to come again from men and women of letters who were determined to restore Spain to the position of intellectual and literary prominence it had not held for a long time. In literature a group of essayists and novelists working in many different fields, known as the 'Generation of '98', would lead the way: Miguel de Unamuno, Azorín, Valle-Inclán, Pío Baroja, Blasco Ibáñez and José Ortega y Gasset – all had in common a desire to shake the Spanish people out of what they saw as apathy and to restore a sense of national pride. The majority of them spoke a language easy to understand that also encouraged food writers and cooks, journalist and chefs to defend the very distinctive food and wine culture the country had inherited from its own rich past, the regional food of Spain.[16]

## CARMENCITA, THE GOOD COOK

To prepare rabbit *final de siglo*, sauté – in a traditional earthenware *cazuela* – chopped onions and tomatoes in some lard. In a frying pan, sauté the pieces of rabbit coated with flour. Transfer the rabbit to the *cazuela* with the onion and tomato, adding an almond *picada* sauce flavoured with lemon rind. This dish is served with small omelettes made with blanched endive leaves. The omelettes are added to the *cazuela* just before serving.

The original recipe belongs to a cookbook written in 1899 by a Catalan mother who was determined to ensure that one day her daughter would be able to prepare food and feed her own family as she should. It is a rich compilation of recipes from the kitchen of a comfortable house in Barcelona. *Carmencita, o la buena cocinera* would become an instant best-seller at a time when publishers were more interested in the food prepared in the kitchens of famous chefs, who were still in most cases influenced by France. On 5 January 1899, Barcelona's most prestigious newspaper, *La Vanguardia*, recommended the book. This was unheard of and many prestigious Catalan chefs protested. The newspaper reported:

> The distinguished Señora Doña Eladia M. de Carpinell has published *Carmencita, o la buena cocinera*, a very useful cookbook that we recommend to our readers for its clarity and the exact measure of the ingredients. It can be purchased from the author at the following address: 1st floor, 2a, 16 De los Angeles Street. It can also be purchased from El Colmado de Padros, 38 Ronda de San Pedro, and from El Colmado de Antonell, 66 Lauria Street [in Catalonia a *colmado* is a food and wine shop].

What Doña Eladia did not know is that the next century would bring years of hunger and desolation to her own city and to the entire country. Nevertheless her book was to be reprinted numerous times.[17]

An illustration from *Carmencita, o la buena cocinera*, 1899.

# SEVEN

# Hunger, Hope and Success

Spain smells as hot bread does, it smells as freshly ironed linen does,
as dust and as the sea. It also smells like the days of the *matanza* in winter
and of fresh fruit in summer, of friendship and of flowers, of pottery before it
is baked, of wine, of coriander, of bull fighting, of fresh milk and of children,
of vinegar, of *pimentón*, of black tobacco, of *anís* liqueur, of sheep
and of many things more . . .
Ismael Díaz Yubero[1]

Even if electricity would bring dramatic changes in the way people lived and
ate, the twentieth century opened in Spain with the heavy economic and
political burdens it had inherited from the previous century.

The accession of Alfonso XIII took place in 1902 when his mother, the
Queen Regent, abdicated. Due to the premature death of his father, Alfonso
XII, he had been king-in-waiting since his birth in 1886. Unfortunately for
Spain, he did not have the upbringing or the strength of character needed to
rule a country in social and economic chaos that was seeking international
recognition. Not even his marriage to an English princess, Victoria Eugénie
of Battenberg, would help. An anecdote recorded by the Spanish press stated
that a wedding cake would be served at the royal wedding banquet for the first
time. It was a foreign tradition after all. The cake, 1.1 metres (43 in.) high and
weighing more than 300 kilograms (660 lb), had been decorated with icing
sugar to represent a Spanish vineyard. It had been prepared in honour of the
new queen by English pastry chefs.

The peculiar parliamentary system in Spain, in which parties and prime
ministers changed as often as the seasons of the year, would aggravate the
situation in which the king found himself. His appointment of Miguel Primo

de Rivera – an aristocrat and an army officer who would later turn dictator – as prime minister would prove to be an unfortunate one. Eventually some of the king's decisions would cost him his crown. At the same time, writers including chefs and cooks were still searching for a national identity. 'Each Spanish *comarca* has a dish good enough to be served at the palaces of the world. Let's ask each one for their recipe, and let us make a repertoire of illustrious Spanish traditional dishes,' HM's Chef had written in 1888 in *La mesa moderna*.[2]

Dionisio Pérez, a well-known writer and passionate defender of the regional food of Spain, chose these words for the first page of a book that was to become a defining moment in the history of Spanish food. A very capable and knowledgeable writer, he was determined to help his country, not only through his numerous articles and publications but by utilizing something uniquely Spanish: the regional food of Spain. He was interested in politics and had a strong nationalistic view of the *Cocinas de España*. Foreign influence, especially from France, had to be left behind once and for all.

His first book, *Guía del buen comer español: historia y singularidad regional de la cocina española*, shows that a true cuisine of Spain existed as long as its regional character was accepted and understood.[3] Criticized for his excessive enthusiasm and for a slight lack of rigour, he was nevertheless admired for his encyclopedic knowledge of the country. This is a book that should be read by all those who wish to understand Spanish food: its ingredients, traditions and diversity. Another two books by the same author, one about oranges written in collaboration with Gregorio Marañón, a renowned physician and historian fascinated by the diversity of Spanish food, and a second one about the classic cuisine of Spain followed: *Naranjas: el arte de prepararlas y comerlas*[4] and *La cocina clásica española: excelencias, amenidades, historia y recetarios*.[5]

Severely criticized by Post-Thebussem as a poor cook but a decent novelist, María Mestayer de Echagüe (1877–1949) took a position some years later on the dilemma of French food versus Spanish regional food that remains unclear. Writing under the name 'Marquesa de Parabere', Maria Mestayer de Echagüe, the daughter of a French diplomat who had served in Bilbao, was to become a celebrated restaurateur and food writer. As she had done all her life, she was able to move freely between two cultures in a cultivated city that had become an industrial and commercial success. Six newspapers and fifteen magazines were being published in Bilbao at the end of the nineteenth century, a figure that would increase in the first quarter of the twentieth century. Even if you were a woman, if you could write well it was easy to succeed in Bilbao.

Perhaps Mestayer de Echagüe's food writing was encouraged by the fact that cooking had become fashionable and all intellectuals professed to be good cooks. In her food writing or as a restaurateur, she might take the side of modernity represented by France, but she might also side with those who defended the regional food of Spain. Her celebrated *Cocina completa*, a cookbook dedicated to French cuisine, would become an instant best-seller, contributing to the success of the restaurant she opened in Madrid in 1936. Other books, such as *Confitería, repostería, entremeses, aperitivos y ensaladas*, are still frequently used by chefs – *entremeses* being cold dishes such as charcuterie, canapés or shellfish, which are served before the first course. In another of her books, *Platos escogidos de la cocina vasca* (Selected Basque Dishes), even if she could not deny her origins and the social class to which she belonged, she would take a national approach. Within days of its publication and ever since, *Platos escogidos* has been heralded by the people of the Basque Country as a serious contribution to their strong food tradition, even if only a limited edition was published by the prestigious Editorial Grijelmo in Bilbao in 1935, and was never reprinted. The Civil War would deny the national and international success the book deserved. Thought to be lost forever when the author's house was ransacked by Franco's Moorish guard in 1937, a copy belonging to the collection of the Basque author José María Busca Isusi was finally found.[6]

*El Amparo: sus platos clásicos* was an original manuscript written by three exceptional Basque cooks, Ursula, Sira and Vicenta de Azcaray, chef-owners of the restaurant of the same name in Bilbao. Featuring classic French and international cuisine, as well as the best of Basque traditional cooking, the sisters' manuscript was published for the first time in 1939 in San Sebastián. It proved that in the early twentieth century a number of restaurants could offer their clients the best of several worlds. This was an idea strongly opposed by those with a nationalist view. El Amparo opened its doors as a *taverna* in 1886, with Felipa de Eguileor, the owner, in charge of the kitchen. Eventually the original modest establishment would be transformed into a fine dining restaurant. By then it was run by Felipa's daughters, the talented Ursula, Sira and Vicenta, who had learned the art of cooking from their mother as well as in a number of professional establishments in France. At El Amparo the sisters delivered succulent and refined authentic food applauded by critics, and especially by the most demanding palates in the city, including a number of prestigious chefs.

The richness of the collection of recipes in *El Amparo* can be seen in the general index of the book: broth and soups, salads and bean dishes, entrées and preserves, side dishes and decorative pasta, sauces and juices, eggs and omelettes, fish dishes, fried dishes, meat dishes in sauce, pork dishes, lamb dishes, game and poultry dishes in sauce, roast meat, roast poultry and game, sausages, refreshing drinks, puddings, ice cream, pastry, patisserie treats, cakes, jams, jellies, fruit preserved in alcohol, and crystallized fruits.

Following fashion, some of the menus, which were prepared with the best products to be found locally and in French markets, were written in perfect French: *Consommé royale, louvine sauce hongroise, bisque d'écrevisses, chateaubriand, vol-au-vent aux perdreaux, gâteaux et fruits variés* and *petites patisseries*. At the same time, Basque specialities described in the Castilian language were demanded by those with a taste for the local: *sopa de pan de chirlas* was a refined bread soup served with clams. *sopa 'verde prado'* was a clear broth in which the finest tapioca was cooked for five minutes, and the sisters specified that it should be prepared with just one teaspoon of tapioca per person. It was coloured and flavoured with spinach purée, asparagus tips and spring peas also known in Bilbao as *arbejillas*. The *huevos empanados* (breaded eggs) and the *huevos fritos en buñuelo* were also specialities of the house.

As usual, seafood, game and all types of meat dishes occupied the main part of the restaurant's offerings. Several Basque recipes prepared with eels, elvers and salt cod were given special treatment. Eels and elvers in particular, which in those days were inexpensive and easy to find, appeared in six different preparations expertly explained by the cooks. There were elvers with peas in a sauce of olive oil, garlic, parsley and dried red peppers; another was the most popular elver recipe of all: *angulas en cazuela*, elvers cooked with olive oil and garlic in an earthenware *cazuela*. The sisters recommended stirring the delicate fish with a wooden or silver fork, making sure they were all cooked at the same time, and never allowing any change from the pure white colour. It is worthy of note that in *El Amparo, la cazuela de angulas* did not include red chilli pepper as is usually the case today. The *cocina de Bilbao* has been always associated with the best *bacalao* (salt cod), a reason why the Azcaray sisters included in their manuscript as many as ten recipes of Basque origin, including two of the best known: *bacalao in salsa verde* (in green sauce) and the baroque *bacalao a la Vizcaína*, its rich deep red colour provided by the elongated dry peppers also called *choriceros* in Rioja and Navarre.

As a reflection of the Basque partiality to game, there were more than thirty dishes cooked with partridge, quail, pheasant, wild duck, pigeon or rabbit, among others, of which quite a few were French, as was the case with the *perdices à la Peregueux*. In the chapter on *reposteria* (patisserie), the *tarta capuchina* may not be necessarily of Basque origin, but brings a clear idea of the Azcaray sisters' versatility in their 'sweet' kitchen drawn from many traditions. It requires a dozen egg yolks, beaten until very spongy and almost

Rice cakes from Bilbao.

white, with the help of a little heat. This is a steamed pudding that, once cold, is dipped in the lightest sugar syrup. The well-known Saint Honoré dessert shared the honours with *tarta de manzana* and *merengues con crema o con fresas* with the *milhojas de crema* or millefeuilles (custard slice). Less French but closer to Portuguese *pastéis de Belém* were the *pasteles de arroz de Bilbao* made by the Azcaray sisters with rice pudding instead of a thick egg custard, as they are also made today all over the Basque Country.[7]

### 'Viva la República'

Alfonso xiii proved to be incapable of dealing with the political instability confronting him. Abandoned by politicians, the army and most importantly by the middle and agrarian classes for whom he never cared, he went into exile in Italy. 'For the famous fidelity of the Spaniards for their monarchs had been broken long before . . . Since 1789 not a single Spanish sovereign had had a natural reign,' wrote Gerald Brenan in *The Spanish Labyrinth* (1943).[8]

Of the immediate predecessors of Alfonso xiii, four monarchs including a Queen Regent had been compelled to abdicate; one, Ferdinand vii, had only been kept on his throne by the French and another, Alfonso xii, had died young.

## Picasso's Table

Nobody would argue with the fact that Pablo Ruiz Picasso (1881–1973), who was born in Málaga and lived life to the full, first in A Coruña (Galicia), then in Barcelona and most of his adult life in Paris, would never stop loving Spanish food – or all food for that matter. It was the food of his childhood and the food cooked by his mother in Andalusia and the food of his beloved Catalonia. It was also the food that brought back memories of summers and winters in Horta, a village up in the wild mountains between Catalonia and Aragon. Here he took care of the animals, collected olives, and painted constantly using the vibrant colours of saffron and also those of the sad days of autumn. They were days of fried *huevos con patatas* (eggs and chips), beans and *butifarra* sausage and above all rice, which he learned to prepare from multiple recipes, all equally tasty and satisfying and which he left behind when attracted by the artificial lights of the big cities. A summer in Gósol in the heart of the Pyrenees in 1906 would bring alive his passion for hunting and for the game dishes that he had left behind in Horta, as well as the *escudellas* and the taste for a good sausage or two.

One day he would leave his country for good. It had become clear that Franco and Picasso did not belong to the same world. For a man of excess and passion, food and cooking would remain a subject the artist would use time and again in numerous paintings and drawings. Today many of the *naturalezas muercas*, the still-lifes of Picasso, together with those of Sánchez Cotán, Velázquez and Meléndez, are located in numerous national museums and private collections all over the world. Apart from Picasso's still-lifes there are more than two hundred other examples of his art dedicated to the *cocina*

Pablo Picasso, *Still-life with Pitcher and Apples*, 1919, oil on canvas. Picasso painted more than 200 pictures of food.

in the broadest sense of the Spanish word: the restaurants he loved to go to with friends, such as Els Quatre Gats in Barcelona or the Catalan, not far from his studio in the Rue Grands-Augustins in Paris; the kitchen utensils he painted in 1896, for example; the ingredients he preferred to cook. During his long life, food would not only become a passion, it was clearly an essential part of the creative language of the artist.[9]

Ploughing in Cuenca, Castile, 1920.

The long-awaited Second Republic not only failed to deal with the problematic agricultural situation that had historically suffocated the country, it could not foresee something equally dangerous: the separate historic interests of the army and the Church.

With the development of industry and trade in the first decades of the twentieth century, conditions in certain parts of the countryside had improved. The introduction of new agricultural technologies increased productivity of crops such as olives, vine and citrus, and even the calorific content of the average diet had improved. The joy would be short-lived as the wheat market crashed, bringing down the economy and especially threatening the two powerhouses of the nation: Catalonia and the Basque Country. Furthermore, since the nineteenth century, wheat, which represented 75 per cent of the country's agricultural output, had started to compete unfavourably on the international market.

Just before the Civil War, the food eaten by Spaniards had been following the same pattern as in the previous century. On one side was the food of the middle classes, which was mostly traditional and provincial, and that of the upper class and aristocracy, which was still influenced by France. On the other side was the food eaten by the urban labourer and the rural peasant, which was still based on pulses and some vegetables, poor-quality flour, pork fat, olive oil, very little meat and salted fish.

Olives and bread
for lunch in Jaen,
Andalusia, before the
Spanish Civil War of
the late 1930s.

Wheat harvest in
Catalonia, 1930s.

A number of writers and historians, including Gerald Brenan, have argued that, during the first part of the twentieth century, the agrarian sector, and its relationship to industry, were Spain's fundamental problems. A large percentage of the population was still working on the land, and the majority could not read or write. Depending on the various systems of land tenure, rainfall and fertility of the area they cultivated, farmers were still barely able to make a living. City workers who had escaped the countryside seeking a better life were confronted with a problem totally out of their control. Galloping inflation was causing rocketing food prices which they could not afford, even if they had been able to find work. The little credibility that politicians in Spain had left came tumbling down as hunger and malnutrition set in. With the popularity of the Church also in decline, people were desperately looking for an alternative. Socialist and especially anarchist ideals had appeared on the horizon. In a period of intellectual expansion, writers and thinkers of the calibre of Pío Baroja and Azorín began to follow these ideas, but their love affair with them would prove to be a short one. Soon it became very clear that too much uncontrolled passion followed by too much brutality would dictate the path that Spain was to follow.

Both kings and governments had tried to resolve the problems related to property and land tenure which had existed in Spain for centuries. Charles III and his ministers naively dreamed of a land divided into small plots owned by the tenants, who would then be able to support their families. In the nineteenth century, several Disentailment Acts were introduced by government to help to reduce the national debt. They also were an attempt to achieve more equitable distribution of arable land. However, the plan failed on both counts when it was confronted with reality, and in particular with the interest of the groups that still owned the land. Less powerful than the aristocracy and the powerful landowners, the Church would become the main target of any possible reform. It would be the newly rich middle class who would benefit as prices fixed by the government for expropriated lands were beyond the reach of the peasantry.

Surprisingly, ten years into the new century, things would improve as the country attempted to industrialize. Some advances had been made in the iron-rich north and in the textile industry in Catalonia, but the mining industry and especially the railways were in the hands of French and English investors, not for the first time their profits growing in non-Spanish banks. While Europe was moving faster and faster towards full industrialization, and countries such as Germany and Italy were each unifying politically, Spain was left behind, still protecting its inefficient agriculture and trying to fragment again. It is fair to say that hope for proper agrarian reform came with the Second Republic in 1931, but it was far too late. Within five years a horrendous civil war would destroy the country and the hopes of its people.

## FEMINISTS AND WOMANHOOD

Many have forgotten the Second Republic that preceded the Spanish Civil War in 1936. Those who benefited from some of the advanced projects undertaken at the time, among them women, praised the achievements brought by the new political system. Women, or at least those women who were prepared to defend their rights, were supported, surprisingly, by a percentage of the intellectual class. In 1933, while the majority of Spanish women were happy to carry on with their duties as mothers and cooks, 6.8 million of them exercised their right to vote in a general election for the first time. A few of them were writers.

> The kitchen is the domestic laboratory where food is prepared
> and therefore should be convenient, safe and economically run.
> It should be located on the lower ground floor, below the rest
> of the rooms. It should contain a food lift capable of supplying
> food speedily to the dining room, avoiding at the same time the
> kitchen smells escaping to the rest of the house. In any case the
> kitchen should be as separate from the bedrooms as possible.
> The kitchen should be spacious and with good light. It should
> be well ventilated as food and in particular pulses are affected by
> dampness. The elimination of bad smells should be done with
> great care. It is convenient to have a separate room for the washing
> up and a separate larder in which to keep groceries and other
> foods. The kitchen should be used exclusively to prepare and cook
> food. The walls should be painted in white with an oil-based paint
> or with emulsion. The floor should be covered with ceramic tiles
> or linoleum. The cooking range should be placed in an area with
> plenty of light, and the cooker hood ample and easy to clean. A
> proper kitchen needs a clock to ensure food is prepared and then
> cooked for the correct time. The wooden tables must be covered
> with zinc and the rest of the furniture should be made also of
> wood but easy to clean. A large table should be placed in the centre
> of the kitchen for placing plates, glasses, etc. to be taken to the
> dining room. Meat should be carved at the same table . . .[10]

The description of this typical kitchen of a comfortably-off family around the 1930s belongs to a cook's manual published in Barcelona in 1931 under the title *¿Quiere usted comer bien?* (Do You Want to Eat Well?) It was written by Carmen de Burgos for domestic cooks, and also for ladies who wished to be involved in the kitchen and running a home. As in the case with Emilia Pardo Bazán, Carmen de Burgos (1867–1932), who also was known as 'Colombine', was not a food writer as such, although she considered herself to be a good housewife capable of entertaining in fine style. Her food was the food cooked in a domestic kitchen with quality ingredients by a skilful and dedicated hired cook who normally lived in.

Barcelona was a city with a strong local culinary tradition which had always shown a natural affinity with France but had also been influenced by other countries, especially Italy. In De Burgos's manual the number of dishes made with pasta, particularly *macarrones* (macaroni), is an indication of the popularity of pasta in Catalonia. She also included recipes with tagliatelle, ravioli and cannelloni. Her recipe for the dish *Macarrones de Vigilia o Divertidos* (a rather contradictory title since *vigilia* means Lent and *divertidos* means amusing in Spanish) is rather original. After boiling in salted water,

*¿Quiere usted comer bien?* by Carmen de Burgos, known as 'Colombine' (1931).

the *macarrones* are sautéed in tomato sauce. Then a layer of the pasta mixture is placed in an earthenware dish known as a *tartera*, covered first with egg in which the yolks and the whites have been separately beaten, and then sprinkled with parmesan cheese. Now further layers are laid on top, making sure that the last layer is egg and cheese. Then the dish is placed in the oven and baked until golden. Colombine also used *macarrones* to accompany other dishes as well as in soups.

Far from being solely a housewife, Colombine was a writer, a journalist and a war correspondent – indeed she was the first Spanish woman to become one. She was also an activist for women's rights whose defence of divorce in particular would antagonize not only the Church but even Franco. She was herself a divorcee. From 1939 to 1974 books and articles by De Burgos would be classified as 'dangerous', making them even more attractive to read.

### Years of Hunger

The old stove blazed with a mixture of wood and refuse, and a great iron pot
stood bubbling upon it. The entire kitchen simmered and was awash with
steam, a steam banked on the long-forgotten juices of real home-cooked
food, swimming aromas of tomatoes, dried beans and garlic sausage, and
boiled chicken peeling on the bone.

Laurie Lee[11]

During the Spanish Civil War (1936–9) and until the early 1950s, for many Spaniards food became a matter of survival and the return to mere subsistence. As a consequence the authentic food of Spain – the food of the *comarcas* and the regions, prepared in the kitchens of the moderately well-off middle classes – suffered from a process of impoverishment. The recovery, if it were ever to happen completely, would require time and professional dedication.

The front cover of Juan Eslava Galán's book *Los años del miedo: la nueva España, 1939–1952* (The Years of Fear: The New Spain, 1939–1952)[12] features four young women dressed in black, one man and one child; all are smiling broadly and holding white bread in their left hands. With their right hands they are giving the Fascist salute. The photograph was probably taken in the early 1940s somewhere in the region of Seville or Zaragoza just after the Civil War. The bread was probably bought on the black market. These areas were rich in wheat and other cereals, as well as pulses, vegetables and fruit, and had survived the war on the nationalist side. If the picture had been taken

Women queue for basic food supplies during the Spanish Civil War of the late 1930s.

in Barcelona, Bilbao or Alicante – all pro-republican areas – white bread would not have been featured, nor would the people have been prepared to be photographed in the first place. During the Civil War socialist ideas had mostly been supported in industrialized areas where the production of food had taken second place.

As a result of this war, all Spaniards suffered deprivation, malnutrition and even starvation. Nothing had prepared them for the years of rationing and queueing that the post-war era would bring, especially for those who had fought on the republican side, many of whom were in prison. Not only did the borders with Europe shut firmly due to the Second World War, transatlantic trade became dangerous, seriously affecting supplies from friendly countries in South America.

Franco had promised Spaniards something he could not deliver: food. With the exception of those who could afford to buy practically anything on that shadowy business that would become an art, the black market, the rest of the population suffered unbearable hardship, especially in large towns and cities. In the countryside things were slightly better. Here at least people could grow vegetables and fruit and kill a chicken or a rabbit, a small wild boar or valuable pig. Rationing was introduced on 14 May 1939, but by 1943 food shortages had reached the critical stage. Apart from this, drought, a word used

Bread rationing during the Years of Hunger of the 1930s and 1940s.

by the government as justification, was not adequate reason for many of the shortages; the main reasons were the poor state of the land and agriculture in general. The transition from liberal to regulated agriculture, which occurred between 1936 and 1954, brought production practically below its pre-Civil War level.

During the Years of Hunger, women worked miracles preparing meals with leftovers, wild foods and lesser-value ingredients. At a time when cookbooks were hardly in demand for obvious reasons, but were considered safe by the official censor, a book published in 1940, *Cocina de recursos* (Resourceful Cooking), became an instant best-seller. Written by Ignasi Domènech, a prestigious chef, restaurant critic and successful author, this was much more than a collection of recipes and ideas. While it was intended primarily to help cooks face the vicissitudes of a world with little food, the author was able to criticize Franco's interventionist policies and incapacity to resolve the situation in a clever and subtle way. A recipe for an omelette is a perfect example of the author's thinking: to utilize ingredients that, during times of plenty, people could not imagine ever existed. His omelette without eggs, *tortilla sin huevo de gallina*, uses instead flour, bicarbonate of soda, parsley, garlic, saffron (if available), celery leaves, water and a few drops of olive oil. He goes even further by preparing a *tortilla de patatas* without eggs and without potatoes. This was an

## *Gachas* and *Hormigos*

*Gachas*, the universal porridge also known as *poleadas*, *puches*, *farapes* and *farinetas*, fed Spaniards since pottery became available in the Iberian Peninsula and until well into the 1950s, when it was often eaten as a substitute for a low-quality bread also known as *pan negro*. It can be said that of all the food capable of combating hunger *gachas* was the most economical and substantial of foodstuffs. All that was needed to obtain nourishment from *gachas* was to pound some grain, blend it with water in a utensil which could support heat, stir constantly while cooking and then eat it while hot. With the passing of time *gachas* has evolved into tastier recipes similar to those eaten before the Civil War, flavoured with cloves of garlic, onions, olive oil, salt and a little water.

Another recipe that caught the imagination of the Spaniards during times of hunger was the historical *hormigo*, also known as *formigo*, *ormigo* and *hormiguillo*. This was an early creative food that could be adapted to the kitchens of the rich and the poor. In its simplest form it is a type of omelette created with bread, milk or water, eggs and olive oil or lard. It was made savoury or sweet. Since medieval times, *Hormigo* has been recorded in different versions by Spanish food writers and cooks including Rupert de Nola and Antonio Salsete. Salsete's recipe for *hormiguillo* does not include cow's milk, bread or even eggs. In his book he advises the reader that there

ingenious invention that would provide a decent alternative to one of the most appreciated dishes in the Spanish culinary tradition. It was made with orange pith, garlic, flour, bicarbonate of soda, white pepper, turmeric, oil and salt.[15]

### DOMÈNECH'S WORLD

Ignasi Domènech's professional approach to food and his influence as a writer cannot be denied, even if some of his early titles, such as *La nueva cocina elegante española*, published for the first time in 1915, had initially damaged his are many ways to prepare *hormiguillo*, although he believes the best one is made with hazelnuts:

> Roast the nuts taking care they do not burn, then remove the shells with a cloth. Pound them and place in a pan with some water. Gently heat. Bring them to the boil once and set aside. Add a little cinnamon, cloves and sugar, which should be also pounded at the same time as the hazelnuts to avoid greasiness. Do not add honey, or salt, neither saffron, nor spices, neither bread nor oil . . .[13]

In the early twentieth century the celebrated Galician authors María Mestayer de Echagüe, Marquesa de Parabere and Manuel María Puga y Parga ('Picadillo'), included in their books recipes for *hormigo* much closer to the idea that this is an omelette made with bread.[14] Today, while its preparation has practically been forgotten, in remote parts of Asturias and Galicia, a hot plate of *hormigos* sprinkled with sugar is still served to mothers after giving birth.

Following a similar recipe but richer and sweeter, *hormigos* are still served during Christmastime in the Portuguese areas of Do Minho or Tras-os-Montes. Here the recipe is made with bread, milk, eggs, lard and some water. Nowadays it also includes port wine, raisins, pine nuts, cinnamon and lime.

reputation.[16] Described as pretentious and full of contradictions, this earlier book could have been easily considered by Dr Thebussem and HM's Chef to be offensive if not treasonable. This was the perfect example of an international cookbook detested by those defending Spanish regional cuisines. As stated on page one, the book was written by 'Ignasi Domènech, director of the magazine *El Gorro Blanco* and ex-chef of their excellencies the Duques de Medinaceli and del Infantado, La Marquesa de Argüelles, Prince von Wrede, the Baron Wedel, Sir Henry Drummond Wolff and the British, Swedish and Norwegian ambassadors'.

In his defence, in the 1930s, Domènech, who was Catalan through and through, published one of the best books ever written on a subject which would have been slightly foreign to him: *La cocina vasca*. A constant traveller, he collected recipes everywhere, brought them up to date, and then returned them to the reader, the chef and the home cook with the style of a journalist – looking beyond the list of ingredients and the method of preparation, and yet making sure as a cook that the recipe worked in a precise way. *Canutillos de crema* is one of the hundreds of recipes he included in *La cocina vasca*. Prepared with thin puff pastry filled with crème pâtissière, *canutillos* are associated with nineteenth-century Bilbao, although they are very popular all over the Basque Country.

What is interesting about Domènech, and also the *aragones* Teodoro Bardají, probably the two most influential Spanish chefs and food writers of the first half of the twentieth century, was their capacity to understand the two different worlds of Spanish food before and after the Spanish Civil War: one still influenced mostly by France, the other very Spanish. The prolific Domènech managed to publish 26 cookbooks in less than half a century.

Teodoro Bardají was a self-made chef, journalist and exceptional writer who brought modernity and innovation to Spanish food in a way that had never been seen before. Contrary to what happened with the popular Domènech, once he became unpopular with publishers, Bardají's intellectual capacity and artistry with cuisine were lost.

Spain, a country trying to recover from the devastation of the Civil War and facing the possibility of entering another war, was compelled to declare a position of neutrality in 1940. In 1947 the country was excluded from an extensive American aid programme that allowed other European countries to rebuild their economies and infrastructure after the Second World War. The dictator Franco was still at the helm. The Marshall Plan, as the aid programme became known, sadly excluded a country in desperate need. In a comic but rather sad film, *Welcome Mr Marshall* (1953), directed by Luis García Berlanga, a small town in central Spain prepares for the visit of American diplomats. The priest, the mayor and other authorities hope all will be forgiven and that economic help will be granted as a result of their efforts. The whole town, decorated as an Andalusian village with its people dressed as *sevillanos* and *cordobeses* (classic stereotypical Spanish dresses), wait in the road impatiently waving small flags with stars and stripes. Eventually a never-ending collection of limousines pass at great speed without stopping.

*Manual de cocina* (1950): a controversial book.

## A CONTROVERSIAL BOOK

In 1950, a cookbook entitled *Manual de cocina* was written by Ana María Herrera. It proved to be very popular at a time when excellent books such as *La cocina de Ellas* by Teodoro Bardají were not reaching readers any more. Herrera was a food teacher working at the Lope de Vega Institute in Madrid under the auspices of the *Sección Femenina del Movimiento*. The *Sección Femenina* was the women's branch of the Fascist Falange movement in Spain. Herrera's book reached the market at a time of serious economic hardship and still limited food availability, which is why the author made certain that all the recipes were prepared with inexpensive ingredients that should be readily available, selecting recipes which were very appetizing and easy to prepare. Furthermore it responded to another important issue: the change in women's circumstances. Women who until then had been in charge of the house and preparing food for the family started going out to work. For them time would become a precious commodity. Supported by Franco's regime, *Manual de cocina* become the perfect book to give newly married women, experienced home cooks and even kitchen professionals. It was also bought by grandmothers to give to their granddaughters one day.

For the *Sección Femenina* this *Manual* had become far too successful, however. The author's name was removed after her retirement and, later, her death. New editions were published as a collective work of the women's section of the Falange. When the institution was disbanded after Franco's death, the book became part of the Ministry of Culture's editorial list, where it would be kept for decades. In 1995, after forty years, the authorship of the *Manual* was returned to Ana María Herrera and her family. Today the *Manual de cocina* remains a cookbook to be found in many Spanish libraries, a bestseller and a classic which has managed to survive the devastating period of a country broken into pieces.

The first part of the book provides general information about ingredients, butchery, carving and fish preparation, as well as an advanced glossary of culinary terms. In the second part, following the seasons of the year, the author provides numerous *minutas*, or menus, for lunch and dinner. This hugely simplifies the cook's task. For example, in one of the menus the author suggests a springtime dinner comprising a substantial potato purée enriched with a little butter and cheese, followed by a hake *timbal* which is made with fresh fish, spinach, milk, butter, olive oil and a little flour.[17] Even if globalization is now seriously impacting well-established Spanish food traditions, Spaniards still prefer to be served their vegetables as a separate course from their meat or fish, as depicted in Ana María Herrera's *Manual de cocina*.

## It All Happened on the Periphery

Despite the efforts of figures such as Bardají, Domènech and other chefs, by the middle of the twentieth century it had become clear that professional Spanish food needed to be updated. It had been stuck in the past for too long, unable to move or moving in a wrong direction following in the footsteps of other traditions, always copying and very seldom creating.

'This country of strange language and malevolent customs, of deep forest and enclosed mountains, where bread is not to be found, nor wine or even something to eat, except milk and cider.' This is a passage believed to have been written by Aymeric Picaud in volume v of the twelfth-century Codex Calixtinus or *Liber Sancti Jacobi* (Book of St James). How could Aymeric have foreseen the promising future of the food of the Basques, and of the rest of Spain for that matter? In the latter part of the twentieth century and until today, thanks to the creative and innovative work of professionals, Spain was to become a world powerhouse of cuisine.

Without a clear 'food capital' to lead the nation's cuisine, but having several strong food *Cocinas*, such as the Basque and the Catalan, which have historically surpassed those of the political centre of the country, the 1970s presented the opportunity to assert their strength. The post-war period and its negative effect on the *Cocinas* had been left behind. More importantly, after almost forty years of dictatorship, democracy was in the air. Both Catalonia and the Basque Country had been historically, geographically and culturally closer to Europe than the rest of Spain, where classic cuisine was now being reinvented. After decades of what has been called 'Post-Escoffier immobility' France was on the move. The rest of the world – and especially the Basque Country – was watching expectantly.

In May 1968, protests in Paris inspired young people to search for alternatives. Among them were a number of French chefs whose names would stand out in the history of contemporary food: Alain Chapel, Michel Guérard, Roger Vergé, the Troigros brothers, and notably Paul Bocuse as far as Basque chefs were concerned. These chefs were to lead a culinary revolution baptized 'nouvelle cuisine' in 1973. Based on a number of precepts, the new movement was to change the world of the kitchen professional dramatically: raw materials of superlative quality and the use of seasonal ingredients were accompanied by a revision of techniques which included shorter cooking times and less use of animal fats. It is important to remember that behind the nouvelle cuisine movement lay a significant desire for chefs to offer their clients healthy food. Having heard Paul Bocuse speak at the 1976 Gastronomic Round Table in Madrid, two Basque chefs – Pedro Subijana and Juan Mari Arzak – were enlightened. They knew that Basque cooking possessed all the inherent elements needed to raise it to its proper place as an interesting and original world cuisine. The journey they started under the banner of *Euskal sukalderitza berria* or *nueva cocina vasca* (new Basque cuisine) was supported initially by a further ten talented Basque chefs. With time they would be followed by hundreds of Spanish professionals, each one showing their own talent and individual style, and reflecting the culinary diversity of the country once again. As Ferran Adrià explained in an article included in the book *Basque, Creative Territory*, published in 2016, the road to change was full of obstacles:

> The domino effect following the emergence of the *nouvelle cuisine* initially left our gastronomy out. We needed a period of transition

first. Little by little, Spain began adapting its structures to bring them up to par with other countries in Western Europe.[18]

In Spain, where each region has kept its own particularities, the new movement would be interpreted in many different ways. In some cases a compromise between the new and the old had to be reached.

The transition mentioned by Adrià would be made possible by *la nueva cocina vasca*, which was by no means a simple copy of nouvelle cuisine. Certainly the dishes that the Basque chefs were creating under the new order were, as now, mostly of Basque inspiration, their ingredients following its distinctive culinary tradition. This is hardly surprising. There are few places where chefs would think about cooking in quite the same terms of idealistic pride and integrity as in the Basque Country. They firmly believe that cooking is part of the heritage of the nation or region, and that the ritual of eating and drinking well is an integral part of Basque identity. What is interesting is that most of the Basque chefs who worked together at the beginning of the project were from San Sebastián, where tradition has not always been so carefully nurtured. For over a century after the French Revolution, international cuisine reigned supreme in San Sebastián to the detriment of more original, indigenous cooking. During the whole of this period, but particularly in the Belle Époque, San Sebastián was the traditional summer holiday resort of the Spanish aristocracy. Their cooks and chefs would pass on their experience and techniques to other professionals and to local women hired to help in the kitchens during the summer months. Many of the Basque chefs involved initially had been influenced by both Basque home cooking and professional international cooking, which was also helping with the new task. Furthermore, most of them belonged to professional families in the business.

A number of recipes from the period of transition in the early 1980s reinforce the point. *Pastel de krabarroka* (scorpionfish), a dish created by Juan Mari Arzak, the owner of the restaurant of the same name, is made with fresh tomato sauce, single cream, eggs, leeks, carrots, a little butter, breadcrumbs, salt and white pepper. This is a classic terrine cooked in a bain-marie and then served cold with mayonnaise made with peanut oil and a dash of sherry vinegar.

Juan José Lapitz, a journalist and Basque author who was a descendant of fishermen who had crossed the Atlantic in search of cod, had also been following the advances of the new movement in the period of transition. His first book, *Comer en Euskalherria*, was published in 1982 and became a classic.

The founding members of the *nueva cocina vasca*.

It was followed by *La cocina moderna en Euskadi*, a compilation of recipes reflecting dishes offered by some of the best restaurants serving modern Basque food at the end of the 1980s, not only in San Sebastián but around Bilbao and Álava.[19] He included restaurants such as Guria, Panier Fleuri and Castillo. At Guria in Bilbao, chef Genaro Pildain, also known as 'El Rey del Bacalao' (the king of cod), prepared *El Bacalao del Chef*, small portions of cod beautifully presented with different delicious sauces from the Basque repertoire: salsa verde, pil-pil and vizcaina. By the time Tatus Fombellida, the only woman among the original twelve chefs of the *nueva cocina* movement, had opened the new Panier Fleuri in San Sebastián, her surname had already become associated with the best food to be found in the city. Instead of breaking completely with the style expected by her family's clientele, she decided to offer at her restaurant a selection of French and Basque dishes once prepared to a high standard at her father's restaurant in the town of Rentería. A new approach much closer to the new Basque movement would mark her trajectory for years to come, even if the names of the dishes prepared with sole or grouper, lobster or woodcock, remained unchanged: *Lenguado 'a la Florentina', Mero 'a la Donostiarra', Homer 'a la Americana'* or *Becada 'al Armagnac'.*

José Juan Castillo, once the owner of the hotel of the same name in Olaberria, Guipúzcoa Province, and another of the founding members of the new movement, is an interesting case. Having dedicated time and effort to the *nueva cocina vasca*, he bought Casa Nicolasa, the emblematic restaurant in San Sebastián, where by public demand he returned to a more traditional Basque food style. Here, under his guidance for 27 years, were served *alubias rojas* (black beans), *marmitako* of potatoes (vegetables and tuna fish), *guibeludiñas a la plancha* (the *Russula virescens* variety of fungi) and delicate braised sweetbreads (*mollejas salteadas*).

Another of the founding chefs, Luis Irizar, opened the first professional catering school in the Basque Country in 1976. His school would play an instrumental role in teaching very successful chefs such as Pedro Subijana. In 1990 Subijana, chef-patron of the restaurant Akelarre in San Sebastián, accepted an invitation from the Spanish government to cook for the British press at the Dorchester hotel in London. For the first time Spain was using modern gastronomy as an instrument of promotion. A recipe for *lubina a la pimienta verde* (sea bass with green peppercorns) delighted the guests, although it still reflected the classic French influence on a San Sebastián chef. Fish loins were cooked in a light sauce with shallots, green peppercorns, olive oil, some butter, Basque apple brandy and a little cream. Over time local tradition and the modern approach have become more integrated. Subijana's *ensalada de tomate del país y bonito marinado* (salad of local tomatoes and marinated bonito) may appear to be a very simple dish, but in fact it is not. This is a celebration of summer: the ripeness of the tomatoes and the high-quality fillets of the most appreciated tuna fish in the whole of Spain, the *bonito del Norte* (*Thunnus alalunga*). The bonito, which is less fatty than the rest of the tuna family, is first marinated for several hours in lemon rind and a moderate amount of apple vinegar. Two sauces are then prepared, one made with tomatoes seasoned with salt and pepper and a few drops of lemon juice, another made with green peppers which need to be cooked for a few minutes beforehand. Plating is equally important. First a few slices of the tomato (properly seasoned) are lightly covered with the two sauces, then the marinated fish is carefully placed on top.

Pedro Subijana, Akelarre, San Sebastián, one of the founding members of
the *nueva cocina vasca*.

## On the Mediterranean and Beyond

In her book *Comer en Catalunya*, the journalist Carmen Casas affirmed that
the best Catalan food was still to be found in the north of the region, in the
*comarca* of El Ampurdán, which is in the province of Girona on the border
with France.[20] Time would prove that her statement had to be extended to
other parts of the Catalan Autonomy. Since then several Catalan chefs have
become legends: the late Santi Santamaría, the unstoppable Ferran Adrià,
Carme Ruscalleda and the Roca brothers, among others.

When Casas made his claim, top Catalan restaurants – and they were
numerous – were holding onto their strong regional tradition but were already
developing a more modern approach: Agut d'Avignon (Barcelona), Eldorado
Petit, El Motel and El Racó de Can Fabes (Santi Santamaría's restaurant) were
by then also included in this list. Their chefs would be followed a decade later
by a younger generation working in Barcelona and in Girona. They were still
cooking food with a strong Mediterranean character, but their kitchens were
already in tune with the principles of nouvelle cuisine and *nueva cocina vasca*.
Soon the restaurants Florian, Roig Robí and Azulete would become the talk
of the town not just because their chefs happened to be beautiful women but
because their food, and particularly the way it was presented, was exceptional.[21]
By then another young chef was already destined to influence the rest of the
world. He was Ferran Adrià.

Santi Santamaría, who died in 2011 aged 53, had opened El Racó de Can Fabes in San Celoni, in the province of Barcelona, in 1981. He was another Spanish chef who initially followed the *nouvelle cuisine* movement. In 1994 El Racó de Can Fabes was awarded three Michelin stars. This was a first for Catalonia. By then he was also a well-known author and journalist. In a moving piece published by *The Telegraph* as a celebration of Santamaría's life on 17 February 2011, the journalist described the poetic effects of eating at Can Fabes:

> It stirred memories of his mother spreading out the special white cloth she used for feasts . . . Using only fire he would perform the magic of turning raw food into meals. The result could be shrimp that makes you lose your senses, or a fish and potato soup that would put the moon on your plate.

Eventually Santamaría's passion for local ingredients and the threat to what he considered the best of Mediterranean food and Spanish gastronomy would bring controversy and a split in the professional culinary community. In his book *Cocina al desnudo* (Cooking Laid Bare),[22] he lamented the rise of fast food and furiously attacked the style of molecular cooking actively promoted by Adrià. For many this was an unnecessarily harsh book at a time when Spanish avant-garde gastronomy had obtained international recognition and acclaim, even if some of the questions it raised, particularly the safety of some ingredients, were also being questioned. Did envy bring out the worst in him? For those who knew him well this was totally out of character. He was a defender of local ingredients and Mediterranean food culture, as Adrià had been at the beginning of his career: real food from a historical tradition that tasted of the sea and the mountains; fish from the afternoon market at the nearest port; mushrooms and lamb from the closest sierras; sausages and fresh truffles from the town of Vic in the foothills of the Pyrenees; all elevated to the realms of hedonism by a professional local chef.

A little more than 100 kilometres north, in Josep Pla's beloved Ampurdán, Ferran Adrià, adopting a very different approach, was also delighting his customers at the restaurant El Bulli. The results were spectacular. The road he was following was totally original. Would Josep Pla, considered the best narrator of contemporary Catalan literature, exceptional food critic and defender of traditional Catalan food, have approved of what was happening at El Bulli? Who knows; we should never underestimate the capacity of brilliant people who love food, even Pla. Perhaps he did at the beginning, before El

Bulli became the centre of attention of thousands of young chefs, older chefs and food critics, and before extreme avant-garde cooking placed Adrià on the front cover of *Time* magazine. In Spain the world of professional food had been divided into two: before and after.

La Hacienda del Bulli – the original name of the restaurant – situated in a classic Costa Brava cove 7 kilometres from the port of Roses, had become well-known among French and German food lovers. It was a Mediterranean restaurant serving good French food owned by Hans Schilling, a German doctor, and his Czechoslovakian wife, Marketta. The Schillings had a French bulldog, a breed known as Bulli.

In 1975, Jean-Louis Neichel was taken on as head chef and manager. Neichel was strongly influenced by Alain Chapel, and his arrival was to mark the direction that would later allow this restaurant to become arguably the most innovative and creative in the world. In 1976 El Bulli was granted its first Michelin star. A second soon followed. The style here was fine dining with a strong French influence.

In 1981 Juli Soler, a new manager and man of vision, hired a 22-year-old Catalan chef with little experience but plenty of talent: Ferran Adrià – more an instinctive chef than a dedicated one. Soler also decided to shorten the name of the restaurant. El Bulli was about to start developing a style of its own as both Soler and Adrià embarked on a long learning process that would take them to the best restaurants in the world, and which would influence their own unique style and way of thinking. As Neichel had done before and with the full approval of the Schillings, Adrià spent months working abroad. By 1987 the young chef had become responsible for El Bulli's kitchen.

During the summer the restaurant would be open to the public for lunch and dinner. In winter Adrià and his brigade would create the menu for the following year. At the beginning it was clear that inspiration was drawn from the Mediterranean, or more precisely from El Ampurdán and the seaside port of Roses, an area of delicious rice dishes, fish, goose with pears or turnips and the more elaborate style of cuisine known in Spanish as *mar and montaña*, a term often translated into English as more or less 'surf and turf'. Within a short period of time, the influence of nouvelle cuisine, and other cuisines such as the Japanese, were clearly in evidence. A recipe for *tempura de pistachos* served at the restaurant was a good example of the latter. Can a pistachio shell be eaten and be delicious? Adrià's answer was yes, and the rest of the world agreed.

Adrià's first book, *El Bulli: El Sabor del Mediterráneo*, published in 1993, offered a taste of what was going to be a perpetually evolving career. The book's index included an explanation of how the preparation of the dishes followed

*El Bulli: Cooking in Progress*, poster, 2010.

a new path involving a number of processes: the 'inspiration' based on a form of art; the 'adaptation' of recipes that already existed; and the preparation of dishes from various elements previously assembled in a rather random way. Adrià called the latter process 'association'.[23] The recipe collection was presented in sections: *Tapitas, Mar y Montaña, Subasta de Roses, El Bulli* and *Recetas Básicas* (Small Tapas, Sea and Mountain (or surf and turf), the Roses Fish Market, El Bulli and Basic Recipes). At the restaurant a number of *tapitas* were often served before lunch and dinner on a splendid terrace looking over the sea: small pieces of art made with exciting combinations of ingredients and textures offered, more often than not, with a glass of sherry – the only wine capable of matching them perfectly. *Coca* with *escalibada* of aubergines, bacon and rabbit ribs, *costillitas; dátiles de mar* (local mussels) *en gelée* with a soup of fennel; sea urchins *gratinados*; cuttlefish with marrowbone and sorrel . . .

Ferran Adrià, the man who revolutionized food in the professional kitchen.

There was nothing new about the concept of *mar y montaña* when Adrià decided to include several recipes belonging to the El Ampurdán repertoire in his first book. In Catalonia, combinations of salty and sweet, sweet and sour, and fish and meat date back to medieval times. In his first book the chef wrote: 'Without this liaison my cuisine would probably have never existed.' Considered a total triumph by chefs and critics, *Tuétano con caviar*, roasted marrowbone with a generous portion of caviar on top on a bed of cauliflower purée, was 'an outstanding dish' according to Paul Bocuse. Other dishes, such as partridge *escabeche* with lobster and scallops with foie gras, were also included. The pig's trotters with calçots (a type of onion shoot) and the *espardenyes* (sea cucumber) and ceps were as complicated as they were appreciated by a discerning public. Many books would follow. Under Adrià's guidance new techniques would be openly discussed and implemented by his followers, but at times misunderstood by critics and other chefs. Controversy would often follow him as he imparted new concepts in his articles and public discussions. Unheard-of products were constantly being added to the larder of his impressive *taller* (workshop) in Barcelona. Most importantly, while all of this was happening, scores of young chefs from all over Spain and from many other countries were being trained in the kitchen at El Bulli beneath a magnificent sculpture of a bull's head.

After years at the cutting edge of innovation, El Bulli, probably the world's most famous restaurant of its era, served dinner to a group of friends for the last time in 2011. Ferran Adrià, the late Juli Soler and El Bulli had done their work. Its successor is Can Roca, a leading international restaurant in its own right. Here the Roca brothers offer a very different food proposition compared with that of the El Bulli era, but creativity and innovation are still at the heart of everything they do.

Adrià, never short of words or new ideas, is now focusing exclusively on education and the future world of food. He does not have to wait for history to endorse his great contribution; he already has a fabulous and fundamental role in the history of food. Now he thinks and talks.

Thanks to the first and second generation of revolutionary Basque and Catalan chefs as well as many other chefs working all over the country, *la restauración española* (the restaurant and hotel sectors) are still advancing at an equal or faster pace than the rest of the world. This has not been the case since medieval times, when Catalonia reigned supreme in the Mediterranean world. Those who influenced them in the first place are now watching a third generation of talented Spanish chefs: Elena Arzak, the daughter of Juan Mari; Andoni Luis Aduriz at Mugaritz in the Basque Country; Nacho Manzano at

Nacho Manzano's modern approach to traditional food.

Casa Marcial in Asturias; and Francis Paniego at El Echaurren in Rioja, among many others, belong to this generation. Spanish chefs are now shining not only in Spanish restaurants but in other countries where they head up many well-known kitchens. Furthermore, inspectors and food lovers are now also searching for other types of food experiences. In the last few years, Spanish chefs have been even freer to develop their own personal styles. Some have decided to follow in the footsteps of their masters; others have chosen to return to their own environment – to the food of their mothers and the ingredients grown in their own vegetable gardens. They know precisely what to do and how to convince others to do the same, their menus now written in Basque, Castilian, Catalan or Galician.

# EIGHT

# The *Cocinas* of Spain

Until well into the twentieth century, many chefs and food writers had defended the validity of the regional kitchens of Spain. They believed that having been able to save themselves from the cosmopolitan invasion, these traditions had become the true representatives of the genuine food of Spain. The same people however would not have been aware that by 2017 referring to Regional Spain had become politically incorrect. As mentioned at the beginning of this book, politically the regional map of the country changed in 1978 into the map of the Autonomies, as established in the new Constitution approved by the large majority of Spaniards. Should *Las Cocinas de España* retain the word 'regional' as they always have, or should they just be named *Cocinas de España* in the different languages spoken in different parts of the country? Such a pity that Larra, Bardají, Domènech, La Marquesa de Parabere, His Majesty's Chef, Pla and many others are no longer with us, as they would have had some answers to a rather complex question.

Some of the *Cocinas* share many ingredients, and some are stronger and more distinctive than others; the foods of their individual cooking pots are layered with geography, climatic conditions, water and soil, tradition and, of course, history. These aspects should be taken into consideration when drawing the map of the *Cocinas*, leaving behind individual nationalistic claims and sensibilities, and it is important to acknowledge them. Admitting and defending their individuality, the *Cocinas* also shared centuries of history and culture. They are all part of the complex food map of the Iberian Peninsula and the Balearic and Canary islands. They all include a *cocido* and a *tortilla de patatas*, two of the very few dishes that could be considered 'national'. They also include the fashionable tapas, a tasty plate of rice, good bread, fiesta food and a glass of local wine.

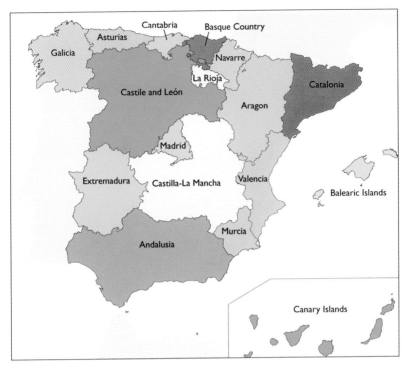

The autonomous communities of Spain in 1978.

## LAS COCINAS DE ESPAÑA PAST AND PRESENT

Fairly recently a journalist asked a renowned Basque chef where he liked to eat when travelling in Catalonia with other chefs. He replied, 'Hispània', the restaurant where the sisters Paquita and Lolita Rexach have been cooking authentic Catalan dishes for the last fifty years. If the question had been about where he loved eating with his friends in the Basque Country, he probably would have replied: 'in a Gastronomic Society in San Sebastián'.

Spaniards have managed, in an extraordinary way, to remain emotionally attached to the places of their birth and the food of their childhoods. In Spain, every village and town has its own special dishes or versions of a dish which are considered by locals, particularly those living abroad, as the best food man can eat, especially if they have been prepared by their mothers. This may not be unique to Spain, but here it is definitely an element to take into serious consideration when talking about Spanish food. This *localismo* is based on dishes prepared following the food traditions of people's place of birth, or rather of the *comarcas*. *Comarcas* are natural areas – defined by their geography, climate, soil, agriculture and market towns – in control of a number of municipalities. With the arrival of the railway in the nineteenth century and the opening of major roads from the 1950s, the *Cocinas* experienced influences from outside their own locality almost for the first time. With internal migrations in medieval times – from the north to repopulate the south and from the poorer south to the industrial north and northeast in more recent times – local dishes may have crossed the natural barriers earlier.

To understand the *Cocinas de España*, it is necessary to go back and identify the unique character of each part of the country. With such diversity, this is complicated. The best way to travel through the patchwork of *Cocinas* is to draw an imaginary food map which would allow one to pass through the natural *comarcas*, discovering landscapes and market towns, people, ingredients, recipes and even cooking utensils. Even if modern transport and newly designed roads have broken down the natural barriers that once encouraged and protected individuality, particularly in the countryside, many local markets are still offering food grown locally with a small percentage of produce from neighbouring areas brought in by itinerant traders. Unfortunately this is under threat.

## From the Roaring Seas to the Highlands

From Galicia to the border with France, roaring seas, ancient mountains and the best pastures to be found in the peninsula are permanent features shared by 'Green Spain'. Here corn, known in Spanish as *maíz*, has been grown for human as well as animal consumption since it arrived from the Americas. These regions share a passion for white, red or black beans, for pork and pork products, and for cheese: Ttetilla in Galicia, Cabrales in Asturias, Quesucos in Cantabria and Idiázabal in the Basque Country are some of the best-known. Owing to the damp winters, hocks of pork, chorizos and black puddings are traditionally smoked in the farmhouses of Galicia and Asturias. In Cantabria and the Basque Country, smoking is less popular. Seafood caught in the Bay of Biscay or across the Atlantic is always in demand: shellfish, hake, monkfish, turbot, white bonito, sardines and anchovies, octopus and squid. Looking at the land from the sea or from the high mountains, it is easy to assume that there are few differences between the northern regions. This is not the case. Even if they are all affected by mist and mystery, long history and legend, the character of the people, their language and the way they cook is in each one as distinctive as it is original.

In Galicia and Asturias, corn is kept in the traditional *hórreos.*

## GALICIA, ASTURIAS, CANTABRIA AND THE BASQUE COUNTRY

Scents of sea and wood fires, of pine and eucalyptus, of seafood and cornbread, hang in the air in the Galician countryside. Tall cabbages, whose leaves will grace warming broths and substantial stews, decorate the land of the northwestern corner of the Iberian Peninsula, a land divided up by ancient heritage laws. *Minifundia* have left their enduring mark on the landscape, as has the wild and rugged nature of the coast. Since early times invaders and settlers believed that this was the *finis terrae*, the very end of a world, chosen for settlement by Celts. Inland, the Christian city of Santiago de Compostela awaits the arrival of pilgrims with a promise of salvation. They look forward to kissing the robe of the saint and to having a long rest, sharing a glass of Albariño, Valdeorras or Ribeiro wine, all locally produced, and a portion of the best Spanish omelette to be found in Spain. During their stay, good bread and an array of dishes cooked with potatoes, chestnuts, beef, turnip tops, cured and smoked pork products and especially fish and shellfish will be offered by hundreds of small restaurants, their doors permanently open in a medieval university town which is accustomed to attending to the needs of the passing visitor. All along the coast, the grey

### *Cocido*

If there is one dish which is truly representative of the *Cocinas*, then *cocido*, also known as *olla*, has to be the one. The Castilian word *cocido* comes from the verb *cocer*, to boil. This is not a single dish, it is a family of dishes in which the names and ingredients (which can include vegetables, pulses, pasta in most cases, meats and sausages) change in accordance with local cooking traditions and the language spoken in different parts of the country: *cocido madrileño*, *escudella i can d'olla* in Catalonia, *pote* in Asturias, *cocido montañés* in Cantabria and *puchero* in Andalusia. The quantity and quality of the meats, which normally include beef, poultry and sausages, give an indication of the economic position of the family. Some *cocidos* are served in three different courses: soup, followed by vegetables with pulses, then sausages and meat. Normally pasta is added to the broth to make the soup. In Madrid, a freshly made tomato sauce is normally cooked to accompany the meats, which after a prolonged period of cooking tend to become slightly dry. The chickpea is a fundamental part of Castilian and Andalusian *cocidos*, but in Galicia, Asturias and even Catalonia they are cooked with different types of bean such as haricots or the Catalan *ganchet*.

Some historians affirm that given how easy it is to make, and the number of ingredients used, *cocido* may have appeared spontaneously in different places as a way of making the most of local products. Other historians see the dish as a less ostentatious derivative of the medieval *olla podrida*, or even that

stone houses and the multitude of shades of green and rainy greys contrast with the brilliant, luminous hues of water and shores of the *rías* (inlets) these remain unchanged in Galicia. At last the images of women in black walking behind their oxen are beginning to fade.

For the fishermen, life has also changed beyond recognition, but not necessarily for the best. The Spanish fishing fleet is no longer what it once was, forced to change by competition and quotas. However, Galicia is dotted with fishing ports and *lonjas* where fish is auctioned twice a day, supplying its origins are to be found in the *adafina*, the Sephardi dish cooked on Fridays to eat on the Sabbath. To prepare *adafina*, Jewish cooks wilted spinach or sorrel leaves in olive oil together with pieces of lamb or goat, a few handfuls of previously soaked chickpeas and a number of whole eggs in their shells. It was then covered with water and seasoned. To follow Jewish law relating to the Sabbath, the dish was cooked over the dying embers of a fire. The lid was covered with hot embers, which helped cook the dish very gently and in such a way that it would remain hot until the following day.

In the late 1950s the introduction of the pressure cooker brought freedom to the Spanish housewife, especially in the cities. Even today, as the oven is rarely used to cook stews, pressure cookers are still widely used in the preparation of traditional recipes which require prolonged cooking times. Away from the home, it is difficult but not impossible to find a restaurant in Madrid serving a good *cocido madrileño*. At its best, *cocido* has to be served as soon as it is ready, otherwise the tenderness of the chickpeas and the texture of the potatos and the meat will be affected. In the realm of the perfect *cocido*, reheating is a forbidden word. Even these days local restaurants, known as *restaurantes económicos*, still serve different traditional dishes, including many *cocidos* and stews almost every day of the week: Monday *cocido madrileño*, Tuesday *pote asturiano*, Wednesday *escudella*, Thursday lentils with chorizo, Friday *potaje de vigilia*, Saturdays *fabada* and Sundays *arroz* or *paella*.

restaurants and both local markets and those in major cities in the interior, especially Madrid. In Galicia seafood is a profitable business, and is skilfully cooked in many different ways. Hake, fried or stewed with potatoes and *ajada*, a hot sauce made with olive oil, garlic and *pimentón*, is as popular as fresh scallops and mussels. In recent decades they have been successfully farmed in the sheltered waters of large inlets of the sea which decorate the Galician coast. These *rías* are often compared with the romantic fjords of Norway. Galician mussels and scallops share the market with flavoursome small crabs known as *nécoras* as well as the freshest langoustines. As the tide recedes down long beaches of fine sand, other types of pilgrim appear on the horizon: they are women searching for clams and razor clams hiding in the sand and in the shallows. From the cliffs, brave men venture onto the partially uncovered wave-battered rocks, looking for native mussels and goose barnacles. In Spain goose barnacles or *percebes* are considered the sea's most precious food.

In inland Galicia, everyday hearty food starts with a cabbage and potato broth known as *caldo*, flavoured with a small portion of *unto* (pork fat) which imparts the very characteristic flavour loved or hated by outsiders. There are as many versions of this broth as there are houses, bars and restaurants where it is served. The name *caldo*, interestingly enough, is also given to another dish much closer to the traditional *ollas* and *cocidos* prepared all over Spain. This dish is made with white beans, potatoes, vegetables and flavoursome pieces of pork which may come from the ribs, tail, ears or hock, as well as a generous piece of the local chorizo. Pork and greens are the basis of another classic Galician dish, *Lacón con grelos*, which is cooked with turnip tops and salted and smoked *lacón*, the Galician name for the forelegs of a pig.

Galicia, considered not so long ago as one of the poorest regions in the country, has never stinted on the joyous and food-filled celebrations that mark the summer months. There are a thousand different festivals and *romerías* (processions of holy icons) during which picnics are held in honour of patron saints and the Virgin Mary. Octopus is festive food in Galicia. Any excuse will prompt the lighting of fires under large copper pans where good-sized locally caught octopus are boiled. *Pulpo á feira* is prepared on specialized food stalls, with freshly boiled octopus placed on a bed of boiled potatoes dressed with olive oil and *pimentón*. This dish is usually served on a wooden plate. *Empanada* pies are equally celebrated. Nobody from Galicia could imagine a summer excursion, a day by the sea or a family reunion without them. Depending on the season, *empanadas* made with corn- or wheat-flour dough are filled with *sardinillas*, tuna fish, mussels or cockles, or with salt cod flavoured with sultanas and saffron. Others are made with pigeon, hare, rabbit or chicken. Fresh chestnuts, found in abundance in the region, are also used by local cooks to make rich sauces and to stuff game birds and capons. As in many other parts of Spain, capons and not turkeys are served at Christmas, stuffed with dried apricots, plums and sweet chestnuts. Stuffed capons are roasted in the oven, coated with a little lard and served with a delicate chestnut purée. Some food writers have recently associated the *tarta de Santiago* made with almonds with the large Sephardi community that lived in Galicia before the expulsion of the Jews. However, so far there has been no written evidence to support this.

Since the fourteenth century, the heir to the Spanish Crown has borne the title of Prince or Princess of Asturias. The Principality of Asturias is located between the regions of Galicia, Cantabria and León. This is a world of classic pastoral beauty covered much of the time by mists. Its narrow coastal strip is dotted with some of the most romantic spots in the north, giving way to a wall of high mountains pierced with valleys which are only disturbed by the occasional sound of mining. The food here is hearty and substantial having for centuries fed farmers, seamen and miners. Perhaps the main difference between Asturias and other regions bordering the Bay of Biscay is that the influence of the land is greater than that of the sea. In Asturias to be a farmer is really something to be proud of, more so than in the other regions. This does not mean that fishing is unimportant, but here it takes second place to the tending of the land.

In Asturias and in the rest of Spain old cereals from the hulled wheat family have now become fashionable including einkorn (*Triticum monococcum*), emmer (*T. dicoccum*) and spelt (*T. spelta*). Discoveries in Asturias are causing academics to review their thoughts on the subject of wheat. Asturias is affected by Atlantic weather, and until fairly recently has been considered of little interest to those studying Neolithic farming and

In the port of Cudilleros in Asturias, people enjoy cider and *pitxin* (monkfish) beneath umbrellas in the square.

257

the areas in which wheat traditionally thrived. Now archaeologists have found cereal pollen dating back to 5000 BC in Asturias. This is because of the particular characteristics of hulled wheat, which enabled it to adapt to the adverse climatic conditions there. Hulled wheat has tough glumes, which protect the grains from the weather and during storage. It can grow in poor soils and is resistant to disease. Asturias is now the only part of Spain where old cereals are cultivated as they were centuries ago. Here farmers are still harvesting by plucking the ears by hand or using traditional *mesorias* made with wooden sticks.

It is often said that the Asturian kitchen relates to the rest of the *Cocinas* with two main dishes: *pote* and *caldereta*. *Pote* is another version of the family of *cocidos*. *Caldereta* is the local variation of a fish and potato stew cooked by fisherman in both Atlantic and Mediterranean Spain. But it is in the food of Galicia, northwest France, and to a lesser extent Ireland where affinities with Asturias can really be found; after all this is Celtic land.

In the bars of Oviedo, the capital city of Asturias, lightly fried monkfish known as *pixin* served with a glass or two of the local cider appears on every menu. Cider is used as a main ingredient in many fish dishes. Bream cooked in cider (*chopa a la sidra*) is an excellent example. Another dish that has become synonymous with this area is *fabes con almejas*, beans with clams. Away from the sea, fast-running rivers, their waters tumbling down from the mountains, are rich in trout and salmon. Maize is used in many recipes: trout is first coated with maize flour and then fried in oil flavoured with bacon. Maize or corn flour is also used to make *tortos*, a type of flat bread similar to a Mexican tortilla and usually fried. In Asturias maize or corn bread known as *borona* is as popular as *farrapes*, a tasty type of porridge prepared with maize flour, water and salt which in the past fed the poorest of the poor.

The assimilation of American products into Asturian cuisine was fast and successful. Maize was brought to Asturias in 1604 and was immediately planted in areas where wheat was difficult to grow. By the end of the seventeenth century it had improved the local diet substantially. As in Galicia, it would be impossible to imagine the Asturian countryside without *hórreos*, the traditional wooden and granite barns on stilts where the harvested cobs of maize are stored. A dish that should be eaten in the winter months, *fabada* is essentially a bean dish flavoured with smoked cured meats which the food historians Néstor Luján and Juan Perucho,[1] along many other food writers, have considered as one of the pillars of the *Cocinas*. The best Asturian beans, known as *fabes* and not to be confused with the original pre-American 'fava' bean, are a very specific variety of American bean known as *de La Granja*.[2]

The stunning orange colour of this dish is given by the chorizo, the smoked black pudding with a pinch of saffron.

In the capital Oviedo, patisseries are as visited as the cathedral and San Francisco Square in the heart of the city. With the exception of rice pudding, biscuits and apple or hazelnut cakes, very few sweets and desserts are made at home. The lacey, paper-thin *frixuelos* – also known in Asturias as *fiyuelas* and *fayueles* (pancakes), which have always been associated with Carnival – are cooked all over the Principality. They are also prepared in many other parts of the country with different names: *filloas* in Galicia and *hojuelas* in Castile. Seventeenth-century royal chef Francisco Martínez Montiño includes in his book *Arte de cozina, pastelería, vizcochería y conservería* a recipe he calls *fruta de fisuelos*, with milk, wine, flour, eggs and salt cooked in plenty of lard and sprinkled with honey or sugar.[3] It is possible that he served this dish to his employer, the prince of Asturias, the future Philip III. As a very meticulous cook, Montiño provides the reader with plenty of details related to the consistency and colour *frixuelos* should have when ready. In Asturias rice pudding, its origin lost in time, is served with a distinctive light crust of burned sugar. *Casadieles* are fried pastries filled with cream of walnuts and are believed to be of Roman origin, but most modern Asturian patisserie and confectionary date back to the nineteenth century. The *carbayones* from Oviedo are made with puff pastry, lemon zest and almonds.

Situated between Asturias and the Basque Country, Cantabria is a land of milk and lemons, its past strongly linked to Castile as it was Castile's main access to the sea. It is today a successful *autonomía* where high mountains are never far away. The Picos de Europa watch over the life of many picturesque valleys, but here the mountains are set back further than in Asturias, making the transition between mountains and sea gentler and less aggressive.

*Montañés* is a word spoken in Cantabria with respect. It refers to where the mountain people come from, as well as to a hearty *cocido* in which the local green cabbage is as important as the meat and the chickpeas. Associated also with Cantabria is a dish called *olla ferroviaria*. Its name derives from a large utensil which incorporates a charcoal stove. This cooker was used by train drivers and conductors to cook food while travelling on the railway. As the train continued steaming along the tracks on its journey, the tantalizing smell of food cooked at the front joined the aroma of the *tortilla de patatas*, roasted legs of cold chicken and apples usually brought by the passengers. Wine produced further south was normally carried by men in a leather *bota* which from time to time was passed around to fellow travellers. Despite the long-ago disappearance of the ingenious stove, different *ollas ferroviarias* can be tasted at a local competition that takes place in the Cantabrian town of Mataportera once a year.

Laredo, Comillas, Santander (the capital city of Cantabria) and above all the historic Santillana del Mar attract thousands of visitors looking for good food and the prehistoric Altamira caves during the summer months. In Laredo the spectacle of large barbecues on the beach is as attractive as the irresistible aroma of fresh sardines in season, grilled fast over red-hot embers. The Cantabrians can fry fish as well as the Andalusians from whom they learned the skill in the first place. *Rabas* is the local name for crispy but tender squid fried in olive oil with a difference. Cooks here do not cut the squid into rings but into the shape of a potato chip.

Anchovies are a good reason to visit a particular village or bar at the beginning of the summer. If they are fresh they are known as *bocartes*, but if they are preserved in salt local people call them *anchoas*. Across the bay from Laredo, Santoña is a place where people have Italian names almost as much as Castilian ones. In the nineteenth century a number of Sicilian families moved to the area, bringing with them a cottage industry that soon became one of the most important businesses on the northern coast. They knew how to preserve anchovies in salt better than the locals.

Based mostly on dairy products, desserts are prepared by home cooks, and the same dishes are served at well-attended traditional restaurants. *Leche frita*, or fried milk, sounds rather unappealing and yet deserves credit. At its best it is prepared with the lightest béchamel, made with butter and milk from a local farm, flour, sugar and the peel of local lemons. As it sets it is cut into small squares, coated lightly with flour to retain its shape, dipped in egg and fried in olive oil. Surprisingly lemons thrive in the Cantabrian countryside not far from the sea and not far from the natural border that separates Cantabria from the Basque Country.

Ask any Spaniard where you will find the best food in Spain and the answer will be the Basque Country. This is a place where the perfect duality between man and food is the norm to the point where it has become an obsession. Here everybody is a potential cook whether amateur or professional, man or woman.

The land where the enigmatic Basques have lived since prehistoric times lies close to the western end of the Pyrenees. Three of the six historic Basque provinces are in France to the north of this mountain range. Along the coast to the west are the provinces of Guipúzcoa and Vizcaya. Alava, the third of the Spanish Basque provinces, is inland. Even if they all speak the same language and share a passion for peppers, French Basques prefer to cook with meat whereas a large percentage of Spanish Basque recipes are cooked with fish.[4]

Preserving fish is
an art passed from
generation to
generation all along
the Cantabrian coast.

Preserving fish is an art passed from generation to generation all along the Cantabrian coast.

It would be difficult to define Basque regional cuisine precisely. Basque cooking has several different sources of inspiration, ranging from peasant dishes to the cuisine of the high bourgeoisie, and it is true to its culinary traditions and practices. There are slight variations between the cooking in Álava in the interior and Guipúzcoa and Vizcaya by the coast, but they all pride themselves on using local produce in season. Come spring the first young peas, the smaller the better, appear in the market, supplied from the vegetable gardens of the *caseríos* (local farms). Recipes such as *guisantes salteados con cebolletas* (tiny peas sautéed with spring onions) do not need the helping hand of ham, which is so often used in Spanish recipes cooked with vegetables and beans. In the early autumn, tender beans also known in Navarre and Rioja as *pochas* for their light colour command the same attention, although it is the black bean – the *alubia* of Tolosa, a town in Guipúzcoa – which has always been one of the main pillars of the food of the *caserío*. In the Basque Country and northern Navarre, *caseríos* are dotted here and there every few kilometres. These isolated farmsteads are independent economic and social units, and have remained at the heart of rural life in this part of the country. In Basque symbolism they represent goodness, protecting all that is inside. Each one has its own name, normally called after the family to which they belong. Here, *alubias*, not so long ago eaten every day of the year, are cooked with pork belly, onion, a little olive oil, pork ribs, black pudding, local cabbage and garlic. They are served with a few preserved *piparra* chillies picked while still green.

Over the centuries, Basque men have searched out places where they can eat and drink and meet their male friends. In the Basque Country, cider houses dating back to the Middle Ages and gastronomic societies from the nineteenth century are still going strong. In small towns such as Astigarraga, not far from San Sebastián, cider houses are normally open to the public from January through to April, when the cider is ready for bottling. Here cider is tasted by clients directly from the large wooden vats where it ferments. Sometimes the customers bring *chuletones* (ribs of beef) or large sea bream to be grilled in the communal kitchen of the cider house, or they try the dishes offered by the kitchen which have become synonymous with this type of establishment, such as fried cod and salt cod omelette. Cod omelette, infinitely more delicious that it sounds, is made with slow-fried sweet onions and green peppers, flaked desalted cod and eggs.

> Apart from the techniques used in the preparation of fish, Basque cuisine utilizes special techniques to prepare meat, vegetables and innumerable desserts and preserves, and yet what gives it its unique personality and dignity is, without doubt, the preparation and cooking of the products of the sea.

Spanish scientist, historian, philosopher and writer Gregorio Marañon wrote these words in 1979 in the introduction to the book *La cocina de Nicolasa*.

In the Basque Country people speak about the quality, diversity and freshness of fish as much as they talk about the weather, and with the same deep passion that they feel about politics. At Christmas time, elvers *(angulas)* and bream *(besugos)* reach sky-high prices. It takes only a minute to prepare elvers in an earthenware *cazuelita* with olive oil, garlic and dried chilli pepper.

When summer arrives it is time for celebrating the arrival of tuna. *Marmitako* is a fisherman's stew cooked with potatoes, tomatoes, green peppers and light-coloured tuna fish known as *bonito del Norte* (albacore, or longfin tuna). Fresh anchovies *al estilo de Bermeo* is a dish to share with friends. Each person takes three or four fresh anchovies, and in turn cooks them for a minute or so in a pot filled with hot olive oil flavoured with chilli pepper and garlic.

Whether fried or baked in the oven or cooked in a rich sauce, hake is highly appreciated by Basques as long as it is truly fresh, but it takes the patience and light touch of a Gastronomic Society cook to transform a *merluza en salsa verde* (hake in green sauce) into a very respectable dish. These egalitarian societies where men gather to play cards, to sing and most importantly to cook for themselves are to be found all over the Basque Country, Navarre and Rioja. They were founded almost two centuries ago, but radical changes in the way modern Basques live are threatening their existence. Gastronomic societies are places where women have never, until fairly recently, been allowed to enter. Now they can be invited by members on certain days of the week to have lunch or dinner, although entry to the kitchen area remains forbidden. To those who defend the true spirit of the societies, 'women disrupt the harmony,' they say. For them this is a man's space, created by men who prepare food for their sole enjoyment or the enjoyment of other men, learned from their mothers and grandmothers, cooked more often than not in the traditional earthenware *cazuelas*. Apart from fish, small game is another speciality of the societies.

Some food writers may say that the popularity of game dishes in the Basque Country is more a consequence of the local shooting tradition than a true appreciation of game, but this may not necessarily be the case. In the Basque Country the cooking of game dishes is clearly influenced by France as well as by the cooking of northern Navarre and Rioja. *Codornices con salsa de manzana* (quail cooked with a sauce made with apples, carrots, onions, leeks, white wine, cider and the local brandy) is a dish that encapsulates the thinking behind Basque food, the cider house and the gastronomic society.

On the evening of 19 January, the gastronomic societies of San Sebastián open their doors to their members for the celebration of *La Tamborrada*, probably the most important festival of the year. This is when small processions of drummers in military costumes and chef's whites parade during the entire night through the old part of the town. Each procession of drummers and chefs, or *Tamborrada*, belongs to a gastronomic society. Later all of them will serve dinner. There are many different stories about the origins of the *Tamborrada*. Some believe it goes back to the Napoleonic Wars when there were more soldiers than civilians occupying the walled city of San Sebastián. At five o'clock each morning, the city bakers would fetch water from one of the town's public drinking fountains while the changing of the guard took place. From time to time, half teasingly, the bakers would beat out a rhythm on their pitchers and water barrels to echo the guard's drums. Do the cooks of the present-day *Tamborrada* represent those bakers of the past? Perhaps they do. Other versions are equally defended by some people. Are the origins of the

People dressed up as chefs and soldiers to celebrate *La Tamborrada* festival in San Sebastián.

*Tamborrada* associated with the comical *charangas* of Carnival that mocked authority with their singing while parading the streets in fancy dress? One thing is for certain, one of San Sebastián's earliest gastronomic societies, the Unión Artesana, was one of the original organizers in 1871 of the festival as it exists today. On 19 January, traditional desserts such as cheese with walnuts and quince paste, followed by *mamia* (junket), *pastel vasco* and almond-paste *frangipane*, are served at the Societies.

Not far from San Sebastián, at the foothills of the Pyrenees, away on the *caseríos* in Navarre, the ancient *intzaursalsa*, a sweet soup made with walnuts, sugar, cinnamon, water and milk, is prepared by the Basque *amona*, the grandmother. The walnuts are wrapped in a piece of thick white cloth, then crushed with a wooden mallet until they form a smooth paste. Then the walnut paste is cooked in boiling water with the cinnamon until the water has nearly evaporated, at which point the milk and sugar are added. The mixture is cooked until it thickens to form a light cream and it is then served sprinkled with a little ground cinnamon.

## AROUND THE PYRENEES

Many small towns were built along the Spanish Pyrenees, in northern Navarre, northern Aragon and northwest Catalonia. Their names are associated with the Catholic Church, the pilgrim trail to Santiago, and medieval battles between the French and the Basques: Jaca, La Seu d'Urgell, Roncesvalles.

Two different branches of the *Camino de Santiago* start in the Pyrenees on the way to Rioja and Castile-León. One starts in Roncesvalles in Navarre, the other in Jaca in Aragon. They join at Puente la Reina, a little town 'in the loveliest countryside on earth' as described by Adam Hopkins in his evocative book *Spanish Journeys*.[5]

In medieval times religious orders coming from France opened a number of monasteries and hospitals where simple food was served free of charge to the hundreds of pilgrims who crossed the Pyrenees on their long journey to Santiago. In spring, as the snows begin to melt in the high mountains and the pilgrims begin again their crossing of the border, local enthusiasts follow the quiet pursuits of river fishing and mushroom gathering.

### ALTO EBRO: A VEGETABLE PATCH BY THE RIVER

The River Ebro flows from Cantabria to the Mediterranean Sea, and transforms dry land into lush fields of vegetables extending for hundreds of kilometres through the regions of Rioja, southern Navarre and Aragon, an area known as Alto Ebro. All along this fertile land, irrigation systems installed by the Arabs in the tenth century are still in use. Throughout the year, seasonal vegetables are made into local dishes such as *menestra* and *cardoen salsa de almendras* (cardoon in almond sauce), which is served at Christmas time. *Menestras* are a family of dishes, prepared depending on the seasons, with five or six different types of vegetables – peas, artichokes, asparagus, cardoon, broad beans, borage and the white parts of chard – each one adding a different flavour and a different texture. Some of the vegetables are first boiled separately; others, such as the white of chard, are fried, having first been boiled and then coated with flour and egg. The dish comes together with a light sauce made with onions, flour and some liquid from boiling the asparagus. It is also flavoured by a *sofrito* made of garlic and small pieces of ham.

Dishes cooked with bread, salt cod, lamb and above all peppers share the food culture of this part of the country. Many of the dishes made with bread as a main ingredient are common not only in this area but in the rest of Spain. *Sopa* is the generic name both for soup and for the bread that is used to make the ubiquitous *migas*. Originally prepared by shepherds in the open air, *migas* were already eaten in Roman times. Ujué in Navarre is a hill-top village known for its thirteenth-century church and for the quality of its bread and *migas*. At Ujué this humble food has become a special dish which attracts hundreds of visitors to local restaurants each weekend. The cut-up pieces of dried bread are first moistened with water and left overnight to become light and fluffy. Then they are cooked in a large iron pan with a few spoonfuls of homemade tomato sauce and small pieces of chorizo and *panceta*. In early autumn, grapes replace some of the cured meats.

As ever, salt cod coming from the Atlantic fishing ports is eaten today in the Alto Ebro as it was in previous centuries, but it is a much more interesting product. Now it reaches the market with less salt and higher water content. *Bacalao con leche* is cod cooked with milk, onions and pine nuts, while *bacalao al ajoarriero* is mainly flavoured with red peppers. Along the Ebro a historical recipe for *conejo con anís* (rabbit with aniseed, cinnamon and black pepper) is still prepared in a number of villages. Less ancient but equally traditional is *cordero al chilindrón*, lamb cooked with a rich sauce made with dried red peppers, green peppers, parsley, garlic and very often potatoes. Many towns and villages in the area smell of the peppers which can be seen hanging on balconies, drying in the sun. Peppers of all colours, shapes and different names are prepared in many dishes in Navarre and Rioja: stuffed *piquillo* peppers, roasted *entrevarados* (variegated purple-green and red) or the *pimientos del cristal* used for bottling. White asparagus is equally celebrated in the spring, served with home-made mayonnaise or poached with a dash of vinegar. The artichokes of Tudela, a town famous for the quality of its vegetables, are equally

*Cogollos* are grown by the side of the River Ebro in Navarre.

in demand. Recently some restaurants have started to serve pink cardoon, an old variety rescued by local chefs almost from extinction, the same cardoon that was beautifully painted by Sánchez Cotán in the seventeenth century. Traditionally it is cooked at Christmastime with a rich almond sauce. The *crema de alubias*, a classic dish made with colourful white-and-red *caparrón* beans, belly of pork, leeks, carrots, green peppers and onion, is as often made in restaurants as it is in private houses with an old-fashioned pressure cooker. Slow-roasted *gorrín* is the name given in Navarre to suckling pig. It is served with a tantalizing thin crackling.

In Rioja, Navarre and Aragon, vines grown for producing wine share the land with olive groves, fruit orchards and vegetable gardens. The vine is pruned in early winter and nothing is wasted. Vine shoots are used as fuel for grilling thin *txistorra* sausages, local chorizo and lamb chops, the last of which are the main attraction at the vintage festival that takes place each year in Logroño, the capital city of Rioja, on 21 September. Thousands of lamb chops are grilled in every street of the city in honour of Saint Michael, the patron saint of the wine-maker.

In the Alto Ebro, wineries open their doors to visitors looking for one or two cases of good wine and something to eat. On the menu, *patatas a la riojana* flavoured with local chorizo, potato omelette, stuffed peppers and especially *chuletillas* (lamb chops) are always available. In the last decade, some bodegas have invested in state-of-the-art restaurants and hotels offering local specialities, ultra-modern dishes and wine tastings.

## Castille: The Power Engine of the Old Country

At the heart of Castile, the peninsula's high plateau has always watched over the rest of the country. Once the top dog and most powerful of all the old Spanish kingdoms, modern Castile has now been divided into two separate autonomies: Castile-León and Castile-La Mancha.

In the twelfth century, pilgrims felt that travelling along the Camino de Santiago took them away from luscious foods, making gluttonous obesity vanish and generally restraining appetites of the flesh. Centuries later, the Camino de Santiago still attracts thousands of pilgrims. They know that nothing will take away the luscious food they deserve. Having left Navarre behind at the beginning of their journey, many pilgrims would have been travelling on the main route of the Camino de Santiago for hundreds of kilometres, first in Rioja, then on the northern side of the River Douro as it crosses the provinces of Burgos, Valladolid and León before reaching Galicia and Santiago de Compostela, their final destination. Taking the longer route, they would have travelled past hundreds of Romanesque chapels, their size and simple architectural style competing with two of the most impressive edifices of Christianity, the Gothic cathedrals of León and Burgos. The provinces of Avila, Zamora, Soria, Segovia, Valladolid and Salamanca are also part of Castile-León. With the exception of Rioja and certain parts of the Basque Country, which now belong to their own autonomies, the whole of modern Castile-León practically coincides with that of the old kingdoms of the same names, finally unified by the Christians in the early thirteenth century.

It is almost impossible to provide a complete guide to the food traditions of such a large expanse. At least they all share a passion for lamb, pork and charcuterie, excellent bread, pulses and the wines of five Denominations of Origin: Ribera del Duero [Douro], Toro, Rueda, Cigales and El Bierzo. Not far from El Bierzo, *cocido maragato* from the Comarca of La Maragatería in León is made in the same way as other *cocidos* in Castile, but here the meat is eaten first and the soup last. Apparently during the War of Independence from Napoleon's France at the beginning of the nineteenth century, a group of people were getting ready to enjoy the soup of a substantial *cocido* when they were disturbed by the proximity of the enemy. A life-and-death decision had to be taken, so they ate the important part first, the meat and sausages, sadly leaving behind the chickpeas and of course the soup.

The economy of Castile-León has always depended on its capacity to produce some of the best cereals and breads in the country. At bread shops, many specialities can be purchased: *molletas*, *hogazas*, *teleras* and the *Torta de Aranda de Duero*. The festive *hornazo*, baked at Easter, is stuffed with boiled eggs, chorizo and cured ham. Large areas of Castile-León were selected by the Romans to improve the production of cereals, to make bread and to feed the Roman army legions. They were the same areas of land that would later be known as the granary of the country, *la tierra del pan* and *la tierra de campos*, in the province of Zamora, where bread has traditionally been made with two types of dough. Spongy breads characterized by a crunchy and rather brittle crust are made with what is known as *flama* dough. Breads preferred by those with very long memories and a true attachment to the Castilian land are made with *candeal* flour, which is also the name of the dough. *Candeal* bread is made with little water, which produces a dough that cannot be kneaded. Home bakers have to stretch the dough several times with a rolling pin as if making puff pastry. *Candeal* doughs are only raised once. This bread has a dense, shiny, very smooth crust. If it is decorated with artistic motifs lightly carved on the surface it is called *pan lechugino*. Both *flama* and *candeal* doughs are normally made into large round loaves known as *hogazas* in which deep cuts are made with a knife before baking; this helps to break the crust.

Pulses, once the food of the poor and also loved by powerful Castilians, have become the food of those who can afford it, since many are now sold at prohibitive prices under their own Denomination of Origin. The *judía del Barco* is a very creamy bean produced in Ávila. The small *arrocina* bean and large *judión* are also highly prized.

In the whole of Castile, roasting meat in wood-fired ovens has always been an art. Roasting at such high temperatures requires a special skill handed down from fathers to sons. They roast milk-fed lamb, kid and suckling pig (*cordero lechal, cabrito* and *cochinillo*). Wednesday is market day in the small town of Roa in Ribera del Duero, where excellent red wines are produced, and it is also the only day of the week that the local *mesón* serves meals to the public. By popular demand, the menu never changes and probably never will: roast lamb, freshly baked bread and a fresh salad of lettuce, tomatoes and onions dressed with olive oil, vinegar and salt. By two o'clock the queues of people waiting for a table stretch all the way back to the market, several streets away. The bread is baked overnight in the same oven which later in the day will be used to roast the meat. Large round loaves with a firm crust, orangey colour and a spongy texture are just perfect for mopping up the flavoursome meat juices. Whole lambs are roasted in large oval earthenware dishes with a little water and salt.

Lamb roasted in an earthenware *cazuela* in Castile.

269

The city of Segovia is famous for its magnificent Roman aqueduct and above all a number of emblematic restaurants serving *cochinillo*, the speciality of the town. This is not easy to roast. The thin skin needs to become crispy while the meat underneath remains juicy. To prove its extreme tenderness, chefs carve the *cochinillo* at a sideboard in front of their clients using a dinner plate instead of a knife.

A fresh cheese and the best-known black pudding of the country – *queso de Burgos* and *morcilla de Burgos* – are in demand all over Spain. Celtiberian in origin, the city of Burgos would become, in the eleventh century, the capital of Castile. Two centuries later a magnificent Gothic cathedral started to be built. In 1332 King Alfonso XI founded an unusual medieval order in Burgos: the Noble Order of *La Banda* (the sash). Apart from their main Christian duties, all the *caballeros* belonging to this order had to eat clean food slowly, seated and at a table with a tablecloth. They also had to drink with moderation and sleep properly. Around this time, a number of monastic orders, the *Hospalárias*, following the example of the Order of Malta, opened their doors to the sick and poor and especially pilgrims. Eventually more than thirty *Órdenes Hospalárias* were founded north of the River Douro. Among them the Hospital del Rey, a dependent of the powerful monastery of Las Huelgas, was particularly popular with the casual visitor. At the hospital, substantial food and one or two glasses of wine were distributed on the three different floors of the building: soup, meat, white bread and wine, all free of charge and for the love of God. Egg dishes were only given to the privileged and would have been kept under lock and key in the larder. Perhaps this is the reason why eggs are so popular in this part of Spain.

*Huevos escalfados con pisto* are broken eggs with a thick vegetable sauce, prepared by stewing slowly in olive oil, onions, green peppers, courgettes, tomatoes, and potatoes. *Revueltos* (scrambled eggs) are a modern concept from an old recipe. They are made with daring combinations of two or three ingredients along with the eggs. One of these, *revuelto de ajetes y gambas*, is cooked with garlic shoots and fresh prawns.

Castilian potatoes, particularly the yellow-fleshed variety, are cultivated in the provinces of Palencia and Burgos and are preferred for *patatas a la importancia*. This is an inexpensive recipe favoured in the 1950s in schools and hospitals for a very simple reason: it goes a long way. Peeled potatoes are cut into rounds, coated with flour and egg, fried in olive oil and cooked in a light stock or just water. As the liquid reduces it becomes rich and tasty. In the 1970s some innovative chefs altered the recipe by using a light fish stock and clams, and this sold at a very high price. It is interesting how the names of the dishes cooked with potatoes often are accompanied by a description such as *a la importancia* (in an important way), *a lo pobre* (poor man's) or *a la brava* (with a sauce made with tomatoes and chillies).

In northern Castile the paucity of original local desserts is compensated for by the rich tradition of artisan pastries, egg confections, biscuits and small *pastelitos* normally made in convents, local bakeries and patisseries. On Sundays, grandparents and godparents used to buy (some still do) a selection to be eaten at tea-time. Historical *rosquillas* are eaten at fiestas and on saints' days. They are fritters made with eggs, olive oil, sugar, flour, *anis* liqueur and brandy, and sprinkled with icing sugar. *Huesos de santo* (saints' bones) are slightly more elaborate. *Huesos* are pastries made with lemon-juice syrup, toasted almonds, egg whites and icing sugar and filled with egg custard or with runny quince paste. *Almendras garrapiñadas* from Briviesca are almonds coated with a light caramel, while *mantecados de Astorga* in León were prepared for the first time by a nun who left her convent in Ávila and decided to become a successful commercial baker.

Spring is the time to travel in the southern *Meseta*, stretching for hundreds of kilometres and broken by two mountain ranges, the Montes de Toledo to the west and the Sierra de Guadarrama to the north. It has some of the grandeur of the prairies and a magic of its own that inspired the imagination of Cervantes. The Arabs called it *al-Manchara*, meaning flat and dried land, which they embellished by planting saffron crocuses to be gathered in the heart of winter. Since then, come November, families and friends dedicate themselves to the annual harvest of the most expensive spice in the world, saffron. In the early mornings, the aspect of the land at the hardest time of the year is transformed. As the saffron flowers open, swathes of land are converted into magnificent coloured carpets of mauve which intensify with the rising sun. Picking the flowers takes place first thing in the morning by hand. It is a backbreaking task that has to be done efficiently and speedily to preserve intact the three red and yellow stamens inside each flower. Within the same day the stamens will become saffron. To preserve freshness and quality, thousands and thousands of flowers are transported in the early evening to local villages. In each house the members of the family are ready to receive the precious cargo. Once plucked from each flower, the stamens are deposited in fine mesh containers. The most difficult operation, the drying, comes next. The family's father figure does this, and it takes place over a gentle heat before the saffron is stored and made ready for selling. Unfortunately Spanish saffron, which enjoys a high reputation, has been affected by market forces and less than desirable international and national trading practices.

Toledo, the imperial city of the Visigoths, has managed to defeat the passing of time. Little has changed in the city since El Greco painted *The Burial of the Count of Argaz* in the late sixteenth century. In a city of old narrow streets, synagogues, mosques and Christian churches, all still protected by a Moorish wall, modern building development has been forced to keep away. In the countryside, vineyards, garlic fields and olive groves thrive.

It would be fair to say that a couple of decades ago it was almost impossible to find properly cooked regional food in the local restaurants and *ventas* of La Mancha. *La Cocina Manchega*, peasant by nature, had been seriously neglected. Furthermore, a certain amount of confusion and a desire for innovation, not always successful or justified, was in some cases preventing the natural adaptation of this earthy and very substantial food to the modern world, the only way it could have been rescued. Thanks to the quest of a number of local chefs, *la Cocina Manchega* is now coming back renewed and slightly refined but without losing its identity. Everywhere the kitchens of old and new restaurants and bars are trying to follow in the footsteps of fully qualified local chefs fascinated by their own local tradition. *Almoronía*, known as *alboronía* in Andalusia, tastes even better than before. This vegetable dish has retained its association with the Moors and Jews, and is cooked today with tomatoes, green peppers, onions and aubergines and flavoured with cumin, giving each ingredient the correct cooking time – a departure from tradition. Formerly all the ingredients were cooked together almost to a paste with a rather unattractive colour and texture.

In La Mancha many traditional dishes are given interesting names, of which many belong to the realm of irony and metaphor. *Pimentajo* is a dip made with roasted red peppers, pounded ripe tomatoes, garlic, cumin seeds and olive oil. The substantial *sopa de parturienta* made with eggs and ham is still given to mothers after childbirth. Two other traditional recipes, *andrajos* and *ropa vieja*, curious names both meaning 'old clothes', are prepared with leftovers. *Andrajos* is a bean stew made with béchamel, and *ropa vieja* is a stew prepared with meat left from the *cocido*. Some historians believe that the dish known as *duelos y quebrantos* (Hurts and Sorrows) refers to the sadness felt by farmers when losing a sheep or two. Farmers also ate this dish on Saint Peter's day, the day of the year they did their annual accounts. Today it is made with eggs, pieces of fried pork fat, ham and chorizo. *Tojunto* is an abbreviation between *todo* (everything) and *junto* (together). It is a dish in which all the ingredients are cooked together from the start: beef or chicken, rabbit or partridge, onions, garlic, bay leaf, peppercorns, cloves, saffron, peppers, potatoes and a glass of dry white wine.

Purple garlic grows around the town of Las Pedroñeras in the province of Cuenca. Garlic is the protagonist of the traditional garlic soup, *sopa de ajo castellana*, made with bread, *pimentón*, garlic, water and olive oil, enriched with egg. *Gazpachos galianos* or *gazpachos del pastor* is a classic recipe from La Mancha still prepared by shepherds while looking after their sheep or goats. It has very little to do with the well-known *gazpacho andaluz*, which is a vegetarian recipe of Moorish origin. *Galiano* are made with hare, chicken, rabbit, unleavened bread, *pimentón*, salt and pepper.[6]

Game is cooked everywhere in the southern *Meseta* and even modern-style restaurants tend to follow traditional recipes. The shooting of partridges and other small game has regained the popularity it had in the Middle Ages. *Perdices a la toledana*, one of the best recipes known for partridges in Spain, is simplicity itself. First the partridges are sautéed in olive oil previously flavoured with a head of garlic, then the rest of the ingredients are added: bay leaf, black peppercorns and carrots. Wild boar, which is also hunted around the Montes de Toledo, is never available in the market. Hunters gather together to roast their spoils on an open-air spit. At other times, they share the meat to take home and prepare their favourite recipes. *Estofado de jabalí* is a rich stew prepared with large cuts of wild boar.

Marzipan, strongly associated with Toledo since early medieval times, is usually eaten during the Christmas festivities. Chroniclers of the city maintain that to celebrate victory in a battle waged against the Moors by Alfonso VIII of Castile, the nuns of the convent of San Clemente had the idea of making special bread with the sugar and almonds stored in their barns. In Toledo this confection, made by beating almonds and sugar with a *maza* (mallet), was given the name *mazapán* – not a totally original name as any Venetian would rightly say. The *figuritas de mazapán* are made in hundreds of different shapes and symbols reminiscent of the city's multicultural and tolerant past. Minute crescent moons are made at the local *pastelerías*, while little marzipan apples and baby lambs are the speciality of the many convents dotted around the city.

Madrid's heart beats to the tune of the southern *Meseta*. Madrid, or *Magerit*, as the city was known when it was part of the old Visigoth Kingdom of Toledo, became the capital of Spain in 1567 when Philip II moved his court there. Philip, the most powerful and austere king at that time, was apparently partial to fresh air and the aroma of a roasted *cochinillo* coming across the sierras. Even today the most beautiful part of the old city, known as the area of the *Austrias* (Habsburgs), attracts the attention of the *madrileño* and the foreigner looking for an authentic regional taste. This is the Madrid of the Castilian *mesones* and the cosy old restaurants still serving traditional food and wines from La Mancha and Valdepeñas. In the same area, one of the first restaurants of the country, the Hostería Botín, opened its doors in 1626. Today Botín, in Cuchilleros Street, is still serving some of the hearty, peasant-style and very tasty original recipes of the house. Apart from *cocido madrileño*, other recipes associated with Madrid are *callos a la madrileña* (tripe, *madrileño*-style), *judias del Tio Lucas* (Uncle Luke's white beans), *lentejas a la madrileña*, and the humble but succulent *sopas de ajo* (garlic soup). These dishes had to compete with an array of specialities reaching the city from other regions of Spain. As the city grew in the sixteenth and seventeenth centuries, people arriving from all over the country brought with them the recipes associated with their own culinary traditions. Eventually they started to open restaurants with Galician, Basque, Valencian or Andalusian flavours.

With the arrival of the Bourbons, a strong Parisian influence came to Madrid. This would change the infrastructure of the city in the eighteenth century. The city grew again as long avenues and tall houses were built. At the table of the aristocracy the word was foreign refinement. With the arrival of King Charles III, fashionable Madrid turned to Italy. In 1772 José Barbarán, a chef from Verona, opened La Fontana de Oro, a *fonda* (eating house), café and billiard room that become a political enclave and a place to be seen. As for the rest of the population of Madrid, they remained faithful to the hearty food they knew.

Twice a year *madrileños* still gather around the churches of their patron saints: San Isidro el Labrador (the farmer) and San Antonio de la Florida. They pray first for work and for love, and then they eat and dance all night long as their ancestors did. With the war with Napoleonic France (1808), hunger and desperation came to the capital city. By the mid-nineteenth century the Madrid of the aristocracy and upper middle classes was joining the rest of Europe in the search for gastronomic excellence, mainly French in style. The city became a land of both tradition and confusion, particularly in food, where recipes such as *cocido* were served in silver terrines, sharing the menu with elaborate specialities with foreign names and exorbitant prices, without character or hope. Only thirty years ago, the menus served at Spanish embassies all over the world were still showing French names, even in dishes belonging to the regional *cocinas* of Spain. The beginning of the twentieth century was marked by political unrest. In a country where polarization between rich and poor was far too evident, influences by new socialist as well as anarchist ideas were growing. Something had to change and it did. It changed the traditional structure of society into one with a weak aristocracy, a strong upper middle class, a new urban middle class, traders and a growing working class. The traditional local dishes, plus other dishes from the rest of the regions, gained further popularity. Unfortunately the kitchens of famous hotels and restaurants were still serving international food of little interest, headed often by French chefs or their followers. In Madrid, as in many other places, the Spanish Civil War brought hunger and desperation to the city once more. Hope came at the end of the 1970s. Restaurants offering *alta cocina española* (something that had never happened before) were opening their doors to a new type of customer who was taking note of the presence of good food and a good cellar.

To the southwest of Madrid lies Extremadura (Land of Extremes), a land associated with Ibérico hams, conquistadors, Cortés, Pizarro and Núñez de Balboa. Extramadura is also associated with a *cocina* that remains to be discovered. *La Cocina Extremeña* is close to the food of Castile-La Mancha, and yet when it is cooked in small towns and villages, it proves to be as rich in original recipes as it is unknown. It is prepared with some of the best ingredients in the country. Ibérico products are everywhere in the kitchens of Extremadura and this is not surprising. The dehesa forest stretches across the south of the region. Expensive cured hams, shoulders and loins are very thinly sliced to be served as an aperitif. Chorizo, black pudding, the best *manteca* (lard) and tasty cured belly of pork are included in substantial recipes, many of which are flavoured with the local *pimentón*. Since the arrival of the pepper in the peninsula, deep red *pimentón* has enhanced the flavour of popular food and the rather dull colour of traditional charcuterie. Although it is also produced in the region of Murcia in eastern Spain, in the *comarca* of La Vera, *pimentón*, the number one spice in Spanish culinary tradition, is sold smoked and unsmoked, sweet, hot and *agridulce* (sweet and sour).

Not to be confused with Hungarian paprika: *pimentón de La Vera* from Extremadura.

## Serrano and Ibérico Ham

A sixteenth-century painting by 'El Bosco' (Hieronymus Bosch) of the Temptations of St Anthony, showing the saint praying in the company of a small pig, hangs in a gallery at the Prado Museum in Madrid. St Anthony was well known for his passion for animals and especially pigs, letting them roam free in the streets, and hoping charitable people would feed them. Later he would make certain their meat would feed the poor and the infirm.

In Spain pigs have been feeding people throughout the long history of the country, not only in times of misery but of plenty. The Celts in Galicia treasured them as much as the people from the Baetica in the south.

*Serrano* is a generic term Spaniards use to name their cured hams, all hams. It means cured in the high sierras, traditionally after the *matanza*, slaughter, of the pigs. This is a family and local celebration that not so long ago would have mostly taken place in villages and small farms during the winter months. With a few exceptions, mainly in Extremadura and Andalusia, family *matanzas* have practically become a

Sophisticated ingredients such as wild duck liver and truffles have always been available in Extremadura. Large and small game is plentiful in the Sierras of this autonomy. Néstor Luján and Juan Perucho's book *El libro de la cocina española* dedicates a number of pages to game dishes prepared in the region. Among the recipes they selected, partridge cooked with local truffles and rabbit with mushrooms, wine and mountain herbs are two of the best.[7] A manuscript published in Barcelona in 1980, *La mejor cocina extremeña*, by Isabel and Carmen García Hernández,[8] has to be considered as one of the most real and impressive personal records of nineteenth- and twentieth-century Spanish regional food, going back several generations. This is an extensive book containing 586 recipes organized in a random way, sometimes by ingredients, at other times by cooking method. It starts with soups that include meat or ham in the good Spanish way. Vegetable dishes are prepared with asparagus, *tagarninas* (wild cardoon), spinach or cabbage There are also thing of the past. Today the name *serrano* is also associated with hams and shoulders from white European breeds of pigs, of which the majority are produced on a large scale by a competent industry located in many parts of the country. The Jamón de Teruel in Aragon is an excellent sample of a quality Serrano ham guaranteed by a Denomination of Origin. The hams, shoulders and other cured products from the indigenous Ibérico breed, once a national secret kept as such for decades by European and North American regulations, now give pleasure not only to those who live close to the dehesa forest but to others who can afford it. The dehesa is the Ibérico's natural habitat in western Spain, where pigs roam free while acorns carpet the floor of the forest. Ibérico hams and shoulders are from pigs that love fresh acorns and chestnuts, fresh flowers and herbs. They like to siesta and take a daily bath in shallow pools, the muddier the better. Ibérico is protected by a number of Denominations of Origin: Guijuelo in Salamanca, Dehesa de Extremadura in Extremadura and famously Jabugo in Andalusia.

*cocidos, calderetas, macarrones, fideos refritos con salsa de carne, tomate y queso, escabeche, paella* and various *arroces*. By the time the recipes with fish, meat and game are found, it is clear this is the food of a family with means. It appears that the maternal great-grandmother of the authors had worked at one time in the kitchen of a prominent landowner where the food was enriched by the best local as well as imported ingredients. The list of fish dishes includes: *Sopa de Cazón* (small sharks present in both Andalusian and Estremeñan food), stuffed bream, stuffed sardines, macaroni with prawns and clams, macaroni with hake, and a sauce to be served with a cod omelette. The largest section is about meat and meat products, which is not surprising. The description of the preparation of local sausages and other *embutidos* is as impressive as the number of pages dedicated to preserving vegetables and fruit: old-fashioned pastries, ice cream, fresh lemonade, a number of liqueurs and even a recipe to make toilet soap are also part of the collection. *Leche merengada* can also be found here. This is a popular Spanish drink which is served very cold. It is made with milk, lemon zest, sugar, egg white and cinnamon, a perfect blend of meringue and milk, infused with citrus and spice.

## Along the Mediterranean Shore

From northern Catalonia to Murcia, a large percentage of the land and its people belong to the Mediterranean world of the olive and the vine, the pestle and mortar, and the sweet ñora pepper. By the time peppers reached the peninsula the Crown of Aragon's expansionist adventures in the Mediterranean were over. They had lasted almost 400 years, during which food had been enriched beyond people's dreams in most parts of Catalonia, the Spanish *Levante*, the Balearics and Murcia.

In the ninth century, when war prevailed in a divided Christian Spain, 'Wilfred the Shaggy', a visionary and rather ambitious Sardinian nobleman, founded the house of Barcelona. His intention was clear. He wanted to unify the surrounding territories under one ruler. He could never have imagined how extensive the new territory would become. Ramon Berenguer, one of his descendants, would marry Petronila, queen of the powerful Kingdom of Aragon. Here the history of the Aragonese-Catalan Mediterranean expansion and its culinary exchange began.[9]

Catalan cooking has reached modern times almost intact. Logically throughout the centuries it has been influenced by other cultures connected with this land by geography or history. As a result of the devastation caused by the Spanish Civil War in the late 1930s, some original Catalan recipes were unfortunately lost or mercilessly altered. Following the growing interest in authenticity, helped by chefs, critics and writers, these recipes are coming back. The Arab influence on medieval Catalan cuisine is still visible, even if some of the ingredients are no longer in use, rose water for instance. Almonds, dried fruit, fresh fruit, fresh and dried herbs, cinnamon, saffron or the peel of citrus fruits have remained.

Contrary to the food culture of other parts of Spain, mostly transmitted by word of mouth, Catalan food enjoyed by the elite was perpetuated in some of the oldest European cookbooks known from the fourteenth and fifteenth centuries. Among these are the *Sent Soví* and the *Llibre de coch*, which include recipes such as *morterol* from the word *mortero* (pestle), made with different meats, almond milk, eggs and spices, and *carabasses a la morisca*, made with pumpkin, lard, almond milk, meat broth, cheese, egg yolks, coriander and '*salsa fina*' (ginger, cinnamon, white pepper, cloves, mace, nutmeg and saffron).[10]

## Pasta

The Arabs were responsible for the introduction of the pasta called *fidaws* (*fideos*) to Spain. Guilds of pasta-makers, known as *fideuers*, have been registered in Mediterranean Spain since the early Middle Ages. Since that time and even earlier, pasta in many different shapes has been present in the country's diet. Fourteenth-century Catalan cookbooks have recipes for *aletria*, derived from the Arabic *itria*, given as an alternative name for *fideo*.

Spaniards cook pasta with great regularity. The thinnest *fideo*, *cabello de angel* (angel-hair pasta), is added to soups. *Fideo gordo*, similar to Italian *spaghettini* but only a few centimetres long, is served with clams in Asturias and in fishermen's stews flavoured with saffron in Andalusia. In the Spanish *Levante*, at a beach resort called Gandía in the province of Alicante, a competition takes place every summer for best *fideua* dish of the year — a relatively modern dish cooked in a *paella* pan with fish, shellfish and a thin *fideo*. Since then, other types of pasta of mainly Italian origin have enriched the original Arab repertoire. Somehow lacking the authentic Italian touch, dishes known as *canalones*, *espaguetis* and *macarrones* as they are called in Spain are nevertheless the legacy of the large number of Italian cooks who came to work for the newly wealthy Catalan and northern Spanish industrial bourgeoisie in the nineteenth century. *Canalons a la barcelonesa*, the interpretation of the classic Italian recipe *Cannelloni Rossini*, are cooked in the city with an indisputable Catalan style. The *canalons*, which have previously been boiled for a few minutes in water, are stuffed with a rich mixture of *sofrito* (onion, garlic and tomato) and meat: finely ground chicken, chicken livers, pork and veal are sautéed in the *sofrito* together with egg yolks and breadcrumbs. The mixture is flavoured with thyme and nutmeg then seasoned with salt and black pepper. *Canalons a la barcelonesa* are baked in the oven with a classic béchamel and grated parmesan cheese on top.

From the twelfth to the late fifteenth centuries, the effects of the Kingdom of Aragon's expansion in the Mediterranean world became evident. Sicily was incorporated in the thirteenth, Sardinia in the fourteenth, and Naples in the fifteenth century. The Crown of Aragon lost some of its dominance in the Mediterranean. This affected the traffic in spices and the Mediterranean culinary traditions which had benefited oriental Spain. As a result Catalan food closed in on itself for almost two hundred years. It is true that from the end of the eighteenth to the late nineteenth century, professional Italian and French chefs refined the restaurant scene in Barcelona, but perhaps fortuitously in the rest of the region the splendid *ruralismo* of the food of the Catalan *comarcas* was safe for generations to come.

In reality, *La Cocina Catalana* cannot be just defined as Mediterranean – it is far too diverse. Half of the land lies 500 metres (1,640 ft) above sea level in almost impossible terrain. Here they do not cook with olive oil but with pork fat, and yet in the coastal areas the Mediterranean rules the kitchen with a distinct and unique personality. The respected Catalan journalist and author Josep Pla, who travelled extensively in France and Italy, wrote: 'How is it possible to compare or associate our food with France's bourgeois cuisine, the use of butter and the abundance of beef dishes?'[11] It would be fair to say that Pla was talking about the *cocina* of El Ampurdan in northern Catalonia, and the *cocina* he describes as *cocina familiar*.

In the city of Barcelona things were different from the rest of Catalonia, where food was mainly cooked at home. From the eighteenth century onwards the city had enjoyed something rare even in Madrid or Seville, the professional restaurant. A hundred years later, prestigious restaurants with French and Italian names were serving food to be compared with Europe's best. They shared space with those offering dishes preferred by the Catalan bourgeoisie: *zarzuela de peix* (fish and shellfish stew), *bacalla a la llauna* (cod cooked in a tin), as well as a number of dishes influenced by Valencia rather more than Italy such as *arroz negre*, rice made with artichokes or cuttlefish ink. As new trends originating in Spain and other countries became popular, classic French and Italian restaurants almost disappeared, although in the case of the Italians, the Catalan passion for pasta cooked with a Catalan accent would not change. In Barcelona cannelloni is so appreciated that it has become synonymous with Christmas festivities. Catalonia has several pasta dishes, including some based on short macaroni, that reflect their Arab heritage.

One thing that the Catalans and the French have in common is a passion for quality ingredients and for weekly markets. On the whole, Catalan markets are faring better than most in other parts of Spain. In every village or small town, itinerant and permanent markets offer a great local selection of fruit and vegetables, cheeses and hams, breads, biscuits, honey, quince paste, pulses – already dried or still in their pods – and fresh and dried herbs. In spring and autumn, the insatiable appetite of the Catalans for fungi, only to be compared with the Basque taste for *setas*, is fully satisfied. At local bars and restaurants the substantial Catalan breakfast, consisting of a rich variety of cured meat and omelettes, bean dishes and *pa amb tomàquet* (bread and tomato), are more often than not served with red or rosé wine drunk from the traditional glass *porrón*.

In large towns and cities, covered markets of architectural interest, trading morning and evening six days a week, still attract a large percentage of the population. They are threatened now by the high value of property, the integration of women into the professional world, and the advance of the supermarket into Spanish life, but in the city of Barcelona 27 daily markets are thriving, including the famous Saint Joseph or La Boquería in Las Ramblas. Some markets are much more than a place to buy vegetables or meat; they share the space with numerous small restaurants serving breakfast, lunch and dinner to traders, clients and tourists. These apparently humble restaurants are the protectors of many authentic Catalan dishes. Some are prepared with ingredients purchased in the market: razor clams, squid or fresh *butifarra* sausages; others are stews made with fish, meat or beans often flavoured with one of the great Catalan sauces. The sauce *picada* can be made with different combinations of ingredients: chicken or fish liver, garlic, almonds, saffron,

La Boquería.

cinnamon, bread and even sweet biscuits. *Sofrito* is made with onions or with onions and tomatoes. *Romesco* is a combination of ñora peppers and garlic, among other ingredients. This sauce should not be confused with the fish stew known by the same name in the province of Tarragona. The medieval *allioli* is a perfect emulsion of garlic and olive oil.

In Catalonia, food starts normally with a piece or two of bread and tomato. In local restaurants all over the country clients often also request one of the specialities *a la plancha* (on a hot plate) which have previously been marinated with olive oil, lemon juice, parsley and garlic or served with *allioli*. Tender artichokes also cooked *a la plancha* are at their best in early spring. Distinguished Catalan dishes are prepared in renowned local restaurants, especially in areas of inland Catalonia: *anec amb peres* (duck with pears) and *escudella i carn d'olla* (broth and vegetable and meat stew) are two of the best known. *Escudella* in its simple form used to feed Catalan peasantry six days a week. Festive *escudella* of the same name is a celebration of meat: veal shank, chicken and pork (belly, snout, ear, trotter and bones). Many other ingredients are also included: chickpeas, potatoes, four or five different types of vegetables, breadcrumbs, parsley, black pepper, saffron and salt. It is served like other *cocidos* in two parts, a rich soup followed by the meat, sausages and vegetables.

Tarragona, the fourth of the Catalan provinces, is well known for its Roman past and its architecture, its almond and hazelnut trees, aromatic herbs and the acclaimed wines produced in the whole region. At the Carthusian monastery of Scala Dei, which dates back to the twelfth century, monks made a sweet wine which was used in the mass. In 1988 the late Australian journalist Tony Lord wrote in his book *The New Wines of Spain* the following words:

> De Muller, a bodega based near the harbour of Tarragona, has been supplying the Popes with these wines for over a century. They are sweet, fortified *Moscatel* or *Macabeo* wines, allowed to mature in old American oak casks, developing with time a deep raisin flavour.[12]

The province of Tarragona is also known for the festival of the *calçot* (a sweet onion which is roasted in the streets and served with *romesco* sauce). Rice is produced in the delta of the River Ebro.

On the other side of the river is the Spanish *Levante* and the provinces of Castellón de la Plana, Valencia and Alicante. They occupy a narrow stretch of land bordering the Mediterranean Sea. High sierras to the west bring diversity and much-needed rainwater to the region. In the sierras, pine and oak forests, wild flowers and herbs have adorned the land here since ancient times. In between the coast and the highlands lie some of the most fertile lands of Iberia where cotton, oranges, lemons and of course rice are cultivated.

It could be said that food culture in the Spanish *Levante*, including the region of Murcia further south, has been hiding behind 'a plate of rice' prepared with different ingredients and methods of cooking. These rice dishes were born a long time ago out of the necessity among the people living on the coast, where swamps and marshes restricted the growing of other crops. In the Albufera lagoon, not far from the city of Valencia, rice and eels became a solution to poverty and hunger.

There is much more to the food of the *Levante* than rice, oranges and fresh vegetables. The strong personality of many *comarcas*, whether they are located inland or by the coast, has maintained a unique *cocina* with a history which is seldom appreciated or associated with the region by outsiders. In Morella, in the *comarca* of Els Ports in the province of Castellón de la Plana, black truffles and *cecina* (cured beef) are sold. Lightly cured *cecina* is served with a few drops of olive oil and freshly ground black pepper: 'Morella was traditionally a thriving Jewish community. The Jews loved ham, but couldn't eat pork. So they made their ham from oxen and the tradition hangs on.'[13] *Patatas a la morellana*, an alternative to roasted potatoes, come from the same town. Peeled, cut into halves and with a few deep incisions in the flesh, these potatoes are marinated for a few hours with a pounded dressing made with olive oil, fresh garlic, and sweet *pimentón* and then roasted with the skins placed on top. Another early sweet recipe believed to be of Jewish origin, *flaó* is a small pastry filled with ricotta or unsalted fresh sheep's milk cheese. The pastry is made with flour, water, olive oil, sugar and a dash of *aguardiente* (local eau de vie), and the filling with fresh cheese, almonds, eggs, sugar and cinnamon. *Flaó* from Morella is very different from the cheese tart of the same name baked on the islands of Ibiza and Formentera since medieval times.

The Moors brought gunpowder and fireworks to the Spanish *Levante*. Since then firework-makers of Valencia, the capital city, have come to rank as the best in the world alongside the Chinese masters. Mouths drop open in anticipation as the first rocket announces the beginning of yet another multicoloured feast of light and noise, accompanied by *buñuelo* fritters and iced *horchata*, a drink made with tiger nuts.

*Las Fallas*, a hymn to rejuvenation and the start of spring, is the name given in Valencia to the biggest and noisiest fiesta of all. It is also the name of the large sculptured effigies made of wood and cardboard which are destined to be burned. The origin of the *Fallas* can be found in the celebrations of the local carpenters' guild that used to take place to commemorate their patron

## Cooking with Rice

In Mediterranean Spain there are hundreds of dishes based on rice. They are cooked with stock or water, and with a whole range of possible ingredients to select from depending on the dish to be prepared – vegetables, pulses, nuts, seafood, poultry, meat, game, charcuterie, herbs and spices including *pimentón*, ñora pepper and saffron.

Spanish rice dishes are not only distinguished by the ingredients but by the utensil in which they are cooked, by the method of preparation and by the amount of liquid added. Dry dishes (*arroz seco*) are cooked in flat *paella* pans or deep enamel dishes over a flame or in earthenware casseroles in the oven. The moist *arroces melosos* (honey-textured rice) is prepared in deeper pans while the *arroces caldosos* (with broth) are cooked in clay pots or metal cauldrons over a flame. The amount of liquid added to the rice depends on the type of dish chosen – usually twice the volume for dry, two and a half times for *meloso* and three times for soupy.

*Paella valenciana*, the well-known Spanish dish, is cooked in a *paella* pan, on a wood fire if possible. The dish originated in the fields around the Albufera lagoon in Valencia, and has become a festive offering often cooked by men in the open air. Most people outside Spain and even in Spain believe that it is made with shellfish, chicken or pork and even sausages, but this is heresy to purist cooks born in Valencia. Originally, *paella* was a peasant dish cooked with whatever was found in the fields around the Albufera lagoon. As the area and the people progressed, chicken, rabbit and snails (they could be substituted by a sprig of rosemary) became some of the main ingredients of Valencian *paella*.

It is not easy to prepare *paella*. The meat has to be sautéed first in olive oil at a high temperature in the *paella* pan, before chopped tomatoes and some sweet *pimentón* are stirred in. Then the right quantity of cold water is added. Next are added three different types of beans, including the lima bean, known locally as *garrafón*, together with a few stamens of saffron, previously dissolved in some of the stock. As saffron imparts more flavour than colour, it should be used sparingly. With the stock boiling and the meat almost tender, the rice is sprinkled evenly by hand without stirring. After twenty minutes or so the fire will have died down, and the rice will have absorbed the liquid completely while the grains remain separate, firm and full of flavour.

Other rice dishes are known as *arroces*. If they are cooked with fish or shellfish they need a substantial stock prepared beforehand. This should always be added hot, once the rice is already in the pan. In the case of *arroces de pescado y marisco*, more often than not the stock is flavoured with the sweet ñora pepper.

Cooking in the open air: an authentic *paella valenciana* with rabbit, chicken and beans. The stock will be completely absorbed by the rice.

saint Joseph, by burning unwanted timber and wood shavings in the streets. Today, more than six hundred or so objects of popular art, based on political or social satire and made by local artists, are burnt every year in the main squares of Valencia on the night of 19 March.

The central market of Valencia was built in the old Arab quarter, near the mosque, in a maze of narrow streets and little squares that today are still the most attractive part of the city. From the fifteenth century onwards the marketplace was the nerve centre of the city. It awoke at dawn with the arrival of cartloads of fruit and vegetables from the country. Genoese and Catalan sailors, ladies and their maids, students and everyone who wanted to watch or be part of the spectacle of city life would frequent the place. King Alfonso XIII opened the modern Central Market in 1928. The style of the architecture is essentially modernist with a few turn-of-the century touches. The construction is a mixture of brick, ironwork, *Buñol* stone and marble, Mediterranean mosaics and multicoloured glass windows. It is worth losing oneself down the alleyways that run throughout the market to see the rich arrays of fruit and vegetables displayed with intuitive artistry and sold with pride. Come winter, fresh olives are sold together with the herbs needed to give them flavour when curing, especially fennel. In the market most of the stallholders are women, splendid in their lace aprons and perfect hair.

This market, arguably the most beautiful in Spain, smells of mountain herbs and curing hams. The bread stalls also sell sweet potato pies, aniseed rolls and all sorts of pastries and *pastelitos*. In the fish section the pale *galera* (mantis shrimp) is purchased to make substantial soups and stocks. In his *Tio Pepe Guide to the Seafood of Spain and Portugal*, Alan Davidson said:

> An oddity, not a real shrimp, not a crab, but a creature belonging to a different order, *Stomatopoda*. As this name indicates, its front legs are extensions of its mouth; and it is the marine counterpart of the praying mantis.[14]

Freshwater eels are another speciality of the market rarely seen in other parts of the country. They are sold from big metal tanks where they can be seen writhing about in the fresh water. The eels when they are sold are humanely dispatched in front of the customer with one blow from a sharp knife, so their freshness is guaranteed. *Anguilas all-i-pebre* (garlic and peppers) is a tasty dish to have in one of the local restaurants on the island of El Palmar, which sits in the freshwater Albufera lagoon in Valencia. This dish is also popular in Majorca.

It would be impossible to understand *la Cocina Valenciana* without a salad. Bread and olives accompany numerous salads prepared with fresh leaves, pickles and many *salazones* such as tuna *mojama* and grey mullet roe or *huevas*. The seasons are fundamental to the composition and quality of a salad. The base of a fresh salad tends to be leaves of a plain or frisée lettuce or tender leaves of young cabbages. Valencians believe that dressing a salad is an art requiring an understanding of the role played by each ingredient. In popular belief traditional Spanish dressings have few ingredients but need four people to prepare them: a generous person for the olive oil, a miser for the vinegar, a counsellor for the salt and a mad person to mix it.

An interesting dish from the city of Alcoy in Alicante further south, made during the *Fiesta de Moros y Cristianos*, is the *olleta de music* (musicians' pot) made with haricot beans, black pudding, ham bone and chard. *Giraboix* ('to turn the pestle') belongs to the *mar i montaña* tradition. It is made with salt cod, potatoes, black pudding and other cured sausages as well as artichokes, onions, ñora peppers, tomatoes and hard-boiled eggs. *Coques* (flatbreads with toppings) are as traditional in the *Levante* as they are in Catalonia and the Balearic Islands. Here also they can be sweet or savoury, plain or stuffed, with many different ingredients. *Coque amb tonyna* is covered with a *sofrito* sauce known as *fritanga* made with salted or fresh tuna fish, fresh peppers, bay leaf, tomatoes and pine nuts. The bread dough is made with flour, lard and hot olive oil. Lard gives a light texture to the dough. Until ten or fifteen years ago, housewives made *coques* every day at home; today practically all are made on an industrial basis or in local bread shops.

There are two celebrations in the Levantine calendar, and for that matter in the rest of Spain, at which food becomes as important as the *fiesta* itself. The celebrations take place over a period of several days or even weeks: from Christmas to Epiphany and from Palm Sunday to Easter Sunday. Even if today the biggest feast of all starts around 10 p.m. with the celebration of Christmas Eve (*Nochebuena*), not so long ago it was necessary to wait until after Midnight Mass to enjoy the first of the many banquets that would take place during the long period of these festivities. Christmas Eve was a day of abstinence in the Catholic calendar for adults. After mass, the family gathered around the open hearth in traditional farmhouses. With large iron *parrillas* in place and the hot coals glowing red, the people of the *Levante* celebrated with lamb chops, cold *embutido* sausages and hams. Greens came in the form of large endive salads, aromatic crushed olives and bowlfuls of *allioli*. Some families served extravagant festive *cocidos*, made with the classy combination of vegetables, sausages and other meat. Festive *cocidos* included (and still do) *pilotes de Nadal*, meatballs the size of an orange made with minced pork, pork lard, breadcrumbs, cheese, cinnamon and garlic, but there are many variations on the theme. Sweet green winter melons, already peeled and cut into slices, are still served for dessert. The fruit is followed by Christmas sweets: sugared almonds and pine nuts, small pieces of hard Alicante and soft Jijona *turrón* (nougat), and dried fruit covered with chocolate. Among the traditional Easter sweets, *coques de Pascua* (*monas* in the rest of the country) are made with a type of brioche bread dough where boiled eggs are placed at the centre before baking. These *coques* are essentially made with flour, eggs, yeast, water, olive oil and sugar.

Easter Sunday brings to the table vegetable *menestras* and *albóndigas de bacalao*, fish balls made with cod, boiled potatoes, parsley, eggs and pine nuts. Also related to the Easter celebrations is *arnadi*, believed to be one of the oldest puddings known in the peninsula. It appears that *arnadi* made around the Játiva area is also of Jewish origin. Játiva had a large Jewish community and fabulous vegetable gardens. *Arnadi* as we know it today is made with large pumpkins cut in half and filled with sugar, peeled almonds, walnuts, sultanas, a little olive oil and a dash of black pepper; then they are placed in the oven. After an hour or so, the pulp becomes caramelized; it is scooped out and left to drain overnight in a large clean tea towel. *Arnadi* is served decorated with almonds.

The syrup obtained by boiling down grape or fig must is known in Spain as *arrope* (arrop) in the Catalan language. Another traditional and almost forgotten delicacy is the *arrop i talladetes* that travelling sellers brought to the villages and small towns not so long ago. *Talladetes* are small pieces of pumpkin, plums, peaches and other fruits hardened by placing them overnight in a very light mixture of lime and water. Boiling first in water for a few minutes softens the fruit inside. Once the *arrop* is almost ready and still on the heat, the *talladetes* are added. *Buñuelos* made with puff pastry are not unique to the lands of Valencia. They are prepared all over Spain. In Catalonia they belong to the traditional repertoire of light pastries cooked at home to celebrate festive days such as Saint Joseph's or Saint Dionisio's day. They are also fried in speciality shops. The common *buñuelo*, the most popular of all, is made with flour, water and a little yeast. Once the dough is ready, small portions are fried in olive oil until they become very fluffy and golden in colour. They are eaten hot with icing sugar on top. *Buñuelos de viento* are made with a scalded dough softened with the addition of beaten eggs. Scalded dough is prepared by bringing water and olive oil to the boil. Then the flour is added little by little, stirring constantly until the dough is obtained. Once it cools down, the eggs are added to dilute and soften the dough. *Buñuelos* are also made with a soft pumpkin paste.

Across the water from Valencia, the Balearic Islands, in the Mediterranean, have always attracted visitors and invaders. Strategically positioned and easily reached by the main players of the ancient world, the islands became a playground for travellers, warriors and agriculturists, their legacy still to be seen today. Following Roman and Greek traditions, cured olives are perfumed with wild fennel. With the sweetest almonds they make ice-cream and eighteenth-century *panellets* to celebrate All Saints days. There are hundreds of different preparations, many of which cannot deny their Middle Eastern origin, although the *panellets*, which include almonds, potato or sweet potato, are also associated with northern European sweet traditions.

The Aragonese and Catalan federation first, and the English and French colonizers afterwards, would enrich the larder and table of the islands even further. The two largest islands, Majorca and Minorca, are very fertile, and Ibiza is well known for its beaches and for sea salt, *flor de sal*. Formentera and Cabrera, which are quite small, share an inventive culinary approach based on seafood, and have always faced a scarcity of fresh produce. The Majorcan tradition is strongly connected with the Catalan lands. However, Minorca, the minor island, as it was called by the Romans, has retained a British and to a lesser extent French character which is non-existent on the big island. In 1713 Minorca became part of the British Empire as a consequence of the Treaty of Utrecht. With the British came the valuable Frisian cow and a healthy production of cow's milk. Until then this would have been unthinkable in a land of goats and sheep. Soon dairy farming, established mainly for the production of butter and cheese, would improve the life of the farming community. In Minorca gin was originally distilled for the benefit of the large contingent of British sailors and soldiers present on the island during the eighteenth century, and would become part of the British legacy. In 1802, after a short period in French hands when lobster and *mahonesa* became a favourite dish, Minorca and its capital city Mahon were returned to Spain.

The Aragonese chef Teodoro Bardají, who in 1928 wrote a booklet under the title *La salsa mahonesa*, was adamant about the origins and nationality of what he considered to be the queen of all cold sauces:

> *Mahonesa* sauce and not *mayonesa* is the name of this ointment, a legitimate daughter of the *all-y-oli*, so popular in Valencia, the Balearic Islands, Catalonia, Aragon, and practically all Spain . . .

*Mahonesa* was born for the world, a sauce that is more or less the ancient *ajolio* without the unpleasant taste of garlic, refined and tuned to please the most delicate palates.[15]

Spaniards believe the French military commander, the Duke of Richelieu, tried this *pèbre lemosin* during the siege of Mahon; it pleased him and he took the recipe to France.

Since the late 1950s landowners and growers in the islands, particularly the large islands, have been subject to a constant temptation to sell their land to property developers and the tourist industry. It is interesting that in the Balearic Islands, men traditionally inherited land destined for cultivation, while the coastal strips were given to women. This eventually made the women very rich and very popular. Since the late 1960s potato fields and acres of vegetables have been replaced by golf courses and pretty villas whose owners are attracted by colourful local markets where food, pottery and local lace are as much in demand as the purple carrot, the small sweet aubergine and the *tomatiga de ramellet*. The *tomatiga* is a variety of tomato which is grown without irrigation and is kept in a semi-dried state during the winter months hanging on strings from porches and ceilings. Also in demand are Mediterranean herbs, both fresh and dried, fresh almonds, local olive oil, wine and liqueurs. Speciality breads are made with characteristically unsalted dough. Cheeses made from Majorcan and Minorcan cow's milk and a superb selection of charcuterie including *sobrasada* are unique to the islands. The best *sobrasada* is made with finely minced belly fat and minced pork meat from the Majorcan *porc negre*. Come October, freshly picked green olives are gently crushed with a wooden mallet, then placed in water for a couple of hours and drained. Later they are transferred to a glass or ceramic container and covered completely with brine, fresh thyme, lemon leaves, garlic, cloves, bay leaves and the distinguished wild fennel.

There are more than six hundred traditional recipes in the islands. Some specialists believe that what distinguishes the *Cocina Balear* from other Spanish *cocinas* is the way food was prepared in the past more than the local ingredients. Contrary to what happens for instance in Andalusia, food is seldom fried. This is all about gentle cooking at a moderate temperature.

Founded as a Roman camp, raided by the Vandals, conquered by the Byzantine Empire, colonized by the Moors and reconquered by James I of Aragon in the thirteenth century, Palma de Mallorca is a modern city with an impressive Gothic cathedral. Apart from the success of the tourist industry, agriculture has managed, almost by a miracle, to maintain a strong second

A woman hangs strings of tomatoes from the rafters for storage.

position in economic terms. On this island, pigs and not cattle have been the success story behind a rich food culture, especially the black pig, the *porc negre mallorquí*. Majorcan black pigs are hairier than the black *extremeño* or Andalusian counterparts, with comical large floppy bits hanging from their necks. It is known that George Sand spent the winter of 1836 in Majorca taking care of her lover, Chopin, who was suffering from tuberculosis. Even if she professed a dislike of the local food, she would become aware of the importance of the pig and pork products in the life and diet of the island. Compared with the recent success of Ibérico pigs, little is known about the equally special black pig of Majorca. They do not eat acorns but thrive on a diet of alfalfa grass, raisins, fresh herbs and beans. In Majorca, fresh pork is rarely used in the kitchen, with a few exceptions. *Lomo en salsa dulce* (loin of pork with a sweet sauce) and *lomo en salsa de granadas* (loin in a sauce of pomegranate) are two good exceptions, as is *porcella*, which is suckling pig stuffed with a mixture of pork trotters, liver and heart, breadcrumbs, different spices and herbs. *Frito mallorquín* is made with pig's offal, potatoes and fennel. Unusually, even roast lamb is first brushed with pork fat instead of olive oil. Based on the Spanish belief that the pig is a walking banquet, in the Balearic Islands charcuterie has always been a serious matter, including *porc de xuia* (*xuia* means lard and by extension the slaughtering of the pig). *Camayot* is prepared with different pork, blood, pancetta and pork fat, seasoned with black pepper, *pimentón* and other spices.

Away from meat and fish, cultivated and wild vegetables are an essential part of the islanders' diet: samphire and nettles, chicory and St John's wort are as appreciated as artichokes and chard. The Majorcan variety of aubergine has a light colour and is very sweet. Aubergines are stuffed with meat or fish, covered with béchamel and served with a vegetable *pisto*. *Tumbet* is made with local tomatoes, peppers and aubergines. Bread features in *sopas mallorquinas*, a dish that derives from an ancient vegetarian soup, made with bread and cabbage, that once fed the peasantry daily. Today these soups are made with chopped leeks, onions, tomatoes, garlic, peppers, cabbage and bread. *Pa amb oli* (bread and oil) is the title of a book by Tomás Graves. The son of the poet Robert Graves, Tomás, who was born on Majorca, dedicated his book to the Balearic answer to the Catalan *pa amb tomàquet* in a poorer form, without tomatoes. 'In the Balearics and everywhere else in the Mediterranean, we'd been eating bread and oil for over two thousand years before the tomato knocked at the kitchen door,' he said.[16] Sweet and savoury *cocas*, pastries and pies are prepared with the whitest pork *manteca* (lard), except in Lent when olive oil is used. *Cocorrois* are pies often stuffed with spinach, currants, pine nuts, olive oil, *pimentón* and sea salt.

Apart from sweet *cocas* made with a few drops of *anís* liqueur, pine nuts and sugar, cakes and pastries benefit from tasty fruit gathered in season. The *coca d'albercos* (apricots) is not a *coca* in the Catalan and Valencian sense, it is a flan or open pie that originated on the island of Ibiza. It is always made with lard. The *ensaimada* is a unique pastry, a superior delicacy that cannot be successfully mass-produced. The name derives from the Majorcan *saïm* (best-quality lard). Only those who are prepared to knead, pull, push and stretch a dough until large bubbles of air are formed inside can succeed. After two more fermentations and extra pulling and stretching, multiple layers of dough, each one brushed with the thinnest layer of lard, would be ready to be rolled into the characteristic shape of the *ensaimada* before baking. The origin of this pastry has allowed the imagination of writers and painters to fly free. Some believe the origin of the *ensaimada* is lost in the darkness of the Middle Ages and the times of Moors and Christians – its shape, resembling a Middle Eastern turban, converted to Christianity. Meanwhile, war has been declared between Majorca and an alliance of Ibiza and Formentera. The reputation of the two smaller islands has been stained by Majorca's claim to ownership of the distinguished *flaó*, which is a true *Ibicenca* speciality. In the Balearics *flaó* is an open tart made with flour, olive oil, *anís* liqueur, aniseed and water, filled with a light cream made of sugar, eggs, fresh local cheese and mint leaves, and baked in the oven. So far the cooks from Morella in the province of Castellón de la Plana have not participated in the dispute, despite having historical claims to the origin of *flaó*.

## ANDALUSIA

In the past, the idea of Andalusia as a land of watery *gazpacho* and *pescaito frito*, miserable and hungry, was promulgated not only in Spain but abroad. As far as food was concerned this was far from the truth.

Thousands of pages have been written about the southern part of the Iberian Peninsula, and yet so little justice has been done to the food cooked by the people who have sung and danced to give pleasure to themselves and others since antiquity. In reality the food of one of the most charismatic lands in Europe encapsulates the richness given by layer upon layer of a unique cultural legacy almost impossible to equal. This is a vast territory close to Africa. It is Mediterranean and Atlantic all at the same time, blessed with a magnificent clear light that makes buildings and land look constantly at their best. In the high sierras pine and acorn forest embellish the dehesas where the Iberian pig roams free. In the valleys cherry and orange blossom overwhelms the senses.

The 'Four Kingdoms of Andalusia' was a collective name given in the eighteenth century to the possessions of the Crown of Castile in the territory occupied by modern Andalusia: the Kingdom of Cordoba, the Kingdom of Jaen, the Kingdom of Seville (Seville, Cádiz and Huelva) and the Kingdom of Granada (Granada, Almería and Málaga). This is an old division, which helps the understanding of the complex mosaic of Andalusian food.

The terms *Cocina Mozárabe* or *Cocina Andalusí* are used frequently in Cordoba and Granada and not only in these provinces. *Mozárabe* is the name given to the Iberian Christians who lived under Moorish rule in Al-Andalus, including some Arab and Berber Christians. In the kitchen it encapsulates a number of recipes associated with food prepared in Andalusia and some parts of Morocco during the Islamic invasion and even after. *Cabrito a la miel* (kid cooked with honey) is considered by some the most relevant dish of the *Mozárabe* group of dishes. *Albóndigas mozárabes con salsa de almendras y azafrán* (meatballs with almonds and saffron) and *rape mozárabe* (monkfish with pine nuts and sultanas) are equally revealing. Away from the touristic world of the city of Cordoba, a rather fascinating rice dish known these days as *paella de campiña* is not a *paella* at all. It is cooked in an *olla* or deep pot with ham, belly of pork, chicken, chorizo, black pepper, cloves, onions, roasted garlic, bay leaf, rice and water.

Just as beautiful as Cordoba and as relevant in the history of Spain or perhaps more, Seville is not the best place when searching for fine dining. Seville is the undisputed capital of the *tapa*, a word that in the last few years has become internationally recognized. Authentic tapas can now be found in London or New York, but something is missing and always will be when cooked outside Spain. *Tapas* are much more than small portions of food prepared with Spanish ingredients and a unique local character. In their most original and pure form they are much more than food, they are a way of living which is practically impossible to imitate. It is believed that the tradition of tapas was born in the nineteenth century in the district of Triana on the right bank of the Guadalquivir River in Seville. Moving from bar to bar, talking to the bartender or any other person for that matter, while having a *copita* (a glass of Fino or Manzanilla sherry) and enjoying for free a few olives or a piece of local charcuterie, is what *Sevillanos* love most; the essence of a very social and pleasurable exercise. There is also the possibility of ordering one or two tapas more clearly advertised on a blackboard or recited by the waiter, for which one has to pay. Larger portions or *raciones* can also be ordered for sharing among friends. The word *tapas* derives from the verb *tapar*, to cover, as originally it was a custom to cover the glass *copita* with a slice of ham or chorizo offered free by the bartender.

*Gazpacho andaluz*, or summer gazpacho.

In the bright mornings of Seville, bars and *cafeterías*, especially those located inside food markets, are never empty. Coffee or even *carajillo* (with the addition of a little brandy) is often accompanied by a toasted *mollete*: bread drizzled with olive oil or generously spread with *manteca colorá* (pork lard coloured with *pimentón*). *Churro* fritters served with a hot cup of chocolate are also eaten at that time of day. The day's grazing in coffee shops and bars is normally complemented by lunch and dinner at home, particularly during the winter months. *Freidurías* (fried fish shops), which are particularly good in Seville, offer the possibility of eating on the premises or taking away fish fried in olive oil – never greasy, always crispy. Following a traditional repertoire that has changed little across society in Seville, home cooking tends to be uncomplicated and always flavoursome. *Puchero*, from the Latin *pultarius*, is not made with flour and water; it is the Andalusian version of the *cocido*. It contains a little meat, salted pork bones, vegetables and chickpeas. *Gazpachuelo* is not a cold soup and it does not have tomatoes. This is a sophisticated hot soup made with egg whites, king prawns and hake. *Arroz a la sevillana* is an expensive dish and clearly not a *paella*. It is a festive dish made with crayfish, monkfish, clams and squid, ham, chorizo, garlic, peas, parsley, roasted red peppers, onions and olive oil.

The Aljarafe is an area to the west of Seville, the Roman *Vergetum* (orchard) from where large quantities of olive oil and sweet wine were exported to Rome.

The *arroz dulce de Aljarafe* is a recipe made with prawns and monkfish, as well as tomatoes, onions, celery, rice, cumin seeds and sweet local wine. Olives feature in the classic *pollo a la sevillana*, in which the chicken is fried first and then marinated in a blend of rosemary and mint before being gently cooked in an earthenware *cazuela*. Then finally the olives are added. Originally this dish had a beautiful yellow colour given to it by the addition of *flores de jaramago* (arugula) of the Brassicaceae family. *Pestiños* are pastries with a clear *Andalusí* provenance, rarely prepared by the home cook nowadays. They are bought from renowned local patisseries on festive days. These are a hymn to olive oil flavoured with the peel of a bitter orange in which small portions of dough, rolled in a characteristic shape, are fried. The dough is made with flour, white wine, cinnamon, aniseed, sesame seeds, toasted almonds, walnuts, *anís* liqueur, eggs, yeast and honey. Sweet to the extreme, the *yemas de San Leandro* is Seville's ultimate gift. They are made with egg yolks, sugar syrup, sugar fondant and lemon following a recipe dating back to the sixteenth century, and sold by the nuns in charge of the kitchen of San Leandro's famous convent in the heart of the city. Leaving Seville on the way to Mérida in Extremadura, a short detour will lead to the Sierra de Aracena and the village of Jabugo in the foothills of the romantic and once dangerous Sierra Morena. In Jabugo a Denomination of Origin protects the production of cured hams, shoulders, loins and charcuterie. This is the kingdom of the Ibérico pig and the dehesa, the ancient oak forest that extends all the way into the heart of Extremadura further to the north.

In the southwest of Andalusia, not far from the Pillars of Hercules, *La Tacita de Plata* (the small silver cup) is another name given to the most ancient of all Spanish cities, Cádiz. The old city of the Phoenicians lies on the end of a narrow spit of land hemmed in by the sea. This capricious geography has been a deterrent for expansion and a protector of the past. At the very end of the spit, churches with whitewashed walls and golden *cúpulas* embellish the picturesque Viña and Santa María quarters where narrow winding streets lead to small square plazas and the main covered market where life is busy and affable. Across the bay, Puerto de Santa María and Sánlucar de Barrameda belong to the same world as Jerez de la Frontera further inland, the world of the classic wine, sherry. Around the bay some of the best vegetables in the country are grown in the *navazos*. *Navazos* are sand dunes that receive fresh water from underground, caused externally by the pressure of the rising tide of the sea. They are planted with an array of produce, much of which originally arrived from the Americas with seafarers and missionaries. After all, so many of the adventures across the Atlantic had started from here. Nothing is missing in this food-rich part of the country. The ancient *Almadraba* fishing-net system guarantees a supply of tuna captured as they arrive from the Atlantic Ocean and pass along the coast. From the mouth of the Guadalquivir River to the Cape of Trafalgar, fish and shellfish are abundant: king or tiger prawns (*langostinos*), large prawns (*camarones), acedias* (sole), *hortiguillas* (sea anemone), *corvinas* (meagre) and *dentones* (dentex), among others.

In Jerez de la Frontera several food traditions are to be found, some of which would never intermix. Two books, *Cooking with Sherry* by Lalo Grosso de Macpherson[17] and *La cocina gitana de Jerez* by Manuel Valencia,[18] speak for themselves. Lalo is of Bostonian stock on her mother's side and Andalusian on her father's. Her husband is of Scottish descent and she was educated in England. Eventually she became a successful caterer working in Jerez for a number of bodegas: Osborne, Gonzalez Byass and Domecq. In Jerez the food of the upper classes has been influenced by the French and British as well as the local aristocracy, and is prepared most of the time by professional cooks with a good dash of sherry and more often than not with a rich sauce with a Spanish or foreign name.[19]

Manuel Valencia is a prestigious chef of Gypsy origin who defends innovation and has already made an outstanding contribution by updating the original food of his ancestors. In his book, he has recorded detailed information of the food prepared by Gypsies during hard times and good times. Records going back to the early fifteenth century located Gypsy groups in the area. Some historians believe Gypsies crossed the Pyrenees from France, others that they came from Africa. In 1499 they were forced to abandon their nomad life and take up residence in a fixed place, to find work and to dress in accordance with the Spanish custom. This proved to be an almost impossible task. Several centuries later, mostly by force, they would find work in the local *cortijos* or farmhouses around Jerez where they tended the vineyards. As payment they could have shelter for their families and a plate of beans with olive oil flavoured with pork belly. The rest of their food came from the wild – after all they had always been expert gatherers of the food that nature gives for free. They prepared *jongo* and *jeta* (wild champignon and oyster mushrooms) as well as *tagarninas* (Spanish oyster thistle), following a recipe known as *esparragás* (the same as they do with wild asparagus), boiled and then tossed in a sauce made with olive oil, garlic, fried bread and *pimentón*. Many original Gypsy recipes may have disappeared, but outside the markets Gypsy women still sell *tagarninas* and also snails called *cabrillas*, together with the aromatic herbs they use to prepare them. With the profits they buy fresh sardines, anchovies and mackerel and what are now called 'forgotten cuts' such as beef skirt. Recipes cooked with *gandingas* (oxtail, pig's cheeks and tripe) have remained part of their diet.[18]

To the east of Cádiz, just beyond Cape Trafalgar, is the port of Barbate and the fishing village of Azahara de los Atunes. Gibraltar, Málaga and the old Kingdom of Granada are within easy reach. In the city of Málaga, straw boater hats, fine lace blouses and little painted cotton parasols may have almost been forgotten, but after decades of neglect the good old food enjoyed by Málaga's great-grandparents has started to be rescued by professional cooks and food writers. Being aware of the sorry state of gastronomy faced by Málaga at the beginning of the 1980s, Enrique Mapelli, a local lawyer, decided to take action by publishing an extensive collection of local recipes and a number of articles on the subject by well-known authors. He had realized that home cooking was where Málaga's food excels. *La cocina malagueña* existed beyond the *gazpacho* and the *pescaito frito* served in beach bars known as *chiringuitos*. It also existed beyond the international food repertoire that was served at official ceremonies and the tables of the rich.

*Arroz a la parte* (rice served in different parts) is no longer cooked on a hearth or in the open air as it was a century ago. Rice is cooked in a rich broth previously prepared in one pot with a variety of fish and shellfish which are removed before the rice is added. Then the rice is flavoured with a sauce made with sautéed garlic, pounded fried bread, hot chillies, parsley, oregano and wine. In a very traditional Spanish way it is served in three different courses: the broth, the fish and shellfish, and the rice. *Patatas a lo pobre* appear everywhere. They are fried potatoes cut into rounds flavoured with a pounded sauce made with black pepper, cumin, breadcrumbs, water, a dash of vinegar and *pimentón*, previously heated in the same oil in which the potatoes were fried.

The essence of the food of Málaga is still encapsulated in a plate of sardines enjoyed at the *Moraga*, a social event where friends gather together with a simple purpose: to eat fresh sardines by the beach on a warm summer night. Freshly caught sardines are impaled on metal skewers placed vertically around a lively fire, and watched by people patiently waiting while drinking a glass of the local wine so admired by Mapelli. In his *Papeles* he includes a recipe for turkey written by the Countess of Pardo Bazán to celebrate the virtues of Málaga wines. *Pavipollo al Vino de Málaga* is cooked with belly of pork, onions and carrots, wine and broth, as well as bay leaf and thyme. *Pasas, higos secos* (sultanas and dried figs) and almonds from Málaga are often listed as ingredients in local recipes. Almonds are the essence of *ajo blanco*, the same recipe which is prepared in Cordoba, but in Málaga fresh grapes (*uvas*) are added before serving. Considered also as a *gazpacho*, *ajo blanco con uvas* is all about sweet, and a few bitter, almonds, garlic, bread, olive oil, vinegar, water and salt.

Inland, at the crossroads of Seville, Málaga and Granada, history began early in Antequera. Dolmens built between 2500 and 1800 BC stand guard outside this intriguing city. This is the same Antequera whose name was taken by young Fernando, Prince of Castile, after a long battle against the Moors, the same prince who would found the Order of the Jar and the Griffin in the early fifteenth century. The very Christian *mantecados de Antequera* is a classic recipe still prepared in the convents of La Perla and Belen and associated with the extensive Andalusian Christmas sweet tradition. The original recipe calls for lightly toasted flour, sugar, pork lard, eggs, cinnamon and sesame seeds, although almonds are sometimes included too.

Once in Antequera it is easy to reach the city of Granada, the mighty palace of the Alhambra and the tapas bars in El Albayzín. At the heart of the city, Albayzín is one of the oldest centres of Muslim culture and a great place to taste some of the most distinguished dishes of *la Cocina Granadina*. Not far from the city, Las Alpujarras and the fertile lands of El Valle de Lecrín have been celebrated by authors such as Gerald Brenan and Benavides Barajas. When April arrives at what was the last stronghold of Moorish and *Morisco* Spain, broad beans (*habas*) and small artichokes are in full production. At this time of the year they are small and very tender. The *habas verdes a la granadina* are often served in local bars and restaurants. Broad beans are first boiled and drained and then cooked in a tomato, onion and garlic sauce with some water. Extra flavour is given by a *ramillete albaicinero* (bay leaf, mint and parsley) and half a dozen artichokes, cut into quarters. Once the artichokes are tender, cumin seeds, saffron and black pepper are added. Other recipes with Mozarabic flavour are *cocido de hinojo* (fennel *cocido*) and *patitas de cordero en salsa de almendras* (lamb trotters in almond sauce).

*South from Granada* is an autobiographical book Gerald Brenan wrote in Yegen, a remote village in the Alpujarras where he lived for years. Here Brenan, a renowned author and Hispanist, gives a comprehensive description of his kitchen and storerooms, where grapes were kept from September to April hanging from the ceiling. A number of baskets of persimmons and quinces, oranges and lemons, and one or two Alpujarra hams, were also kept in the store.

> Then came the vegetables – dried tomatoes and egg plants, cut into slices and laid out on shelves, pimientos hung from the ceiling, jars of home-cured olives and of dried apricots and figs, chick peas and lentils.

## An Anchovy Called Victoria

In his passionate and exaggerated fashion, Dionisio Pérez (Post-Thebussem) wrote in his *Guía del buen comer español* about the anchovies caught off the coast of Málaga between the towns of Estepona and Nerja. As far as he was concerned they were the best in the world, a statement probably objected to by people from Laredo in Cantabria, or Bermeo in the Basque Country, two fishing ports equally passionate about one of the most exquisite fish men can taste. In the nineteenth century, anchovies from Málaga had caught the imagination not only of food writers and gastronomes but of well-known novelists such as Pedro Antonio de Alarcón. According to De Alarcón, as with Dionisio Pérez, in Málaga anchovies were simply superior. One thing these writers never mentioned was that, to confuse the traveller, in Málaga anchovies are called *boquerones* as well as *Victorianos*, referring to the time they are fished, around the patron saint's day of the Virgin of the Victory of Málaga, on 8 September. They are celebrated in style in a festival taking place where the tantalizing smell of freshly cooked anchovies fills the streets of El Rincón de la Victoria, a typical municipality on the Costa del Sol. Here hundreds of visitors, some local, others from countries around the world, can taste a number of recipes prepared with the Victoria *boquerón*. The list of recipes is pretty impressive. Anchovies fried in plenty of hot olive oil (*boquerones fritos*) require an expertise in which Andalusian women excel. Any leftover fried *boquerones* are often dressed with garlic, saffron, cumin, oregano, vinegar or lemon and olive oil. Homemade *boquerones en vinagre* are prepared just as they come from the sea, raw, gently cleaned and filleted, cured for a number of hours with salt, vinegar and water, and then washed and served with a dash of olive oil, chopped parsley and garlic.

Brenan also mentioned that, apart from pork products, kid killed from time to time and festive ham from Trevelez, little meat was eaten in Las Alpujarras in those days. 'Fish came up on mules from the coast on most nights of the year – sardines, anchovies, horse mackerel, octopus or cuttlefish,' he added. Talking about Spanish cooking at the beginning of the 1950s, Brenan explained: 'The merits or otherwise of Spanish cooking are a matter on which people differ.'[20] The dish he preferred himself was *cazuela*, a stew of rice, potatoes and green vegetables cooked with fish or meat, with tomatoes, peppers, onions, garlic, almonds and saffron. He loved salads and summer and winter *gazpachos*. He detested the local *cocido* or the Yegen's version of the *puchero* as well as some of the dishes prepared with salt cod, if it was of lower quality. He also enjoyed recipes prepared with rabbit, hare and partridges as much as he loved the local bread: 'It has a taste and sweetness like no other bread in the world.' He imagined this was due to the ripeness of the grain before it was harvested.

Today, many years later, some of the ingredients and recipes mentioned by Brenan are still prepared by local people living in Las Alpujarras, a place of outstanding beauty and character that attracts foreign and Spanish visitors to southern Granada. Another cookbook, recently published, has already gained recognition by food writers and critics. *Las Chimeneas: Recipes and Stories from an Alpujarran Village*, by David and Emma Illsley, gives another example of the attachment of the Andalusians to food which has never left its origins and traditions behind. In the kitchen of Las Chimeneas, the name of a small hotel and restaurant at the heart of the Alpujarras, *cazuelas* are cooked with *fideo* pasta instead of rice all year around and in early spring broad beans with local ham are also prepared in *cazuela*. The original salad known as *remojón*, with oranges, waxy potatoes and best-quality salt cod, black olives and pomegranate seeds, is as authentic as the *berenjenas con caña de miel* (aubergines with molasses). One thing is certain: even if, as Brenan professed, he did not like *pucheros*, he would have loved *puchero de hinojo*, with beans, fennel and pork stew prepared frequently by Soli and Conchi, two cooks who have always worked at Las Chimeneas.[21]

### The Canary Islands

About 145 kilometres (90 mi.) to the west of the Moroccan coastline, out into the Atlantic Ocean, the Canary Islands became instrumental as a port of call on the way to the Americas. From 1492, Spanish vessels would stop in the islands for food, water and rest before crossing the ocean. Much earlier, the archipelago and its legendary association with Atlantis had fascinated antiquity. Plato apparently believed in the existence of the lost continent, and Ptolemy accurately located the islands, advising seafarers that beyond the island of Hierro was nothing but the end of the world. Not until the early fourteenth century and the arrival of a large number of Europeans would the islands be acknowledged as part of the known world. With the signing of the Treaty of Alcácovas on 4 September 1479 came peace between Spain and Portugal, ending the cruel War of the Castilian Succession. Among other agreements they decided that Portugal would take the Azores along with the Cape Verde Islands, Madeira and Guinea. Spain opted for the Canary Islands, until then just a playground for Spanish, Portuguese, Genoese and Flemish traders.

Since then and even before, the words *Guanche* and *Canaria* have been surrounded by mystery and legend. *Guanche* was the name given by Spaniards to the original inhabitants of the island of Tenerife and, later on, of the whole archipelago. The origin of the name of the islands is proving to be another area of disagreement among modern historians. Does it comes from the Latin and refer to the large communities of seals (*Monachus monachus*), also known as *canes marinos* (sea dogs), that every year came to the area (and still do), hunting for squid and as a place to give birth to their young? Or does it come from the word *Canari*? The Canarii were a Berber tribe from the Atlas mountain range in Africa, banished to the islands by the Romans as punishment for their rebellion. From that moment and until the Middle Ages, having failed to provide incentives and riches to possible European settlers, the islands would be lost, stuck almost in the Stone Age for centuries. Within a few centuries of the arrival of the Europeans, as had happened before to the Tainos in the Caribbean, the *Guanches* would disappear altogether from this earth.

Soon sugar cane from Africa was planted in large areas to be cultivated and collected by *Moriscos* and African slaves. It thrived in the soil and climate of some of the islands. At the same time, vineyards planted on the island of Tenerife started to produce the rich Malvasías that would attract English and Irish merchants dealing in the wine trade. Potatoes and chillies came to the islands with the Atlantic food exchange. *Papa* and the small *papita* are the names given in the Canaries to the potato of the Andes. They found an ideal habitat in those islands since they had a decent rainfall, especially Tenerife. Already by the middle of the sixteenth century, barrels of potatoes were exported from Gran Canaria and Tenerife to Flanders. López de Gómara had recorded their existence thirty years after their first sighting in Peru by Francisco Pizarro in 1532, so the introduction of potatoes into the Old World

In Tenerife, grilled *cherna* is served with *arrugada* potatoes and *mojo picón*.

could have happened first in the Canaries and not directly into mainland Spain.[22]

Tomatoes were another crop that succeeded in the islands. By the nineteenth century the Canary Islands were exporting huge quantities of tomatoes to Britain and northern Europe. Nevertheless, until well into the same century, a large proportion of the islanders ate badly and very seldom hot food. Wood was scarce and too costly, as was meat. Their diet was based on bread and *gofio*, a flour made from lower-quality roasted grains and even beans or fern root. Best bread was made from barley. Fern root was also an important part of the diet of the *Guanches*, supplemented with goat's fat and meat, milk and fish. Contrary to early reports and the original belief of the Europeans, the *Guanches* knew how to prepare food in a rather sophisticated way. They roasted meat and fish to make it palatable and digestible, they kept fat in ceramic pots, and they toasted their ground barley, which they would then boil in water and milk and serve with honey.

What we understand today as *Cocina Canaria* is a conglomerate of different dishes of which the best belong to the *Cocina Canaria Tradicional* influenced by the food of the Iberian Peninsula and in particular Andalusia and some Caribbean flavours. *Conejo en salmorejo* is prepared with grilled rabbit first marinated with garlic, cumin, pepper and salt, olive oil, vinegar and wine. *Papas arrugadas* (potatoes in sea salt, boiled almost dry until wrinkled) are served with different *mojos* or sauces clearly of Caribbean or Mexican origin. *Mojo picón* is red and very hot. It is made with cumin, garlic, olive oil, vinegar, tomatoes and red chillies. *Mojo Verde*, which normally accompanies fish dishes, is made with coriander. Rich soups are prepared with the fish called *sama (Dentex dentex)* and potatoes, cumin and saffron. *Escabeche de pescado* is prepared with oranges, almonds and raisins, which is a departure from the ingredients used for the same dish in Andalusia. On the contrary the use of certain spices established a clear relationship between the Canaries and southern Spain: cinnamon, aniseed, nutmeg, cloves, black pepper, ginger, cumin and saffron. Rice with chicken is as popular here as in Seville, and *empanadilla* pies stuffed with meat are as popular in the Canaries as in the rest of Spain. The *huevos moles* (soft eggs) prepared in the whole archipelago are of clear Portuguese origin adapted to the local taste. They are made with egg yolks, sugar, water, Malvasia wine and cinnamon. This is a creamy mixture of sugar syrup and egg yolks thickened while stirring constantly in a *baño maría*.

Meanwhile, *gofio* flour, the salvation of the original Canary Islanders, has remained the food which their descendants identify with their past. Reminiscent of the importance that bread made with wheat has always had in the peninsula, *gofio* made with barley, or even maize flour, added to milk or to popular dishes is what people of the Canary Islands still like to eat almost every day. [23]

## Spanish Regional Cheeses

Until a decade ago, and with the sole exception of Manchego, Spanish cheeses were virtually unknown outside Spain or even outside their own production areas, and yet cheeses of extraordinary character with a long history are made in every part of the country. Spanish cheese culture is a combination of old traditions and new techniques. Over the last thirty years food enthusiasts and cheese-makers have been rescuing cheeses from the verge of extinction and completing a unique map. Today this map includes more than a hundred varieties, of which over twenty belong to a 'Protected Designation of Origin' that guarantees their authenticity. The great range of cheeses produced in Spain reflects the diversity of the landscapes and the animals that are kept and fed in different parts of the country.

Sheep and goats are found everywhere in Spain. Goats are particularly well adapted to the harsh conditions of the Mediterranean coast which stretches from Catalonia to the Strait of Gibraltar. Sheep have historically dominated the interior – the Meseta, Navarre, Aragon and Extremadura – while dairy cows thrive in the lush green north, from Galicia to the foothills of the Pyrenees. Many cheeses in Spain exist in two or three variants: *fresco*, freshly made; *semicurado*, with a short maturation period; and *curado*, the fully matured cheese.

A large proportion of Spanish cheeses, around half of the total varieties, are produced in the north, where rainfall creates the perfect habitat for dairy cattle. Indigenous breeds such as the Rubia Gallega and the Asturiana share the land with the Friesian and other foreign breeds. Some farmers also keep a small number of sheep and goats, and blend the different milks to make cheese during the seasons when poor pastures are reflected in the lower quality of cow's milk. This practice follows the tradition of shepherds who would take all of their livestock to the highlands in summer, making cheeses from two or even three different types of milk.

In Galicia, Asturias and especially in Cantabria, ownership of two or three milk cows was, until only a few years ago, the dream of any family in the countryside. From these treasured animals, kept close to the house, would come milk to sell to the local dairy and some for home consumption as fresh milk, homemade cheese and, if any was left, delicious festive puddings. Some women are still making cheese in their own farmhouses as they have always done, but they are fewer and fewer. EU regulations do not allow the selling of milk to local dairies from farmers with fewer than seven cows and for many this has ended an ancient and cherished way of life.

Galician tetilla cheese, named after its remarkable shape (supposedly like a girl's breast), is popular all over Spain, with a smooth, buttery texture and a taste somewhere between lactic and sweet. *Queso de Arzúa*, similar to Tetilla but with a rounded shape, is a traditional homemade cheese. *San Simon* from Lugo is one of the very few smoked cheeses in Spain. Today both small artisan and industrial producers are mushrooming, allowing widespread distribution of these cheeses, but a Galician will still shop at the local market where farmers sell delicious, irregularly shaped cheeses, made with milk from their own cows.

Further east, the valleys and hamlets of Asturias, especially around the stunning Picos de Europa, a succession of saw-bladed mountain crests at the heart of the Cantabrian range, offer a diversity of cheeses that is unrivalled not only in the rest of the Iberian Peninsula but in many other cheese-producing countries. *Afuega'l pitu* is a hand-moulded fresh or matured semi-soft cheese made in a characteristic cone shape. Its unusual name, taken from the local dialect, means to 'choke a cockerel' and refers to the texture of this cheese, which is so creamy and thick that it would be impossible for a cockerel to swallow!

Pungent and flavoursome, a number of blue cheeses, such as La Peral, Gamonedo and, above all, the highly prized Cabrales are matured in the limestone caves of Asturias. Cabrales is normally made with unpasteurized cow's milk (not goat's, as the name might suggest), but at certain times of the year it is also made with a blend of cow's, goat's and sheep's milk. The cold temperature and high humidity found in the caves all year round encourage the natural development of the *Penicillium* mould from the rind to spread into the heart of the cheese, unusual in blue cheeses.

Easier to find outside Spain, Valdeón is also a blue cheese. Creamier and less capricious than Cabrales, it is made on the border with Castile-León. It is distinguished by the layers of maple leaves that are still used to protect and store these cheeses.

Historically, cheese production was not confined to smallholders and shepherds. Monastic orders were also fundamental in the development of regional cheeses. Many monasteries dotted around the Cantabrian sierras and valleys are still making local cheeses as they did in medieval times. Cóbreces is a small village on the Cantabrian coast, renowned for the juicy lemons that decorate its gardens and streets. Here the local monastery supplements its income by selling *queso de nata* (cream cheese) and *quesucos*, small, creamy cow's milk cheeses of unique character. In the Pas Valley, also in Cantabria, *queso de las Garmillas* is a fragile, creamy cheese made without pressing that has to be sold between two pieces of greaseproof paper. Local chefs are encouraging the production of this cheese for its delicacy and ease of adaptation to new kitchen concepts and recipes.

It would be unimaginable to end a meal in a Basque gastronomic society or a gathering at a local cider house without a piece of smoked Idiazábal and a few walnuts. Idiazábal has been produced in local farmhouses and by Basque shepherds from the beginning of time. The name Idiazábal derives from a small area in the province of Guipúzcoa at the heart of the sierras of Urbia and the Aralar. Unsmoked, Idiazábal has a uniquely pure ewe's milk character derived from the animals feeding in rich summer pastures. The smoked version is more traditional and stems from the time when these cheeses were smoked simply by maturing in the hearth of the shepherd's chilly summer retreat high up in the mountains.

Closer to the Pyrenees, the cow shares the pasture with the sheep. The Roncal, one of the most beautiful valleys of Navarre, gives its name to one of Spain's oldest cheeses made by local shepherds. Roncal is similar in shape to other traditional hard sheep's milk cheeses, such as Manchego, but it has a very distinct aroma derived from the fresh grass and wildflowers that permanently cover the steep slopes of the mountain range and valleys where the sheep spend their life. The wandering nature of sheep dictates a unique and rigorous way of life for their companion and keeper, the shepherd, who became a romantic figure in Spanish literature and folklore, as well as a highly skilled cheese-maker.

Sheep are a major feature of the landscape in Extremadura, Castile-León and Castile-La Mancha, where many indigenous breeds are found: the Churra in Castille-León and the Manchega are two of the best known. The Merino, once bred mainly for its excellent wool and delicious meat, is also behind some of Spain's most distinctive cheeses. One day each year in early winter, all the traffic on one of Madrid's main arteries stops to make way for large flocks of sheep en route from the north to the south of the central plateau. Bringing the sheep through the city is a defiant gesture, the annual reminder of a right granted by the Castilian King Alfonso VI in the twelfth century to the shepherds of Spain.

Two classic sheep's milk cheeses, Zamorano produced in the northern Meseta, and Manchego from La Mancha in the southern Meseta, have a memorable past. The Romans in Hispania ate cheeses produced in the

Mesetas and encouraged its production. The first mention of cheese in the Castilian language appeared in the document *Noticia de Kesos*, written by Friar Jimeno, who was working in the ninth century in the convent of San Justo in Rozuela, León. Abu Zacarías, writing about Spanish agriculture in the twelfth century, mentions the emphasis given by the Arabs to the improvement of livestock, particularly sheep, in central Spain. The Arabs were more interested in mutton, but the cheese called *al-Muyabbana* made by local shepherds, the Manchego of today, was also in demand. With the taking of the Moorish capital of Toledo by King Alfonso VI in the eleventh century, the economic, religious and social structure of central Spain changed dramatically. After the Christian military occupation there followed a slow process of amalgamation of the typical small farms owned by Arabs, Jews and Christians alike into estates for the nobles at Alfonso's court. As the Christian armies moved south, many areas until then cultivated by the Moors became vacant. Repopulating the land became a complicated matter. Few of his subjects from Castile-León were keen to leave their homes for a harder life in a harsher countryside, so they sought substantial rewards for moving south. Alfonso was able to offer them vast tracts of land for herding sheep to produce wool – a very lucrative industry at the time. Cheese-making became marginal. Wool production continued to dominate in La Mancha until the

Woven esparto-grass *pleitas* imprint the characteristic patterns of many Castilian cheeses.

Manchego cheese is made with milk from the Manchega breed of sheep.

seventeenth century, when expansion of the population brought the land over to cereal farming. Eventually the winter pastures became a thing of the past and the huge migrating flocks disappeared. The migrating shepherds gave way to the farmers of the land. The production of wool decreased, but meat and Manchego cheese production rose in importance.

Extremadura has always been the winter refuge of the sheep of the Meseta. Today local farmers use milk from Merino sheep to produce two cheeses with personality: Torta del Casar and Queso de La Serena, which are at their best from November to June when the pastures are richest. The most sought-after are made by artisans with a vegetable rennet obtained from the local *Cynara cardunculos*, a type of artichoke. The *Cynara* produces a deliciously runny cheese with a characteristic slight bitterness which is rather unusual.

In the eastern part of the country in Mediterranean Spain, the goat reigns supreme, providing soft, fresh cheeses and hard, mature varieties. Fresh goat's milk cheeses are made today to supply local and urban demand, as they have been since Roman times. Trade flourished for centuries between major cities and ports from Catalonia to the Pillars of Hercules in Cádiz Province. *Mató* is a fresh cheese produced in many farms in Catalonia, a perfect dessert cheese served with honey (*mel i mató*) or with dried fruit and nuts.

In Valencia some cheeses take their name from the mould or cloth in which they are prepared, like *cassoleta* (a wooden mould in the shape of a small volcano) or *servilleta* (napkin), a cheese very close to Greek feta. Some are so fresh that the whey still runs from them, while others are matured to make them less fragile. Murcia cheeses, which are named after that region, were not so long ago only produced by shepherds. A cured version, *Murcia al vino*, is dipped in wine to provide a unique colour to the rind.

The supremacy of the goat in Mediterranean Spain is challenged only in the Balearics, especially on the island of Minorca. Here, in the face of capricious weather, windy and rainy in winter, hot and dry in summer, the local farmers rely more on grazing dairy cattle than on cultivation of the land. Their cheeses were greatly improved when the British occupied the islands during the seventeenth century and introduced to Minorca more productive breeds of cow. Mahón, the main town of Minorca, gives its name to the best cheese produced in the islands by far. Artisan Mahón is made with unpasteurized milk in a characteristically square shape, using a cotton cloth. Traditionally the rind of this cheese is coated with olive oil or butter, or with a blend of butter and sweet *pimentón* for an attractive orange colour. Slightly acidic and a little salty, Mahon cheese has a pleasant floury texture that resembles Parmesan when well matured.

The Canary Islands have an especially fine tradition of hard goat's milk cheeses. Each island has its own, but Lanzarote produces one of the most distinguished goat's cheeses of Spain, Majorero. This is a large, round cheese with a complex flavour of mature fruit, marked with an image of a palm leaf on the rind.

'With bread, cheese and wine the journey will be done,' is often said in Spain by the older generation. Yet there is much more than these good things to the journey taken by the *Cocinas de España* throughout the centuries. We can also say that from prehistoric Atapuerca to the early 1970s, food in Spain progressed slowly in a constant search for identity. Having now found this identity and still as diverse as ever, the food of Spain has reached adulthood as well as a prestige that is difficult to equal. What is also important is that Spaniards have become much more adventurous and now enjoy eating away from their own local *cocinas* as they travel off the beaten track to find places of interest. Sometimes what they find is a type of traditional food associated with a particular area and at other times a more creative and innovative gastronomic offering. What is difficult to predict is where Spain is going from here in all matters related to food. Today the winds of disruption caused by political and economic uncertainty are blowing again not only in Europe, but in many other parts of the world, and are already affecting

Spain in some sectors of the food and restaurant trades. Let's hope that the interest in quality already associated with the country and the dedication of its professionals will allow Spain to adjust to the possible changes, hopefully without compromising more than is necessary. In a few years only history will be able to tell what has happened.

# References

## Introduction

1 J. H. Elliott, *Imperial Spain: 1469–1716* (London, 2002), p. 13.

## ONE: A Land at the Edge of the Unknown

1 Roger Collins, *Spain: An Oxford Archaeological Guide* (Oxford, 1998).
2 José Miguel de Barandiarán and Jesús Altuna, *Selected Writings of José Miguel de Barandiarán: Basque Prehistory and Ethnography* (Reno, NV, 2007), pp. 39–45.
3 María José Sevilla, *Life and Food in the Basque Country* (London, 1989), pp. 70–71.
4 Mattias Jakobsson et al., 'Ancient Genomes Link Early Farmers from Atapuerca in Spain to Modern-day Basques', *PNAS* (*Proceedings of the National Academy of Sciences of the United States of America*), CXII/38 (2015).
5 Jan Read, *The Wines of Spain* (London, 1982), p. 27.
6 Sebastián Celestino and Carolina López-Ruiz, *Tartessos and the Phoenicians in Iberia* (Oxford, 2016), pp. viii, 70–72, 191–6.
7 H. C. Hamilton and W. Falconer, trans., *The Geography of Strabo*, vol. III (London, 1857).
8 Carmen Gasset Loring, *El arte de comer en Roma: alimentos de hombres manjares de dioses* (Merida, 2004).
9 Cato, *Cato: On Farming* [1998], trans. Andrew Dalby, ebook (London, 2016).
10 Mark Cartwright, 'Trade in the Roman World', *Ancient History Encyclopedia* at www.ancient.eu, 12 April 2018.
11 Eloy Terrón, *España encrucijada de culturas alimentarias* (Madrid, 1992), pp. 45–6.
12 Paul Fouracre, ed., *The New Cambridge Medieval History: c. 500–700*, vol. I (Cambridge, 2005), p. 357.
13 Stephen A. Barney et al., eds and trans., *The Etymologies of Isidore of Seville* (Cambridge, 2009).

## TWO: Moors, Jews and Christians

1 Garci Rodríguez de Montalvo, *Amadís de Gaula* (Barcelona, 1999).
2 Juan Lalaguna, *A Traveller's History of Spain* (London, 2011), pp. 22–3.
3 Joseph F. O'Callaghan, *History of Medieval Spain* (New York, 1983), pp. 49–54.

4  Emilio Lafuente y Alcántara, *Ajbar Machmua: crónica anónima del siglo XI, dada a luz por primera vez* (Charleston, SC, 2011).

5  Lucie Bolens, *La cocina andaluza un arte de vivir: siglos XI–XIII*, trans. Asensio Moreno (Madrid, 1992), pp. 43–6, 49–51, 71–2.

6  José Moreno Villa, *Cornucopia de México* (Mexico City, 2002), p. 381.

7  Manuel Martínez Llopis, *La dulcería española: recetarios histórico y popular* (Madrid, 1990), pp. 20–24.

8  Juan Antonio Llorente, *History of the Inquisition of Spain from the Time of Its Establishment to the Reign of Ferdinand VII*, ebook (London, 1826).

9  Elena Romero, *Coplas sefardíes: primera selección* (Cordoba, 1988).

10  Harold McGee, *On Food and Cooking: An Encyclopedia of Kitchen, Science, History and Culture* (London, 2004).

11  Gil Marks, *Encyclopedia of Jewish Food* (New York, 2010), p. 561.

12  Martinez Llopis, *La dulcería española*, pp. 24–5.

13  Carolyn A. Nadeau, 'Contributions of Medieval Food Manuals to Spain's Culinary Heritage', *Cincinnati Romance Review*, XXXIII (2012).

14  'Nunca dexaron el comer a costunbre judaica de manjarejos e olletas de adefinas e manjarejos de cebollas e ajos refritos con aceite; e la carnen guisaven con aceite, o lo echaven en lugar de tocino e de grosura, por escusar el tocino. El aceite con la carne e cosas que guisan hace oler muy mal el resuello, e así sus casas e puertas hedían muy mal a aquellos manjarejos: e ellos esomismo tenían el olor de los judíos, por causa de los manjares . . . No comían puerco sino en lugar focoso, comían carne en las cuaresmas e vigilias e quatro tenporas en secreto . . . comían el pan cenceño, al tiempo de los judios e carnes tajale.' Andrés Bernáldez, *Memorias del reinado de los Reyes Católicos, que escribía el bachiller Andrés Bernáldez, cura de los palacios*, ed. Manuel Gómez-Moreno and Juan de M. Carriazo (Madrid, 1962), pp. 96–7. In Spain olive oil and the fat from pigs, of which *manteca de cerdo* or rendered pork fat (lard) is the best, have always been used for cooking and pastry-making in different parts of the country.

15  Jaime Roig, *Spill o Llibre de les Dones. Edición crítica con las variantes de todas las publicadas y las de MS de la Vaticana, prólogo, estudio y comentarios por Roque Chabés* (Barcelona, 1905).

THREE: Life in the Castle

1  Juan Cruz Cruz, *Gastronomía medieval*, vol. II: *Dietética, Arnaldo de Vilanova: Régimen de Salud* (Navarre, 1995), pp. 8–9.

2  Rudolf Grewe, *Llibre de Sent Soví, llibre de totes maneres de potages de menjar*, ed. Amadeu Soveranas and Juan Santanach, 2nd edn (Barcelona, 2009).

3  Francesc Eiximenis, *Lo Crestià* [1379–1484] (Barcelona, 1983).

4  Eiximenis, *Com usar bé de beure e menjar: normes morals contigudes en el Terç del Crestià*, ed. Jorge J. E. Gracia (Barcelona, 1925).

5  Enrique de Villena, *Arte cisoria*, ed. Felipe-Benicio Navarro (Barcelona, 2006).

6  Angus Mackay, 'The Late Middle Ages, 1250–1500', in *Spain: A History*, ed. Raymond Carr (Oxford, 2000), p. 108.

7  Julius Klein, *La Mesta: A Study in Economic History between 1273 and 1836* (Cambridge, MA, 1920).

8  Henry Kamen, '*Vicissitudes of a World Power, 1500–1700*', in Carr, ed., *Spain*, p. 53.

9 Eloy Terrón, *España encrucijada de culturas alimentarias: su papel en la difusión de los cultivos americanos* (Madrid, 1992), p. 71.

10 José Pardo Tomás and María Luz López Terrada, *Las primeras noticias sobre plantas americanas en las relaciones de viajes y crónicas de Indias* (Valencia, 1993).

11 Manuel Zapata Nicolas, *El pimiento para pimentón* (Madrid, 1992).

12 Bernabé Cobo, *Historia del nuevo mundo* [1653], Google ebook (Seville, 1891).

13 Carolyn A. Nadeau, *Food Matters: Alonso Quijano's Diet and the Discourse of Food in Early Modern Spain* (Toronto, 2016), p. 90.

14 Garcilaso de la Vega (El Inca), *Royal Commentaries of the Incas and General History of Peru*, ed. Karen Spalding, trans. Harold V. Livermore (Indianapolis, IN, 2006).

15 Redcliffe Salaman, *History and Social Influence of the Potato*, ed. J. G. Hawkes (Cambridge, 1985), pp. 68–72.

16 José de Acosta, *Historia natural y moral de las Indias* [1590], ebook (Madrid, 2008).

17 Sophie D. Coe, *The True History of Chocolate* (London, 1996), p. 133.

18 Martha Figueroa de Dueñas, *Xocoalt: Chocolate, la aportacíon de México al mundo, recetas e historia* (Mexico City, 1995), p. 11.

19 Diego de Landa, *Yucatan Before and After the Conquest*, trans. William Gates (Mineola, NY, 2014).

20 Gabriel Alonso de Herrera, *Libro de agricultura general de Gabriel Alonso de Herrera*, ed. Real Sociedad Económica Matrileña (Madrid, 1818–19).

21 Text trans. Robin Carroll-Mann, 2001.

22 Ibid.

23 Juan Cruz Cruz, *Gastronomia medieval*, vol. I: *Cocina, Ruperto de Nola: Libro de los Guisados* (Navarre, 1995), pp. 74–6.

## FOUR: A Golden Age

1 Juan Sorapán de Rieros, *Medicina española en proverbios vulgares de nuestra lengua* (Madrid, 1616).

2 Otto Cartellieri, *The Court of Burgundy* (Abington, 2014).

3 Diana L. Hayes, 'Reflections on Slavery', in Charles E. Curran, *Changes in Official Catholic Moral Teaching* (Mahwah, NJ, 2003), pp. 65–9.

4 Nicholas P. Cushner, *Lords of the Land: Sugar, Wine and Jesuit Estates of Coastal Peru, 1600–1767* (Albany, NY, 1980), pp. 38–40.

5 Mitchell Barken, *Pottery from Spanish Shipwrecks, 1500–1800* (Pensacola, FL, 1994).

6 Regina Grafe, 'Popish Habits vs. Nutritional Need: Fasting and Fish Consumption in Iberia in the Early Modern Period', *Discussion Papers in Economic and Social History*, 55 (Oxford, 2004).

7 Rosa García-Orellán, *Terranova: The Spanish Cod Fishery on the Grand Banks of Newfoundland in the Twentieth Century* (Irvine, CA, 2010).

8 Julio Camba, *La casa de Lúculo o el arte de comer* (Madrid, 2010), p. 45.

9 Juan Ruiz, *Libro del Buen Amor* [1432], ed. Raymond S. Willis (Princeton, NJ, 1972).

10 Francisco Abad Nebot, 'Materiales para la historia del concepto de siglo de oro en la literatura española', *Analecta Malacitana*, III/2 (1980), pp. 309–30.

11 'Yo señora, pues me paresco a mi aguela que a mi señora madre y por amor de mi aguela me llamaron a mi Aldonza, y si está mi aguela bivia, sabía más que no sé, que ella me mostró guissar, que en su poder deprendi hacer fideos, empanadillas, alcuzcuz con garbanzos, arroz entero, seco, grasso, albondiguillas redondas y apretadas con culantro

verde, que se conocían las que yo hazía entre ciento. Mira, señora tía que su padre de
mi padre dezía: !Estas son de mano de mi hija Aldonza! Pues adobado no hacía? Sobre
que cuantos traperos avía en la cal de la Heria querian provallo, y maxime cuando era
un buen pecho de carnero. Y !que miel! Pensa, señora que la teniamos de Adamuz y
zafran de Penafiel, y lo mejor de la Andaluzia venía en casa d'esta mi aguela. Sabía hacer
hojuelas, prestinos, rosquillas de alfaxor, textones de cañamones y de ajonjoli, nuégados
. . .' José Carlos Capel, *Pícaros, ollas, inquisidores y monjes* (Barcelona, 1985), p. 186.

12  Linnette Fourquet-Reed, 'Protofeminismo erótico-culinario en *Retrato de la
Lozana Andaluza*', *Centro Virtual Cervantes*, AISO, Actas VII (2005), at
https://cvc.cervantes.es.

13  Juan Luis Vives, *The Education of a Christian Woman: A Sixteenth-century Manual*,
ed. and trans. Charles Fantazzin (Chicago, IL, and London, 2000).

14  Miguel de Cervantes, *Don Quixote* (Part II), trans. Edith Crossman (London, 2004),
pp. 582–91.

15  María del Carmen Simón Palmer, *Alimentación y sus circunstancias en el Real Alcázar
de Madrid* (Madrid, 1982), pp. 45–53.

16  Carolyn A. Nadeau, 'Early Modern Spanish Cookbooks: The Curious Case of Diego
Granado', *Food and Language Proceedings of the Oxford Symposium on Food and
Cooking*, ed. Richard Hoskings (Totnes, 2009).

17  Domingo Hernández de Maceras, *Libro del arte de cocina* [1607] (Valladolid, 2004),
pp. 3–71.

18  William B. Jordan and Peter Cherry, *Spanish Still Life from Velázquez to Goya*
(London, 1995), p. 36.

## FIVE: Madrid, Versailles, Naples and, Best of All, Chocolate

1  María de los Angeles Pérez Samper, *Mesas y cocinas en la España del siglo XVIII* (Jijón,
2011), p. 153.

2  Eva Celada, *La Cocina de la Casa Real* (Barcelona, 2004), p. 26.

3  Ken Albala, *Beans: A History* (Oxford and New York, 2007), pp. 71, 19.

4  William B. Jordan and Peter Cherry, *Spanish Still Life from Velázquez to Goya*
(London, 1995), pp. 152–62.

5  Fernando García de Cortázar and José Manuel González Vargas, *Breve Historia de
España* (Madrid, 2015), pp. 342–7.

6  Montesquieu, 'Consideraciones Sobre las Riquezas de España' [*c.* 1727–8], ed.
Antonio Hermosa Andújar, *Araucaria*, XXXIX (2018), pp. 11–17.

7  Montesquieu, *The Spirit of the Laws*, ed. Anne M. Cohler (Cambridge, 1989).

8  'En el mismo instante que forzado de la obediencia me hallé en el empleo de la
cocina, sin director que me enseñara lo necesario para el cumplimiento de mi oficio,
determine, cuando bien instruido, escribir un pequeno resumen or cartilla de
cocina, para que los recien profesos, que del noviciado no salen bastante instruidos,
encuentren en él sin el rubor de preguntar que acuse su ignorancia quanto pueda
ocurrirles en su oficina.' Juan Altimiras, *Nuevo arte de cocina sacado de la Escuela de la
Experiencia Económica* (Madrid, 1791), p. 21.

9  Antonio Salsete, *El cocinero religioso*, ed. Manuel Sarobe Puello (Pamplona, 1995),
p. 112.

10  Christopher Columbus, *The 'Diario' of Christopher Columbus's First Voyage, 1492–1493*,
ed. and trans. Olive Dunn and James E. Kelly Jr (Norman, OK, and London, 1989).

11  Enriqueta Quiroz, 'Del mercado a la cocina: La alimentacíon en la Ciudad de Mexico en el siglo XVII: entre tradición y cambio', in Pilar Gonzalbo Aizpuru, *Historia de la vida cotidiana en Mexico*, vol. III (Mexico City, 2005), pp. 17–44.

12  Elisa Vargas Lugo, *Recetario novohispano, México, siglo XVIII* (Anónimo) (Mexico City, 2010); Dominga de Guzman, *Recetario de Dominga de Guzman* [1750] (Mexico City, 1996); Jerónimo de San Pelayo, *El libro de cocina del Hermano Fray Gerónimo de San Pelayo, México, siglo XVIII* (Mexico City, 2003).

13  María Paz Moreno, *De la Página al Plato*: *El Libro de Cocina en España* (Gijón, 2012), p. 60.

14  Zarela Martínez, *The Food and Life of Oaxaca: Traditional Recipes from Mexico's Heart* (New York, 1997), pp. 160–61.

15  María del Carmen Simón Palmer, 'La Dulcería en la Biblioteca Nacional de España', in *La Cocina en su Tinta*, exh. cat. (Madrid, 2010), pp. 63–81.

16  Fernando Serrano Larráyoz, ed., *Confitería y gastronomía en el regalo de la vida humana de Juan Vallés*, vols IV–VI (Pamplona, 2008).

17  Miguel de Baeza, *Los cuatro libros del arte de confitería* [1592], ed. Antonio Pareja (2014).

18  Juan de la Mata, 'El café disipa y destruye los vapores del vino, ayuda á la digestion, conforta los espíritus, é impide dormir con exceso', in Mata, *Arte de repostería* [1791] (Valladolid, 2003).

19  Joseph Townsend, *A Journey through Spain in the Years 1786 and 1787, with Particular Attention to the Agriculture, Manufacturers and Remarks in Passing through a Part of France* (London, 1791), pp. 265–6.

20  Carolyn A. Nadeau, *Food Matters: Alonso Quijano's Diet and the Discourse of Food in Early Modern Spain* (Toronto, 2016), p. 96.

21  Sidney Mintz, *Sweetness and Power: The Place of Sugar in Modern History* (New York, 1985).

22  Joan de Déu Domènech, *Chocolate todos los días. a la mesa con el Barón de Malda: un estilo de vida del siglo XVIII* (Albacete, 2004), p. 255.

23  Tom Burns in David Mitchell, *Travellers in Spain: An Illustrated Anthology* (Fuengirola, 2004), p. 1.

24  Ibid., p. 8.

25  Madame d'Aulnoy, *Travels into Spain*, Google ebook (London, 2014).

## six: Politics at the Table

1  Néstor Luján, *Historia de la gastronomía* (Barcelona, 1988), p. 156.

2  Lucien Solvay, *L'Art espagnol: Précédé d'une introduction sur l'Espagne et les Espagnols*, ed. J. Rouan (Paris, 1887).

3  Leonard T. Perry, 'La Mesa Española en el Madrid de Larra', *Mester*, X/1 (Los Angeles, CA, 1981), pp. 58–65.

4  Isabel González Turmo, *200 años de cocina* (Madrid, 2013), pp. 65–8.

5  María Carme Queralt, *La cuynera catalana* [1851], Google ebook (London, 2013).

6  Richard Ford, *Manual para viajeros por España y lectores en casa: observaciones generals* (Madrid, 2008).

7  Fernando García de Cortázar and José Manuel González Vesga, *Breve historia de España* (Barcelona, 2013), pp. 456–7.

8  'Je crois que Madrid est le lieu de la terre où l'on prend de meilleur café; que cette

boisson est délicieuse! plus délicieuse cent fois que toutes les liqueurs du monde . . .
le café égaie, anime, exalte, électrife; le café peuple la tête d'idées . . .' Jean-Marie-
Jérôme Fleuriot de Langle, *Voyage de Figaro, en Espagne* (Saint Malo, 1784).

9  Edward Henry Strobel, *The Spanish Revolution, 1868–75* (Boston, MA, 1898).

10  Fernando Sánchez Gómez, *La cocina de la crítica: historia, teoría y práctica de la crítica gastronómica como género periodístico* (Seattle, WA, 2013), p. 124.

11  Mariano Pardo de Figueroa, *La mesa moderna: cartas sobre el comedor y la cocina cambiadas entre el Doctor Thebussem y un cocinero de S.M.* (Valladolid, 2010), pp. 23–39.

12  Angel Muro, *El practicón: tratado completo de cocina al alcance de todos y aprovechamiento de sobras* [1894] (Madrid, 1982).

13  María Paz Moreno, 'La Cocina Antigua de Emilia Pardo Bazán: Dulce Venganza e Intencionalidad Múltiple en un Recetario Ilustrado', *La tribuna, cadernos de estudios da Casa Museo Emilia Pardo Bazán*, 4 (2006), pp. 243–6; Emilia Pardo Bazán, *La cocina española moderna* (Madrid, 1917).

14  Rebecca Ingram, 'Popular Tradition and Bourgeois Elegance in Emilia Pardo Bazán's *Cocina Española*', *Bulletin of Hispanic Studies*, XCI/3 (2014), pp. 261–4.

15  Lara Anderson, *Cooking up the Nation* (Woodbridge, 2013), p. 105.

16  Alvaro Escribano and Pedro Fraile Balbín, 'The Spanish 1898 Disaster: The Drift towards National Protectionism', *Economic History and Institutions, Series 01. Working Paper* (Madrid, 1998), pp. 98–103.

17  Eladia M. Carpinell, *Carmencita o la buena cocinera: manual práctico de cocina española, americana, francesa* (Barcelona, 1899), pp. 65–6.

## SEVEN: Hunger, Hope and Success

1  Ismael Díaz Yubero, *Sabores de España* (Madrid, 1998), p. 9.

2  Mariano Pardo de Figueroa, *La mesa moderna: cartas sobre el comedor y la cocina cambiadas entre el Doctor Thebussem y un cocinero de S.M.* (Valladolid, 2010), p. 180.

3  Dionisio Pérez, *Guía del buen comer español: historia y singularidad regional de la cocina española* [1929] (Seville, 2010).

4  Dionisio Pérez and Gregorio Marañón, *Naranjas: el arte de prepararlas y comerlas* (Madrid, 1993).

5  Dionisio Pérez, *La cocina clásica española* (Huesca, 1994).

6  Maria Mestager de Echague (Marquesa de Parabere), *Platos escogidos de la cocina vasca* (Bilbao, 1940).

7  Ursula, Sira y Vicenta de Azcaray y Eguileor, *El amparo: sus platos clásicos* (San Sebastián, 2010), p. 217.

8  Gerald Brenan, *The Spanish Labyrinth: An Account of the Social and Political Background of the Spanish Civil War* (Cambridge, 1969), p. 86.

9  Ermine Herscher and Agnes Carbonell, *En la mesa de Picasso* (Barcelona, 1996).

10  Carmen de Burgos ('Colombine'), *Quiere usted comer bien?* (Barcelona, 1931), pp. 5–6.

11  Laurie Lee, *A Moment of War* (London, 1992), pp. 115–18.

12  Juan Eslava Galán, *Los años del miedo: la Nueva España (1939–52)* (Barcelona, 2008).

13  Antonio Salsete, *El cocinero religioso*, ed. Victor Manuel Sarobe Pueyo (Pamplona, 1995), p. 124.

14  Manuel María Puga y Parga (Picadillo), *La cocina práctica* (A Coruña, 1926), p. 15.

15 Ignacio Domènech, *Cocina de recursos* (Gijón, 2011).

16 Ignacio Domènech, *La nueva cocina elegante española* (Madrid, 1915).

17 Ana María Herrera, *Manual de cocina (recetario)* (Madrid, 2009), pp. 47–8.

18 Pedro Subijana et al., *Basque, Creative Territory: From New Basque Cuisine to the Basque Culinary Centre, a Fascinating 40-year Journey* (Madrid, 2016), pp. 15–17.

19 Juan José Lapitz, *La cocina moderna en Euskadi* (Madrid, 1987), pp. 27–55.

20 Carmen Casas, *Comer en Catalunya* (Madrid, 1980), p. 170.

21 Caroline Hobhouse, *Great European Chefs* (London, 1990), pp. 174–88.

22 Santi Santamaría, *La cocina al desnudo* (Barcelona, 2008).

23 Ferran Adrià, *El Bulli: El sabor del Mediterráneo* (Barcelona, 1993), pp. 15–71.

## EIGHT: The *Cocinas* of Spain

1 Néstor Luján and Juan Perucho, *El libro de la cocina española, gastronomía e historia* (Barcelona, 2003), p. 158.

2 Ken Albala, *Beans: A History* (Oxford, 2007), p. 198.

3 Francisco Martínez Montiño, *Arte de cozina, pastelería, vizcochería y conservería* (Madrid, 1617).

4 Nicolasa Pradera (with Preface by Gregorio Marañon), *La cocina de Nicolasa* (San Sebastián, 2010).

5 Adam Hopkins, *Spanish Journeys: A Portrait of Spain* (London, 1992), p. 45.

6 Lorenzo Díaz, *La cocina del Quijote* (Madrid, 2005), p. 80.

7 Luján and Perucho, *El libro de la cocina española*, p. 395.

8 Isabel and Carmen García Hernández, *La mejor cocina extremeña escrita por dos autoras* (Barcelona, 1989), pp. 53–86.

9 Colman Andrews, *Catalan Cuisine* (London, 1988), pp. 15–17.

10 Josep Lladonosa i Giró, *La cocina medieval* (Barcelona, 1984), pp. 71–80.

11 Josep Pla, *Lo que hemos comido* (Barcelona, 1997), p. 18.

12 Tony Lord, *The New Wines of Spain* (Bromley, 1988), p. 51.

13 D. E. Pohren, *Adventures in Taste: The Wines and Folk Food of Spain* (Seville, 1970), p. 193.

14 Alan Davidson, *The Tio Pepe Guide to the Seafood of Spain and Portugal* (Jerez de la Frontera, 1992), p. 141.

15 Teodoro Bardají, *La salsa mahonesa: recopilación de opiniones acerca del nombre tan discutido de esta salsa fría . . .* (Madrid, 1928).

16 Tomás Graves, *Bread and Oil* (London, 2006), p. 107.

17 Lalo Grosso de Macpherson, *Cooking with Sherry* (Madrid, 1987).

18 Manuel Valencia, *La cocina gitana de Jerez: tradición y varguandia* (Jerez de la Frontera, 2006), pp. 18–20, 34–35.

19 Enrique Mapelli, *Papeles de gastronomía malagueña* (Málaga, 1982), pp. 101, 142, 239, 31.

20 Gerald Brenan, *South from Granada* (Cambridge, 1957), p. 125.

21 David and Emma Illsley, *Las Chimeneas: Recipes and Stories from an Alpujarran Village* (London, 2016), pp. 31, 136.

22 J. G. Hawkes and J. Francisco-Ortega, 'The Early History of the Potato in Europe', *Euphytica*, LXX/1–2 (1993), pp. 1–7.

23 José Juan Jiménez Gonzalez, *La tribu de los canarii, arqueología, antiguedad y renacimiento* (Santa Cruz de Tenerife, 2014), pp. 173–4.

# Select Bibliography

Abu Zakariyya'Yaliya ibn Muhammad ibn al-'Auwam, Sevillano, *Kitab al-falahab, Libro de Agricultura*, trans. José Antonio Banqueri [1802], e-book (Madrid, 2011)

Agulló, Ferràn, *Libre de la cocina Catalana* [1924] (Barcelona, 1995)

Ainsworth Means, Philip, *The Spanish Main: Focus of Envy, 1492–1700* (New York, 1935)

Alcala-Zamora, José, *La vida cotidiana en la España de Velázquez* (Madrid, 1999)

Aldala, Ken, *Food in Early Modern Europe* (Santa Barbara, CA, 2003)

Allard, Jeanne, 'La Cuisine Espagnole au Siècle d'Or', *Mélanges de la Casa de Velázquez*, XXIV (1988), pp. 177–90

Almodóvar, Miguel Angel, *Yantares de cuando la electricidad acabó con las mulas* (Madrid, 2011)

Alperi, Magdalena, *Guía de la cocina asturiana* (Gijon, 1987)

Apicio, *La cocina en la Antigua Roma*, ed. Primitiva Flores Santamaría and María Esperanza Torrego (Madrid, 1985)

Aram, Bethany, *Juana the Mad: Sovereignty and Dynasty in Renaissance Europe* (Baltimore, MD, 2005)

——, and Bartolomé Yun Casadilla, eds, *Global Goods and the Spanish Empire, 1492–1824* (London, 2014)

Arbelos, Carlos, *Gastronomía de las tres culturas, recetas y relatos* (Granada, 2004)

Azorín, *Al margen de los clásicos* (Madrid, 2005)

Azurmendi, Mikel, *El fuego de los símbolos: artificios sagrados del imaginario de la cultura vasca tradicional* (San Sebastian, 1988)

Badi, Méri, *La cocina judeo-española*, trans. Carmen Casas (Barcelona, 1985)

Balfour, Sebastian, 'Spain from 1931 to the Present', in Raymond Carr, ed., *Spain: A History* (Oxford, 2000)

Balzola, Asun, and Alicia Ríos, *Cuentos rellenos* (Madrid, 1999)

Barandiaran, José Manuel, *La alimentación doméstica en Vasconia*, ed. Ander Monterola (Bilbao, 1990)

Bardají, Teodoro, *La cocina de ellas* (Huesca, 2002)

——, *Indice culinario* (Huesca, 2003)

Barragán Mohacho, Nieves, and Eddie and Sam Hart, *Barrafina: A Spanish Cookbook* (London, 2011)

Benavides Barajas, Luis, *Al-Andalus, la cocina y su historia, reinos de taifas, norte de Africa, Judíos, Mudéjares y Moriscos* (Motril, 1996)

——, *Al-Andalus, el Cristianismo, Mozárabes y Muladíes* (Motril, 1995)

Bennison, Vicky, *The Taste of a Place: Mallorca* (London, 2003)

Bermúdez de Castro, José María, *El chico de la Gran Dolina* (Barcelona, 2010)

Bettónica, Luis, *Cocina regional española: trescientos platos presentados por grandes maestros de cocina* (Barcelona, 1981)

Blasco Ibañez, Vicente, *Cañas y barro* (Madrid, 2005)

Bonnín, Xesc, *La cocina mallorquina: pueblo a pueblo, puerta a puerta* (Mallorca, 2006)

Bray, Xavier, *Enciclopedia del Museo del Prado* (Madrid, 2006)

Brenan, Gerald, *The Face of Spain* (London, 2006)

Burns, Jimmy, *Spain: A Literary Companion* (Malaga, 2006)

Butrón, Inés, *Comer en España: de la subsistencia a la vanguardia* (Barcelona, 2011)

Cabrol, Fernand, 'Canonical Hours', in *The Catholic Encyclopedia*, vol. VII (New York, 1910)

Capel, José Carlos, and Lourdes Plana, *El desafío de la cocina Española: tres décadas de evolución* (Barcelona, 2006)

Caro Baroja, Julio, 'De la Vida Rural Vasca', *Estudios Vascos*, V (San Sebastian, 1989)

——, *Los Vascos* (Madrid, 1971)

Carr, Raymond, *Modern Spain, 1875–1980* (Oxford, 1980)

Casas, Carmen, *Damas guisan y ganan* (Barcelona, 1986)

Castellano, Rafael, *La cocina romántica: una interpretación del XIX a través de la gastronomía* (Barcelona, 1985)

Chela, José H., *Cincuenta recetas fundamentales de la cocina canaria* (Santa Cruz de Tenerife, 2004)

Chetwode, Penelope, *Two Middle-aged Ladies in Andalusia* (London, 2002)

Cieza de León, Pedro de, *Crónica del Peru* (Lima, 1986)

Civitello, Linda, *Cuisine and Culture: A History of Food and People* (London, 2003)

Cobo, Bernabé, *Historia del Nuevo Mundo*, trans. Roland Hamilton (Austin, TX, 1983)

Collins, Roger, *Visigothic Spain, 409–711* (Hoboken, NJ, 2004)

Columbus, Christopher, *The Log of Christopher Columbus* [1492], trans. Robert H. Fuson (Camden, ME, 1991)

Cooper, John, *Eat and Be Satisfied: A Social History of Jewish Food* (Northvale, NJ, and Jerusalem, 1993)

Corcuera, Mikel, *25 años de la Nueva Cocina Vasca* (Bilbao, 2003)

Cordon, Faustino, *Cocinar hizo al hombre* (Barcelona, 1989)

Cruz Cruz, Juan, 'La cocina mediterránea en el inicio del renacimiento: Martino da Como "Libro de Arte Culinaria"', in Ruperto de Nola, *Libro de guisados* (Huesca, 1998)

Cunqueiro, Alvaro, *La cocina gallega* (Vigo, 2004)

Dawson, Samuel Edward, *The Lines of Demarcation of Pope Alexander VI and the Treaty of Tordesillas, AD 1493 and 1494* (Ottawa and Toronto, 1899)

De Benitez, Ana María, *Pre-Hispanic Cooking* (Mexico City, 1974)

De Herrera, Alonso, *Ancient Agriculture: Roots and Applications of Sustainable Farming* [1513] (Layton, UT, 2006)

De Miguel, Amando, *Sobre Gustos y Sabores: Los Españoles y la Comida* (Madrid, 2004)

Del Corral, José, *Ayer y hoy de la gastronomía madrileña* (Madrid, 1992)

Delgado, Carlos, *Cien recetas magistrales: diez grandes chefs de la cocina española* (Madrid, 1985)

Della Rocca, Giorgio, *Viajar y comer por el maestrazgo* (Vinaroz, 1985)

Díaz, Lorenzo, *La cocina del Barroco: la gastronomía del Siglo de Oro en Lope, Cervantes y Quevedo* (Madrid, 2003)

Díaz del Castillo, Bernal, *Historia verdadera de la conquista de la Nueva España* [1632] (Madrid, 1955)

Doménech, I., and F. Marti, *Ayunos y abstinencias: cocina de Cuaresma* (Barcelona, 1982)

Domingo, Xavier, *La mesa del buscón* (Barcelona, 1981)

Domínguez, Martí, *Els nostres menjars* (Valencia, 1979)

Domínguez Ortiz, Antonio, *Carlos III y la España de la ilustración* (Madrid, 2005)

——, *La sociedad Española en el siglo XVII* (Madrid, 1992)

Eichberger, Dagmar, Anne-Marie Legaré and Wim Husken, eds, *Women at the Burgundian Court: Presence and Influence* (Turnhout, 2011)

Eléxpuru, Inés, *La cocina de Al-Andalus* (Madrid, 1994)

Escoffier, A., *A Guide to Modern Cookery*, trans. James B. Herdon Jr (London, 1907)

Espada, Arcadi, *Las dos hermanas: medio siglo del restaurante hispània* (Barcelona, 2008)

Fàbrega Colom, Jaume, *Cuina monàstica* (Barcelona, 2013)

Fatacciu, Irene, 'Atlantic History and Spanish Consumer Goods in the Eighteenth Century: The Assimilation of Exotic Drinks and the Fragmentation of European Identities', *Nuevo Mundo, Mundos Nuevos* (27 June 2012)

Fear, A. T., *Prehistoric and Roman Spain*, in Raymond Carr, ed., *Spain: A History* (Oxford, 2000)

Fidalgo, José Antonio, *Asturias: cocina de mar y monte* (Oviedo, 2004)

Fletcher, Richard, *The Early Middle Ages, 700–1250*, in Raymond Carr, ed., *Spain: A History* (Oxford, 2000)

Font Poquet, Miquel S., *Cuina i menjar a Mallorca: història i receptes* (Palma de Mallorca, 2005)

García Armendáriz, José Ignacio, *Agronomía y Tradición Clásica: Columela en España* (Seville, 1994)

García Mercandal, José, *Lo Que España Llevó a América* (Madrid, 1958)

García Paris, Julia, *Intercambio y difusion de plantas de consumo entre el nuevo y el viejo mundo* (Madrid, 1991)

Gautier, Théophile, *A Romantic in Spain* (Oxford, 2001)

Gitlitz, David M., *Secrecy and Deceit: The Religion of the Crypto-Jews* (Albuquerque, NM, 2002)

Glick, Thomas F., *Irrigation and Society in Medieval Valencia* (Cambridge, MA, 1970)

Gonzalbo Aizpuru, Pilar, *Historia de la vida cotidiana en Mexico*, vol. III: *El siglo XVIII: entre tradición y cambio* (Mexico City, 2005)

González, Echegaray J., and L. G. Freeman, 'Las escavaciones de la Cueva del Juyo (Cantabria)', *Kobie* (Serie Paleoantropología), XX (1992–3)

Gracia, Jorge J. E., 'Rules and Regulations for Drinking Wine in Francesc Eiximenis' "Terç del Crestià" (1384)', *Traditio: Studies in Ancient and Medieval History, Thought, and Religion*, XXXII/1 (1976), pp. 369–85

Granado, Diego, *Libro del arte de cocina* (Madrid, 1971)

Grewe, Rudolf, 'The Arrival of the Tomato in Spain and Italy: Early Recipes', *The Journal of Gastronomy*, VIII/2 (1987), pp. 67–81

——, 'Hispano-Arabic Cuisine in the Twelfth Century', in *Du manuscrit à la table: Essais sur la cuisine au Moyen Age et rèpertoire des manuscrits médiévaux contenant des recettes culinaires*, ed. Carole Lambert (Montreal, 1992), pp. 141–8

——, *Llibre de Sent Soví: receptari de cuina* (Barcelona, 1979)

Haranburo Altuna, Luis, *Historia de la alimentación y de la cocina en el pais vasco, de Santimamiñe a Arzak* (Alegia, Guipúzkoa, 2009), pp. 264–6

Hayward, Vicky, *New Art of Cookery: A Spanish Friar's Kitchen Notebook by Juan Altamiras* (London, 2017)

Herr, Richard, 'Flow and Ebb, 1700–1833', in Raymond Carr, ed., *Spain: A History* (Oxford, 2000)

Herrera, A. M., *Recetario para olla a presión y batidora eléctrica* (Madrid, 1961)

Herrero y Ayora, Melchora, and Florencia Herrero y Ayora, *El arte de la cocina: fórmulas (para desayunos, tes, meriendas y refrescos)* (Madrid, 1914)

Huertas Ballejo, Lorenzo, 'Historia de la producción de vinos y piscos en el Peru', *Revista Universum*, IX/2 (Talca, 2004), pp. 44–61

Huici Miranda, Ambrosio, trans., *La cocina hispano-magrebí durante la* época *almohade: según un manuscrito anónimo del siglo XIII,* a preliminary study by Manuela Marín (Gijón, 2005)

Humboldt, Alexander von, *Ensayo político sobre el reino de la Nueva España* (Mexico, 1978)

Johnson, Lyman L., and Mark A. Burkholder, *Colonial Latin America* (Oxford, 1990)

Juan de Corral, Caty, *Cocina balear* (León, 2000)

——, *Recetas con Angel* (Madrid, 1994)

Juderías, Alfredo, *Viaje por la cocina hispano-judía* (Madrid, 1990)

Kamen, Henry, *The Disinherited, Exile and the Making of Spanish Culture, 1492–1975* (New York, 2007)

——, *The Spanish Inquisition: A Historical Revision* (New Haven, CT, 1999)

Keay, S. J., *Roman Spain (Exploring the Roman World)* (Oakland, CA, 1988)

Kurkanski, Mark, *The Basque History of the World* (London, 2000)

Lacoste, Pablo, 'La vid y el vino en América del Sur: el desplazamiento de los polos vitivinícolas (Siglos XVI al XX)', *Revista Universum*, XIX/2 (2004), pp. 62–93

Lana, Benjamín, *La Cucina de Nacho Manzano* (Barcelona, 2016)

Lladonosa Giró, Josep, *Cocina de Ayer, Delicias de Hoy* (Barcelona, 1984)

López Castro, José Luis, 'El poblamiento rural fenicio en el sur de la península ibérica entre los siglos VI a III A.C.', *Gerión*, XXVI/1 (2009), pp. 149–82

López Mendiazábal, Isaac, *Breve historia del país vasco* (Buenos Aires, 1945)

Luard, Elisabeth, *The Rich Tradition of European Peasant Cookery* (London, 1986)

Luján, Néstor, *El menjar (Coneixer Catalunya)* (Madrid, 1979)

Mackay, Angus, *The Late Middle Ages: From Frontier to Empire, 1000–1500* (New York, 1977)

March Ferrer, Lourdes, *El Libro de la paella y los arroces* (Madrid, 1985)

Marín, Manuela, and David Waines, *La alimentación en las culturas islámicas* (Madrid, 1994)

Marti Gilabert, Francisco, *La desamortización española* (Madrid, 2003)

Martínez Yopis, Manuel, *Historia de la gastronomía española* (Huesca, 1995)

——, and Luis Irizar, *Las cocinas de españa* (Madrid, 1990)

Mendel, Janet, *Traditional Spanish Cooking* (London, 2006)

Menéndez Pidal, Ramón, *Crónicas Generales de España* [1898] (Whitefish, MT, 2010)

Menocal, María Rosa, *The Ornament of the World: How Muslims, Jews and Christians Created a Culture of Tolerance in Medieval Spain* (New York, 2002)

Miguel-Prendes, Sol, 'Chivalric Identity in Enrique de Villena's *Arte Cisoria*', *La Corónica: A Journal of Medieval Hispanic Languages, Literatures and Cultures*, XXXII/1 (2003), pp. 307–42

Monardes, Nicolás, *La historia medicinal de las cosas que se traen de nuestras Indias Occidentales, 1565, 1569 and 1580* (Madrid, 1989)

Montanary, Massimo, *The Culture of Food*, trans. Carl Ipsen (Oxford, 1994)

——, *El hambre y la abundancia, historia y cultura de la alimentación en Europa* (Barcelona, 1993)

Morris, Jan, *The Presence of Spain* (London, 1988)

Motos Pérez, Isaac, 'Lo Que Se Olvida: 1499–1978', *Anales de Historia Contemporánea*, XXV (2009)

Muñoz Molina, Antonio, *Córdoba de los omegas* (Seville, 1991)

Norwich, John Julius, *The Middle Sea* (London, 2006)

Obermaier, Hugo, *El hombre fósil* (Madrid, 1985)

Ortega, Simone, and Inés Ortega, *1080 Recipes* (London, 2007)

Ortega, Teresa María, ed., *Jornaleras, campesinas y agricultoras: la historia agrarian desde una perspectiva de género* (Zaragoza, 2015)

Pan-Montojo, Juan, 'Spanish Agriculture, 1931–1955. Crisis, Wars and New Policies in the Reshaping of Rural Society', in *War, Agriculture, and Food: Rural Europe from the 1930s to the 1950s*, ed. Paul Brassley, Yves Segers and Leen van Molle (New York, 2012), Chapter Five

Pelauzy, M. A., *Spanish Folk Crafts* (Barcelona, 1982)

Pérez Samper, María de los Angeles, 'Los recetarios de cocina (siglos XV–XVIII)', in *Codici del gusto* (Milan, 1992), pp. 154–75

Pisa, José Maria, *El azafrán en Aragón y la gastronomía* (Huesca, 2009)

——, *Bibliografía de la paella* (Huesca, 2012)

Pla, Josep, *Lo que hemos comido* (Barcelona, 1997)

Pritchett, V. S., *The Spanish Temper* (London, 1973)

Quiróz, Enriqueta, 'Comer en Nueva España: privilegios y pesares de la sociedad en el siglo XVIII', *Historia y Memoria*, 8 (2014)

Remie Constable, Olivia, 'Food and Meaning: Christian Understanding of Muslim Food and Food Ways in Spain, 1250–1550', *Viator, Medieval and Renaissance Studies*, XLIV/3 (2013), pp. 199–235

Revel, Jean-François, *Un Festín de Palabras*, trans. Lola Gavarrón and Mauro Armiño (Barcelona, 1996)

Rios, Alicia, and Lourdes March, *The Heritage of Spanish Cooking* (London, 1992)

Roca, Joan, *La cocina catalana de toda la vida: las mejores recetas de mi madre* (Barcelona, 2004)

Rose, Susan, *The Wine Trade in Medieval Europe, 1000–1500* (London, 2011)

Sánchez, Marisa, and Francis Paniego, *Echaurren: el sabor de la memoria* (Barcelona, 2008)

Sánchez Martinez, Verónica, 'La fiesta del gusto: construcción de México a través de sus comidas', *Opción*, XXII/51 (Maracaibo, 2006)

Sand, George, *A Winter in Majorca* [1842], trans. Robert Graves (Valldemossa, Mallorca, 1956)

Santamaría, Santi, *Palabra de cocinero: un chef en vanguardia* (Barcelona, 2005)

Santich, Barbara, *The Original Mediterranean Cuisine: Medieval Recipes for Today* (Totnes, 1995)

Seaver, Henry Latimer, *The Great Revolt in Castile: A Study of the Comunero Movement of 1520–1521* (Cambridge, 1928)

Serradilla Muñoz, José V., *La mesa del emperador: recetario de Carlos V en Yuste* (Barcelona, 1997)

Serrano Larráyoz, Fernando, *Un recetario navarro de cocina y repostería (Siglo XIX)* (Gijon, 2011)

Settle, Mary Lee, *Spanish Recognitions: The Roads to the Present* (New York, 2004, and Oxford, 2015)

Sevilla, María José, 'Pasus: A Basque Kitchen' in Alan Davidson, *The Cook's Room* (London, 1991)

Shaul, Moshé, Aldina Quintana and Zelda Ovadia, *El gizado sefaradí* (Zaragoza, 1995)

Sokolov, Raymond, *Why We Eat What We Eat* (New York, 1991)

Spataro, Michela, and Alexander Villing, eds, *Ceramics, Cuisine and Culture: The Archaeology and Science of Kitchen Pottery in the Ancient Mediterranean World* (Oxford, 2015)

Subijana, Pedro, *Akelarre: New Basque Cuisine* (London, 2017)

Sueiro, Jorge Victor, *Comer en Galicia* (Madrid, 1989)

Tannahill, Reay, *Food in History* (New York, 1998)

Thibaut i Comelade, Eliana, *La cuina medieval a l'abast* (Barcelona, 2006)

Thomas, Hugh, *The Spanish Civil War* (London, 1965)

Torre Enciso, Cipriano, *Cocina gallega 'enxebre': así se come y bebe en Galicia* (Madrid, 1982)

Vallverdù-Poch, Josep, et al., 'The Abric Romaní Site and the Capellades Region', in *High Resolution Archaeology and Neanderthal Behavior: Time and Space in Level J of Abric Romaní (Capellades, Spain)*, ed. Eudald Carbonell i Roura (2012), pp. 19–46

Van Hensbergen, Gijs, *In the Kitchens of Castile* (London, 1992)

Vázquez Montalbán, Manuel, *Las recetas de Carvalho* (Barcelona, 2004)

Vázquez Ramil, Raquel, *Mujeres y educación en la España contemporánea: La Institución Libre de Enseñanza y la Residencia de Señoritas de Madrid* (Madrid, 2012)

Vicens Vives, Jaume, *Aproximación a la historia de España* (Madrid, 1952)

——, *España contemporánea, 1814–1953* (Barcelona, 2012)

Watson, Andrew M., 'The Arab Agriculture Revolution and Its Diffusion: 700–1100', *Journal of Economic History*, XXXIV/1 (1974), pp. 8–35

Weiss Adamson, Melitta, *Food in Medieval Times* (Westport, CT, 2004)

Welch, Kathryn, ed., *Appian's Roman History: Empire and Civil War* (Wales, 2015)

Wittmayer Baron, Salo, *A Social and Religious History of the Jews*, 2nd edn (New York, 1969)

Zamora, Margarita, *Language, Authority and Indigenous History in the Comentarios Reales de los Incas* (Cambridge, MA, 1988)

Zapata, Lydia, et al., 'Early Neolithic Agriculture in the Iberian Peninsula', *Journal of World Prehistory*, XVIII/4 (2004)

# Acknowledgements

This book is the result of many years working on the food and wines of Spain. I am indebted to a long list of people who have greatly influenced the writing and the publication of this book: members of my family, food writers and journalists, academics and photographers, as well as cooks with long memories of Spain, chefs, and food and wine producers.

The list must start with Michael Leaman, Publisher at Reaktion Books. Michael has dedicated time and effort to this series of books, 'Foods and Nations', which is contributing to the understanding of life and food in many countries of the world. He has guided me when needed, making me as selective and precise as possible, not an easy matter when dealing with a Spanish writer together with the cultural richness of Spain. David Swan, my husband, Patricia Langton, an editor and journalist, and Sarah Codrington, a historian and exceptional linguist, have made certain that the English grammar I have used is as it should be. Furthermore I have to express my gratitude to Martha Jay, the Managing Editor for Reaktion Books. She has been patient, talented and indispensible. My son Daniel J. Taylor deserves several medals for being able to cope with my fight with modern technology.

The list would be incomplete without the names of people who initially encouraged me to look further into the food and wine of my country, starting with the novelist and outstanding marketing man Patrick Gooch and of course Juan Calabozo, who worked as Commercial Counsellor at the Spanish Embassy in London. The talented Cathy Boriac, publisher of the acclaimed magazine *Spain Gourmetour*, proved to be equally influential, as were other journalists of the calibre of the late Michael Bateman, Michael Raffael and Philippa Davenport, among others.

The Oxford Symposium on Food and Cookery, which I have attended for the last thirty years, has proved to be a great source of original research and contacts. At Oxford I have been able to admire the work of many true specialists whose influence has benefited my work and the way I think about the history of food and food writing: Alan Davidson, with whom I shared a passion for fish; Sophie Coe with the history of chocolate; Jane Grigson with vegetables and pulses; and Claudia Roden with the world of Sepharad. At Oxford I met Vicky Hayward, who has become a defender of, and authority on, Spanish food and Spanish culture. A long time ago we developed together a taste for the world of Basque food – a shared experience not to be forgotten. My friendship with Elisabeth Luard, who understands Spain so well, and Jill Norman, a woman of wisdom and talent, began at Oxford many years ago. In recent years I met at one of the lectures of Carolyn Nadeau, whose writings about food in Spain's medieval and Baroque eras are as relevant as the very many contributions of

Charles Perry on the food of Al-Andalus. I have listened to Professor Paz Moreno, whose contribution to women's writing in Spain and the Americas has opened new avenues to writers such as myself. The library of the Instituto Cervantes in London and the library in the small Andalusian town of Aracena have proved to be a great help when l have been looking for something different to add.

I have been lucky to meet a number of Spanish historians who have included food in their work: the late Néstor Luján and his friend Juan Perucho, the prolific Julian Fernández Armesto, the distinguished Julio Caro Baroja and the very thorough Ismael Díaz Yubero. Unfortunately I was never able to meet Josep Pla or Gerald Brenan (who could be considered almost Spanish). Josep Pla's *Lo Que Hemos Comido* and Brenan's *The Spanish Labyrinth* and *South from Granada* are essential reading for furthering an understanding of the complex issues of *localismo* and the Spanish agrarian question.

I must mention two chefs with whom I have shared great dishes and, even better, discussions on the subject of the evolution of food in the professional kitchens of Spain: Pedro Subijana and the late Santi Santamaría. Their numerous books and articles speak for themselves.

I am also very grateful to a number of academics who include Spanish food in their research and publications: in Spain, María del Carmen Simón Palmer and María de los Angeles Pérez Samper; in the u.s., Tom Perry, Ken Albala and Rebecca Ingram. I am equally grateful to Lara Anderson, Senior Lecturer in Spanish and Latin American Studies at the University of Melbourne. Her comments on the *Cocinas de España* made me review my original thoughts on the regional food of Spain.

Another group includes the names of a number of Spanish and non-Spanish historians whose work on the history of Spain has occupied a prime space on my desk for the last six years. I will be forever grateful to the writings of Joseph F. O'Callaghan, Fernando García de Cortázar, José Luis Roig, Paul Preston, Henry Kamen, Raymond Carr, and particularly John H. Elliot and the late Jaume Vicens Vives.

Searching for the illustrations has proved to be a rather fascinating occupation, new to me, where I have found a number of generous and talented friends. Among others I must mention Juan Manuel García Ballesteros and Luz Gutiérrez Porras, who has allowed me to search the photographic archives at the Ministry of Agriculture in Madrid; Francisco Javier Suárez Padrán, who specializes on the subject of American food products in Tenerife; Oskar Alonso in San Sebastián; Santiago Mendioroz in Brussels; and Julián Fernández Larraburou at Navarre's Department of Tourism.

# Photo Acknowledgements

The author and publishers wish to express their thanks to the below sources of illustrative material and/or permission to reproduce it.

Alamy: pp. 15 (José Lucas), 21 (blickwinkel), 29 (David Noton Photography), 32 (Danita Delimont), 35 (Classic Image), 116 (The Florida Collection), 194 (blickwinkel), 232 (World History Archive), 246 (Everett Collection, Inc); AKG Images: pp. 225 (Musée Picasso/© Sucession Picasso/DACS, London 2019); Oscar Alonso Algote: p. 264; Annual (CC by 3.0): p. 18; A. Barra (CC by SA 4.0): p. 38; Markus Bernet (CC by SA 3.0): p. 257; © The British Library Board: p. 62; Juan Mari Camino: p. 241; Cellers Scala Dei, Catalonia: p. 89; Diego Delso (CC by SA 4.0): p. 253; Dungdung: p. 281; © Juantxo Egaña/Akelarre: p. 243; Eurocarne: p. 113; Getty Images: p. 291 (Fran & Jean Shor/National Geographic); Jglamela (CC by SA 4.0): p. 215; Lucy Hollis: p. 251; Kunsthistorisches Museum: p. 125; Louvre, Paris: p. 132; Photo courtesy of Nacho Manzano: p. 249; Ministerio de Agricultura, Pesca y Alimentación. Secretaría General Técnica: pp. 88, 96 (Javier López Linaje), 226, 227 top and bottom, 309 (Courtesy Fernando Fernández); Museo de Teruel, Aragon: p. 77 middle; Museum of the Americas, Madrid: p. 101; Museum of Fine Arts, Budapest: p. 114; The Museum of Fine Arts, Houston: p. 137 top (Accession number 94.245); Museo Nacional del Prado, Madrid: pp. 77 top, 85, 146, 157, 178, 193; Museo Nacional y Centro de Investigaciones de Altamira, Cantabria: p. 12; Paul Munhoven: p. 40 (CC by SA 3.0); NASA/JPL/NIMA: p. 92; Patrimonio Nacional de España: p. 153; National Gallery, Dublin: p. 148; National Museum, Warsaw: p. 136; PixofSpain (ICEX Inversion y Exportaciones): pp. 49, 247 (Pablo Neustadt); Rasbak (CC by SA 3.0): p. 16; María José Sevilla: pp. 68, 97, 129, 137 bottom, 156, 205, 218, 223, 303; Scottish National Galleries: p. 147 (Accession Number: NG 2180); Servicio de Marketing Turístico, Reino de Navarra: p. 266; Shutterstock: p. 43 (Inu); David Swan: pp. 13, 27, 41, 50, 52, 53 bottom, 57, 64, 76, 171, 176, 189, 214, 230, 233, 237, 261, 275, 308; Tamorlan (CC by 3.0): pp. 183, 185, 205, 295; Jo Soc De Torrent (CC by SA 2.0): p. 285; Daniel James Taylor: p. 251; UNESCO: p. 51 (José Jordan); Rufino Uribe (CC by SA 2.0): p. 118; Contando Estrellas por Vigo: p. 210 (CC by SA 2.0); Valdavia (CC by SA 3.0): p. 269; Villa Romana La Olmeda, Palencia: p. 30 (CC by SA 3.0 IGO).

# Index